THE
NEW MUSLIM
BROTHERHOOD
IN THE
WEST

Columbia Studies in Terrorism and Irregular Warfare

Columbia Studies in Terrorism and Irregular Warfare
Bruce Hoffman, Series Editor

This series seeks to fill a conspicuous gap in the burgeoning literature on terrorism, guerrilla warfare, and insurgency. The series adheres to the highest standards of scholarship and discourse and publishes books that elucidate the strategy, operations, means, motivations, and effects posed by terrorist, guerrilla, and insurgent organizations and movements. It thereby provides a solid and increasingly expanding foundation of knowledge on these subjects for students, established scholars, and informed reading audiences alike.

Ami Pedahzur, *The Israeli Secret Services and the Struggle Against Terrorism*

Ami Pedahzur and Arie Perliger, *Jewish Terrorism in Israel*

THE
NEW MUSLIM
BROTHERHOOD
IN THE
WEST

Lorenzo Vidino

COLUMBIA UNIVERSITY PRESS
NEW YORK

Columbia University Press
Publishers Since 1893
New York   Chichester, West Sussex
Copyright © 2010 Columbia University Press
All rights reserved
Library of Congress Cataloging-in-Publication Data
Vidino, Lorenzo.
The new Muslim Brotherhood in the West / Lorenzo Vidino.
p.   cm. — (Columbia studies in terrorism and irregular warfare)
Includes bibliographical references and index.
ISBN 978-0-231-15126-9 (cloth : alk. paper) — ISBN 978-0-231-52229-8 (electronic)
1. Muslims—Western countries—Politics and government. 2. Islam and politics—
Western countries. 3. Islamic fundamentalism—Western countries. 4. Terrorism—
Religious aspects—Islam. I. Title. II. Series.
D842.42.M87V53   2010
322′.1091821—dc22
2009052517
♾
Columbia University Press books are printed on permanent and durable acid-free
paper.
This book was printed on paper with recycled content.
Printed in the United States of America
c 10 9 8 7 6 5 4 3 2 1

Contents

Acknowledgments

This book is the fruit of nine years of research, dozens of trips that have led me to sixteen countries in four continents, and more than two hundred interviews with government officials, scholars, journalists, and activists who were kind enough to sacrifice some of their time and share their thoughts with me. Aside from the many people who helped me that I cannot publicly acknowledge, I would like to mention, in strictly alphabetical order: Pernille Ammitzbøll, Jeffrey Bale, Ibrahim Barzawi, Daniel and David Beran, David Draper, Ryan Evans, Alice Falk, Doug Farah, Dean Godson, Husain Haqqani, Evan Kohlmann, Josh Lefkowitz, Robert Leiken, Stefan Meining, Steven Merley, Herbert Müller, Raffaello Pantucci, Jonathan Paris, Angel Rabasa, Ibrahim Ramadan, Dave Rich, Udi Rosen, Ronald Sandee, Cynthia Sanders, Morten Skjoldager, Tamar Tesler, Edward Valla, Nasser Weddady, Michael Wildes, and Barbara Zollner. I am also very grateful to the many leaders of the Muslim Brotherhood and legacy groups in the West who agreed to talk to me. Among them I would like to thank in particular Kamal Helbawy and Yussuf Nada, whose insights were priceless.

Many individuals and institutions have supported my research in various ways. Among them, I cannot thank enough some of the faculty and personnel at the Fletcher School of Law and Diplomacy: Andrew Hess, William Martel, Anna Seleny, Vali Nasr, Linda Batista, Bernie Kelley-Leccese, and Jenifer Burckett-Picker. Robert Pfaltzgraff and the people at IFPA have been equally exceptional. I am very grateful also to Nadia Schadlow and Marin Strmecki at the Smith Richardson Foundation for believing in this project. The support received from Harvard University's Belfer Center (in particular from Monica Duffy Toft, Steven Miller, and Susan Lynch) and the U.S. Institute of Peace (thanks to Chantal De Jonge Oudraat, Lili Cole, and Shira Lowinger) has been crucial in the latest stages of my work. I would also like to acknowledge Anne Routon and Leslie Kriesel at Columbia University Press for their support and patience. Finally, my most heartfelt thanks go to the two people without whom this book would have not been possible, two extraordinary mentors whose friendship I deeply cherish: Bruce Hoffman and Richard Shultz.

This book is dedicated to my family. To Ellie, Marco, Jonathan, Ruth, Jack, Orna, and Nike, for their patience and encouragement. To my parents, for their infinite love and support. And to Jessica, love of my life, for being who she is.

THE
NEW MUSLIM
BROTHERHOOD
IN THE
WEST

1

Who Speaks for Western Muslims?

No American Muslim leader ever had better access to the U.S. political establishment than Abdurahman Alamoudi. After his arrival in the United States as a student in 1980, the Eritrean-born biochemist involved himself in various American Muslim organizations, assuming leadership positions in several of them.[1] By the end of the decade he had settled in Washington, where he began to develop an impressive network of contacts within the upper echelons of the American political establishment. In 1990, Alamoudi cofounded the American Muslim Council (AMC) and soon became a regular visitor to the White House, establishing cordial relationships with both Republican and Democratic administrations. He held frequent meetings with members of Congress and even managed to successfully lobby Congress to host, for the first time in history, the opening invocation from an Islamic leader.[2]

By the mid-1990s Alamoudi had become a staple of Washington's political life.[3] His organization planned events with interfaith groups, dealing with the country's Protestant, Catholic, and Jewish leaders at the highest levels. Representatives and senators, bishops, and media personalities, eager to establish relations with American Muslims, enthusiastically attended AMC's events, which often were held in Washington's most prestigious hotels.[4] After extensive meetings the Department of Defense put Alamoudi in the powerful position of training and vetting the imams who attend to the religious needs of American Muslims serving in the military.[5] His organization was praised by the FBI as "the most mainstream Muslim group in the United States," and the State Department even appointed him as a goodwill ambassador, routinely asking him to travel throughout the world representing American Muslims.[6] Washington's establishment considered Alamoudi a successful, representative, and moderate Muslim leader who could be a spokesman and model for the American Muslim community.

In 2003, however, an unexpected discovery during a routine customs screening at London's Heathrow Airport undid Alamoudi's accomplishments. He was found to have concealed $340,000 in his suitcase. An investigation revealed that Alamoudi had been illegally importing funds from Libya since 1995 and that part of the money was intended to support a murky plot—conceived by the Libyan government and two London-based Saudi dissidents linked to al Qaeda—to assassinate Saudi Crown Prince Abdallah. A year later Alamoudi pled guilty to all charges and was sentenced to twenty-three years in jail.[7] The investigation also revealed Alamoudi's financial dealings with U.S.-designated terrorist organizations such as Hamas and al Qaeda, for which the Treasury Department accused him of fund-raising in the United States.[8]

To many in Washington, Alamoudi's ties did not come as a complete shock. Since the 1990s, in fact, law enforcement agencies had been quietly monitoring his links to elements suspected of terrorist ties.[9] In addition, over the years, Alamoudi had repeatedly made comments that clearly displayed his sympathies for Islamist outfits banned in the United States. Once, authorities intercepted a phone conversation in which Alamoudi told his interlocutor that the 1998 attacks perpetrated by al Qaeda against American embassies in East Africa had been "wrong," but only because "many African Muslims have died and not a single American died."[10] Alamoudi had also expressed his political views in public venues. In October 2000, speaking at a rally in Washington's Lafayette Park, just a block away from the White House, he proudly proclaimed: "Hear that, Bill Clinton, we are all supporters of Hamas! I wish they added that I am also a supporter of Hezbollah!"[11]

The case of Abdurahman Alamoudi and AMC raises a number of questions. In 1996 AMC claimed to have 5,000 members, out of a population of American Muslims that the group itself estimated, quite generously, at 7 million.[12] How could the head of an organization that by its own calculations represented no more than 0.07 percent of the American Muslim population, whose leadership had never in any way been elected by the Muslim community, have become the de facto spokesman for American Muslims, testifying before Congress and expressing views in the media on behalf of the whole community? The extraordinarily poor judgment of large segments of the American political establishment requires some explanation. Why would U.S. authorities, who were or should have been aware of Alamoudi's views and ties to suspect groups, embrace him and his organization as a model for American Muslims?

Though the height of Alamoudi's fall makes his case unique, the issues raised by his case are hardly limited to him or to the United States. Rather, they highlight a situation that is common to virtually all Western countries, whose governments have been attempting for the past twenty years to identify representative and, in their view, moderate interlocutors within their Muslim communities. While circumstances and experiences vary from country to country, most display similar patterns and difficulties. Particularly after 9/11, the debate over which individuals and organizations Western governments should engage as the representatives of their local Muslim communities has been intense and seemingly unending. As the story of Alamoudi dramatically shows, such choices are not easy—for reasons that lie in the internal dynamics of Western Muslim communities and in the intricacies of how Western governments decide such matters.

The Birth of Western Islam

The year 710 marked the first contact between Europe and the then nascent Muslim world.[13] Raiders led by the legendary commander Tariq ibn Ziyad crossed from North Africa to the Iberian peninsula and began a drive into the continent that ended just twenty-two years later, when Charles Martel defeated them in Poitiers. The following thirteen centuries have been characterized by continuous tensions and conflicts between Europe and the Muslim world. In the Middle Ages, when Europe was in a state of cultural and economic crisis and Islamic civilization at its peak, Muslims seemed to have the upper hand. Although they never managed to penetrate into the heart of Europe, they occupied or battled in its southern and southeastern extremities. By the seventeenth century, fortunes appeared to reverse; the decline of Muslim influence began with the 1699 Treaty of Karlowitz, which was signed by the Ottomans after their second unsuccessful siege of Vienna. European powers slowly surpassed Muslim powers in economic, scientific, cultural, and military achievements and began their expansion into Muslim lands. By the end of World War I, only a few pockets of this territory were free of their direct or indirect control.

The end of World War II heralded a new era of Muslim-European relations. European countries slowly came to realize that they could no longer afford empires and, more or less reluctantly, granted independence to their colonies in the Muslim world. Moreover, the economic boom that followed the war created a need in European countries for cheap, unskilled labor—satisfied with immigrants who came largely from Muslim countries. Thus large numbers of Algerians, Tunisians, and Moroccans found jobs in France, a country with which they had historical ties, as did Pakistanis and Indians in Great Britain and Turks in Germany. Belgium, the Netherlands, and the Scandinavian countries also attracted Muslim workers. Both sides envisioned this migratory movement as a temporary and mutually advantageous solution to pressing economic problems. The Europeans assumed that immigrant workers would stay for only a few years, contribute to the region's economic growth, and then go back to their countries of origin. By the same token, migrant workers originally planned to use the fruits of their hard labor to build a new life for themselves in their home countries. European governments did not feel the need to devise policies to accommodate and integrate individuals who would soon return to their countries of origin, and Muslims limited their religious life to a few makeshift mosques, leading some experts to speak of "cellar Islam."[14] Muslims, and consequently Islam, therefore remained in effect an invisible presence in Europe.[15]

The situation changed significantly in the 1970s. In the wake of the economic downturn triggered by the 1974 oil crisis, most European countries restricted immigration.[16] Yet, even as regulations reduced the influx of new laborers, family reunification laws enacted throughout Europe allowed migrant workers to be joined by their spouses and children. Rather than returning to their home countries, the vast majority decided to settle permanently in Europe with their extended families. Since then, Europe's Muslim population has grown steadily. To the first wave of immigrants has been added a second and even a third generation of European-born Muslims, most of them citizens of their country of birth. As large numbers of asylum seekers have joined legal and illegal immigrants, the Muslim presence has expanded to areas of southern Europe it had not previously reached. Today, virtually all European countries host a Muslim minority, and the best estimates put the number of Muslims living in Western Europe at between 15 and 20 million—making Islam the continent's second religion.[17]

With the arrival of women and children, Muslims and non-Muslims began to interact not only in factories but also in schools, hospitals, and housing projects, with public administrations and local institutions.[18] Muslims began expressing the need to build mosques, to have their faith taught in public schools, to celebrate weddings and funerals according to Islamic tradition, to find *halal* butchers, and so on. As they transitioned from being temporary laborers to permanent residents and then to citizens, Islam left the cellars and became more visible.[19] Having become a stable presence in Europe, Muslims grew more vocal in demanding that their faith be accommodated into European societies and that they be accorded the same rights as other religious groups.

The history of Islam in North America is in some respects different from that of Europe. A small Muslim presence had always existed in the United States, as some slaves from West Africa had Islamic practices that they maintained throughout their captivity.[20] From the late nineteenth century to the present, waves of Muslim immigrants from the Middle East, South Asia, and the Balkans have settled in North America, albeit in numbers proportionally lower than those of most European countries. As a result, the American Muslim population, currently gauged at between 3 and 5 million, is extremely diverse, dominated by no single ethnic or national group. Particularly noteworthy is the high number of converts— estimated as more than 40 percent of the country's Muslim population.[21] A large percentage of the converts are African Americans, who often adhere to particularistic forms of Islam, such as those espoused by the Nation of Islam.

The distinctions between American and European Islam go beyond immigration patterns and ethnicity. Whereas Muslim immigrants to Europe were and, to a large degree, still are uneducated and unskilled laborers, the vast majority of Muslims who have settled in the United States and Canada are well-educated professionals, many of whom initially left their homelands to study at American universities. Most belong to the middle and upper middle classes; unlike European Muslims, who generally languish at the bottom of measures of economic integration, the average American Muslim household's income is equal to, if not higher than, that of the average non-Muslim American household, and the percentage of Muslim college graduates is more than double the national percentage.[22] While large segments of European Muslim communities contend with deprivation and marginalization, American Muslims generally have integrated more easily into the mainstream culture both socially and economically. Moreover, the American tradition of religious freedom and diversity creates an environment in which the accommodation of Islam presents fewer problems than in Europe.

Despite such differences, Islam in both Europe and North America has experienced a remarkable surge in numbers and thus in visibility over the past three decades. As large communities have formed in most Western countries, policy makers have had to address the governance of Islam.[23] All Western countries recognize religious freedom, but they have fundamentally different ways of accommodating and regulating religion, most developed over centuries of often tense interactions between various churches and the state.[24] The rights and obligations of both parties have gradually been defined in models that range from the state churches of England and various Scandinavian countries to the rigid separation (verging on antagonism) between religion and state that characterizes the French system. Because Islam, as a newcomer to the West, had to adapt to these different and long-established patterns, its governance varies significantly from country to country.[25]

A Leaderless Community

A major issue facing several Western countries is the legal status of Islam.[26] All states fully guarantee individual freedom of religion, but they may take different approaches to organized religion. In such countries as the United States, Great Britain, or the Netherlands, religious groups can constitute themselves and conduct their activities without the need of any government authorization. But in several European countries, only those recognized by the government can enjoy various legal and fiscal benefits. Germany, Italy, Spain, and Belgium are among those that rely on a concordat system: religious groups must undergo a vetting process that ensures their compatibility with the values of the state and must sign an agreement with the state to gain the rights that have been traditionally granted to Christian churches. Few of the different approaches to the legal recognition of Islam have been free of difficulties and controversies.

Most other aspects of the governance of Islam in the West, particularly in Europe, have also posed serious problems. With rare exceptions, Western countries are still struggling to determine if and how to teach Islam to Muslim children in public schools. The construction of mosques and Muslim cemeteries often spurs political confrontations because the relevant laws are unclear. Despite the efforts of some countries, the qualifications and legal status of most imams preaching in Western mosques are unregulated, creating problems of inequitable treatment of Muslim clerics and allowing the infiltration of radicals.

The reasons for these problems are many—the massive increase in the number of Muslims living in the West during a relatively brief period; the tendency of any debate concerning Islam to become politicized and unusually heated—particularly in the post–9/11 world; and the resistance of various political forces to many, if not all, concessions to Islam have all played a role. Another crucial factor, perhaps less obvious, is that nearly all Western Muslim communities lack unified leadership. Most other religious confessions, from minority Christian churches to Jewish and Buddhist groups, have been able to identify leaders—often through umbrella organizations—who could legitimately be seen as representative and could speak to policy makers seeking to extend to them the legal and financial benefits traditionally accorded major Christian churches.

The task of finding interlocutors within the various Muslim communities of the West, in contrast, has been excruciatingly difficult. Many governments deal with a vast array of organizations fighting to become the anointed representatives of the Muslim community and unwilling to cooperate with their competitors. Which of these should sit at the table with the government to negotiate issues such as regulating the slaughter of animals according to the *halal* method or drafting legislation to allow Muslims not to work on Friday? Which should be asked to partner with the government to draft programs to teach Islam in public schools or to train imams? As one commentator stated, "When government officials look for a responsible interlocutor, they find that the Muslim voice is a cacophony rather than a chorus."[27]

This cacophony is the direct by-product of the extreme diversity of Western Muslim communities, which are deeply divided by ethnicity, national origin, language, sect, and political opinion.[28] Indeed, many wonder if it would be more appropriate to speak of "Muslim communities" rather than a single Muslim community.[29] Though some of the divisions (particularly those along ethno-linguistic lines) are slowly diminishing as new generations of Western-born Muslims come of age, they are reflected in the high number of distinct organizations created over the past few decades.

To navigate this complex landscape, the myriad of Muslim organizations operating in the West must be labeled and categorized, even though the exercise unavoidably lends itself to oversimplification. One major distinction can be drawn between secular and religious organizations. During the first phase of Muslim immigration, most organizations were established primarily on the basis of cultural and ethnic ties; religion was relegated to a secondary role. Workers' associations, cultural circles, and so-called *amicales* were founded—mainly by North African and Turkish immigrants—to provide services for their members and maintain the community's cultural traditions. Usually divided by nationality, with close relations to their home country, they often operated under the auspices of their embassies.

Such organizations are, in a sense, called "Muslim" only descriptively: their members are Muslim, but their focus is not religious. Though the younger generations are less attracted to associations so closely bound to the countries of their parents' birth, these groups still represent an important fraction of the West's Muslim organizations. Other groupings often focus on specific issues, such as women's rights or conditions in a particular neighborhood. Over the past twenty years, however, the number of Islamic religious organizations has significantly increased, a development stimulated by several factors. In the Muslim world, the decline of nationalism, commonly dated to the early 1970s, coincided with a return to various forms of Islamic piety. In the West, first-, second-, and third-generation Muslim immigrants struggling to adjust to life in the West have also come to see Islam as a provider of cultural identity.

Religious organizations are even more diverse than their secular counterparts. A first important division is along sectarian lines, though not—as in parts of the Islamic world—between Sunni and Shia. With the exception of some concentrations of Lebanese, Pakistani, and Iranian Shia (the latter form a particularly sizable community in the United States), the vast majority of Muslims living in the West are Sunni, but they hardly form a monolithic block. Indeed, because Sunni Islam refuses to accept the existence of a central authority (unlike Catholicism and, to a lesser extent, Shia Islam), its very nature encourages organizations to mushroom and compete with one another to attract supporters.[30]

A second principle of differentiation, equally important in explaining the fragmentation of organized Islam in the West, is ethnicity—or, more specifically, nationality.[31] Almost as strictly as the secular associations, the religious organizations tend to split along national lines rather than into the four main ethnic groups of Muslim immigrants (Arab, Turkish, Indo-Pakistani, and sub-Saharan African). Other ethnic groups, such as African Americans, Kurds, Albanians, and Somalis, also generally have their own mosques and organizations. Divisions based on nation of origin and ethnicity are becoming less sharp as a second and third generation of Western-born Muslims comes of age, but they continue to exist and are a major obstacle to the creation of a unified Muslim leadership.

Finally, divisions among religious organizations are produced by their links to foreign actors and transnational movements. Since the early days of Muslim immigration to the West, outside forces have sought to influence the development of Western Islam by employing both their financial largesse and their ideology. The two forces that have been most active and successful at this, while at the same time competing, often viciously, with each other, are so-called embassy Islam and the global Islamist movement.

"Embassy Islam" is the term often used to describe the networks established by the governments of a handful of Muslim countries that have seen millions of their citizens migrate to the West. Eager for political, financial, and security reasons to maintain control over their expatriate communities, the governments of Turkey, Algeria, Morocco, and, to a lesser extent, Tunisia and Egypt have created institutions to serve the cultural, educational, and religious needs of their citizens living in Europe. Conceived (and perceived) as the *longae manus* of the government, such institutions generally preach what is widely considered a moderate interpretation of Islam and attempt to reinforce the believers' links to their homeland. Particularly extensive is the network established in Europe by the Turkish state, whose Ministry of Religious Affairs (*Diyanet İşleri Başkanlığı*, commonly referred to as *Diyanet*) runs hundreds of mosques and has more than 1,200 imams in all Western European countries with a sizable Turkish immigrant community.[32]

The global Islamist movement has also actively sought to influence Western Islam. Transnational movements such as the Muslim Brotherhood and the South Asia–based Jamat-e-Islami began establishing small and often informal networks in Europe and North America in the 1950s, initially using the West simply as a sanctuary from the recurring persecutions to which they were subject in most of the Muslim world. Over time, such networks became part of a more ambitious plan, aimed at the rest of the Muslim population of the West, to spread their vision of Islam as a comprehensive system of life. Organizations that belong to this loose and diverse ideological movement, which is the main subject of this book, have achieved remarkable successes over the past twenty years, often gaining high visibility through their activism.

The dynamics of the relationships among these diverse and ever-evolving secular and religious organizations are complex, ranging from occasional cooperation to outright confrontation, though competition is the normal state of affairs. The West is a new religious market for Islam, and organizations vie for influence both within the Muslim community and with Western establishments. This panorama is ever-changing, as the importance and visibility of the organizations rise and fall, reflecting not necessarily the numbers of their adherents but rather the means they possess.

Indeed, the vast majority of Western Muslims are connected with no organization. Separate studies conducted in several countries have consistently found that no more than 10 to 12 percent of Muslims are actively engaged in or even belong to a Muslim group, indicating the presence of a silent majority who do not feel represented by any of the competing organizations.[33] Moreover, while exact numbers and percentages cannot be determined, studies suggest that most Western Muslims can be categorized as "cultural" or "sociological" Muslims.[34] They interpret their faith much as do most contemporary Westerners, particularly Europeans: as purely cultural, a family tradition and a source of identity, but not as the center of their lives. Some might be agnostics; others could be indifferent to religion or simply accept that Islam shapes some rites of passage (such as marriage) without exerting a general influence on day-to-day life.

But many religious and practicing Muslims also remain independent of organizations. Particularly among the second and third generations, they have shaped new, individualized ways of living their faith; these hybrid forms often merge traditional elements of Islam with aspects of Western life and are completely independent of any structure.[35] Others practice more orthodox forms of Islam and might regularly frequent a mosque of their choosing, but they do not recognize themselves in any of the Muslim organizations operating in the West.

The Search for Partners

Because of the community's internal fragmentation and the widespread reluctance of individuals to affiliate, no organization operating in the West has succeeded in attracting anything close to a majority of Muslims. Some communities in certain cities or regions have been able to create umbrella organizations that seem to legitimately represent the majority of the local Muslim population.[36] Yet in no Western country have Muslims been able to create a truly representative organization at the national level.

This lack of unified leadership has significantly hampered the process of governance of Islam in the many countries whose constitutions require that a religious group be recognized by the state in order to enjoy a variety of rights and benefits. The process of recognition has been fairly straightforward in the few European countries that for historical reasons have a well-established Muslim minority. For example, in some Eastern European countries, such as Bulgaria and Romania, a mufti represents both political and spiritual authority. Even though the mufti's leadership may be (and often is) challenged by competing forces inside the Muslim community, the institutional structure establishes a formal point of contact for the Bulgarian and Romanian governments. In Greece, the status of the Muslim community was set out in the 1923 Lausanne peace treaty with Turkey. The arrangement was well suited for dealings with the sizable Turkish Muslim minority of Thrace, but has become increasingly inadequate to manage the state's relationship with the new Greek Muslim community, which is composed largely of immigrants.[37] More recently, Austria, Spain, and Belgium have enacted legislation that identifies a representative body to serve as the Muslim community's official interlocutor with the state. Though the day-to-day implementation of such measures has not always gone smoothly, they represent the most advanced approaches to institutionalizing Islam; most Western countries have not moved beyond debate and experimentation.

To date, European and North American governments have used different tactics to ameliorate this situation. Some have selected, almost arbitrarily, one Muslim organization with which they deal exclusively in almost all initiatives. Others have encouraged the formation of national umbrella organizations. France and Italy have decided to form representative bodies to serve as each government's official partner (elected according to a controversial formula based on mosques' square meters and government-appointed, respectively). No country has yet found a satisfactory solution, and policy makers in all Western countries are seeking better ways to engage their Muslim communities.

In establishing relations with any religious community, Western authorities seek an interlocutor that meets two basic requirements: representativeness and reliability.[38] That is, the interlocutor (be it one organization, an umbrella organization, or some kind of collective body) must be recognized by a majority of the members of the religious community as their legitimate representative. At the same time, the interlocutor must accept the basic constitutional framework of the country, even while possibly holding positions that are in conflict with the government's: to be judged reliable, the interlocutor must participate fairly and accept the rules of the political process (a requirement vaguely corresponding to the concept of a loyal opposition in the Anglo-Saxon tradition).[39]

To these minimum conditions, Western governments seem to have added an additional requirement that applies only to Muslim organizations: moderation. To be sure, issues of cultural integration and extremism may also arise among other religious groups, but they have appeared particularly salient in Muslim communities, especially in Europe. Western governments have ignored the apparently discriminatory nature of this added demand and placed particular emphasis on finding representatives of the Muslim community who embrace values that are compatible with the country's and encourage integration.

The search for "moderate Muslims"—a term that is as fashionable as it is inherently controversial, vague, and subjective—has been one of the guiding principles in Western governments' efforts to find interlocutors. And although problems of extremism and radicalization have existed for decades, they have become paramount in the post–9/11 environment. Events such as the July 2005 London bombings, the November 2004 assassination of Theo van Gogh, and the arrests of hundreds of Western-born

Muslims who have joined terrorist organizations since 9/11 have only made the need to partner with "moderate" Muslim leaders more urgent. Western policy makers now share a broad understanding that for the security of their countries it is crucially important to improve relations with their own Muslim population, and that to do so, they must find counterparts who not only represent the Muslim community but also can help decrease radicalization and alienation within it.

Some commentators have harshly judged Western governments' efforts to find partners who fit their agenda. Several voices in Western Muslim communities reject any institutionalization, particularly if conditioned on arbitrary requirements of "moderation," fearing it could create a sort of tutelary relationship that will subjugate Islam to Western governments.[40] In an article with the telling title "Good imam bad imam: civic religion and national integration in Britain after 9/11," Jonathan Birt criticizes the British government, which had previously devoted little attention to the Muslim community, for attempting to mold the country's Muslim leadership into a sort of "civic religion" modeled on the Church of England.[41] "The good imam," writes Birt, "is now to embody civic virtues, interfaith tolerance, professional managerial and pastoral skills, possibly become involved in inner city regeneration, work as an agent of national integration (most importantly on behalf of his young unruly flock), and wage a jihad against extremism."

Such censure is not completely unjustified. But attempts to ensure that the primary loyalty of members of religious movements is to the state have a long tradition in the West, dating back to the birth of the nation-state.[42] The demand that citizens integrate, without necessarily assimilating, and embrace some core values is hardly new, unreasonable, or discriminatory. Moreover, the process of institutionalization is in the best interests not only of the state but also of the Muslim community. Indeed, it is necessary if the community is to receive the same rights and benefits enjoyed by other religious groups, completing Islam's natural progress toward inclusion among Europe's religions.[43]

Limited Options

Islam has rapidly become Europe's second religion, yet most European countries lack clear rules that would provide for equal rights for Muslims on matters such as public education, construction of places of worship, and the legal status of clerics. Often the difficulty can be ascribed to the Muslim community's lack of unified leadership, though many Muslims blame discrimination against them. Whatever the actual effects of discrimination, its perception by many European Muslims is a very important and troubling phenomenon, as it creates a sense of alienation that can easily be exploited by the most radical voices in the community.

Given this situation, all governments are now looking at ways to at once regulate Islam and integrate it into their societies. The "benign neglect" formerly exhibited by most European governments has turned into a proactive, and in some cases hyperactive, attempt to encourage the development of a form of Islam that authorities deem compatible with life in a Western, multicultural society.[44] Though the modalities of this new interventionist approach vary from country to country, reflecting their different legal traditions, historical experiences of state-church relations, and local conditions, in all cases the governments understand the necessity of working with the Muslim community. In order to develop a curriculum to teach Islam in public schools, train imams, or implement counter-radicalization programs, they need the help of Muslim organizations and leaders who would, ideally, meet the desired requirements of representativeness, reliability, and moderation.

Yet because of the extreme fragmentation of Western Muslim communities, no organization can legitimately claim to fully meet the first, basic requirement: representativeness. The two types that, in most cases, come closest are those backed by Muslim governments and those linked to transnational Islamist movements. Neither has the general support that would even remotely qualify it to serve as sole representative of the whole Muslim community, but they alone have the organizational apparatus and control over a network of mosques that give them the appearance of possessing a nationwide following in most Western countries.

Though virtually nonexistent in America, organizations created or supported by Muslim governments have worked with European governments for decades. Several European governments, for example, have concluded agreements with the Turkish *Diyanet* and organizational outgrowths of various North African governments, allowing their employees to run mosques or teach Islam to Muslim pupils in public schools. But as European governments attempt to foster a European form of Islam, the idea of relying on such associations has increasingly seemed inappropriate. Many of today's European Muslims are European citizens; how could they be represented by the employees or the ambassadors of a foreign country? Even though the moderate and often secularist interpretation of Islam generally espoused by these organizations is appreciated, there is a growing understanding that only authentically European Muslim organizations that act independently of foreign influences can become representatives of Europe's Muslim communities.

This intrinsic unsuitability of "embassy Islam" has led many policy makers to turn their attention to the other obvious candidate: transnational Islamist organizations. These groups are not merely "Islamic"—that is, associations of Muslims who come together for mainly religious reasons—but "Islamist": their attempt to mobilize Muslims is based on the core belief that Islam should not be limited to the private sphere but should encompass all aspects of life, including the public and social.[45] Islamist organizations are, therefore, Islamic organizations that reject the view that Islam should be simply an individual matter; they subscribe to an all-encompassing interpretation that mixes politics and religion, presenting Islam as a complete system (*nizam Islami*).

The universe of Islamist organizations and movements is extremely diverse, both in the Muslim world and in the West, and a first distinction must be made between rejectionist and participationist movements.[46] The former are those that declare any system not based on a strict interpretation of the *sharia* as un-Islamic and refuse to take part in it. They include violent organizations such as al Qaeda as well as groups, such as Hizb ut Tahrir, that express their opposition to democracy but do not, at least openly, resort to or advocate violent means to further their agenda. Rejectionist movements, particularly those using violence, have received extraordinary amounts of attention over the past few years. Policy makers and commentators universally condemn them, though they often debate the causes of the rejectionists' positions and the best strategies for confronting their organizations.

Assessing participationist Islamist movements is much more complicated. These Islamists, well exemplified by Abdurahman Alamoudi, publicly declare their acceptance of democratic processes and actively seek to participate in them. Policy makers and analysts are split over the genuineness of this stance. An accurate judgment is vitally important because, unlike rejectionist groups, participationist movements make a claim to the leadership of Western Muslim communities. Having built an extensive network throughout the West over the past fifty years, these Islamist movements often present themselves as representatives of local communities and seek to interact with Western elites as such. Despite their relatively small numbers and the lack of any clear indication that they have the support of a significant percentage of Western Muslim communities, their activism and capacity for mobilization put them at the forefront of the battle for the leadership of Western Islam.[47]

Given the deficiencies of their competition, participationist Islamist organizations are by default the main candidates to become the privileged interlocutors of Western governments. Understanding their history, nature, and aims is therefore crucial. Is their stated desire to participate in the democratic process genuine, or simply tactical? Do they meet the criteria of reliability and moderation required by Western governments? What are Western governments' attitudes toward them? What elements influence them? Although no definitive assessment of the complex and ever-evolving reality of participationist Islamists can be made, this book will attempt to provide as much information and analysis as possible to answer these critical questions.

2

The Western Brotherhood

The Founder

The history of what is today commonly referred to as modern political Islam or Islamic revivalism starts in the late nineteenth century, when thinkers such as Jamal al-Din al-Afghani, Mohammed Abduh, and Rashid Rida began addressing the reasons for the Muslim world's state of crisis. At a time when Europeans were exerting their colonial influence in most of the Islamic world, Muslims were asking themselves why their power and culture were in decline. Many thinkers and rulers argued that their religiosity had kept them back and that the military, economic, technological, and cultural advantages of the West could be overcome only by emulating its industrialism and secularism. But al Afghani and his disciples offered an opposing analysis. The humiliating state of inferiority in which the *ummah* (community of those who affirm Islam) found itself, they argued, should be attributed to its loss of piety. Muslims had gone astray and adopted foreign ways of life. The only way for them to regain their rightful position of glory was, therefore, to revert to the mores of their past, imitating the early followers of the prophet Mohammed, the pious forefathers (in Arabic, *as-Salaf as-Saalih*, from which comes the term "Salafi," commonly used to identify both the nineteenth-century revivalists and various contemporary Islamist trends).[1]

Al Afghani and his disciples' contribution to modern Islamist thought cannot be overstated. Yet for all their merits in framing a narrative that identified the Muslim world's weaknesses and their solutions, the nineteenth-century reformers remained largely isolated from the masses and were unable to create a movement that would spread their ideas. The "popularization of Islamic discourse," as the American Islamist thinker and activist Jamal Barzinji defined it, came only in the 1930s and 1940s, thanks to the genius of Hassan al Banna and Abul A'ala Mawdudi.[2] Operating respectively in Egypt and the Asian subcontinent, al Banna and Mawdudi applied a modern organizational model to the message of the nineteenth-century reformers. The result was the birth of the modern Islamist movement.

The foundation of the Muslim Brotherhood (*Al Ikhwan al Muslimeen*) represents a fundamental milestone in the development of this movement. Hassan al Banna was a twenty-two-year-old schoolteacher with a deep faith and a gift for oratory when he founded the organization in 1928 in Ismailiya.[3] Al Banna had previously lived in northern Egypt and in Cairo, where he had been outraged by the impact of British colonialism on Egyptian society. Disillusioned by the apathy of the Islamic establishment, which he saw as failing to defend Islam from the secular and materialistic influences that were sweeping Egypt, al Banna started preaching in coffee shops, small mosques, schools, and anywhere else he and his early followers could find an audience.[4] Like most of the grassroots movements that sprang up in Egypt at the time, the Brotherhood was strongly opposed to colonial rule and advocated Egyptian independence. But while most anti-British movements took inspiration from an array of Western-imported ideologies, from nationalism to socialism, the Brotherhood was basing its discourse on Islam. Creating what would become the motto of generations of Islamists ("Islam is the solution," *al-Islam huwa al-hal*), al Banna saw the answer to the Western "military-political-ethical-social invasion" of the Muslim world as "resistance to foreign domination through the exaltation of Islam."[5]

For al Banna the foreign presence that was strangling Egypt and, more broadly, the whole Muslim world was identified less with European armies than with European ideas.[6] Blind imitation of Western lifestyles and customs introduced the poisons that weakened Muslim societies. And no imitation was more malign than that of Western legal systems. Since the arrival of European merchants and armies, rulers throughout the Muslim world had slowly but inexorably replaced the traditional provisions of *sharia* with rules taken from Western codes in an effort to modernize the social and commercial life of their lands. Al Banna considered the replacement of *sharia* with man-made laws not merely a symbol of the Muslim rulers' cultural surrender to the West, but, most important, a heretical act. In al Banna's view, God was the only sovereign and lawmaker; thus any other source of legislation was illegitimate. Men could only interpret God's law; creating law was man's attempt to substitute himself for God. *Sharia* was a perfect and all-encompassing system, the implementation of which would guarantee social justice and harmony.

Al Banna viewed Islam as complete and all-embracing, governing all aspects of private and public life. For him Islam was not just "empty acts of prostration" but "politics, society, economy, law and culture."[7] "Those who think that these teachings [of Islam] are concerned only with the spiritual or ritualistic aspects are mistaken in this belief," said al Banna, "because Islam is a faith and a ritual, a nation and a nationality, a religion and a state, spirit and deed, holy text and sword."[8] Solutions to all problems of the *ummah* could be found in this complete system: only when Muslims had fully implemented Islam would they regain their natural and God-given position of prominence in the world. The Islamic state was "more complete, more pure, more lofty, and more exalted than anything that can be found in the utterances of Westerners and the books of Europeans."[9] Islam, according to al Banna, included the virtues of all other systems and none of their flaws.

Al Banna's reference to Islam's mythical past as the cure for the *ummah*'s ills does not contradict his embrace of modernity. Al Banna believed that modernity itself could benefit the *ummah*, but firmly rejected the axiom that modernization equaled Westernization and secularization. Modernity and progress, the nineteenth-century Salafist reformers had argued, are perfectly compatible with Islam, which is not a stagnant faith. But any modernization must come on Islamic terms, not as a blind imitation of the West. The best way to modernize and to confront the military and cultural threat coming from the West was, paradoxically, to refer to the past. Only a modernization that took inspiration from Islam's glorious history could enable the *ummah* to compete with the West.

Nowhere was al Banna's embrace of modernity more evident than in his approach to political activism. Al Banna's Brotherhood was the first organization to attempt to simultaneously modernize and re-Islamize the Muslim community, developing a comprehensive plan of action to implement the ideas of the nineteenth century Salafists. Unlike his predecessors, al

Banna was able to create a modern and effective political organization that, within a few years, generated a mass movement. In less than twenty years, the Brotherhood was estimated to have over half a million members and an even larger number of sympathizers spread throughout Egypt.[10] The group attracted many from the city proletariat and the recently urbanized, well-educated, but frustrated lower middle class of government employees, white-collar workers, and university graduates with few employment prospects.[11]

An explanation for the organization's success unquestionably lies in the power of its message, a sort of anticolonial nationalism based not on an ethnic origin but on a common faith. Nostalgic references to the Islamic past played on the senses of pride and frustration simultaneously felt by most Egyptians. But the group's ideological appeal accounts for only part of its success, and such massive growth at the grassroots level can be explained only by the organizational genius of al Banna. Borrowing, whether consciously or not is unclear, from other popular movements of the era, such as communism and fascism, al Banna established an organizational framework that had no precedents in the Muslim world. At first the spread of his ideas was favored by the seemingly indefatigable propaganda efforts of the early Brothers. In a few years the organization grew more sophisticated, creating a capillary structure that soon included mosques, professional organizations, charities, social services, and publications. Internally, the Brotherhood subdivided itself into a myriad of suborganizations and committees, each with a very precise structure and goal. Some committees were in charge of finances, others focused on women or youth, and still others on propaganda or training new cadres. Some operated at the local level, others as part of a central structure, but all fell into a very precise hierarchy. Externally, the Brotherhood devoted itself tirelessly to the social and charitable work necessary to build support in the population, occupying the spaces that the state or competing Islamic organizations could or would not fill.

Establishing a model that would be used over the following decades by Islamist movements throughout the world, the Brotherhood used its immense apparatus to further its main mission: *dawa*. *Dawa*, or invitation to God, is commonly interpreted as the individual duty of all Muslims to spread their faith by calling people to Islam, but al Banna viewed it more broadly. Muslims too should be its target. Al Banna believed that his coreligionists had been so corrupted by foreign traditions that they had to be reintroduced to "real Islam." Mawdudi, al Banna's ideological counterpart in South Asia, had introduced the differentiation between "Muslims by choice" and "Muslims by chance" to address this issue.[12] The latter are those who are only nominally Muslim—aside from a few external gestures, they do not live according to Islamic teachings. It was, according to al Banna and Mawdudi, the duty of the "Muslims by choice" to bring the "Muslims by chance" to a wholesome Islamic lifestyle through *dawa*.

Here the organizational genius of al Banna is once again evident. He had established an extensive network of *dawa* organizations that could tailor their message to their audiences, reaching all strata of society. But he also devised a long-term social engineering program that, in his mind, would lead to a bottom-up Islamization of society.[13] This process would begin with the construction of the authentic Muslim individual, a pious man or woman guided by deep faith and a sense of social justice. Muslim individuals would form authentic Muslim families and, consequently, a truly Muslim society. Once society had been Islamized, a genuinely Muslim government and Muslim state based on the teachings of *sharia* would automatically follow. Only the state would have the strength to unite all Muslims, regain all Muslim lands from foreign hands, and restore Muslim honor. This newly rebuilt empire would be ready for the last step: the God-given mandate of spreading Islam worldwide, as, in al Banna's view, the faith's message knew no boundary—it was meant for the whole of humanity.

Al Banna's teachings became vague when he attempted to define the nature of the Islamic state or describe the steps necessary to establish it. Yet he was quite meticulous in outlining the first steps of his seven-pronged plan. He perfectly understood the need to focus on the youth and students in particular, taking advantage of their innate activism and frustration. He highlighted training loyal and competent cadres, "equipping the Islamic personality with the qualities that are needed for the advancement of the movement."[14] Finally, he understood the importance of having an extensive propaganda system and a viable financial apparatus to support it.

The Brotherhood's crisp message and relentless propaganda soon attracted followers outside Egypt. Foreign students who had been fascinated by the Brotherhood while studying in Cairo's prestigious universities began circulating the group's teachings in their homelands. Soon entities espousing al Banna's worldview and maintaining varying degrees of formal affiliation to the Egyptian Brotherhood began appearing throughout the Muslim world. Some, particularly in the Levant and in Yemen, were established as formal national branches of the Brotherhood; others were linked to it only by an ideological affiliation and personal connections.[15] In 1941, the Indian-born journalist Abul A'ala Mawdudi established the Jamat-e-Islami, a corresponding movement in South Asia. Within two decades the Brotherhood had managed to become not only a primary political force in Egypt but also a relevant ideological movement throughout the Muslim world.

The Troubles

Al Banna's public message called for the establishment of an Islamic state through "Islamization from below," a slow process that saw the creation of a purely Islamic system of government only as the natural consequence of the peaceful Islamization of the majority of the population. Yet parts of the Brotherhood seemed not to have patience to await the fruits of their *dawa* and, almost from the organization's inception, developed a secret apparatus that planned to use violence to further their goals. Al Banna himself soon formed a Special Section, the existence of which was unknown to most of the Brotherhood, to train members in paramilitary skills and weapons use. Initially the Special Section carried out attacks against British interests in the country, and some members participated in the 1948 war in Palestine against the newly formed state of Israel.[16]

But soon the Special Section extended its violent actions against domestic targets, bombing sites owned by or linked to Egyptian Jews and killing prominent politicians, judges, and government officials.[17] Tensions reached their peak when members of the Brotherhood were accused of killing Prime Minister Mahmud Fahmi al Nuqrashi, and Egyptian authorities banned the organization in December 1948. The ban escalated the confrontation between the Brotherhood and the Egyptian state, which the Brothers accused of having sold out to the British and not respecting the Islamic identity of the country. A few weeks later, members of the Egyptian security forces killed al Banna; several of the Brotherhood's top leaders were incarcerated and summarily tried. The Brothers had lost the first of many battles they would fight with the Egyptian government over subsequent decades.

The loss of al Banna's organizational genius dealt a significant blow to the Brotherhood, which nevertheless managed to survive and attempted to take advantage of the huge changes in Egyptian politics that soon followed. In July 1952, Gamal Abdel Nasser and the Free Officers overthrew King Farouk and established a republic. The move initially filled the hearts of the surviving Brothers with hope. Many Free Officers had close ties to the Brotherhood, having fought together in the Palestine war, and some Brothers contributed significantly to the planning of the 1952 coup.[18] They hoped to exploit these personal ties to influence the Free Officers, a group of ambitious men driven by nationalist and anticolonial feelings, but devoid of a real ideology. In the Brotherhood's vision, Nasser and the Free Officers could finally give an Islamic direction to the Egyptian state.

The alliance lasted for just a few months. In 1953 the Brotherhood was the only political organization authorized to operate when the government ordered the dissolution of all Egyptian parties, but the Brothers' insistence on the introduction of *sharia* and more Islam soon began to drive a wedge between the Brotherhood and the government. After a few months it became clear that Nasser and his Revolutionary Command Council had no intention of implementing the Brothers' vision of an Islamic state, and Nasser began to perceive them as a threat to his regime.[19] In January 1954 he banned the Brotherhood, initiating a violent confrontation similar to the one that had taken al Banna's life. In October of the same year Nasser was the victim of an assassination attempt while speaking in his native Alexandria. The unsuccessful plot gave him enormous prestige and provided him with the political opportunity to dismantle an organization that had posed significant challenges to his power. Over the years many have questioned whether members of the Brotherhood were indeed behind the assassination attempt. Unquestionably, even if some were, the entire organization would not have been aware of the plot. Nevertheless, the Alexandria incident opened a dramatic phase of the Brotherhood's history, characterized by sweeping arrests, prolonged detentions, concentration camps, summary military tribunals, and widespread torture.

The crackdown of 1954 was just one of many that would be imposed by the Egyptian regime against the Brotherhood over the next fifty years.[20] Egyptian authorities have alternated phases of severe repression, during which thousands of members have been arrested and, in many cases, tortured and executed, with periods of tolerance. The Brothers have survived through all these trials, demonstrating a remarkable resilience. Nevertheless, the crackdowns of the 1950s and 1960s caused major changes, spurring three developments that have marked the organization's recent history and more generally, the trajectory of the global Islamist movement.

The first development was the violent radicalization of a part of the Brotherhood. Deprived of al Banna's leadership, the Brotherhood of the late 1950s and early 1960s found a new ideological leader in another schoolteacher, Said Qutb. Qutb did not possess al Banna's charisma and organizational skills, but his literary ability compensated for these deficiencies. Originally only a minor player, Qutb gained a following among the Brothers thanks to his writings from behind bars. At a time when thousands of Brothers were languishing in jail and the formal leadership of the organization was proving itself ineffective—a former judge, Hassan Ismail al Hudaiby, had been elected as al Banna's successor, but his role was quite weak—Qutb's incendiary writings drew many members of the Brotherhood to embrace more radical views.

In works that have become classics of the Islamist movement, such as *In the Shade of the Quran* and *Milestones*, Qutb examines the situation of Muslims, concurring with al Banna's analysis of the problems. Qutb also agrees with al Banna that religion must be a "dominant master: powerful, dictating, honored and respected; ruling, not ruled, leading, not led."[21] Foreign influences and secularism (which he refers to as a Western schizophrenia) have led most Muslims to a state of pre-Islamic ignorance (*jahiliya*) that is the cause of the *ummah*'s weakness. But Qutb's contribution to Islamist thought was not so much in the diagnosis as in the cure. Al Banna believed that once his organization had properly Islamized the people, the Islamic state would naturally arise. Although he had always flirted, in both words and deeds, with the idea of using violence, he had never elaborated a conceptual framework and religious justification for doing so. Qutb developed the doctrine that would lead large segments of the global Islamist movement to embrace violence.

Qutb's analysis, unquestionably influenced by the horrors he witnessed in detention, is that the situation is so dire that Muslims cannot and should not wait.[22] Islamization from below is too slow a process, impeded by the intervention of local authorities and foreign powers. Therefore the only solution lies in the concepts of *takfir* and *jihad*. *Takfir* is the practice of declaring a Muslim a non-Muslim, and Qutb claims that it applies to the current Muslim rulers who, by refusing to implement *sharia* and establish authentic Islamic states, have in effect abandoned Islam. In Qutb's view, "true" Muslims are obligated to overthrow and kill such rulers in order to establish an Islamic state. *Dawa* cannot do what *jihad*, in this case defined as violent confrontation, can accomplish.[23] A small group of true Muslims, vaguely resembling the revolutionary vanguard envisioned by Lenin, should spearhead the fight against apostate rulers.

Qutb was never able to implement his vision and, after years in jail, he was hanged in 1966.[24] His martyrdom only increased his popularity. Qutb's doctrine, and particularly his religious justification of violence, has influenced generations of militants throughout the Muslim world. In Egypt, members of the Brotherhood broke with the group and formed bands such as the Gamaa Islamiya and the Egyptian Islamic Jihad, which aimed at using violence to overthrow the regime. Globally, Qutb's teachings on *takfir* and *jihad* have inspired the actions of most *jihadist* groups, making him the undisputed ideological forefather of modern Islamist terrorism.[25]

Whereas after the persecutions of the 1950s and 1960s one part of the Brotherhood decided to follow Qutb's path and engage in an all-out confrontation with the Egyptian government, in a second major development, another group opted for accommodation. By the late 1960s several leaders of the organization began to publicly eschew violence against the regime, beginning a long process of normalization that is still under way. Many point to a book written by the then *murshid* (spiritual guide) of the Brotherhood, Hassan al Hudaiby, as making a clean break with the Qutbist phase. *Preachers, Not Judges*, never mentions Qutb but rejects his doctrine of *takfir* and argues for reverting to al Banna's focus on education.[26] Hudaiby states that the Brothers should not judge other Muslims, a role that is reserved for God, but should simply focus on educating them on true Islam.[27] Adopting his teachings, the Brotherhood opted for a nonviolent opposition that focused on societal reform through grassroots education.[28] The shift crystallized in the late 1970s, when Umar al Tilmisani, the charismatic and astute third leader of the Brotherhood, began cooperating with the Egyptian government, opting for a policy of moderation and gradualism and accepting a place within the political process.[29] The accommodationist wing, which soon gained the leadership of the organization, understood that any sort of violent confrontation would have seen them on the losing side and led to further persecutions. These "Neo Muslim

Brethren" therefore decided to focus on *dawa*, implementing the bottom-up Islamization detailed by al Banna.[30]

Nasser's death in 1970 and the rise to power of Anwar Sadat gradually allowed more room for the Brothers to conduct their activities. Since then, the organization has endured periodic crackdowns, albeit minor, inevitably followed by periods of relaxation during which the Brotherhood, while never officially allowed to operate as a formal organization, is tolerated. The Neo Brothers have established a *modus vivendi* with the government; while still officially banned, they participate in elections, having successfully integrated into the country's political life. They still aim at Islamizing society but declare their intent to do so without resorting to violence.

The final consequence of the Nasserist crackdowns, and the one that interests us the most, was the emigration of large numbers of Brotherhood members. Many fled the persecution in Egypt and found a golden refuge in countries of the Arab Gulf whose economies were booming, thanks to their oil wealth. There the Brothers became teachers, lawyers, administrators, and bankers, taking intellectual jobs that the cash-rich but educationally underdeveloped Gulf countries had to fill in great numbers. The highly conservative kingdom of Saudi Arabia proved to be a paradise for them. Although the Saudi monarchy, careful to prevent any challenge to its absolute control of internal affairs, never allowed them to establish a formal branch of the Brotherhood, they found the country an ideal sanctuary.

The relationship between the Brothers and the Saudis was, at least at the beginning, a match made in heaven. The Saudis had the funds but lacked the educated class required to translate their newfound wealth into geopolitical influence. Motivated and highly educated, the Brothers seemed the ideal candidates to transform Wahhabism, the highly conservative Saudi interpretation of Islam, into a global ideology. Even though they had some theological differences with Saudi Wahhabism, these were put aside by the common desire to spread Islam throughout the world. Soon the Brothers began to put the Saudis' wealth to good use. Some funds went to finance the activities of the Brotherhood in Egypt, which was struggling to stay afloat. But larger amounts went to the creation of Islamic centers, publications, and organizations worldwide. Saudi financial patronage and Brotherhood brainpower led to the formation of the Muslim World League (MWL, 1962), the World Assembly of Muslim Youth (WAMY, 1972), and other multimillion-dollar *dawa* organizations that spread the Saudis' and the Brothers' interpretation of Islam.[31] With Saudi money, *dawa* could now be done globally and on an unprecedented scale.

Though the Arab Gulf was the perfect haven and a seemingly inexhaustible gold mine, not all Brothers who had chosen to leave Egypt decided to settle there. Smaller numbers, also coming from other Muslim countries, relocated in Europe and North America, hoping to receive political asylum or attracted by the option of furthering their studies at local universities. These "Western Brothers" founded some of the first Muslim organizations in the West—at the time, little more than student groups with a few dozen members. Nevertheless, such individuals and organizations represent the first seeds of political Islam in the West, and knowing their history and development is crucial to understanding the dynamics of today's Muslim communities.

The Pioneers

The first active presence of the *Ikhwan* in the West can be dated to the 1950s, when small, scattered groups of Brothers from Egypt and other Middle Eastern countries began concentrating in various European and North American cities. A handful of these pioneers were hardened Brotherhood members who sought refuge in the West after fleeing persecution in their native countries. The majority were students, members of the educated, urban middle classes who had already joined or flirted with the idea of joining the Brotherhood in their home countries.[32] They were a small, dispersed contingent of militants whose move reflected not a centralized plan but rather personal decisions that brought them to spend some years or the rest of their lives in the West. The Brotherhood, at the time barely able to withstand Nasser's pressure, had no strategy to establish an organic presence in the West and hardly kept tabs on what its affiliates were doing there.

Despite their isolation from the mother group in the Middle East, the first Brotherhood members and sympathizers who settled in the West became immediately active. Most were university students and, loyal to al Banna's organizational creed, they formed the first Muslim student organizations. Most Western cities lacked Muslim places of worship, and the Brothers' mosques, generally little more than garages or small meeting rooms on university campuses, often became the first religious facilities for Western Muslims. The West's freedoms allowed the Brothers to conduct the activities for which they had been persecuted in their home countries; with little funding but plenty of enthusiasm, they published magazines and organized lectures, meetings, and all sorts of events through which to spread their ideology. Their activism soon attracted other Muslim students and small numbers of Muslim immigrant laborers who had not had contact with the Brotherhood in their home countries.

Two figures stand out among the pioneers: Said Ramadan and Yussuf Nada. Born in 1926 in a village north of Cairo, Ramadan had joined the Muslim Brotherhood at the age of fourteen.[33] In 1946, upon obtaining his law license from the University of Cairo, Ramadan became al Banna's personal secretary and began the publication of *Al Shihab*, the organization's official magazine. In 1948 Ramadan fought in Palestine among Arab volunteers, was briefly appointed by King Abdallah of Jordan as head of Jerusalem's military corps, and opened the first branch of the Brotherhood in the holy city.[34] He then traveled to the newly established state of Pakistan, where, despite his young age, he competed for the office of secretary general of the World Muslim Congress. Al Banna's assassination and King Farouk's crackdown on the Brotherhood convinced Ramadan to remain in Pakistan, where he worked as a "cultural ambassador" to the Arab world. He became a respected and influential intellectual, hosting a weekly radio program, publishing booklets, and interacting with Mawdudi, the founder of Jamat-e-Islami.[35]

In the early 1950s, after King Farouk's ban on the Brotherhood was lifted by Nasser, Ramadan returned to Egypt, where he began to publish *Al Muslimoon*, one of the most important magazines of Islamist thought. When Nasser began to crack down, Ramadan was briefly imprisoned along with many other *Ikhwan* leaders. Realizing he could not continue his activities in Egypt, he left the country and, after short sojourns in various Middle Eastern countries, decided to permanently move to Europe with his wife, Wafa, Hassan al Banna's eldest daughter. Ramadan enrolled at the University of Cologne, in Germany, where he obtained his graduate degree in law with a dissertation on Islamic law. The choice of West Germany was not uncommon among Brothers fleeing the Middle East at the time.[36] Some members of the Muslim Brotherhood had established links to Germany during World War II, when the Grand Mufti of Jerusalem, Haj Amin al

Husseini, moved to Berlin and aided the Nazi regime in its anti-Jewish propaganda.[37] Moreover, most of them were attracted by the prestige of the country's technical faculties, and many decided to further their studies in Germany's engineering, architecture, or medical schools.

Soon Ramadan left Germany and settled in Geneva, where in 1961 he founded the local Islamic Center. Quiet, free, and visited by wealthy Gulf Arabs during their summer vacations, the Swiss city was the perfect place for Ramadan. The center, which soon became one of the main headquarters of the Muslim Brotherhood in Europe, was the first of a score that he planned to establish throughout the continent, with the financial support of Saudi Arabia. Ramadan, in fact, had been one of the driving forces behind the establishment of the Muslim World League, the Saudi government-funded transnational body created with the aim of spreading the Saudi interpretation of Islam worldwide.[38] He soon became one of the Saudis' main point men in the West, traveling with a Saudi diplomatic passport to organize the scattered groups of refugee Brothers and sympathetic students who had settled in various European cities and in the United States.[39]

Ramadan's and most of the pioneers' hearts were still in their native countries; they viewed their sojourn in the West as only a temporary exile before returning home as victors and often compared their experience to the prophet Mohammed's exile in Medina after being persecuted in his native Mecca. Yet, while Ramadan never ceased to dream of returning to Egypt, he was among the first Brothers to recognize the potential benefits that operating in the West could have for the Islamist movement worldwide. The West was not just the ideal sanctuary, where the Brothers could freely fund-raise and spread their message, but also a place where they could come to control the local Muslim population. With scant competition from other currents of Islamic thought and local governments reluctant to interfere in religious affairs, the West presented opportunities that the Brothers could not enjoy in any Muslim country. Ramadan understood that the financial and organizational resources of the Brotherhood could gain them a position of prominence among Western Muslims.

A confirmation of Ramadan's analysis soon came from Munich, where a group of Arab students contacted him to seek his help in constructing a mosque.[40] The Mosque Construction Commission, the body that was trying to raise the funds for the new structure, had become the focus of a struggle between the Arab students and a group of Muslims who had stayed in Munich after fighting alongside the Nazis during World War II.[41] Originally from Central Asia and the Caucasus, the ex-soldiers embraced an interpretation of Islam that clashed with the more militant Arab views. By 1960 Ramadan, thanks to his Saudi funding, had secured for himself the position of chairman of the commission; by 1973, when the mosque was completed, the Brotherhood, with its finances, determination, and organization, had completely eclipsed other influences over the mosque.[42]

The Brotherhood-dominated Mosque Construction Commission became a permanent organization, which later changed its name to Islamic Society of Germany (Islamische Gemeinschaft Deutschland, IGD). Ramadan headed the organization for ten years; then, after the stewardship of Pakistani national Fazal Yazdani, one of the students who had originally contacted Ramadan, the Syrian-born Ghaleb Himmat, took the helm. Soon Munich became another sanctuary for the Brotherhood in Europe; particularly during Ramadan and other Islamic holidays, the mosque was a meeting point for members and sympathizers throughout Europe. Indeed, three of the eight *murshid* the Egyptian Brotherhood has had throughout its history spent significant time in the German city.[43] And it was in Munich that Himmat met Yussuf Nada, another member of the Egyptian Brotherhood who, like Said Ramadan, would shape the development of the *Ikhwan* in the West.[44] The meeting started a political and financial symbiosis between the two men that lasted for more than forty years.

The scion of a wealthy family from Alexandria, Nada joined the Brotherhood as a teenager and at age of twenty-three was among the thousands of *Ikhwan* imprisoned by Nasser after 1954.[45] After two years in prison Nada left Egypt, never to live there again. Barely escaping the 1969 coup d'état in Libya, he settled in Austria, where he set up a profitable dairy business. While building a multimillion-dollar financial empire between the Middle East and Europe, Nada remained involved in the vicissitudes of the Brotherhood. In the 1970s the *murshid* Umar Tilmisani named him the head of the Brotherhood's external relations.[46] Using the high-profile connections made through his business activities and traveling without restrictions, thanks to his Italian passport, Nada shuttled across the world to represent the Brotherhood's interests in meeting with many Muslim leaders, from heads of Islamic movements to heads of state. Nada's gigantic mansion in Campione d'Italia, an upscale Italian enclave in Swiss territory, has been described by many, including Nada himself, as a sort of unofficial foreign ministry of the Brotherhood.[47]

Nada's skills as a businessman enabled him to play a key role in the financial aspects of the Brotherhood's establishment in the West. In the late 1960s he became a sponsor of several Brotherhood activities, from organizations in the United States to mosques in Europe. He also became a mentor for several younger Brothers, whom he hired to work in some of his many companies, connecting them to his networks of Arab Gulf billionaires. Finally, in the 1980s, Nada and Himmat, who lives in a smaller villa right next to Nada's in Campione d'Italia, cofounded Bank al Taqwa, a financial institution widely believed to have served as the Brotherhood's clearinghouse in the West. According to European and American authorities, they used al Taqwa and an extensive network of companies to finance dozens of Brotherhood-related projects throughout the West. Both Himmat and Nada, whom the U.S. Treasury Department accuses of having funded Hamas and al Qaeda, were designated as terrorism financiers in 2001 by various Western countries and by the United Nations, even though no case against them has been brought in any court of law.[48]

Building Networks

As the personal stories of Ramadan and Nada show, the arrival of the first Brothers was hardly the first phase of a concerted plot of the Muslim Brotherhood to Islamize the West. Yet the interaction of these and other charismatic refugees with many enthusiastic students who either had flirted with the Brotherhood during the first years of their studies in the Middle East or had discovered its ideology on Western campuses bore unforeseen fruit. The small organizations they spontaneously formed soon developed beyond their most optimistic expectations and outgrew the status of student clubs. By the late 1970s the founders of such groups who had decided to stay in the West understood the necessity of creating new organizations that fulfilled the needs of the growing Muslim population, not just students. They steadily founded scores of associations that mirrored al Banna's model from the 1930s, establishing youth and women's branches, magazines and propaganda committees, schools and think tanks.

This mature phase of the "Western Brotherhood" coincided with epochal events worldwide. In the Middle East, Arab nationalism, having suffered the humiliating defeat of the 1967 war against Israel, had largely lost its appeal, to the benefit of Islamism. Sadat's new policy of gradual reconciliation had also allowed the accommodationist wing of the Brotherhood, the so-called New Brothers, to reorganize themselves. Finally, with continuing immigration and family reunifications, the numbers of the once invisible Muslim communities living in the West soared. These new populations had to fulfill their spiritual needs, seeking places of worship, Islamic literature, and all sorts of guidance as Muslim minorities in non-Muslim countries.

The combination of these factors led the Western Brothers to acquire a new outlook and confidence, drastically changing their perception of the role of Muslims in the West. In various seminars held in Europe, top Brotherhood scholars started to redefine some centuries-old religious qualifications, stating that the traditional distinction between *dar al Islam* (land of Islam) and *dar al harb* (land of war) did not reflect the current reality.[49] While the West could not be considered *dar al Islam*, because *sharia* was not enforced there, it could not be considered *dar al harb* either, because Muslims were allowed to practice Islam freely and were not persecuted. The scholars decided, therefore, to create a new legal category. They concluded that the West should be considered *dar al dawa* (land of preaching), a territory where Muslims live as a minority, are respected, and have the affirmative duty to spread their religion peacefully.[50]

The implications of this decision go far beyond the realm of theology. By redefining the nature of the Muslim presence in the West, the Brothers also changed the nature of their own role in it. Establishing an Islamic state in the Muslim world was still an important aspect of their agenda, but they began to focus more on Islamizing the West's growing Muslim population. This more ambitious aim led the Western Brothers to more sophisticated activities. Whereas earlier they had each operated in their adoptive country independently, by the 1970s the scattered clusters of Brothers settled throughout the West began meeting to coordinate, at least loosely, their actions. One of the first known meetings of Western Brothers took place in London's theater district in 1973.[51] The small and informal gathering, sponsored by the Saudi embassy, was convened to establish some form of collaboration among Islamist leaders in Europe. The same year, with the financial and political backing of Saudi Arabia and other Muslim countries, the Islamic Council of Europe was founded.[52]

Headquartered in London's posh Belgravia neighborhood, the Council became extremely active throughout the 1970s and 1980s, promoting high-profile conferences about Islam, providing financial support to Muslim organizations throughout Europe, and lobbying with European institutions in favor of Muslim minorities.[53] The director, Salem Azzam, was the scion of one of Egypt's most prestigious families; after being expelled from Egypt, he entered the Saudi diplomatic corps and eventually reached the position of Ambassador and Minister Plenipotentiary at the Saudi embassy in London.[54] Thanks to Azzam's close ties to royal families and elites in the Arab world, the Council served as a powerful lobbying arm of political Islam in Europe, financing an array of Islamic centers and establishing relationships with European institutions. It soon came to be known among British Muslims as the "Islamic jet set," for its members had no basis of popular support in the community but shuttled between lavish conferences and high-profile meetings with various heads of state.[55]

Financially supported by the Muslim World League, the Council also represented one of the first European-based Muslim organizations to transcend ethnic differences; although Arabs like Azzam and Said Ramadan were the leaders, South Asian activists also played an important role.[56] Since the early 1960s, Britain had hosted a small network of organizations linked to the Pakistani-based Jamat-e-Islami, the organization founded by Mawdudi in 1941. While the Brotherhood had settled in most European countries, Jamat-e-Islami established a presence only in Britain, the only country with a large South Asian population. There they created the UK Islamic Mission in 1962, and the Islamic Foundation, one of the first Islamic research centers in Europe, in 1973. Located initially in Leicester and subsequently in the nearby village of Markfield, the Islamic Foundation immediately became active in printing and translating the works of Mawdudi, Qutb, and other theorists of the Islamic revival. Over time it established the largest private Islamic library in Europe and organized numerous interfaith and academic programs, often in partnership with non-Muslim organizations.[57]

The Islamic Council of Europe and the Islamic Foundation of Leicester were among the first initiatives that tied the Western Brothers to the Jamat-e-Islami. Historical, personal, and, most important, ideological links had always existed between them. "We consider ourselves as an integral part of the Brotherhood and the Islamic movement in Egypt, Sudan and Malaysia," confirmed Qazi Ahmad Hussain, head of Jamat-e-Islami in Pakistan. "Our nation is one. The intellectual foundation of our movement is one: based on the Quran and the Sunna, and on the teachings of imam Hassan al Banna and Mawdudi."[58] A crucial figure in this alliance has been Khurshid Ahmad, another pioneer whose importance compares to that of Ramadan and Nada. An early follower of Mawdudi, Ahmad rose to the position of vice-president of the Jamat-e-Islami and had a prestigious career as a member of the Pakistani senate and a minister of planning in Zia ul-Haq's government.[59] Assigned by the party the task of engaging in "the propagation of Islam in Europe, Africa, and America," between 1968 and 1978 he lived in Britain.[60] There he served on the executive board of the Islamic Council of Europe and founded the Islamic Foundation of Leicester. He became a key player in the informal networks of Islamic revivalists who lived in Europe, cementing his and his organization's symbiosis with the Western Brothers by joining the governing council of the Munich mosque.[61] While the rest of the Muslim community was still rigidly divided along national lines, the revivalists, driven by their belief in the unity of the *ummah*, were able to transcend ethnic differences and work together to implement a common vision.

The informal network of like-minded Western-based Islamic revivalists that revolved around the Islamic Council of Europe took an additional step toward increased coordination in July 1977, after a conference held in Lugano. The charming Swiss lake town had always been the headquarters of Yussuf Nada's business activities and, by his own admission, the wealthy "foreign minister" of the Brotherhood played a key role in organizing the meeting.[62] The First International Conference on the Islamization of Knowledge brought together some thirty leaders of the global Islamist movement.[63] Among the most prominent attendees were the ubiquitous Khurshid Ahmad; Abdul Hamid Abu Sulayman, one of the founders of WAMY; and Yussuf al Qaradawi, a member of the Egyptian Brotherhood who had settled in Qatar and was establishing himself as a very influential cleric in the oil-rich emirate.

A particularly important role in the Lugano meeting was played by American-based members of the Islamic movement. Members and sympathizers of the Brotherhood first settled in the United States in the late

1950s; in 1963 they were instrumental in forming the Muslim Student Association (MSA), which started as a small group comprising about a hundred students from various universities throughout the Midwest.[64] Particularly active among the pioneers who settled in America were three young Iraqi Kurds: Jamal Barzinji, Ahmed Totonji, and Hisham al Talib. They had left Iraq as the regime began cracking down on the local branch of the Brotherhood; they studied in the United Kingdom and then moved to the United States in the late 1960s.[65] Once in America the three Kurds took high-profile roles in Brotherhood-linked organizations both in the United States and worldwide. Totonji and al Talib served as secretary general of the International Islamic Federation of Student Organizations (IIFSO), a Kuwaiti-based umbrella organization for worldwide Muslim student groups and a forerunner of the Saudi WAMY.[66] Al Talib later served also as secretary general of WAMY itself. IIFSO and WAMY were among the most active and best funded youth multinational organizations sponsored by Gulf countries to propagate their interpretation of Islam worldwide.[67]

Domestically the three Kurds were no less active. Aside from their involvement in the daily management of the MSA (of which Barzinji served as president and chair of the Planning and Organization Committee, Totonji as chairman, and al Talib as founding member), they also masterminded the creation of a web of affiliated organizations.[68] In 1973 they set up the North American Islamic Trust (NAIT), initially headed by al Talib and Barzinji, whose purpose was to financially support the activities of the MSA.[69] The MSA began developing a network of suborganizations and professional orders, from the Association of Muslim Scientists and Engineers (AMSE) to the Association of Muslim Social Scientists (AMSS), which published the American Journal of Islamic Social Sciences.[70] Like their European counterparts, the American Brothers soon realized that their needs could not be met by a student organization; they therefore established the Islamic Society of North America (ISNA), an umbrella organization designed to include all others.[71] ISNA, NAIT, and MSA soon established their headquarters on a multimillion-dollar, 42-acre site in suburban Indianapolis, which came to be used for conferences of all their affiliated entities.[72]

The three Kurds' success in building a myriad of entities was due largely to their activism and vision, but the financial angle cannot be overlooked. Throughout the 1970s and the early 1980s the men worked for various companies owned by Nada and were introduced to his network of wealthy

Arab Gulf donors.[73] The relationship was so close that Nada purchased a home in Indianapolis (and three of his four children were born in the United States), and more than thirty years later, he still refers to the three—Barzinji, Totonji, and al Talib—affectionately as "my boys."[74] The 1977 Lugano meeting, which had been formally convened by the Association of Muslim Social Scientists, entrusted the three with an additional responsibility. The attendees had agreed that, in order to solidify their position in the West, the Brothers had to develop a scientific methodology to refine the spread of Islamist thought. Acknowledging the Muslim world's inferiority in scientific, military, and cultural knowledge, they sought ways to close this intellectual gap.[75] Their answer lay in the concept of the "Islamization of knowledge," a quest to analyze social and political issues from an Islamic perspective.[76] Crucial in this endeavor was the creation of a think tank, the International Institute of Islamic Thought (IIIT), which the attendees of the Lugano meeting decided to base in the United States. IIIT's first board consisted of WAMY founder and University of Pennsylvania graduate Abu Sulayman, Barzinji, the American-based scholar and Muslim World League founder Taha al Alwani, and Anwar Ibrahim, who would later become Deputy Prime Minister of Malaysia (1993–1998). IIIT was formally incorporated in Pennsylvania in 1980 (it later moved to suburban Washington, D.C.), and its first board meeting was held in Barzinji's Maryland home.[77] Along with the Islamic Foundation of Leicester and various Saudi and Gulf organizations, IIIT served as a catalyst for the spread of revivalist ideology, focusing on translating into various Western languages and disseminating the works of al Banna, Qutb, Mawdudi, and other key Islamist thinkers.

The roles of treasurer and director were given to Ismail Faruqi, the Harvard-educated scion of a prominent Palestinian family from Jaffo who had obtained tenure at Philadelphia's Temple University.[78] Originally a pan-Arabist, Faruqi had embraced an Islamist worldview in the United States after interacting with the leadership of the MSA. Thanks to his remarkable intellectual vivacity, Faruqi soon became a pivotal figure in the pioneering networks of the American Brotherhood, turning Temple University into an important hub of Islamist thought. Several young Islamists, often benefiting from scholarships from WAMY and other Saudi organizations, studied under him at Temple; his suburban Philadelphia home, out of which he ran most of IIIT's activities, was the Islamic version of a nineteenth-century Paris salon. In 1986 Faruqi and his wife were killed in their home by one of Faruqi's disciples, an African American convert to Islam, for reasons that remain unclear.

Who's a Brother?

From their modest beginnings in the early 1960s the American Brothers have made impressive gains. The cluster of no more than a few dozen activists, all of whom serve on the myriad of interlocking boards and committees, has managed to develop an extremely effective organizational apparatus. IIIT has become a global entity, with branches on all continents.[79] Its conferences are often cosponsored by top American universities and think tanks and are frequently attended by government officials. Its affiliated educational institution, the Virginia-based Graduate School of Islamic and Social Sciences, trains hundreds of imams and was officially tasked by the Pentagon to endorse Muslim chaplains to serve in the U.S. military.[80] ISNA organizes the largest annual gathering of American Muslims, attended by no fewer than 30,000 people every year. Its leaders are invited to end-of-Ramadan dinners at the White House and regularly meet with top government officials.

The American Brothers' success is hardly the exception, and its pattern of development from small student groups to influential and multifunctional network of organizations has been paralleled in most Western countries. Throughout the West the Muslim organizations that began as small groups established by the pioneering Brothers in the 1960s and 1970s have grown exponentially, both in terms of their influence on the wider Muslim community and in access to Western political, intellectual, and media elites. The Islamic Foundation of Leicester hosts annual dinners, during one of which even the Prince of Wales, sitting beside Khurshid Ahmad, lavished praises on its scholarship.[81] The Islamic Society of Germany, the organization founded by Said Ramadan after the Brothers' takeover of the Mosque Construction Commission and then headed by Himmat for twenty years until his designation by the United Nations as a terrorism financier, claims to control a large number of the country's mosques, and its leaders often speak before the European Parliament.

Before analyzing the reasons for the Western Brotherhood's success, it is necessary to address a persistent terminological problem. When experts

speak about Brotherhood networks in the West, their analyses and specu-
lations often collide confusingly with an undeniable fact: there is no formal Muslim Brotherhood organization in the West. Moreover, individuals
and organizations commonly identified by governments and commentators as "members of the Muslim Brotherhood" or "affiliated to the Muslim
Brotherhood" often vigorously challenge such characterization, in some
cases even by legal means. This is easy to understand. In the West having
an affiliation with the Brotherhood is not illegal, as it is in Egypt, Syria,
and other Middle Eastern countries. Yet the linkage, even on a purely ideological level, affects how an organization is perceived and, consequently, its
relationship with Western political establishments.

To clarify the situation requires analyzing the evolution of both the Muslim Brotherhood and its Western offshoots. In the 1930s Hassan al Banna
did create an organization with a well-defined hierarchy and a ceremony in
which new members pledged their allegiance before formally joining. Although this organizational structure was limited to Egypt, in the 1940s the
Brotherhood created a Section for Liaison with the Islamic World.[82] Operated by a director, two deputies, and a secretary, and inserted in the complex formal structure of the Brotherhood, the section had nine permanent
committees; six dealt with various geographical areas in the Muslim world,
and others oversaw regions where Muslims were a minority, such as the
Soviet Union, Europe, and the Americas. As the Brotherhood's ideas were
spreading throughout the world, al Banna tried to form a multinational
organization, but the waves of crackdowns under first the Egyptian monarchy and later the Nasserist regime prevented the Brotherhood from implementing his plan; the idea was shelved.[83]

In the 1970s, as its members were being released from jail and the organization was slowly regaining the ability to plan activities under the less restrictive regime of Sadat, the Egyptian Brotherhood again worked to create
a more structured international organization.[84] "The Brotherhood organisations in Kuwait [sic], Jordan, Lebanon, Syria and Iraq agreed to join the
Egyptians, with their headquarters in Egypt and the *murshid* as leader," recalls Abdelwahab al Affendi, a London-based academic and former member of the National Islamic Front, Sudan's Islamist party.[85] In 1982 a formal
International Organization of the Muslim Brotherhood was established
as "a comprehensive Islamic body working to establish Allah's religion on
earth," composed of several institutions (a General Guide, a Guidance Bu-

reau, and a Shura Council) assigned to coordinate the activities of the various branches.[86] Uniting some of the top leaders of Brotherhood branches from several countries of the Arab world—but with the Egyptians always dominating—the International Organization aimed at crafting a unified strategy for the movement, arbitrating internal conflicts, and dividing funds. The experiment failed. Travel bans and other security restrictions prevented members of the various branches from traveling freely and meeting regularly. Most important, the attempt to create a multinational organization failed because of the reluctance of all branches to accept the leading role the Egyptians had reserved for themselves. If the Egyptians had in mind a sort of Soviet-style "Muslim Comintern," with Cairo in place of Moscow, other branches and affiliates rejected the idea, opting for more decentralization.[87]

The repeated failures of the Egyptian Brotherhood to create a Cairo-dominated transnational structure highlight one undeniable truth: a formal International Organization of the Muslim Brotherhood still exists, but it is hardly a fully functioning, all-overseeing Muslim command center.[88] Over the past fifty years the ideology and methodology envisioned by al Banna and then refined and re-elaborated by scores of other scholars, many of whom lacked any formal affiliation with the Brotherhood, has influenced generations of Muslim activists who have created all sorts of organizations throughout the world. Yet the operational influence exerted by the Egyptian Muslim Brotherhood over them is minimal to nonexistent, even though all groups recognize their intellectual debt to it.

Therefore, today the term "Muslim Brotherhood" can simultaneously encapsulate various realities. It is still an organization with a formal structure in Egypt and in various Middle Eastern countries, where some groups do view themselves as local branches. But, most notably, the Brotherhood is also a global ideological movement in which like-minded individuals interact through an informal yet very sophisticated international network of personal, financial, and especially ideological ties. Mohammed Akef, the *murshid* of the Egyptian branch of the Muslim Brotherhood until January 2010, describes it as "a global movement whose members cooperate with each other throughout the world, based on the same religious worldview—the spread of Islam, until it rules the world."[89]

The idea of creating a global movement rather than a formally structured organization has been present since the early days. Al Banna himself had stated that he saw the Brotherhood not as a political party but rather "as an idea and a creed, a system and a syllabus, which is why we are not bounded by a place or a group of people and can never be until the Day of Judgment."[90] Since the 1940s the Brotherhood's message has spread to virtually all other Muslim countries and the rest of the world. In each country the movement took different forms, adapting to the local political conditions. In Middle Eastern countries where it was tolerated, it existed as a political party; in those where it was persecuted, it remained an underground movement, devoted to *dawa* and, in some cases, to violence. In Palestine it took a peculiar turn and became Hamas, which, as the Hamas Charter states, is the official Palestinian branch of the Brotherhood.[91] In the West, it took locally familiar forms, such as civil rights groups and religious and lobbying organizations.

All these entities work according to a common vision but in complete operational independence. There are consultations and constant communication, but each is free to pursue its goals as it deems appropriate. Therefore the international Muslim Brotherhood is today most properly identified not as a group or even a loose federation, but simply as an ideological movement, in which different branches choose their own tactics to achieve their short-term goals in complete independence. What binds them together is a deep belief in Islam as a comprehensive way of life that, in the long term, they hope to turn into a political system using different methods in different times and places. Taking full advantage of the benefits of globalization and modern technology, they constitute a perfect example of modern transnational activism: informal, heterogeneous, and in constant evolution.[92]

In a 2008 interview, Mohamed Habib, first deputy chairman of the Egyptian Muslim Brotherhood, confirmed this analysis of the organizations that locate themselves in the Brotherhood's galaxy. "There are entities that exist in many countries all over the world," said Habib. "These entities have the same ideology, principle and objectives but they work in different circumstances and different contexts. So, it is reasonable to have decentralization in action so that every entity works according to its circumstances and according to the problems it is facing and in their framework."[93] Habib added that such decentralization serves two objectives: "First: It adds flexibility to [the] movement. Second: It focuses on action. Every entity in its own country can issue its own decision because it is more aware of the problems, circumstances and context in which they are working. However, there is some centralization in some issues. These entities can have dialogue when there is a common cause that faces Arabs or Muslims over their central issues like the Palestinian cause. At that time, all of them must cooperate for it." Habib's view is confirmed by a member of the Union of Islamic Organizations of France (UOIF, the country's Western Brotherhood offshoot), interviewed by Brigitte Maréchal: "I think that the basis of this ideology, is precisely the ability to be adaptable. . . . So . . . in the Palestinian context, that means . . . making things blow up . . . bombs. And in the context of the French Republic, it means . . . talking about lay status."[94]

Like any movement that spans continents and has millions of affiliates, the global Muslim Brotherhood is hardly a monolithic block. Personal and ideological divisions are common. Divergences emerge on how the movement should try to achieve its goals and, in some cases, even on what those goals should actually be. Issues such as the First Gulf War or the *hijab* (head scarf) controversy in France have spurred strong internal debates, which in some cases have degenerated into personal feuds. Senior scholars and activists often vie with one another over theological issues, political positions, access to financial sources, and leadership of the movement. Despite these inevitable differences, their deep belief in the inherent political nature of Islam and their adoption of al Banna's organization-focused methodology in order to implement it make them part of the informal transnational movement of the Muslim Brotherhood.

Terminology can be deceiving. As already noted, most individuals and organizations, particularly in the West, will publicly reject any "formal" or "organic" link to the Brotherhood. By doing so, they are indeed stating a true fact, but they are also playing with words. Senior members of the Brotherhood have repeatedly made clear that it is not a structured organization of card-carrying members, but rather an ideological movement that transcends formal affiliation. Membership comes by adopting certain ideas and methods, not by swearing allegiance or signing one's name in a secret registry. Already in al Banna's mind, despite his almost obsessive focus on organization, the ideological message of the Brotherhood was much more important than formal affiliations: "Leave aside appearances and formalities. Let the principle and priority of our union be thought, morality, action. We are brothers in the service of Islam, we are the Muslim Brotherhood."[95] Sixty years later, the former *murshid* of the Egyptian Brotherhood,

Mohammed Akef, confirms that "a person who is in the global arena and believes in the Muslim Brotherhood's path is considered part of us and we are part of him."[96] Yussuf Nada believes that describing the Muslim Brotherhood even as an informal movement is too confining and prefers to see it as a "common way of thinking."[97] Dr. Abd El Monem Abou El Fotouh, a member of the Egyptian Brotherhood's Guidance Council, refers to the Brotherhood as "an international school of thought," acknowledging that, whereas the Brothers have been unable to build an international organization, they have been very successful at creating an informal network of groups and individuals that have the same understanding of Islam and the same vision for the future.[98]

Identifying Indicators: A Methodological Attempt

In an interview with Xavier Ternisien, a French expert on religions, Mohammed Akef clearly described how the Brotherhood transcends formalities such as official affiliation.[99] "We do not have an international organization; we have an organization through our perception of things," explained the *murshid*. "We are present in every country. Everywhere there are people who believe in the message of the Muslim Brothers. In France, the Union of Islamic Organizations of France (UOIF) does not belong to the organization of the Brothers. They follow their own laws and rules. There are many organizations that do not belong to the Muslim Brothers. For example, sheikh al Qaradawi. He is not a Muslim Brother, but he was formed according to the doctrine of the Brothers. The doctrine of the Brothers is a written doctrine that has been translated in all languages." Confirming the informality of the movement's ties, Akef elsewhere referred to the UOIF as "our brothers in France."[100] Finally, in a 2005 interview, Akef explained that European Ikhwan organizations have no direct link to the Egyptian branch, yet they coordinate actions with them. He concluded with a telling remark: "We have the tendency not to make distinctions among us."[101]

Though members of the Egyptian branch of the Muslim Brotherhood may still take an oath of allegiance when they join, these formalities do not apply in the West. The absence of official affiliations makes the identification of members of what I am calling the global Muslim Brotherhood movement particularly challenging. The task is even more difficult in the

West, where individuals and organizations, aware of the negative stigma that any possible link to the Muslim Brotherhood can have, have gone to great lengths to sever or hide such ties. Governments and commentators have endlessly debated whether the organizations founded by the Brotherhood's pioneers and their offshoots—established decades ago and increasingly guided by a second generation of mostly Western-born leaders—can be described as Muslim Brotherhood entities. The answer can be given only by refining the question. If identification with the Brotherhood is defined by a formal membership or affiliation, then the Brotherhood is not present in the West aside from such pioneers as Nada and a few others. But if what matters is adherence to a set of ideas and methods, as Brotherhood leaders themselves consistently maintain, then the Brotherhood is very much active in Europe and North America.

Given the lack of formal affiliation and the conscious effort by the Western Brothers to downplay or deny even their ideological links to the Muslim Brotherhood, identifying an organization as part of the movement is difficult. Nevertheless, there are a number of indicators that, though not conclusive, help efforts to assess whether a certain group belongs to the global movement.

1. History

The most obvious indicator of affiliation to the global Muslim Brotherhood movement is in the group's past. An organization that was established by self-avowed or widely known Muslim Brotherhood members is quite likely to embrace the Brotherhood's ideology, no matter how distant in time its foundation was. They may have changed their tactics in order to adapt to the circumstances, their thinking on many issues might have evolved, but rarely do organizations started by Brotherhood members lose the basic ideological imprint of their founders.

2. Adoption of the Brotherhood's Methodology

Belonging to the global Muslim Brotherhood movement is determined by a belief not only in its credo but also in its methodology. *Dawa* is the not exclusive domain of the Brotherhood; many competing Islamic organizations make efforts to spread their faith.[102] Similarly, relentless activism and a determination to exert influence both within the Muslim community and over Western elites are common to other Islamic trends. However, the creation of an extensive array of suborganizations, each designed for a well-specified task, seems to be a distinguishing trait of the Western Brothers. A synoptic look at the organizational chart of various Western Muslim organizations shows similarities and a level of sophistication not found in any other Islamic trend.

An almost obsessive focus on education seems to be another characteristic of the Muslim Brotherhood and, consequently, of the Western Brothers. As al Banna did in the past, today's Western Brothers consider the formation and indoctrination of trained cadres a crucial step for the success of the movement. *Tarbiya*, the systematic training of members and potential members in Islamic texts and in the methodologies of political activism, is a cornerstone of al Banna's strategic thinking to which many Western Brotherhood organizations devote significant attention. Most regularly organize leadership seminars in which experienced activists teach effective *dawa* techniques and the tactics of political mobilization, and some even possess a permanent *tarbiya* committee. It must be noted that although most members of Brotherhood organizations, in the West and in the Muslim world, study the Quran and other religious texts, their education tends to be focused more on political aspects. Only a very small minority has a formal and extensive education in traditional religious studies.

Moreover, Western Brotherhood organizations tend to follow a pattern used by Islamist groups in the Muslim world and adopt the "paramosque" structure.[103] Rather than being a simple place of worship, their mosque is the center of the community, a forum for social, religious, educational, and political engagement. Even though such multiplicity of activities is not exclusive to Islamic centers controlled by Western Brothers, it reflects their vision of religion as a comprehensive system encompassing all aspects of life. According to Mohammed Akram, a self-avowed member of the American wing of the Brotherhood, Islamic centers should become a place for "study, family, battalion [*sic*], course, seminar, visit, sport, school, social club, women gathering, kindergarten, the office of domestic political resolution and the center for distributing our newspapers, magazines, books."[104] In every major American city, the Islamic center is to become, according to

Akram, "the axis of our Movement"—"the base for our rise" necessary to "educate us, prepare us and supply our battalions in addition to being the 'niche' of our prayers." All the activities of the paramosque, from football games to field trips, from lectures to initiatives to clean up local parks and neighborhoods, are designed to forge a sense of community and advance the movement's message. Carry Wickham perfectly described this process in the setting of urban Cairo. "A group of my committed friends and I will think of getting two or three other guys from our neighborhoods more involved," said a Brotherhood militant she interviewed. "So we invite them to play soccer, but of course it's not only soccer; we also talk to them about right and wrong. They see that we play fair, that we don't cheat, that we set a good example, and gradually, gently, over time, we try to show them the right path."[105] The dynamics are virtually identical in neighborhoods with large Muslim populations in London, Marseille, New York, or any other Western city.

3. Muslim Brotherhood Literature Predominant at Events/Bookstores

In pursuing their goal of the "Islamization of knowledge," the Western Brothers have devoted particular attention to the translation, publication, and extensive dissemination of texts written by Islamist authors. The works of al Banna, Mawdudi, and Qutb, or modern scholars like Yussuf al Qaradawi, Faysal Mawlawi, and Khurshid Ahmad, are sold at bargain prices or handed out for free at bookstores and conferences. The availability of such texts in a certain venue does not make the organization controlling it a part of the Western Brotherhood. But organizations that regularly recommend, advertise, and subsidize their publication are in most cases part of it. The position of prominence given to the texts of Islamist authors and their active promotion are clear indicators.

4. Frequent Interaction with Other Brotherhood Organizations

In the early 1970s the pioneers scattered in various Western countries began to interact with one another. Some had known each other from their home countries, but most established connections only through the conferences organized by groups such as the Muslim World League, IIFSO, WAMY, or the Islamic Council of Europe. Senior members of the Brotherhood such as Said Ramadan and Yussuf Nada, who spent decades traveling throughout the West and the Muslim world, also played a significant role in introducing activists operating in different countries. The result of these decades of interactions is the formation of an impressive network based largely on informal ties.

Conferences have been enormously effective. Since the 1970s Islamist scholars and activists have constantly traveled to attend the many conferences organized on a regular basis by the entities of the network, creating an informal circle where everybody knows everybody and generating the intellectual exchanges that make Islamist thinking so vibrant.[106] Thousands of Muslims regularly gather at Western Brothers' conferences to hear such stars of the circuit as al Qaradawi, Mawlawi, Khurshid Ahmad, and Taha al Alwani. But these events are also where personal connections are made, weekends during which long nights are spent talking, meeting like-minded individuals, and even arranging marriages.

Marriages are, in fact, one of the ways the personal relations among leaders of the Western Brotherhood are built. The leaders of the Western Brotherhood comprise no more than a few hundred figures whose names appear on the boards of the same intricate web of organizations, conference panels, and initiatives. A significant number of them have cemented such relationships by intermarriage, solidifying networks and literally helping to generate the next leaders. One of Yussuf Nada's daughters, for example, married the son of Yussuf al Qaradawi, while another married the son of Issam al Attar, the Aachen-based leader of one of the branches of the Syrian Muslim Brotherhood.[107] In some cases marriages provide interethnic linkages between Western-based Islamists, as in the case of Ibrahim el Zayat, the heir of Said Ramadan and Ghaleb Himmat at the head of the Islamic Society of Germany, who is married to Sabiha Erbakan, the nephew of Turkish Islamism's godfather Necmettin Erbakan. Daughters and wives of the leaders often head Brotherhood-linked women's organizations. All these family ties reinforce the network and enable the Western Brothers to control a myriad of organizations.

In essence, the Western Brotherhood is composed of connections and collaborations established around interlocking personal relationships.[108] It hardly corresponds to a well-defined master plan or a finely tuned conspiracy, but originates from the interaction of a small group of smart, educated, and motivated individuals. United by a common ideology and driven by a deep belief in a religious/political worldview, they slowly came together and found ways to cooperate. More than just a pure ideological movement, this small network is joined by marriage, business ties, old friendships, and, most important, a common vision. Technology and modern communication have also contributed to the creation of this "Islamic jet set." An organization's consistent and protracted involvement in this ever-evolving social network that transcends borders and linguistic barriers is a good indicator of its affiliation to the Western Brotherhood's network.

5. Financial Ties

Funding is one of the main factors that have set the Western Brotherhood apart from its competitors in the Western Muslim ideological marketplace. For decades the Brothers were among the preferred recipients of Saudi and Arab Gulf largesse. Beyond simple donations, the Brothers' financial interaction with Arab Gulf elites has provided a bonanza. Several top Brotherhood leaders such as Yussuf Nada have become extremely successful businessmen and have devoted parts of their financial empires to the spread of the movement. Moreover, Western-based Brotherhood thinkers such as Khurshid Ahmad, Gamal Attia, and Mahmoud Abu Saud have been at the forefront of the creation of the *sharia*-compliant system of banking that has spread throughout the Muslim world since the 1970s.[109] Today, many Brothers, whether Western or Middle East-based, sit on the *sharia* boards of large Islamic banks and investment companies, obtaining lucrative compensation and establishing important connections with Muslim financial and political elites. The Brothers have also established their own financial institutions—mostly in London, Geneva, and Luxembourg—directed by Western-educated *Ikhwan* according to Islamic principles. One of the first in Europe was the now dissolved Islamic Bank International of Denmark, set up in the early 1980s in Copenhagen by key Brotherhood figures. Its board included activists such as the Luxembourg-based financier and close friend of Nada, Gamal Attia; Hassan Abuelela, the late head of the Islamic Center of Stuttgart and a board member of the Islamic Society of Germany; and the U.S.-based Mahmoud Abu Saud.[110] Highlighting the Brothers' powerful ties, also listed on the board were then United Arab Emirates' Minister of Justice and Islamic Affairs, Sheik Mohamed Abdul Rahman al Bakr, and the personal advisor to the emir of Kuwait, Abdul Rahman Salem al Ateeqy.

The financial pipeline originating in the Middle East has never fully dried up, but occasional political disagreements and pressure from Western governments have recently diminished the flow. The Saudi government no longer funnels millions into the Brothers' coffers, so wealthy Emirati and, in particular, Qatari families are now the largest institutional funders of their activities. But over the past few decades, the Western Brothers have been also able to supplement and, in some cases, replace foreign donations with self-generated funds. As noted above, already in 1973 the American wing of the Western Brotherhood had established its financial arm, the North American Islamic Trust. The European Brothers followed suit in 1996, creating the Europe Trust, devoted to raising funds for its various activities. Officially established as an independent charity, the Europe Trust was incorporated in Markfield, the headquarters of the Islamic Foundation of Leicester, the Jamat-e-Islami think tank.[111] Its trustees are senior members of the Brotherhood-linked organizations of each large European country, from Ahmed Jaballah of the Union of Islamic Organizations of France to Ibrahim El Zayat of the Islamic Society of Germany.[112] A regular flow of funds to and from organizations such as NAIT or the Europe Trust is a good indicator of an affiliation with the Western Brotherhood.

6. Informal Allegiance to Yussuf al Qaradawi

In 2006 the *Wall Street Journal*, echoing what many both in the Muslim world and in the West have said, referred to Yussuf al Qaradawi as "the nearest thing Sunni Islam has to a pope."[113] The comparison might be somewhat overblown, as the Egyptian cleric's popularity is relatively low in non-Arab parts of the Muslim world, but it underscores the level of influence reached by al Qaradawi. Born in 1926, he joined the Brotherhood as a teenager and suffered through all its early waves of persecution by the Egyptian government.[114] In the early 1960s, after graduating from al Azhar's

Faculty of Theology, he left Egypt for Qatar, where he began teaching and, with his theological knowledge and charisma, built a network of loyal supporters and financial backers among the wealthy elites of the Arab Gulf countries.[115] A prolific writer (he has published more than thirty books), gifted orator, and exceptional networker, today al Qaradawi oversees an Islamic ideological holding that comprises schools, think tanks, publications, and Web sites. His weekly program on Al Jazeera, *Sharia and Life*, has millions of viewers and his books and sermons are widely circulated throughout the Muslim world.

From this powerful position al Qaradawi seems to have built a new movement parallel to, albeit not necessarily in competition with, the "traditional" Muslim Brotherhood and put himself firmly at the head of it. Al Qaradawi was among the first members of the Egyptian Brotherhood to follow Tilmisani's accommodationist turn in the 1970s and articulate the preference for *dawa* over *jihad* as a means to create an Islamic state.[116] Sheltered from the disturbances of the Egyptian regime and coddled by Arab Gulf elites, al Qaradawi has been able to establish his own network of followers who espouse his message of *wassatteyya*, a sort of political and religious middle way between secularism and what he refers to as extremism, which advocates the centrality of Islam while rejecting violence.[117]

Thanks to his influence and prestige, the scholar-cum-activist has become the spiritual father of this new global Islamist movement whose followers could be referred to as New Brothers. While firmly referring to the principles of al Banna and other Islamist thinkers, al Qaradawi takes a position of functional and intellectual independence from the Brotherhood as an organization, as was attested in 2004 by his refusal to become the *murshid* of the Egyptian Muslim Brotherhood.[118] Some members attempted to downplay the embarrassing refusal. "Sheikh al-Qaradawi is an influential scholar and one of the Muslim Brotherhood's spiritual leaders in the world," said Abd El Monem Abou El Fotouh. "Any Muslim Brother would be honored to have him as supreme guide, but he turned down the offer for the post, citing health and other reasons, as he did in the past."[119] The real reasons for the refusal seem to have more to do with al Qaradawi's personal ambitions and vision than with his health. Many speculate that the position he has carved out is much more important than that of *murshid* of the Egyptian Brotherhood: presiding unchallenged at the head of the informal global Muslim Brotherhood network. Al Qaradawi himself seemed to cite his higher ambitions in justifying his refusal, explaining that "the MB [*sic*] asked me to be a chairman, but I preferred to be a spiritual guide for the entire nation [intended as *ummah*]."[120] Al Qaradawi's networks, united by informal ties rather than formal membership, operate in complete symbiosis, parallel or occasionally in opposition to the Egyptian Brotherhood and its International Organization, depending on the circumstances.

The Western Brothers play a crucial role in the global network led by al Qaradawi.[121] It is evident that most of their networks and organizations ideologically refer to him rather than to the *murshid* of the Egyptian branch. Though al Qaradawi might not be the pope of Sunni Islam, he unquestionably is the pope of the New Brothers and their Western branches. This is shown by the importance given to his sermons and *fatwas* on the Web sites of Western Brotherhood organizations and by the quantity of his books sold in their bookstores. The cleric sits on the boards of many New Western Brotherhood organizations from America to Europe and is welcomed with the highest honors during his occasional visits to Europe (the U.S. government banned al Qaradawi from its territory in the mid-1990s). Al Qaradawi's popularity among Western Muslims goes well beyond the Western Brothers. Nevertheless, consistent ideological references and any organizational link to him are good indicators of an affiliation with the Western Brotherhood.

7. Membership in Brotherhood Superstructures

The New Western Brotherhood's networks are predominantly informal, built upon personal and ideological ties. The six indicators proposed so far are only telltale signs that an organization belongs to these networks. A seventh indicator, however, allows for a more definitive identification. Albeit limited to the European arena, a superstructure that formally unites all New Western Brotherhood organizations does exist. Predictably, it does not refer to itself as the European Brotherhood umbrella organization, and actually challenges such a definition.[122] Nevertheless, it encompasses all the organizations that in each European country are commonly identified as "Brotherhood" by governments and commentators and possess the six indicators proposed above.

Founded in 1989 with the stated goal of "serving Muslims in European societies," the Federation of Islamic Organizations in Europe (FIOE) is, de facto, the overarching organization for New Western Brotherhood groups in Europe.[123] Its founders and main members are quintessentially New Western Brotherhood organizations such as the French UOIF, the German IGD, and the Muslim Association of Britain, and FIOE's board members include prominent New Western Brothers such as UOIF's Ahmed Dja-ballah and IGD's Ibrahim El Zayat.[124] From its foundation, FIOE, which describes itself as "the largest Islamic organization on the European level," was characterized by the institution-building frenzy typical of the Broth-erhood.[125] Internally, it is divided into a myriad of substructures, with an executive committee supervising the activities of almost two dozen depart-ments devoted to education and *dawa*, women's issues, media, public rela-tions, planning and finance, and so on.[126] FIOE has also spawned an equally impressive array of external organizations, from the European Council for Fatwa and Research to the European Forum for Media Professionals.[127]

In 1990 FIOE and its French component, the UOIF, purchased a castle and 11 hectares of adjacent land in a bucolic part of Burgundy and estab-lished the network's first center of higher learning, the European Institute for Human Sciences (IESH).[128] Inaugurated in 1992 by al Qaradawi, it pro-vides Islamic education to 120 students resident on campus plus 200 stu-dents studying by correspondence each year. In 1996 FIOE, in cooperation with the Saudi-based WAMY, also created the Forum of European Muslim Youth and Student Organizations (FEMYSO), an active youth branch de-voted to lobbying. Originally headed by the ubiquitous Ibrahim El Zayat, FEMYSO has managed to become, in its own words, "the de facto voice of the Muslim youth of Europe." Today it oversees a network of 37 member organizations and maintains relations with institutions such as the Euro-pean Parliament, the Council of Europe, and the United Nations.[129] Stra-tegically headquartered in Brussels in two buildings a few blocks from the EU Commission and other institutions of the European Union, FIOE and FEMYSO enjoy access to the European seats of power that no other Euro-pean Muslim organization can even dream of gaining. Their leaders have often been invited to testify before the European Parliament and to repre-sent the "Muslim point of view" in debates with policy makers.[130]

FIOE's leaders are ambiguous about their connection to the Brother-hood. Ahmed al Rawi, the organization's former president, says that FIOE shares "a common point of view" and has a "good close relationship" with the Brotherhood.[131] Other officials deny any connection.[132] Some Middle East–based affiliates of the organization, however, proudly proclaim that FIOE's ideological and methodological identification with the Brotherhood is complete. "If we move a step forward, and look into targets of the Federation of Islamic Organizations in Europe (FIOE)," wrote Salem Abdul Salam Al Shikhi, a member of FIOE's European Council for Fatwa and Research, "it represents the Muslim Brotherhood's moderate thought taking into consideration European specialty, and working under European regimes and laws."[133]

As usual, the terminological difficulties in defining the nature of the Brotherhood make the identification of organizations related to it controversial. But, as in most cases, the confirmation of affiliation with the Brotherhood, intended as an ideological movement and not as organization, comes from members of the Brotherhood itself. Mohammed Akef has made it clear that FIOE, FEMYSO, and their member organizations fall under the large umbrella of the global Muslim Brotherhood and, more specifically, the trend led by Qaradawi. "These organizations and institutions are independent and autonomous. We do not control them," said Akef in an interview with the Swiss journalist Sylvain Besson. "It is the Brothers abroad that control them. The structures linked to Qaradawi are organizations of the Brotherhood directed by the Brothers of different countries."[134] An organization's membership in the FIOE and in FEMYSO provides a formal indicator of its affiliation with the European wing of the New Western Brothers.

The Power of Thought, Not Numbers

To sum up, what I have termed "New Western Brothers" are those Western-based Islamists who follow the participationist, *dawa*-centric approach envisioned by Tilmisani in the 1970s and perfected by al Qaradawi over the past two decades, and who belong to the informal network that revolves around a handful of key personalities and organizations. The movement defines itself with other descriptors, from Islamic trend (*al tayyar al islami*) to reformist or revivalist school, from Islamic activism to simply Islamic movement (*al haraka al islamiya*).[135] Identifying all the participants as Brothers lends itself to inevitable criticisms. First, it does not give full credit to the contribution of groups such as Jamat-e-Islami or Milli Görüş, which are integral to yet separate from the movement. Second, if not correctly explained, it could give the impression of a structural link with the organization of the Muslim Brotherhood in the Middle East or of a formal structure in the West.

Nevertheless, with the appropriate caveats, "New Western Brothers" best encapsulates the history and the methods of the movement. Understanding that those operating in the West are not subsidiary branches of any Middle East-based organization and that affiliation to the movement is not based on formal membership, it is fair to call them Muslim Brotherhood legacy groups or New Western Brothers. Though the primacy of the legacy of Hassan al Banna is undisputed, the New Western Brothers are now inspired by a heterogeneous ensemble of works and ideas of many thinkers and activists.[136] Each organization acts independently, adapting to the environment in which it operates, but a foundation of commonly accepted principles and goals unites all of them.

The question that logically arises from identifying such networks as New Western Brothers pertains to describing their members. Is everybody who belongs to New Western Brotherhood organizations a Muslim Brother who adopts the Brotherhood's worldview? The answer is clearly no, and it would be simplistic to think otherwise. The core leadership of the groups is still, for the most part, Western Brothers, either first-generation pioneers or second-generation activists who subscribe to the Brotherhood's ideology. But members and, more generally, individuals and organizations that sporadically interact with Western Brotherhood organizations fall into a very different category. Azzam Tamimi, a former spokesman for the Jordanian branch of the Muslim Brotherhood and a longtime Islamist activist in London, perfectly addressed this issue in an interview with *Le Monde Diplomatique*. "The trend over the last decade has been to dissolve organisations started in the 1970s by immigrants, especially among student communities," he explained. "Either people have settled down and been absorbed into open platforms, or they've left. So in the West you have Brotherhood members who have become active in wider-ranging organisations like the Muslim Council of Britain, which represents all Muslims."[137]

Tamimi's claim that the Muslim Council of Britain represents all British Muslims is, as we will see, highly questionable, but it is true that the purity of organizations set up by the early Western Brothers has been diluted with time.[138] The Brotherhood's institution-building frenzy has turned many of the structures created by the pioneers in the 1960s and 1970s into large organizations encompassing (sometimes indirectly) many diverse groups. While some individuals in these groups agree with the Brotherhood's message, many are involved simply because they are attracted by the activities the groups organize or because they lack alternatives. This seems to be particularly true of Western Muslims born in recent decades. Many leaders of the Western Brotherhood have repeatedly warned that the movement has not been able to attract large numbers of second- and third-generation European and North American Muslims and speak of a delegitimation of the old Islamist figures, who in many cases have not been able to engage the younger generations with concepts (or even in languages) they could understand and relate to.[139] Most of the tens of thousands of youngsters who attend Western Brotherhood events, such as the gigantic multiday fairs of the UOIF in Le Bourget, ISNA in Chicago, or London's IslamExpo, do so mostly to spend time in an Islamic environment, meet friends, and, in many cases, find a potential spouse; they do not necessarily subscribe to the Brotherhood's worldview. Even many of those who choose to involve themselves in Islamic activism opt for less dogmatic avenues than the ideological frameworks and the structures created by the early Muslim Brothers.

But, in comparison with competing groups, the Brothers' failure to create a mass movement should be assessed differently. Besides outpacing all rivals in influence among Western elites, the Western Brothers have had enormous success in Muslim communities not through direct membership, which is generally quite limited, but through a diffuse cultural hegemony. Not all attendees of the Western Brothers' conferences will embrace their views, but some will. And there is no other Muslim movement that has the means to organize events even remotely on such a large scale. If a young Muslim or a potential convert wants to know more about Islam, he or she is more likely to have easy access to Brotherhood publications than to those of any other Islamic group. Although their membership has remained fairly small, the Brothers have shown an enormous ability to monopolize the Islamic discourse, making their interpretation of Islam perhaps not yet mainstream but at least the most readily available, and putting their ideological stamp on any Islam-related issue, be it strictly religious or more properly political. Their concepts and positions have been absorbed, often almost unconsciously, by large segments of Western Muslim populations, irrespective of their religious and political views.[140] Moreover, the New Western Brotherhood's success is evident from their access to Western elites. Although they have been unable to create a mass movement, the New Western Brothers have been extremely good at posturing as if they did, thereby gaining a remarkably prominent position in Western Islam.

3

Aims and Methods

Virtually ignored outside of specialized academic and political circles throughout the 1980s and 1990s, since 9/11 Islamism has been the subject of constant and often ill-informed discussion. The heterogeneity of the movement, which arguably encompasses both groups that employ horrifying violence to further a millenarian view of society and modern political organizations that participate in the democratic process and publicly reject violence, has made political Islam particularly difficult to grapple with. Clearly no single assessment can be applied to all, and any analysis must take into consideration the nuances that characterize such diverse forces.

Although experts may disagree about the causes of their actions and the measures to counter them, there is a consensus throughout the Western world in condemning violent groups such as al Qaeda and even rejectionist movements such as Hizb ut Tahrir, which, while not directly espousing violence, openly call for the destruction of democracy and the creation of a strict Islamic state spanning the whole Muslim world (and eventually beyond). The debate becomes much more complicated when it extends to participationist Islamists—whose forefathers and standard-bearers are the Muslim Brothers.[1]

An array of highly respected scholars and commentators subscribe to what could be termed the optimistic view of the Brotherhood and of political Islam more generally. Optimists see the Brotherhood as a religiously conservative yet democratic-leaning movement that has undergone significant changes throughout its history and has now reached maturity—in which it fully rejects violence and engages in the democratic process with remarkable enthusiasm. Nonviolent Islamists' long record of participation in elections in various countries and their nearly consistent condemnation of al Qaeda's terrorist attacks are interpreted as proofs that the movement should be viewed as a reformist force aimed at replacing the authoritarian regimes of the Muslim world with Islamically inspired democracies through political means.

Carry Wickham labels this internal change "Islamist Auto-Reform."[2] While admitting that the opening toward democracy might be opportunistic, Wickham argues that the Islamists' participation in the democratic process has nevertheless triggered a phase of "complex learning," through which they have absorbed some concepts of democracy and revised some of their original views and goals. As some of their more impractical and ideological positions are adapted to fit the realities of daily political life, a new Islamist discourse results. The new generation of democratic-minded Islamists, argue the optimists, represents a powerful and genuinely moderate force that the West should welcome. On this account, while some of their views might be different, they do not pose a threat to the West; indeed, they can be ideal partners in helping to spread democracy in the Muslim world. They could also become allies in the fight against violent groups such as al Qaeda, whose defeat most optimists believe to be a mutual interest of the Brotherhood and the West.[3]

An equally significant group of academics and analysts adopt a diametrically opposed reading of the nature, evolution, and aims of the Brotherhood and like-minded nonviolent Islamist movements. Viewing most, if not all, of their latest shifts toward moderation and nonviolence as an elaborate tactical dissimulation of their real goals, pessimists perceive nonviolent Islamists simply as wolves in sheep's clothing. On this account, the Brotherhood merely portrays itself as a moderate organization seeking to operate within the democratic framework; in reality, it has never abandoned its goal of establishing an Islamic state whose real nature has little to do with democracy.

The Big Test: Islamists and Democracy

Social scientists and political debaters like clear-cut characterizations through which individuals and movements can be placed in predetermined categories: "extremist," "moderate," "fundamentalist," and so on. Such simplifications, often based on highly subjective evaluations, go against the very nature of a movement so complex and constantly evolving. Moreover, the Islamist movement is extremely heterogeneous and its members and affiliates, while adhering to some common principles, differ (and sometimes even quarrel quite harshly) on several issues. Rather than painting the movement with broad-brush definitions, it is therefore more useful to assess its stance on specific matters, starting with the issue that has generated the most heated debate among experts: its position on democracy.

Optimists believe that nonviolent Islamists are a force pushing for reform and democracy in the Muslim world and that, as some Brotherhood leaders have said, the movement's traditional motto, "The Quran is our constitution," is just an emotional slogan used to rally supporters—in reality, its members today embrace the legitimacy of man-made laws and constitutions. Pessimists argue that the Brotherhood "believes in democracy as a political means more than a value or political concept";[4] they believe that the Brothers' renunciation of violence is tactical, dictated by an awareness of their military inferiority to the governments of the region. In public, the Brothers express their full support of democracy and human rights, rejecting violence in order to become part of the system; in fact, they are planning to destroy democratic systems from within.

Without question, today's Islamists hold a much more nuanced position toward democracy than their forefathers. Driven partly by an anticolonial fervor that made them shun any Western influence, many in the early movement rejected democracy as a foreign system incompatible with Islam. "Democracy," stated former Muslim Brotherhood *murshid* Mustapha Mashour in 1981, "contradicts and wages war on Islam. Whoever calls for democracy means they are raising banners contradicting God's plan and fighting Islam."[5] Starting in the early 1990s, the New Brothers began to take a more open approach to the issue of democracy and the replacement of man-made law with *sharia.* Some, particularly among the new generations, claim to have abandoned the idea of an Islamic state based strictly on *sharia,* speaking instead of a democratic system with equal citizenship for all and simply an Islamic cultural background.[6] Others compare themselves to the Christian Democrats of various European countries, embracing democracy while maintaining their religious identity.[7] These frequent invocations of concepts such as democracy, elections, and human rights have led many optimists to conclude that the New Brothers have genuinely taken to the path of democracy and reform.

Yet the optimists have been significantly disappointed by some of the Brotherhood's most recent actions. Pressed by critics who accused them of engaging in propaganda while lacking a concrete political program, over the past few years the Egyptian Brothers have released a series of official documents that present their views and concrete plans for society. In 2004 they released their much anticipated "Initiative for Reform," a platform outlining the Brothers' comprehensive political vision. The document opened with a statement on democracy that clearly marked a major break with the past: "Comprehensive reform cannot be achieved except by implementing democracy, which we believe in, and whose fundamentals we commit ourselves to."[8] However, the core of the document did little to confirm the democratic nature of the Brotherhood's agenda. "We have a specific task," it continued, "to establish God's rule on the basis of our faith. This is our true and effective way to escape all our internal and foreign problems, whether political, economic, social or cultural."[9]

Continued criticism of the vagueness of the Egyptian Brotherhood's political program led the group to draft a new, more detailed platform in 2007.[10] The endeavor generated significant tension between the various wings of the group and the more conservative old guard seems to have prevailed. In any case, the text confirmed the suspicions of the pessimists and disappointed some of the most enthusiastic optimists. An especially controversial section proposed the creation of a council of religious scholars who would express their opinion on the compatibility of legislation with *sharia*.[11] Reminiscent of the powerful Council of Guardians established in Iran after the Islamic revolution, such a body would be empowered to veto any legislation that it deemed against *sharia*, although some members of the group claimed its purported role would be merely advisory.[12] The platform also contained provisions that limited the role of women and non-Muslims in the state it envisioned, barring them from the highest positions of power.[13] Using somewhat ambiguous language, the document recognized equality between men and women "in terms of their human dignity," but added that women should not be burdened "with duties against their nature or role in the family."[14]

The Egyptian Brothers' failure to fully live up to their proclamations of democracy and equal rights does not entail that the global Islamist movement born out of this group has similar views. Many optimists argue that the New Western Brothers, having lived in democratic systems for decades, have absorbed, consciously or not, many democratic principles and even contend that they could possibly influence other Islamists in the Muslim world to embrace them. One leader of the New Western Brotherhood who is often heralded as an active proponent of democracy in the Muslim world is Rashid Ghannouchi. Born in Tunisia, Ghannouchi has spent decades in Europe; he permanently settled in London in the early 1990s after having been repeatedly imprisoned in his home country for his leading role in the Islamist opposition to the Tunisian regime. One of the most respected figures in the New Western Brothers' circles, Ghannouchi is a prolific writer and a highly accomplished public speaker.

Some Islamist thinkers of the first generation, including Mawdudi, had theorized about the possibility of an "Islamic democracy," but Ghannouchi was one of the first modern thinkers to challenge the concept that Western-style democracy is incompatible with Islam. For Ghannouchi, democracy is not an ideology that competes with Islam but simply a tool, a series of procedures for electing, checking, and dismissing a government.[15] As such, democracy is more than compatible with Islam: it perfectly encapsulates the Islamic concept of *shura* (consultation). *Shura* has been invoked by many Muslim thinkers, Islamist and not, to prove that democracy is inherent in Islam, an order given by God himself in the Quran, in the exhortation that Muslims conduct their affairs by mutual consent.[16] The early followers of the prophet Mohammed adhered to the concept and, according to many Muslim thinkers, today's democracy is nothing more than its implementation on a large scale.[17]

Starting from the concept of *shura*, Ghannouchi has developed the idea of "Islamic democracy" and states that democracy actually has an Islamic rather than a Western origin.[18] Though his claim is debatable—Athenian democracy predates the birth of Islam by more than a millennium—it is nevertheless encouraging, as it might show that parts of the Islamist movement are trying to elaborate an Islamic formulation of democracy. Ghannouchi criticizes Westerners for equating democracy to secularism, consistently stating that it is completely compatible with Islam.

Yet, at a second glance, Ghannouchi's interpretation of democracy seems different from what most Westerners would understand from it. The Tunisian thinker says that everyone in his envisioned Islamic democracy would have "equal citizenship," yet he divides this between unqualified citizenship (*muwatanah amah*, available to all non-Muslim citizens) and qualified citizenship (*muwatanah khassah*, available only to Muslims).[19] As John Esposito and John Voll explain, "while the latter enjoy full citizenship, the majority of citizens may choose to have their faith influence public life, and thus the state may prohibit non-Muslims from holding senior positions in government."[20] Ghannouchi states that people would not be forced to embrace Islam, but whoever did not do so would have to pledge loyalty to the state and recognize its legitimacy. He would enjoy personal freedoms pertaining "faith, food, drink, and marriage," but might "be denied some of the rights guaranteed to Muslim citizens."[21]

The "Islamic democracy" advocated by the "democrat within Islamism," as Ghannouchi's biographer calls him, is unquestionably a major improvement from the utter rejection of democracy that the Brotherhood espoused only twenty years ago. But many of its core characteristics can hardly be reconciled with what is traditionally intended as liberal democracy. It is still a state where the basic principle of the equality of citizens is sacrificed in the name of religion. Even the Brothers' concept of *shura*, once analyzed, seems substantially different from how other Muslim intellectuals and most Westerners interpret it. As the Egyptian Brotherhood's platform and the writings of many New Brothers show, many Brothers see *shura* not as a process that involves all citizens but rather as a consultation among experts in Islamic law. The democratic process does indeed take place, but only among a small group of unelected jurisprudents who debate the best interpretation of the *sharia*. It seems apparent that Westerners and the New Muslim Brothers use the same word, "democracy," but their definitions and interpretations are quite different.[22]

Pessimists consider this cleavage between terminology and substance as an example of the Brothers' deceptive tactics. Knowing that certain buzzwords reassure Westerners, Islamists have made the language of democracy, human rights, and social equality their own, but employ it with meanings that seem quite different from those intended by their interlocutors. Semantic tricks, rhetorical artifices, and clever repackaging of their message do not affect the Brothers' goals, which seem unchanged. Statements from various Islamist leaders confirm that the movement's adoption of democracy is not heartfelt but serves strictly tactical purposes. Mustapha Mashur, former *murshid* of the Brotherhood, said that the group might "accept the concept of pluralism for the time being; however, when we will have Islamic rule we might then reject this concept or accept it."[23] Statements like this, as Esposito observes, do "not answer those who wonder whether the espousal of democracy by Islamic movements is a pragmatic, tactical accommodation or a principled position."[24]

An alternative explanation would present the difference between the "Islamic democracy" envisioned by Ghannouchi and the Western concept of liberal democracy as a necessary step in the evolution of the New Brothers' thinking. Considering that only twenty years ago most Islamists viewed democracy as a form of apostasy, a system that, while in some aspects treating non-Muslims and women differently, recognizes basic rights and favors popular participation is a major development and, possibly, a step in the direction of more fully embracing democracy. Moreover, it would be unfair to demand that Muslims should adopt a form of government mirroring the West's. As other regions of the world and civilizations have done, the Muslim world should be able to have political systems that mix democratic principles with local customs without outside criticism. Some New Brothers indeed point to the unfairness of imposing Western principles and standards on Muslim societies. "Will the West accept a different model of democracy in Islamic countries," asks Issam Al Arian, a leader of the second generation of the Egyptian Brotherhood, "a model which uses Islam as a source of authority, where religion is a fundamental core of politics, where the people have the power to appoint, observe and dismiss [the ruler], yet sovereignty belongs to the *sharia*?"[25]

Compared to the early Brothers and today's Salafis, who believe that all lawmaking should be by God, the New Brothers' "Islamic democracy" is unquestionably an advance, which optimists argue will further develop with time. Yet al Arian seems to hint at a crucial milestone that the New Brothers are unlikely to pass. In a liberal democracy a qualified majority can change all laws and all provisions of a constitution. The New Brothers completely reject the idea that even an overwhelming majority can overrule the principles and provisions of the *sharia*, which are God-given and, therefore, immutable. The New Brothers interpret the *sharia* far more flexibly than their predecessors and other contemporary Islamists, but still see it as a permanent superconstitution.

The Egyptian Brotherhood's former *murshid*, Mohammed Akef, is clear in pointing to the core aspects of *sharia* as the main obstacle preventing

"Islamic democracy" from developing into liberal democracy as commonly understood in the West. "The Shura Council can be the paragon of democracy, but [only] democracy of a right kind, [i.e.,] one that honors *shari'a*," he argues. "I distinguish between this kind of democracy and the Western democracy, which allows [a man] to act as he pleases, [even] in contradiction to Allah's commandments."[26] Faysal Mawlawi, the vice president of the FIOE-linked European Council for Fatwa and Research and a historical leader of the New Western Brothers, is similarly clear. "As for the true concept of democracy, it is not our main concern," declares the Lebanese-born cleric. "We Muslims believe in pluralism and political freedom as part and parcel of Islamic teachings. It is worth stressing here that we accept the articles and the principles of democracy that cope with the teachings of Islam and reject those principles that are non-Islamic."[27]

Democracy, according to Mawlawi and the New Brothers, is acceptable as long as it does not conflict with their interpretation of *sharia*. It should not be rejected as a system, but, despite claims made in interviews with Western journalists and scholars, it should not be fully embraced either. Yussuf al Qaradawi, the undisputed spiritual leader of the New Brothers, clearly and comprehensively addressed the issue in a *fatwa* he issued in 2000:

Islam wants this nation to consult with each other, and stand as a united body, so no enemy can penetrate it. This is not what democracy is for. Democracy is a system that can't solve all societal problems. Democracy itself also can make whatever it wants as lawful, or prohibit anything it does not like. In comparison the Shari'ah as a political system has limits. If we are to adopt democracy, we should adopt its best features. These are the issues of methods, guarantees, and manners of a democratic society. As a Muslim society we should adopt it in an Islamic context of a society that seeks to live with its Shariah laws. Our society should abide by what have been made lawful by Allah SW [*Subhanahu wa-ta'ala*, Glorious and Exalted] and abide by what also made unlawful by him SW. In comparison democracy, with a slim majority can cancel all laws and rules. It can even eliminate itself with this type of margin. In fact, in some case democracy may become worse than dictatorship. What I am for is a genuine type of democracy, for a society driven by the laws of Shari'ah that is compatible with the values of freedom, human rights, justice, and equity.[28]

Al Qaradawi affirms a selective adoption of democratic principles, limited by the immutability of God's law. And, according to critics, this position has severe repercussions for basic human rights, highlighting how distant from the concept of liberal democracy the New Brothers are. Like many New Brothers, al Qaradawi refers to values—"freedom, human rights, justice, and equity"—that anybody in the world, and particularly in the West, can subscribe to. His constant invocation of such concepts has won him the praise of many. Ibrahim al Hudaiby, the grandson of the Brotherhood's second *murshid* and a leader of the groups' third generation, has stated that Westerners should embrace al Qaradawi for his "high level of respect for human rights and civil liberties."[29] Western scholars such as John Esposito have described him as a thinker engaged in a "reformist interpretation of Islam and its relationship to democracy, pluralism and human rights," and he has been hailed as a moderate by officials throughout the West.[30]

However, a close analysis of al Qaradawi's writings shows that the Egyptian cleric's interpretation of human rights is diametrically opposed to that of most Westerners. The differences are particularly stark, for example, on the issue of homosexuality. Answering the question of an Austrian Muslim who had asked him about the *sharia*'s position regarding gays, al Qaradawi stated on the extremely popular Web site IslamOnline.net that those who engage in such "depraved practice" should be punished physically, even with the death penalty in some cases. "Such punishments may seem cruel," he responded, but "they have been suggested to maintain the purity of the Islamic society and to keep it clean of perverted elements."[31]

Al Qaradawi disseminated a similarly controversial *fatwa*, also on Islam Online.net, on the issue of religious freedom and, more specifically, on the possibility of converting from Islam to other faiths. First, he identified this phenomenon as a Western conspiracy, indicating that "the ugliest intrigue the enemies of Islam have plotted against Islam has been to try to lure its followers away from it."[32] He then strongly criticized "missionary invaders" who attempt to convert Muslims to Christianity. Such criticism, while not directly a violation of religious freedom, seems to be rather hypocritical, since *dawa* among Christians has been one of the cornerstones of the New Western Brothers' activities for decades and has been advocated by al Qaradawi himself in lengthy treatises and in many of his lectures in Europe and North America.

But the most revealing part of al Qaradawi's *fatwa* on freedom of religion, which summarizes the views expressed in a book he published in Arabic in 1996, is where he clearly identifies leaving Islam with either minor or major apostasy.[33] The former is committed by who those leave Islam as a private matter. In that case, al Qaradawi says the apostate should be given only a "discretionary punishment." But he is inflexible against those who commit major apostasy: that is, those who publicize their conversion and, even worse, attempt to persuade others to leave Islam. Such individuals, he argues in clear terms, must receive the death penalty. "No community accepts that a member thereof changes its identity or turns his or her loyalty to its enemies," states al Qaradawi. "They consider betrayal of one's country a serious crime, and no one has ever called for giving people a right to change their loyalty from a country to another whenever they like." If leaving Islam is like committing treason, Islam is not a religion—the choice of which, in modern Western society, is left to the individual—but a political community, and al Qaradawi goes even further, stating that negligence in punishing apostates jeopardizes the whole community.

The Geographic Peculiarity of the New Western Brothers

Islamist thinkers like al Qaradawi, Mawlawi, and Ghannouchi hold central, albeit often informal, positions in New Western Brotherhood organizations, whose networks also translate and disseminate their writings. Their beliefs about democracy and human rights raise a significant question: How do the New Western Brothers reconcile the ideological primacy they bestow upon thinkers who espouse an imperfect notion of democracy and call for the killing of homosexuals and apostates with the fact that they live in Western, secular democracies?

The answer has to be found in the New Western Brotherhood's unique position as an Islamic movement operating in non-Muslim countries.[34] Initially, the Brothers perceived the West simply as a convenient base of operation from which they could reorganize their struggle, whether through *dawa* or violence, against secular regimes in the Middle East. But by the 1980s, as they understood that a growing Muslim population was to permanently settle in the West, their priorities slowly shifted. While still supporting in words and deeds their counterparts' efforts to establish Islamic states in the Muslim world, they increasingly focused their attention on their new reality. Having redefined the West as *dar al dawa*, they intensified their efforts to spread their interpretation of Islam among Muslim immigrants and Westerners.

To achieve their redefined goals, the New Western Brothers needed to adapt their rich intellectual heritage. Over the last thirty years, they have tried to find ways to contextualize the teachings of their ideological forefathers within their reality of the movement operating freely in non-Muslim societies. It soon became obvious that blindly applying in modern Europe or America what al Banna and Mawdudi had prescribed in Egypt and India in the 1930s made little sense. The ideas of these and other leading thinkers who came after them form a body of invaluable theological and methodological knowledge from which Islamists should draw in all places and in all times. But, although they are revered as eminent leaders, they are not saints and their opinions are not sacred. They can be discussed, reinterpreted, adapted, and even challenged and dismissed as times, places, and circumstances change.[35] The Brotherhood, in the West as elsewhere, is hardly a stagnant movement; flexibility and continuous evolution are two of its core characteristics and strengths.

The New Western Brothers see in al Banna and Mawdudi heroic figures who laid the foundations for a revival of Islam. By the same token, contemporary figures like al Qaradawi, Ghannouchi, and Mawlawi are revered scholars whose thought is highly regarded. But Brotherhood activists working on the streets of twenty-first-century Lyon, Brussels, or Chicago understand that talk about an Islamic state or the punishments to which an apostate should be subjected, while possibly having some emotional appeal, has little practical use. The Brothers' school of thought provides invaluable guidance on several aspects of their faith and activism, starting with the immutable idea of Islam as a comprehensive way of life and a full methodology.[36] Nevertheless, over the last thirty years, one of their struggles has been to reconcile a vision of life shaped by Islam in all its aspects, private and public, with their actual life in secular Western democracies and to make their intellectual references relevant. "For young Muslims who wanted to reflect and act, the literature of the Muslim Brothers was the only one available," explained Tarek Oubrou, one of the UOIF's leading thinkers, speaking of his organization's intellectual evolution. "To us, it emanated from a movement that was reformist, modern, seductive. Since then we have clarified our path and contextualized our action. It is, in effect, a school of thought born in the Muslim world, in a reality that does not correspond to that of a secularized society, like the one we live in. We have shaped our own reading of the relationship between Islam and society."[37]

An interpretative flexibility that has often been criticized by other Islamic currents, such as the Salafis, has allowed the New Western Brothers to adapt their beliefs about the rules that should regulate their ideal Islamic state to their life in the West. They are consistent in explaining that the ideas of Islamist thinkers like al Qaradawi on form of government, minority rights, and other aspects of societal organization are limited to the movement's vision for an Islamic state to be created in any place where Muslims represent the majority. None of these ideas applies to the West, where the movement accepts Muslims' minority status under various forms of government.

If, for example, al Qaradawi is adamant that apostates should be killed, the New Western Brothers have consistently stated that such doctrine is not applicable in the West. They have not repudiated al Qaradawi's analysis, expressly or, more often, tacitly endorsing his view. They have simply stated that such punishment is only to be applied in an Islamic state and not in the West. *Trends*, a magazine published by the Islamic Foundation of Leicester, stated, for example, that leaving Islam is like treason because "Islam is not just a religion but a system for organizing human life. It is an ideology and Muslims are soldiers who carry forward this truth."[38] But the magazine also said that a Muslim living in Britain is free to convert because Islam in Britain is not established and the death penalty can only be applied in an Islamic society. Similarly, a *fatwa* issued by the al Qaradawi-led European Council for Fatwa and Research stated that "executing whoever reverts from Islam is the responsibility of the state and is so to be decided by Islamic governments alone."[39]

By the same token, the New Western Brothers have attempted to contextualize the Brothers' position on homosexuals, indicating that any physical punishment against them should be meted out only in an Islamic state. Taha al Alwani, founder of IIIT and president of ISNA's Fiqh Council of North America, states that homosexuals are "deviants" who should not be given "any opportunity to mix with and corrupt [Muslim] children" or to enter a mosque.[40] Kamal Helbawy argues that homosexuals have a disease and should be subjected to medical treatment.[41] Yet al Alwani, Helbawy, and most New Western Brothers are clear in stating that Muslims have no right to use violence against homosexuals in the West. Only the legitimate government of an established Islamic state can, and must, mete out the religiously mandated punishments against apostates and homosexuals. But no individual Muslim, whether in the Muslim world or, *a fortiori*, in the West, can take that task upon himself.

These positions, held by most New Western Brothers, lend themselves to two opposing interpretations. In one, the Brothers are making a commendable effort to adapt Islamist teachings to Western reality. Their positions on apostasy and homosexuality, for example, are shared by the vast majority of traditional scholars of the four major Islamic schools of jurisprudence. The Brothers, argue optimists, are trying to remain loyal to Islamic texts while attempting to create a framework for the interpretation of some of their most delicate provisions in a Western setting. Labeling them as "fundamentalists" for simply following the letter of the Quran is simplistic and unfair.

The other interpretation is that these positions reveal the incompatibility of the Brotherhood's views with liberal democracy. Moreover, according to some pessimists, they betray the movement's real nature. While trying to reassure Westerners with statements about embracing democracy and human rights, the New Western Brothers at heart believe in the same vision outlined by al Qaradawi. Aware of the repercussions that openly endorsing it would have, they engage in a sort of outsourcing of radicalism. Pessimists accuse the New Western Brothers of playing a deceitful game in which they let non-Western-based thinkers say what they really think about democracy, homosexuality, sexual equality, violence, and relationships with the West. By spinning, downplaying, or refusing to elaborate on such statements, the New Western Brothers maintain their acceptability with Western elites. Yet by maintaining their connections with those who make such comments and disseminating their writings within the Muslim community they are able to tacitly endorse them without compromising themselves.

No matter how their ties to their intellectual heritage are perceived, it is unquestionable that the New Western Brothers' geographical peculiarity has led them to shift their focus and reassess their goals. Optimists and pessimists seem to agree that their main goal is to obtain a position of predominance within Western Muslim communities and become their official or de facto representatives to Western establishments. Any evaluation of how the Brothers seek to use such a position is, of course, open to discussion and largely influenced by the different opinions on the movement. But it is uncontested that the New Western Brothers aim to gradually widen Islamic influence, both within Muslim communities and externally. Although the two fields are closely related, it is perhaps more useful to analyze separately the New Western Brothers' efforts to dominate each.

A useful theoretical framework in which to view the activities and aims of the New Western Brothers, both internally and externally, is provided by social movement theory.[42] Formulated in the 1970s, the theory analyzes the formation, mobilization, and development of social movements by examining various aspects of their activities. In particular, most social movement theorists ascribe the success or failure of a movement to three factors: resource mobilization, framing resonance, and political opportunity. The first describes the capacity of a movement to gather resources, whether human or material, sufficient for its aims. The second corresponds to its ability to frame its message in a way that appeals to its target audience. Finally, "political opportunity" describes the existence of favorable political conditions and the movement's ability to exploit them. Although seldom used to analyze Islamist movements, social movement theory provides extremely useful tools to understand the aims and *modus operandi* of the New Western Brothers.[43]

The Unprecedented Opportunity of Unrestricted *Dawa*

In 1990, Yussuf al Qaradawi published a book entitled *Priorities of the Islamic Movement in the Coming Phase*, which was soon widely circulated in various languages by Western Brotherhood organizations.[44] The 186-page treatise can be considered the manifesto of the Islamic revivalist movement, since, as al Qaradawi explains in the introduction, the "Islamic Movement" is intended to be the "organized, collective work, undertaken by the people, to restore Islam to the leadership of society," with the goal of "reinstating the Islamic caliphate system to the leadership anew as required by Sharia."

After examining the situation of the Islamic Movement throughout the Muslim world, al Qaradawi devotes significant attention to the situation of Muslim populations in the West. Expatriates living in Europe, Australia, and North America "are no longer few in numbers," and their presence not only is permanent but also is destined to grow with new waves of immigration. This can have the positive effect of spreading Islam beyond its traditional abode, but al Qaradawi acknowledges that it can also be problematic. In fact, since the Muslim Nation, and therefore Muslim minorities "scattered throughout the world" does not have a leadership that can guide it, al Qaradawi warns of the risk of "melting"—the possibility that a Muslim minority could lose its Islamic identity and be absorbed by the non-Muslim majority.

Imbued with religious references, al Qaradawi's book is a very lucid political analysis of the situation of Western Muslims and the opportunities that it could offer to the global Muslim Brotherhood network. Like any leader of a religiously conservative movement, he is worried by the fact that millions of his coreligionists live as a minority among populations that not only are of a different religion but also, for the most part, embrace different values. Yet al Qaradawi also sees the lack of any established leadership an unprecedented opportunity for the Islamic Movement, which can "play the role of the missing leadership of the Muslim nation with all its trends and groups."

While in Muslim countries the movement can exercise only limited influence, as it is kept in check by regimes that oppose it, al Qaradawi realizes that no such obstacle prevents it from operating in the free and democratic West. Moreover, if the guarantees of Western political systems allow the Brothers to carry out their *dawa* activities freely, the poor organization of competing Islamic currents in the West puts them in an advantageous position. Finally, the masses of Muslim expatriates, disoriented by the impact of life in non-Muslim societies and often lacking the most basic knowledge about Islam, represent an ideally receptive audience for the movement's propaganda. The combination of these factors leads al Qaradawi to conclude that the Islamist movement can and should play a key role in the life of Western Muslims. The West is a sort of Islamic *tabula rasa*, a virgin territory where the socioreligious structures and limits of the Muslim world do not exist and the Brothers can implement their *dawa* freely, overcoming their competition with their unparalleled means and organization skills.

Written as al Qaradawi himself and other scholars of the global Brotherhood network were redefining the West as *dar al dawa*, *Priorities* is crucial in outlining what the role of the Islamist movement in the West should be. Al Qaradawi sees various purposes, but he is clear in stating that "it is the duty of the Islamic Movement not to leave these expatriates to be swept by the whirlpool of the materialistic trend that prevails in the West."[45] Nurturing Muslims' spirituality and defending them from the cultural assault of un-Islamic principles and customs has been one of the movement's main goals since its foundation. Such a defensive posture becomes even more important for Muslim minorities, as they incur the risk of being culturally absorbed by the host society.

A common theme of the Western Brotherhood's literature and speeches is the moral bankruptcy of the Western world. Like any non-Muslim society, Western society is criticized for not having accepted the only true religion, Islam. But the strongest criticisms of the West are about its abandonment of its own religion, its spiritual decline, and its lax moral customs. Loss of moral values, secularism, sexual promiscuity, and displays of public drunkenness are some of the diseases that the Brothers, like any other religiously conservative movement, see as plagues. Disturbed by these trends, the New Western Brothers often express their desire for religion to play a bigger role in the lives of Westerners, particularly Europeans. Islam is, in the Brothers' mind, the only way of salvation for mankind, but any force or religion that would contribute to moralization of a society in which Muslims live is seen positively.

Allegiance to an Islamic code of ethics, as outlined by the *sharia*, is considered the only way to shield Western Muslims from society's immorality. Yet they acknowledge that the minority status of Muslims in Europe and North America puts them in a particular category, forcing them to compromise between observance of the *sharia* and life in a non-Muslim society. And while there is extensive jurisprudence that addresses the situation of non-Muslim minorities living in *dar al Islam*, very few provisions cover the relatively new situation of Muslims living permanently in non-Muslim countries. For most Western Muslims, this has not been a major issue, either because religion does not play a large role in their lives or because they have found their own ways to reconcile their faith with their Western lifestyles. But many do feel the need for guidance from Islamic scholars about such everyday matters as marriage, prayer, and relations with non-

Muslims. These problems require the development of a new jurisprudence, which has come to be known as *fiqh* (Islamic jurisprudence) for minorities (*fiqh al aqaliyyat*).

Given the lack of intellectual Muslim leadership and structured Islamic clergy in the West, the Brotherhood sees itself as the entity most able to fill this void and create this new *fiqh*.[46] Over the years, the global Muslim Brotherhood network led by al Qaradawi has formed various jurisprudential bodies aimed at disseminating its interpretation of the *sharia*, such as the Dublin-based International Union of Muslim Scholars.[47] In 1997 the network created the European Council for Fatwa and Research. Founded by the FIOE, the Council is described as "an Islamic, specialized and independent entity" with the stated goal of "issuing collective *fatwas* which meet the needs of Muslims in Europe, solve their problems and regulate their interaction with the European communities, all within the regulations and objectives of Shari'a."[48] In practical terms, the Council is a jurisprudential body that issues nonbinding legal advice to Muslims living in Europe, focusing on issues they face as a minority in non-Muslim countries.

The Council is headquartered in Dublin, where it operates in conjunction with the local Islamic Cultural Centre. Both institutions have received the generous financial backing of the Al Maktoum Charity Organisation, headed by Sheikh Hamdan Al Maktoum, UAE Minister of Finance and Industry and Deputy Ruler of Dubai.[49] The Council, which generally meets twice a year in different European venues, comprises thirty-two Islamic scholars from throughout the world, the majority of whom reside within the continent. Its sessions take place behind closed doors, and the clerics deliberate on issues brought forth either by Council members or by European Muslims who ask for advice.

Although it includes representatives from different schools of thought, the Council is created and dominated by the Muslim Brotherhood's global network. As Rachid Ghannouchi has observed, "some members belong to the Brothers, some others do not. What matters is the ideology, not the movement."[50] Its jurisprudence is aimed at guiding Muslims through a "program of perfect life for the individual, the family, society and the state," an expression closely reminiscent of al Banna's multipronged program.[51] Among its members are key figures of the European networks of the New Brothers, such as UOIF's Ahmed Djaballah and Ounis Qourqah, IESH's al Arabi al Bichri, FIOE's Ahmed al Rawi, and Rachid Ghannouchi. Several high-profile scholars from various Arab Gulf countries are also members, most holding positions very close to the *Ikhwan*. Most tellingly, the offices of President and Vice-President are filled, respectively, by Yussuf al Qaradawi and Faysal Mawlawi. The Council is a democratic body in which the majority rules, but actual voting is rarely necessary, as the scholars tend to avoid internal dissent and follow the position of al Qaradawi and the Council's most influential figures.[52]

The Council's *fatwas* are, for the most part, suggestions for individuals who want to follow the requirements of their religion in their new land. Many simply provide guidelines on how to perform certain Islamic rituals in non-Muslim countries, solving dilemmas that are mostly logistical: for example, the problems a Muslim community might find in performing prayers in a building, not originally conceived as a mosque, in which facing Mecca is difficult.[53] Another *fatwa* deals with the problems in timing prayers with sunrise and sunset that might arise for Muslims living in Nordic countries.[54] As most Muslims living in the West have necessarily to deal with the banking system, many decrees attempt to reconcile the need to contract loans, obtain a mortgage, or open a bank account with the Islamic ban on charging interest. On these issues the jurisprudence of the Council is quite liberal and seems to revolve around the Quranic verse that states "Be observant of Allah to the best of your ability."[55] According to Mawlawi's interpretation of the verse, whenever a Western Muslim finds himself in a "legal bind," having to choose between respecting *sharia* and Western law, he or she should opt for the "less detrimental" option.[56] The Council's *fatwa* on banking, for example, urges Muslims to seek all possible "Islamic alternatives," exhorting "Islamic organizations throughout Europe to enter into negotiations with European banks to find formulas that are acceptable."[57] If no alternative is possible and the *haram* (unlawful) transaction is vitally necessary, the Council, drawing on the principle of accommodation, allows the European Muslim to carry it out.

In general, the Council tends to respect European law as much as possible, and espouses a relatively flexible interpretation of Islamic law. In some cases, it even explicitly decrees that European Muslims should follow the laws of European countries and the rulings of their judges, even if those differ from the *sharia*. In case of divorce, for example, the Council ruled that "it is imperative that a Muslim who conducted his Marriage by virtue of those countries' respective laws . . . comply with the rulings of a non-Muslim judge in the event of a divorce."[58] However, in some of its rulings the Council refers only to Islamic law and upholds Islamic principles that are at odds with basic Western concepts such as equality of the sexes and repudiation of domestic violence. A *fatwa* issued in 1997, for example, states that a wife needs her husband's permission to cut her hair, if that the cut is significant and "completely change[s] the appearance of the woman."[59] By the same token, the Council authorizes the husband to prevent his wife from visiting another woman, even if Muslim, "if he felt that this relationship has an adverse effect on his wife, children or marital life in general."[60]

These dicta are not surprising, given the positions held by al Qaradawi on marital relations. In fact, in his hallmark treatise on Islamic law, *The Licit and Illicit in Islam*, al Qaradawi openly states that "the man is the lord of the house and the head of the family." He also claims that when a wife shows "signs of pride or insubordination," her husband is entitled to use violence against her, though the blows should not be hard and should avoid the face.[61] These teachings contradict criminal law and public sentiment in every European country. Significantly, the provisions regarding the treatment of women caused the book to be banned in France in 1995. Charles Pasqua, at the time France's Minister of the Interior, commented that the book deserved the ban because of "its violently anti-Western tones and the theses contrary to the laws and values of the Republic that it contains."[62]

The Council also holds positions that are in conflict with Western civil law regarding marriage and divorce. One *fatwa*, for example, gives the man the unconditional right to divorce, while dictating a set of conditions for the woman to exercise the same right.[63] And in custody cases, the Council views the religious needs of the child as the primary consideration, implying that when a mixed marriage ends in divorce, the child will necessarily be assigned to the Muslim parent.[64] These rulings reflect the thinking of the New Western Brotherhood's leadership and, as such, have been interpreted in diametrically opposite terms by optimists and pessimists. The former see in them a demonstration of the flexibility and lack of dogmatism that sets the New Brothers apart from other Islamist movements. Pessimists stress the incompatibility of some of the rulings with core principles of liberal democracy.

Muslim Identity and the New Western Brothers' *Dawa* Machine

Bodies like the European Council for Fatwa and Research are part of a broader strategy outlined by al Qaradawi in *Priorities*. In order to avoid "melting" and defend Muslims from the moral corruption of the West, he openly calls for the creation of a sort of separate society for Western Muslims. Although he highlights the importance of continuing dialogue with non-Muslims, he advocates founding Muslim communities with "their own religious, educational and recreational establishments." "Try to have your small society within the larger society," he urges, "try to have your own 'Muslim ghetto.'"[65] Al Qaradawi clearly sees the leading role that the Brothers would play. The Islamic movement would have an unprecedented opportunity to at least partly implement its vision, as its local affiliates would run the mosques, schools, and civic organizations that would shape daily life. The New Western Brothers would be the guides of these communities, self-appointed guardians of Islamic orthodoxy spreading their interpretation of Islam through tailored and systematic *dawa* efforts.

Al Qaradawi's and the New Western Brothers' concept of "Muslim ghetto" needs to be further examined, as it is quite different from the idea of a parallel society that Salafis and a few other ultraconservative Muslim groups seek to establish in the West. Most Salafis living in the West see any interaction with non-Muslims as a threat to Muslim identity and aim to create spaces in which Muslims can mentally and, if possible, physically separate themselves from mainstream society. The Brothers, in contrast, do not advocate complete isolation from society but strongly encourage participation in it. Muslims, they argue, should be part of Western society, fully involving themselves in the political debate and participating in elections. Yet the emphasis is always on those forms of participation that are deemed beneficial to the spread of Islam and the success of the Islamic revivalist movement. Other forms of participation that do not serve these purposes or could dilute the Islamic identity of the community are discouraged.

Various treatises, written in Western languages and widely distributed, provide guidelines for this selective interaction. In an essay published by the Islamic Council of Europe, for example, Ali Kettani urges Muslims in the West to create their own geographic and social space inside their host country and argues that the Brotherhood-led network of organizations would direct the life of such enclaves, according to a correct Islamic standard. Interaction with non-Muslims is not forbidden, both to "fulfill the duty of da'wah" and to acquire skills and wealth that can benefit the Muslim community.[66] However, the interaction has to be limited to what is "Islamically unobjectionable." The Brothers urge Muslims to actively participate in the life of Western society, but only insofar as such engagement is necessary to change it in an Islamic fashion. In al Qaradawi's words, Muslims in the West should adopt "a conservatism without isolation, and an openness without melting."[67]

This dichotomy of cultural impermeability and active sociopolitical interaction can be highly risky: the latter can jeopardize the former. The only way the Brothers can ensure that Muslims, having chosen selective interaction over assimilation or the self-ghettoization espoused by the Salafis, will not "melt" into Western society is by instilling in them a strong Islamic identity. As for any social movement, the Islamist movement's success in creating such an identity depends on its ability to conceptualize images, symbols, and a language that will resonate with its target audience.[68] A crucial part of this frame resonance is the creation of the "Other," a separate group of people in relation to whom the identity can be defined. In the Muslim world, Islamist movements have traditionally identified the West and corrupt and secularized elites as the Other.[69] In the West this identification has been easier, as it is more obvious than designating some oblique cultural penetration or other Muslims with different interpretations of Islam.

Forming a sense of identity among a minority that is often visibly different from the majority entails less intellectual work. Positioning itself at the helm of this minority and shaping the characteristics of its identity have been the goals of the New Western Brotherhood over the last thirty years. A strong sense of Islamic identity did not appear among the masses of Muslim immigrants until the mid-1980s, when the crisis of Arab nationalism and other secular ideologies in the Muslim world reverberated in the West and Islam slowly began to replace ethnicity as the main source of *asabiyyah*, or group consciousness, for many Western Muslims. As in the Middle East, the Brothers were quick to seize the moment by offering an identity that transcended ethnic and national barriers: the only division that matters is between non-Muslims and Muslims, as all the latter belong to the transnational *ummah*. The concept turned out to be particularly appealing to many second- and third-generation Western Muslims. Torn between their ancestral traditions, of which they have only indirect knowledge, and their daily life in Western society, in which they do not feel fully accepted, many find particular solace in the knowledge that they belong to a borderless community based on equality and brotherhood.

If a sense of belonging creates individual identity, no other factor has a greater impact on the formation of a collective identity than the existence, or the perception of the existence, of an outside force threatening the community. The New Western Brothers mastered this political concept and showed an unparalleled cunning in becoming the main advocates of causes that outraged the majority of Muslims, even those who did not share the Brotherhood's views. Fostering the idea that Muslims are under siege, discriminated against and victimized by the Other, the New Western Brothers have portrayed themselves as the only voices willing and able to stand up for the community. In doing so they have exploited global political crises, undeniable forms of discrimination that have affected Western Muslims, and cultural tensions that have routinely appeared in most Western countries over the last twenty years.

From the 1988 controversy over Salman Rushdie's *Satanic Verses* to cartoons of the prophet Mohammed printed by Danish daily *Jyllands-Posten* in 2005, from the Israeli-Palestinian conflict to controversies over the veil in various European countries, the New Western Brothers have utilized their superior resources and mobilization skills to lead protests against events that they portrayed as part of a pattern of Western aggression against Muslims and Islam. A "community under siege"—an expression often employed by the New Western Brothers, particularly after 9/11—tends to close ranks, reinforce its communal identity, and rely on aggressive and capable leaders who can defend it.[70] Having nurtured this culture of victimhood, the New Western Brothers, consummate identity entrepreneurs, have been consistent in tapping into the grievances of Western Muslims and presenting themselves as the only force able to "act as the first line of defence for Islam and Muslims all over the world."[71] These mobilization tactics have allowed them to exercise a sort of cultural hegemony over Western Muslim communities. This success is particularly noteworthy in light of the small number of members. Although they control an ever-growing network of mosques and organizations, the membership numbers of Brotherhood legacy organizations in each Western country are limited to a few thousand—a negligible fraction of the Muslim population. Yet in the highly fragmented landscape of Muslim organizations operating in the West, the New Western Brothers far outpace competing trends in organization and influence, if not membership.

This position of disproportionate influence is unquestionably the consequence of this fragmentation of the Muslim community and the poor organization of competing movements. Nevertheless, due credit should be given to the New Western Brothers for their accomplishment. One reason for their success is their ability to secure access to enormous funding. Though in the first phase of its expansion in the West the Brotherhood received most of its funds from Saudi Arabia and other countries in the Arab Gulf, by the late 1990s it had created its own extremely sophisticated financial network to support its activities. Thanks to their rich coffers, Brotherhood-linked organizations have established an impressive and ever-expanding network of mosques, think tanks, organizations, charities, and publications, which operate in each Western country and transnationally. This financial viability allowed the New Western Brothers to establish an array of transnational organizations that worked together to create a global revivalist network and build ties with Western institutions, while most competing Muslim organizations operate only at the local level and with limited means.

Financial resources have also allowed the Brothers to use new technologies to increase their access to Western Muslims. New Brotherhood organizations have created sophisticated and popular Web sites that provide up-to-date information and services in multiple languages. Among them, IslamOnline.net, founded by disciples of al Qaradawi and supported by the Egyptian cleric, is arguably the most popular site among Western Muslims.[72] Operating out of offices in Qatar, Cairo and, since 2008, in Washington, D.C., it employs almost two hundred full-time researchers and two thousand part-time writers. Available in Arabic and English, it offers legal opinions, a *fatwa* bank, discussion forums, and the possibility to ask questions to Islamic scholars such as al Qaradawi and Mawlawi. It also publishes news items with commentary that reflects the perspective of the New Brothers.

Funds are just one of the secrets to the New Western Brotherhood's success. The energy, commitment, and vision of its members are at least as important as material resources. Unlike most Muslim immigrants in the West, New Western Brothers were scions of well-educated families and graduates of some of the West's most prestigious universities—professional community organizers with excellent communication and linguistic skills. Moreover, directly following the personal example of al Banna and the writings of other Islamist thinkers such as Mawdudi, Said Ramadan, Said Hawwa, and al Qaradawi, the New Western Brothers perfectly understood the importance of building institutions and training competent cadres. Islamist scholars have often explained their emphasis on institution building by pointing to their vision of Islam as a social religion. Al Qaradawi has written influential treatises on "organized collective work," which he interprets as a duty "ordained by religion and necessitated by reality."[73] From the very beginning the New Western Brothers adopted this view and established an impressive network of specialized organizations, each devoted to a well-defined goal and structured like a corporation.

An insight into the New Western Brothers' scientific approach to cultural domination of Western Islam comes from a document uncovered in November 2001 in Yussuf Nada's villa in Campione d'Italia. In the weeks immediately following the attacks of 9/11, the United Nations designated Nada as a terrorism financier, and Swiss and Italian authorities opened an investigation of the "foreign minister" of the Brotherhood and conducted a search of his residence. Among the many documents found in Nada's luxurious mansion, they took a particular interest in an Arabic-language piece titled "Toward a Global Strategy for Islamic Politics."[74] Dated December 1982, the document, widely known as "The Project," outlines a meticulous approach the Brothers should use to pursue their goals.

"The Project" asks the Brothers to "employ the necessary scientific and technological resources for planning, organization, implementation and monitoring," "create study and research centers and carry out studies of the political scope of the Islamic movement," and "carry out feasibility studies for different institutions." Provisions encourage followers to "leave a margin so that there is enough flexibility at the local level for issues that do not contradict the general guidelines of the global strategy for Islam" and to "prevent the movement from major confrontations which could encourage its adversaries to retaliate, condemning it fatally." "The Project" also recommends that they "influence the local and global centers of power in service of Islam" and "coordinate the efforts of all those who struggle for Islam in every country and establish quality contact between them, whether they be individuals or groups."

These provisions seem to perfectly describe what has been the *modus operandi* of the New Western Brotherhood over the past twenty to thirty years. Since the 1980s, the New Western Brothers have created a sprawling network of Islamic organizations devoted to all the possible needs of the Western Muslim population, from the purely religious to the more mundane. Umbrella organizations at the national and international level were soon created to coordinate activities. Today the New Western Brothers can be described as professional managers of Islam, well-trained community organizers with prestigious university degrees (in most cases in economics, education, medicine, or engineering rather than in religious studies) who have mastered the arts of communication, politics, and fund raising.

Thanks to their resources, activism, and remarkable intellectual capabilities, groups with historical or ideological links to the Muslim Brotherhood have often overshadowed other organizations in influencing the Muslim community. Even though they enjoy only limited direct support from the Muslim population, they constitute an extremely active and vocal presence and, as such, have gained a prominent position among Western Muslim organizations and created a movement that is unique in being truly pan-European and transatlantic.

Speaking for Islam

The Western Brotherhood's goal appears to be the formation of a cohesive and assertive Western Muslim community, transcending ethnic differences and shaped by a strong pan-Islamic identity defined by the Western Brothers themselves. While remaining committed to its cultural and moral principles, the community should not remain closed on itself but should actively participate in social and political activities. But what are the aims of this interaction? How do the New Western Brothers see themselves and Western Muslim communities in relation to Western society?

Optimists and pessimists seem to agree that it has been the New Western Brothers' desire to be the official or de facto representatives of Western Muslims. Reconceptualizing their position in what they termed *dar al dawa*, the Brothers understood the opportunity they could have as the sole interlocutors of Western governments, media, and intellectual elites on all issues pertaining to Islam. If they were to be the vanguard guiding Muslim communities in their vulnerable position as a minority, they should also represent them to the outside world.

The patterns of relations between Western governments and the New Western Brothers are extremely complex and will be extensively analyzed in chapter 4 and in the case studies. Although the situation differs from country to country, in general terms, the New Western Brothers have been quite successful at portraying themselves as representatives of the Muslim community in the eyes of many Western elites. Today, when Western governments or media attempt to reach out to the Muslim community, it is quite likely that many, if not all, of the organizations or individuals that are engaged belong to some degree to the Western Brotherhood network. Exceptions are not uncommon, but, overall, no other Islamic movement has the political influence and access to elites that the Brothers have obtained over the last twenty years.

The reasons behind Western elites' decisions on the matter will be discussed in the following chapters, but it is now useful to examine what strategies the Brothers have employed to achieve such apparent predominance. Given their small numbers, this position does not seem to reflect their actual standing within Muslim communities. Rather, their role of privileged interlocutors appears to derive, once again, from their phenomenal organizational apparatus and ability to exploit political opportunities. The New Western Brothers have succeeded in convincing large segments of Western elites that they represent local Muslims, despite the lack of any substantial evidence pointing to a mandate to speak on behalf of the entire Muslim community.

Resources unquestionably help in their effort. The New Western Brothers' ability to constantly engage Western elites, either directly or through their active participation in the media, has often made them appear the peak organizations within the Muslim community. No competing organization has been able to organize high-profile events, interact with the Western media, and generally gain as much visibility as the New Western Brothers. Well versed in Islamic theology but sorely lacking knowledge of Western societies, other Islamic trends have experienced severe problems in establishing a permanent dialogue with Western elites. Most of the New Western Brothers might not have the theological background of traditional clerics, but they are personable, highly educated, fluent in Western languages, and knowledgeable in interacting with Westerners, and they have the financial and organizational means to build permanent relationships.

If material resources enable the Brothers to operate on a comparably large scale, their intellectual resources allow them to tailor their actions to the circumstances. Trained political activists, the New Western Brothers have an uncanny ability to understand the political environment surrounding them and devise their actions according to their analysis of what could be most profitable in it. A crucial part of the movement's success, in fact, has been determined by its ability to assess what Western elites were looking for and present itself accordingly.

By the mid-1990s, Western governments stressed the importance of finding an interlocutor that favored the integration of Western Muslims, and the Brothers began to indicate as one of their priorities the creation of a European or American Muslim identity that merged a strong faith with a sense of active citizenship. After 9/11, as Western governments dramatically shifted their attention to security issues, the New Western Brothers began to present themselves as their ideal partners in combating radicalization among Western Muslims.

Flexibility is unquestionably one of the key characteristics of the movement and one of the secrets of their success. As seen, it has been often exhibited in strictly theological matters, allowing *Ikhwan* scholars to justify the violation of secondary principles of the *sharia* in order to advance their cause. But flexibility has also been displayed in more political matters and in the choice of tactics. The New Western Brothers have a remarkable ability to change positions with time, based on a very tactical calculation of what behavior could most benefit their agenda. In the first years of their existence, the *Ikhwan* organizations took very hard and confrontational positions on various issues that involved the Muslim community. These attitudes appear to have been dictated by the strong views of the leaders, as well as by the organizations' desire to make themselves known and gain primacy within the Islamic community.

In 1988, for example, various British-based Jamat-e-Islami–linked organizations vigorously fought for a predominant role in the protests against the publication of Salman Rushdie's *Satanic Verses* that swept the South Asian Muslim community in Great Britain. While their outrage was unquestionably genuine, Islamists appeared to be even more concerned about making sure that other Islamic groups did not take the lead in organizing the protests.[75] Having witnessed how the Rushdie affair helped raise the status of British Islamists, the following year the French *Ikhwan* decided to imitate the tactics of their British counterparts when an opportunity presented itself. As the first nationwide controversy over the use of the *hijab* in public schools erupted in 1989, the Union of Islamic Organizations of France (UOIF), at the time a relatively young and powerless organization, became the most active defender of the right to wear the veil. Hoping to attract the sympathies of the Muslim community, while showing relative disinterest in pursuing a constructive dialogue with the French government, the UOIF organized several protests against the ban and declared that "the Muslims of France could not accept such attacks on their dignity."[76]

Fifteen years later, having reached a position of prominence within France's organized Islam, the UOIF completely changed tactics as it strove to gain the trust of authorities.[77] Realizing that it could obtain more by working within rather than against the system, it decided to avoid head-on confrontations with the government, which can only cause setbacks to its agenda. Therefore, in March 2004, when the French Parliament passed a new, controversial law banning all religious symbols and apparel in public schools, the UOIF kept remarkably quiet, abstaining from participating in the protests that were organized not only in France but also throughout the world.[78] Azzam Tamimi, a leader of the British wing of the Western Brotherhood who was harshly critical of this decision, explained that the UOIF opted for this more moderate position because it is "against any activity that could cause a confrontation with the public powers."[79] Whereas in 1989 the issue of the *hijab* constituted a perfect opportunity to make the UOIF known to the French Muslim community as a strenuous defender of the honor of Muslims, fifteen years later it constituted a dangerous trap to avoid. Since the law passed with overwhelming support of most political forces, the group saw no practical gain in challenging the establishment.

The UOIF's change in tactics highlights the organization's evolution, which, according to its president, Lhaj Thami Breze, can be divided into three phases.[80] After an initial period characterized by the arrival of foreign students in France, the second phase focused on adapting the UOIF's thinking to its reality of Islamic organization permanently operating in a non-Muslim country—a passage epitomized by the symbolic change of name, from Union of Islamic Organizations "in France" to "of France." The final phase is characterized, according to Breze, by the "integration of Islam in the institutional, republican and secular system."[81] Access to power and acceptance as the representatives of French Muslims are the UOIF's priorities today. And in order to achieve this goal, they are ready to sacrifice some of their beliefs. Quintessential pragmatists, the New Western Brothers see no inconsistency in compromising some of their secondary principles to fulfill more important goals.

The New Western Brothers' extreme flexibility is demonstrated not only by their ability to avoid dogmatisms and tailor their actions according to the circumstances but also by their ability to forge tactical alliances with the most disparate political allies. Attracting the harsh criticism of more dogmatic Islamic groups, the New Brothers, and particularly their Western offshoots, have often teamed up with all sorts of political forces that, according to the issue and the circumstances, best served their agenda. It is not unusual for a New Western Brotherhood organization to simultaneously partner with fundamentalist Christian organizations to oppose an adult bookstore, with libertarians to lobby against restrictive counterterrorism policies, with non-Muslim immigrant groups to tackle discrimination issues, and with members of the extreme Left to protest foreign policy decisions. Particularly noteworthy in that sense is, in recent years, the close cooperation between the New Western Brothers and some of the most extreme fringes of the antiwar movement. Despite enormous ideological differences on social issues, the Brothers consider that the advantages they obtain by working with the extreme Left far outweigh the risks involved with being accused of betraying their principles.

Moreover, to appeal to various forces, the New Western Brothers frame issues in different terms according to their target audience. Their opposition to laws and regulations banning the *hijab* in public places, for example, has been justified to the Muslim community using Islamic law, consistently explaining that the veil is a religious requirement for women. In order to obtain the support of Christian and Jewish organizations, the issue is often framed by appealing to the common problem of aggressive and intransigent secularism. With the Left, the opposition is framed through the lenses of multiculturalism, alleging racist persecution of an underprivileged minority on the part of intolerant nativists.[82]

Leveraging Influence

Assuming the position of recognized leaders of Western Muslim communities represents the New Western Brothers' main external goal. How do they intend to use this position? One aim, publicly and proudly declared, is to positively contribute to the future of Western society. Muslims are in the West to stay and, according to the Brothers, have much to add to the development of its modern and multicultural societies. The New Western Brothers encourage Muslims to participate in society and spread their Islamic principles, which ultimately benefit everybody. Highlighting common values, the Brothers present themselves as leaders of a community whose strong faith and moral compass can do much for a moral revival of the rest of society. Muslims, argue Brotherhood leaders, have a lot to offer Western civilization and can help deal with social problems such as family disintegration, crime, and substance abuse.[83]

Presenting themselves as the force that will guide Western Muslim communities on the path to active citizenship is a major attraction to Western elites, who have been eager to find such partners for more than two decades. And most New Western Brothers do sincerely aim at using the movement's predominance to further a process that would benefit both Muslims and Western societies. Muslims, argue many Brothers, are ordered by God to positively affect the behavior of those around them and work for the betterment of society, whether that is Islamic or not. UOIF president Lhaj Thami Breze, for example, emphasizes social pacification as one of his organization's main goals.[84] Breze argues that with its strong Islamic ethos and deep understanding of French culture, the UOIF could play a key role in bridging the gap between the Muslim community and the rest of French society.

Yet the New Western Brothers seem to have additional, less overt goals attached to the establishment of a preferential relationship with Western governments. Despite their unrelenting activism and ample resources, the Brothers have not been able to create a mass movement and attract the allegiance of large numbers of Western Muslims. Although concepts, issues, and frames introduced by the Brothers have reached many, most Western Muslims either actively resist or simply ignore this influence. The Brothers understand that a preferential relationship with Western elites could provide the financial and political capital that would allow them to significantly expand their reach and power inside the community. By leveraging such a relationship, in fact, the Brothers aim at being entrusted by Western governments with administering all aspects of Muslim life in each country. They would, ideally prepare the curricula and select the teachers for Islamic education in public schools; appoint imams in public institutions such as the military, the police, or in prison; and receive subsidies to administer various social services. This position would also allow them to be the official Muslim voice in public debates and in the media, overshadowing competing forces. The powers and legitimacy bestowed upon them by Western governments would give them significantly increased influence over the Muslim community. Making a clever political calculation, the New Western Brothers are attempting to turn their claim of leadership into a self-fulfilling prophecy, seeking to be recognized as representatives of the Muslim community in order to actually become them.

An analysis of the New Western Brothers' activities reveals a third and final objective that the movement seeks to attain through its position of prominence. Once again, this goal has been clearly outlined by al Qaradawi in his seminal 1990 book *Priorities*: "it is necessary for Islam in this age to have a presence in such societies that affect world politics," and the presence of a strong and organized Islamist movement in the West is "required for defending the causes of the Muslim Nation and the Muslim Land against the antagonism and misinformation of anti-Islamic forces and trends."[85]

In other words, al Qaradawi argues that the New Western Brothers have the unprecedented opportunity and the duty to influence Western public opinion and policy makers on all geopolitical issues related to the Muslim world. And indeed, over the last twenty years, the New Western Brothers have consistently tried to take advantage of their position to advance various Islamist causes. From private meetings with senior policy makers to mass street protests, from editorials in major newspapers to high-profile conferences, they have used all their material and intellectual resources to advance the Islamist point of view on several issues and on the nature of the Islamist movement itself. From defending the Islamist regime in Sudan to opposing the wars in Afghanistan and Iraq, from attacking secular rulers throughout the Middle East to presenting various Islamist groups operating in the region as genuine advocates of democracy opposing corrupt dictatorships, they have vocally advocated the many causes of the global Islamist movement within the Muslim community and with Western policy makers and publics.

The one issue that has been embraced by the New Western Brothers with unparalleled intensity and emotion, leading them to invest all their political capital in it, is the Palestinian cause. Upon arriving in the West as refugees or students, the first Brothers advocated supporting the Palestinian struggle against Israel. Some of the first pioneers, like Said Ramadan, had participated in the 1948 Arab-Israeli war and many others, coming from Arab countries bordering with Israel, had strong feelings about the struggle against the Jewish state.[86] But it was in the early 1980s, as the Palestinian cause began to progressively take more religious undertones, that the New Western Brothers, along with the rest of the global Islamist movement, became increasingly involved. The 1982 "Project" found in Nada's home, for example, advocated that the Brotherhood should "perpetuate feelings of disgust toward Jews and deny all coexistence" and, most important, "appropriate the Palestinian cause within the global Islamic movement politically and through the *jihad* because it represents the key that opens the door to the rebirth of the Arab world today."[87] In the late 1980s, with the official foundation of Hamas, an organization whose statute describes it as "one of the wings of the Muslim Brotherhood in Palestine," the global Islamist movement had its own player in the game and directed its worldwide activities to support it.[88]

Since the early 1990s, the New Western Brothers have tried to aid not just the Palestinian cause but more specifically Hamas, in various ways. Within the Muslim community, the Brothers have been consistent in depicting the secular Palestinian leadership of the PLO as corrupt and ineffective and in identifying Hamas as the only force that could liberate Palestine. Their support has gone well beyond words; over the last ten years, the New Western Brothers have established extremely sophisticated transnational networks to collect money for the Palestinian cause. The donations are officially destined to provide aid to the Palestinian population, but many Western governments believe that the actual beneficiary is Hamas and have taken measures to shut these networks down. In the United States, as we will see, the government's case against one of such charities, the Holy Land Foundation, led to the country's largest terrorism financing case ever and the conviction of several prominent American Brotherhood leaders.[89]

Externally, the mobilization of the New Western Brothers has been equally intense, focusing on attempting to influence Western attitudes toward Israel and Hamas. Openly admitting to have used, ironically, Zionist organizations as a model, the New Western Brothers have tried to develop a lobbying apparatus able to reach both public opinion and decision makers. They have attempted to depict Hamas's activities as a legitimate resistance against a cruel oppressor. If within the Muslim community Hamas's struggle is described in religious terms, as a rightful *jihad* against a non-Muslim aggressor, with Westerners it is framed through concepts that can appeal to them, such as anti-imperialism, self-determination, and antiracism. In various countries the Brothers have also tried to draw comparisons that would have particular emotional appeal to locals: in Italy and France, for example, Hamas militants are often compared to the partisans who fought against the Nazis in World War II; in the United States they are compared to George Washington and the American colonists who sought freedom from England.

The New Western Brothers' involvement in the Palestinian and, in particular, Hamas struggle is so strong that it has caused exceptions to two key aspects of their *modus operandi*. First, the Brothers have always publicly downplayed their links to the global Muslim Brotherhood movement, rightly believing that such connections would damage their reputation in the eyes of many Westerners. But their adherence to political or fundraising initiatives of the global movement have revealed links that have caused the Brothers serious political and, in some cases, even legal consequences. Observers, for example, have noted that anti-Israel protests in the West have often been coordinated with those organized by the Muslim Brotherhood in the Middle East. Not surprisingly, London-based Brotherhood activist Kamal Helbawy revealed that, during the January 2009 Israeli attack on Gaza, Brotherhood networks in more than eighty countries coordinated their actions and that the Brothers were able to have protesters sing the same slogans on the same day in Cairo and in London.[90] Similarly, police investigations of Western-based Brotherhood charities have uncovered a large amount of intelligence indicating that the links between the New Western Brothers and other Brotherhood groups throughout the world are much more significant than previously believed.

Moreover, the New Western Brothers' open support of Hamas has led them to justify actions that to most Westerners are morally indefensible.

The Brothers have always striven to present themselves in a reassuring way, to publicly express their views in terms that would seem reasonable and acceptable even to those Westerners who disagreed with them. In their defense of Hamas, however, most Western Brotherhood organizations have been consistent in their refusal to condemn suicide bombings, attacks on Israeli civilians, and other actions that the vast majority of Westerners would clearly perceive as terrorism. The New Western Brothers swing between a full endorsement of such methods and more veiled statements in which they support the right of Palestinians to defend themselves with "any tactic they deem appropriate." In any case, the Brothers have consistently tried to use their influence to portray Hamas's actions as legitimate resistance rather than terrorism. While some Westerners subscribe to this view, it is undeniable that these positions have cost the New Western Brothers significant political capital.

An Islamic Conquest?

The discussion on the motivations of the New Western Brothers has so far focused on the short- and medium-term goals of the movement. But how do the Brothers see themselves and the West in fifty or a hundred years? If in the Muslim world their self-declared aim is the establishment of an Islamic order, whether a pure Islamic state or an "Islamic democracy," as recently envisioned by some New Brothers, what are their aims for the West? Assessing the long-term goals of the Islamist movement is crucial in order to determine how to engage its members, but the process has created enormous divergences among policy makers and commentators.

Pessimists argue that, starting with the forefathers of the movement, Islamists have always expressed their vision of Islam as a religion and a political order given by God for humanity in its entirety, not just for Muslims. And some writings do indicate that several early Islamist thinkers wanted Islam to dominate the whole world. Al Banna, for example, wrote that after the formation of an Islamic state in the Muslim world, "We will not stop at this point, but will pursue this evil force to its own lands, invade its Western heartland, and struggle to overcome it until all the world shouts by the name of the Prophet and the teachings of Islam spread throughout the world. Only then will Muslims achieve their fundamental goal, and there will be no more 'persecution' and all religion will be exclusively for Allah."[91] Similarly, Mawdudi wrote that "Islam wishes to destroy all States and Governments anywhere on the face of the earth which are opposed to the ideology and programme of Islam regardless of the country or the Nation which rules it."[92]

Even though al Banna and Mawdudi are still the celebrated ideological guiding stars of the movement, it cannot be assumed that the New Brothers have adopted all their views. Optimists argue that the movement has significantly evolved over time and the new generations, particularly those who grew up in the West, have refined their ideas on Islam's relationship with the West. Even though they are reluctant to publicly challenge the old leadership, many of these new activists have their own religious and political vision.[93] While still adhering to some of the Brotherhood's intellectual heritage, they are gradually distancing themselves from its most militant aspects and are the agents of a slow, internal reformation to adapt the tradition to the present context. Once this new generation completely takes over, say the optimists, they will move Brotherhood organizations in a new direction and purge their thinking of some of the ideas held by the old guard.

Pessimists argue that the New Brothers' civic participation and pro-integration statements are simply deceitful tactics to further their goals. The New Western Brothers, they argue, have pragmatically understood that expressing their wish to turn the West into part of a global Islamic state would be counterproductive, but still secretly share the founders' dream. Moreover, pessimists point at a series of documents and statements as proof of these real aims. A document often cited to make their case was written in 1992 by Mohammed Akram, a member of the American branch of the Brotherhood. This eighteen-page internal memorandum sent to other American Brothers, "An Explanatory Memorandum on the Strategic Goals for the Group in North America," was introduced as evidence by federal authorities in their terrorism financing case against the Holy Land Foundation.[94]

The tactics and methods outlined, focusing on flexibility, the need for organization, and scientific method, are almost identical to those defined ten years earlier in "The Project." But Akram is more specific than the anonymous earlier author in defining the Brotherhood's goals in the West.

"The process of settlement [in America] is a 'Civilization-Jihadist Process' with all the word means," states Akram. "The Ikhwan must understand that *their work in America is a kind of grand Jihad in eliminating and destroying the Western civilization from within and 'sabotaging' its miserable house* [emphasis added] by their hands and the hands of the believers so that it is eliminated and God's religion is made victorious over all other religions. Without this level of understanding, we are not up to this challenge and have not prepared ourselves for Jihad yet."

Many Brothers, while not challenging their authenticity, downplay the significance of these documents. Nada claims that "The Project" is hardly an official plan of action of the Brotherhood but rather a proposal written by somebody whose name he cannot remember almost thirty years ago and never even disseminated within Brotherhood circles.[95] As for Akram's memorandum, most New Brothers say it reflects only the personal opinions of the author, a mid-level Brotherhood member, and has never been endorsed by the larger movement. Mahdi Bray, the director of the Muslim American Society, a group that traces its origins to the U.S. branch of the Brotherhood, describes Akram's memorandum as "wishful thinking." "I wouldn't be candid if I didn't say there weren't some old-timers who want to hold onto the old way, who say that . . . this should be our model," he explained to the *Dallas Morning News* during the Holy Land Foundation trial. "We said 'So what? It doesn't work here.' We've been very adamant about that."[96]

Pessimists, however, believe that the two documents, written only for internal consumption, offer an invaluable glimpse into the real goals of the New Brothers and debunk their pro-integration façade. Moreover, they argue, the idea that Islam will conquer the West and the rest of the world is hardly limited to a few second-tier militants but has been espoused by several senior Brothers over the past few years. During the same raid that uncovered "The Project," in fact, Swiss authorities found a videocassette with images of a 1993 trip to Afghanistan made by a group of senior Brotherhood leaders to congratulate Afghan Islamist leaders on their victory against the Soviet Union. The group was led by the future *murshid* of the Egyptian Brotherhood, Mustafa Mashour, and included Jamat-e-Islami leader Qazi Ahmad Hussain, al Taqwa founder Ghaleb Himmat, and Yussuf al Qaradawi. Mashour, a widely respected leader who had spent most of the 1980s in Germany, gave a speech that was not supposed to circulate beyond Brotherhood circles. He started by praising the Afghans for their victory and said that *jihad* must continue to liberate other occupied Muslim lands, from Palestine to India and Chechnya. But Mashour did not stop there. "I will assure you," he said, "that as the Soviet Union has fallen, so will America and the West succumb, with the help of God."[97]

In other cases, Brotherhood leaders have had no qualms in publicly expressing their belief and desire that Islam will conquer the West. In 2004, then Egyptian Brotherhood *murshid* Mohammed Akef declared his "complete faith that Islam will invade Europe and America, because Islam has logic and a mission." He added that "Europeans and the Americans will come into the bosom of Islam out of conviction."[98] Al Qaradawi has repeatedly expressed the same view. In a 1995 speech at an Islamic conference in Toledo, Ohio, he stated: "We will conquer Europe, we will conquer America, not through the sword but through dawa."[99] And in a *fatwa* posted on Islamonline.net in 2002 he reiterated the concept: "Islam will return to Europe as a conqueror and victor, after being expelled from it twice. I maintain that the conquest this time will not be by the sword but by preaching and ideology."[100]

Al Qaradawi's idea of an Islamic conquest of the West through *dawa* is hardly new and had been systematically developed during the 1980s and 1990s by many New Western Brothers. Western-based intellectuals who belonged to the Brotherhood network have published extensive treaties outlining methods to achieve this. One of the most prominent and widely read among these authors is the late Khurram Murad, a member of Jamat-e-Islami who in 1978 succeeded Khurshid Ahmed at the helm of the Islamic Foundation of Leicester. In his writings, widely distributed by the foundation in Europe and by ISNA in the United States and today available for free on dozens of Web sites of New Western Brotherhood organizations, Murad outlines his vision for the spread of Islam in the West.[101] But if *dawa* is a duty for all Muslims, Murad, like other Brotherhood *dawa* strategists in the West such as Shamim Siddiqi and Said Hawwa, makes clear that the Islamist movement's *dawa* is meant to "reaffirm and re-emphasize the concept of total change and supremacy of Islam in the Western society as its ultimate objective."[102] That "ultimate objective," reiterates Murad in another article, "should be the establishment of a society based on the Qur'an and the Sunnah."[103]

In 1999, Siddiqi, who served as chairman of the Dawah and Publications Department of the Islamic Circle of North America, wrote an extensive paper about the movement's *dawa* in the United States. America, argued the Indian-born activist, provides a great opportunity: it is "a government of law," a country where "democratic processes are deep-rooted," and the judiciary is "independent and strongly defends and protects human rights."[104] "America," argues Siddiqi, "thus, provides the right environment for the spread of Islam here." He argued that the spread of the Islamic movement in America "will be another front besides the Islamic Movement in the other countries, to pave the way for a success of the movements in the Muslim world." "If an Islamic movement is built up in America which pinpoints the shortcomings of capitalism, elaborates the fallacies of democracy with vivid illustrations of its own system, exposes the devastating consequences of the liberal life-style, there is every possibility that the American people may think of changing over to a better system, a better ideology."[105] Similarly, Ahmad Sakr, MSA founder and former MWL representative to the United Nations, argued that "as a result of our persistent effort, America may become a Muslim country after two or three decades."[106]

Some optimists dismiss these statements as not representative of the current position of the New Western Brothers. In doing so they rely on the many other statements in which New Western Brothers have expressed their desire to live harmoniously with people of other faiths and limited their aims to maintaining the Islamic identity of Western Muslims. Pessimists reply by highlighting that the vision of an Islamic takeover of the West has been expressed consistently and in recent years by senior leaders of the Brotherhood and never directly denounced by New Western Brothers. Pessimists consider this one of the issues in which the Brothers engage in "outsourcing of radicalism," letting non-Western Brotherhood leaders like al Qaradawi say what they believe but cannot say.

It must be noted that the New Brothers have always stated that such a supposed "conquest" will be peaceful. Many political and religious movements hope that the entire world will embrace their vision; similarly, the Brothers, by expressing their desire to "conquer" the West through *dawa*, simply wish that one day all human beings will embrace Islam. Driven by their firm belief in the superiority of Islam to any other religion or system of life, they simply want to spread their message through peaceful means, convinced that all men, once exposed to the beauty of Islam or, better, their interpretation of it, will voluntarily embrace it.[107] "In considering the earth as an arena for Islam," states IIIT's Taha al Alwani in an online *fatwa* on the participation of Muslims in the American political system, "Allah has promised its inheritance to His righteous people, and He has promised that Islam will prevail over other religions."[108] The Brothers are also well aware that immigration, high birth rates, and conversions are contributing to a seemingly unrelenting increase of the Muslim population in Europe and North America. Although they seldom state it openly, the Brothers see such demographic shifts and their *dawa* efforts as the factors that could lead to radical changes in the social, political, and religious makeup of the West.

Understanding that such discourses can make many Westerners uncomfortable, the New Western Brothers have kept a certain ambiguity over their long-term goals. "If the ideal Islamic society remains an objective that most members recognize can never be implemented in Europe," writes Brigitte Maréchal, "others still feel confident that their efforts will bear fruit: they are betting on the demographic rate of increase of the number of Muslims, and on the re-spiritualization of Islam in Europe, in hoping that their ambitions will be realized in a more or less distant future."[109] A quintessentially pragmatic movement, the New Western Brotherhood sees no point in attracting undesired attention by publicly expressing the vision of something that, even in the most optimistic of views, lies far in the future; therefore, they tend to avoid public endorsements of the vision of an Islamic conquest of the West heralded by al Qaradawi and others spiritual leaders.

With no set timetable to reach their goals, the New Western Brothers can go forward implementing their short- and medium-term goals, understanding that loudly enunciating their long-term hopes would lead to the unnecessary scrutiny and confrontations they seek to avoid. But in internal discourses the idea that Islam will, with time—and not through an arcane conspiracy or violence but rather through patient work that entails *dawa* and cozying up to Western elites—become the world's only religion is a constant. In a *fatwa* issued in 2003, Muzammil Siddiqi, a Harvard-educated activist who served as ISNA's president in the late 1990s, perfectly summarized the New Western Brothers' reasons for participating in Western political systems and their final goals:

> By participating in a non-Islamic system, one cannot rule by that which Allah has commanded. But things do not change overnight. Changes

come through patience, wisdom and hard work. I believe that as Muslims, we should participate in the system to safeguard our interests and try to bring gradual change for the right cause, the cause of truth and justice. We must not forget that Allah's rules have to be established in all lands, and all our efforts should lead to that direction.[110]

4

The Governments' Dilemma

The previous chapters have described the New Western Brothers as rational actors operating within the democratic framework to achieve their political goals and as main candidates, thanks to their resources and activism, for the role of representatives of Western Muslim communities. It is now important to see how the New Western Brothers fit into the Western governments' search for interlocutors within the Muslim community. Do the governments perceive the Brothers' desire to participate in the democratic process as based on heartfelt convictions or on tactical calculations? Do they think that the Brothers' ideology is compatible with life in a secular Western democracy? Can they be government interlocutors, reliable middlemen who can help integrate immigrants and the children of immigrants into mainstream society?

The answers to these questions have enormous repercussions on the policies of Western countries determining how to approach Western Muslim communities. Whether the New Western Brotherhood is considered a potential friend, a deceitful enemy, or something in between will shape short- and long-term decisions on domestic policy. Yet the policy making of virtually all Western countries on the issue can only be described as schizophrenic, apparently unable to reach a firm judgment about the Brotherhood's nonviolent Islamism. "The complication is that they [the Muslim Brothers] are a political movement, an economic cadre and in some cases terrorist supporters," stated Juan Zarate, one of America's most senior counterterrorism officials, in a 2004 interview for the *Washington Post*. "They have one foot in our world and one foot in a world hostile to us. How to decipher what is good, bad or suspect is a severe complication."[1]

Zarate's comments reflect the bind in which most Western officials find themselves when assessing the New Western Brothers and, even more, when devising policies toward them. Assessment and engagement are the two components of Western policy making toward Western Brotherhood organizations. Assessment is the first activity, logically and chronologically, within Western governments as they try to determine the nature of the movement. Engagement is the series of decisions taken, in theory following a predetermined assessment, on how to interact with the movement. Policy toward the New Western Brotherhood is complex and characterized by significant differences from one country to another. Nevertheless, common patterns, albeit with differing degrees of intensity and within different time frames, influence it throughout the West.

Assessing the New Western Brothers

Assessments of the New Western Brothers closely resemble those of the global Islamist movement, with analysts split between optimists and pessimists. More specifically, optimists argue that the New Western Brothers are no longer preoccupied with creating Islamic states in the Muslim world, but rather focus on social and political issues concerning Muslims in the West.[2] Their main goals are simply to defend the interests of Western Muslims and to diffuse Islamic values among them. The New Western Brothers are a socially conservative force that, unlike other movements with which they are often mistakenly grouped, encourages the integration of Western Muslim communities, offers a model in which Muslims can live their faith fully and maintain a strong Islamic identity while becoming actively engaged citizens.[3] Moreover, argue the optimists, the New Western Brothers provide young Muslims with positive affirmation, urging them to convey their energy and frustration into the political process rather than into violence or extremism. Governments should harness the New Western Brothers' grassroots activities and cooperate with them on common issues, such as unemployment, crime, drugs, and radicalization.

Pessimists see a much more sinister nature in the New Western Brotherhood. Thanks to their resources and the naiveté of most Westerners, they argue, the New Western Brothers are engaged in a slow but steady social engineering program, aimed at Islamizing Western Muslim populations and ultimately at competing with Western governments for their allegiance. The pessimists accuse the Brothers of being modern-day Trojan horses, engaged in a sort of stealth subversion aimed at weakening Western society from within, patiently laying the foundations for its replacement with an Islamic order.[4] The fact that the New Western Brothers do not use violence but participate with enthusiasm in the democratic process is seen simply as a cold calculation on their part. Realizing they are still a relatively weak force, the Brothers have opted for a different tactic: befriending the establishment.

According to pessimists, officials of Brotherhood-linked organizations have understood that infiltrating the system, rather than attacking it head on, is the best way to obtain what they want; after all, in the West, at least for now, the harsh confrontations mounted by *jihadist* groups such as al Qaeda lead nowhere. New Western Brothers have astutely realized that their most fruitful approach is to cozy up to Western elites and gain their trust. By becoming the privileged partners of the Western establishment, they can gain significant power that will help them further their goals. They are taking advantage of the Western elites' desperate desire to establish a dialogue with any representatives of the Muslim community and putting themselves forward as the voices of Western Muslims, then using the power and legitimacy that comes from such interaction to strengthen their position inside the community.

Pessimists also point to a constant discrepancy between the New Western Brothers' internal and external discourses as a sign of their duplicitous nature. In the media and in dialogues with Western governments, Brotherhood leaders publicly avow the group's dedication to integration and democracy, tailoring their rhetoric to what they know their interlocutors want to hear.[5] Yet, speaking Arabic, Urdu, or Turkish before fellow Muslims, they often drop the veneer and foster an "us versus them" mentality that is the antithesis of integration and tolerance. Even as Brotherhood representatives speak about interfaith dialogue and integration on television, the movement's mosques preach hate and warn worshippers about the evils of Western society. While they publicly condemn the murder of commuters in Madrid and schoolchildren in Russia, they continue to raise money for Hamas and other terrorist organizations. In the words of Alain

Chouet, former head of French foreign intelligence, "Like every fascist movement on the trail of power, the Brotherhood has achieved perfect fluency in double-speak."[6]

Chouet's position seems to encapsulate the views expressed, publicly or privately, by most intelligence and security agencies throughout continental Europe. Belgium's domestic intelligence agency, for example, described the activities of Muslim Brotherhood offshoots in the country in these terms:

> The State Security (Sûreté de l'État) has been following the activities of the Internationalist Muslim Brothers in Belgium since 1982. The Internationalist Muslim Brothers have possessed a clandestine structure in Belgium for more than twenty years. The identity of the members is secret; they operate with the greatest discretion. They seek to spread their ideology within Belgium's Muslim community and they aim in particular at young, second- and third-generation immigrants. In Belgium as in other European countries, they seek to take control of sports, religious, and social associations, and they seek to establish themselves as privileged interlocutors of national and even European authorities in order to manage Islamic affairs. The Muslim Brothers estimate that national authorities will increasingly rely on the representatives of the Islamic community for the management of Islam. Within this framework, they try to impose the designation of people influenced by their ideology in representative bodies. In order to do so they were very active in the electoral process for the members of the body for the management of Islam [in Belgium]. Another aspect of this strategy is to cause or maintain tensions in which they consider that a Muslim or a Muslim organization is a victim of Western values, hence the affair over the Muslim headscarf in public schools.[7]

The AIVD, the Netherlands' domestic intelligence agency, is even more specific in its analysis of the New Western Brotherhood's tactics and aims:

> Not all Muslim Brothers or their sympathizers are recognisable as such. They do not always reveal their religious loyalties and ultra-orthodox agenda to outsiders. Apparently co-operative and moderate in their attitude to Western society, they certainly have no violent intent. But they

are trying to pave the way for ultra-orthodox Islam to play a greater role in the Western world by exercising religious influence over Muslim immigrant communities and by forging good relations with relevant opinion leaders: politicians, civil servants, mainstream social organizations, non-Islamic clerics, academics, journalists and so on. This policy of engagement has been more noticeable in recent years, and might possibly herald a certain liberalisation of the movement's ideas. It presents itself as a widely supported advocate and legitimate representative of the Islamic community. But the ultimate aim—although never stated openly—is to create, then implant and expand, an ultra-orthodox Muslim bloc inside Western Europe.[8]

The position of most intelligence agencies in continental Europe is clear. But governments, lawmakers, and bureaucrats of all levels are not bound by the assessment of their countries' intelligence agencies and often espouse different ideas. Experts within and outside government often influence the policy makers' opinions, leading to a complex, often chaotic situation in which institutions swing erratically between actions that reflect first optimistic and then pessimistic views of the movement. In substance, no Western country has adopted a cohesive assessment followed by all branches of its government. There is no centrally issued white paper or set of internal guidelines sent to all government officials detailing how New Western Brotherhood organizations should be identified, assessed, and eventually engaged. This leads to huge inconsistencies in policies, not only from one country to another but also within each country, where positions diverge from ministry to ministry and even from office to office of the same body.

Engaging the New Western Brothers

An inherently vague term, engagement stands for a variety of forms of contact, from an inconsequential one-time meeting to a stable partnership. The institutions that need to engage representatives of the Muslim communities range from prime ministers and other top government officials to bureaucrats at the local level. Each of them has different aims and priorities and must take into consideration various factors. In some cases they seek to find a range of interlocutors representing the whole spectrum of

the Muslim community; whether the given institution adheres to the optimistic or pessimistic point of view, the local New Western Brotherhood
offshoot is likely to be engaged as one of the representatives. Other institutions might have a more limited aim, to find just one partner in the Muslim community to help them on a certain project or goal. In this case the
institution's assessment of the New Western Brothers is likely to influence
its decision about whether to engage them or not.

At first glance, it would be fair to assume that institutions that adopt the
optimistic point of view tend to consistently engage New Western Brotherhood organizations as partners, while those in the negative camp are opposed to any form of contact. In reality, in most cases the relationship between assessment and engagement is not linear but rather conditioned by
a myriad of external factors and considerations. A governmental body that
takes the optimist position, for example, could decide to refrain from partnering with a New Western Brotherhood organization in order to avoid being criticized by the press. Institutions that adhere to the pessimist point of
view could end up working with them due to political pressures from other
sections of the government or to achieve short-term goals for which they
deem the Brothers' participation necessary.

Given the lack of centralized directives, most governmental bodies have
a large degree of latitude in drafting their own attitudes and policies toward New Western Brotherhood organizations. Several factors, often operating concurrently, influence engagement decisions.

Knowledge/Access to Information

In 2006, Jeff Stein, the national security editor at the Washington-based
Congressional Quarterly, began to conduct a series of interviews with top
U.S. officials about the terrorist threat facing the country. Sensing that
most of the interviewees knew little about the ideology of groups like al
Qaeda and Hezbollah, Stein decided to quiz them about their knowledge
of Islam and Islamism.[9] The results were staggering. Congressman Silves-
tre Reyes, chairman of the House Intelligence Committee, the body supposed to oversee most terrorism matters, was unable to tell the difference
between Sunnis and Shias and argued that al Qaeda's members belonged to
both sects, adding, in an attempt to be precise, that it was "predominantly,

probably Shiite." Scores of top counterterrorism officials interviewed by Stein were equally unable to tell the difference between Sunnis and Shias and some, like the chief of the FBI's national security branch, Willie Hulon, identified Hezbollah as a Sunni organization.[10]

In 2007, reporters at the *Times* of London, suspecting that many British policy makers would not have performed better than their American counterparts, posed them similar questions.[11] Asked whether al Qaeda was Sunni or Shia, Labour MP Brian Iddon, secretary of the British-Palestine parliamentary group, answered, "it attracts all sorts." Conservative MP Gary Streeter, chairman of his party's international office and vice-chair of the All-Party Friends of Islam parliamentary group, confessed he did not know what the difference between Sunnis and Shias was and failed to identify Mahmoud Ahmedinejad as president of Iran.

Although informed and knowledgeable policy makers do exist in both the United States and Great Britain, these investigations revealed a pervasive ignorance among many of the top officials in charge of issues that have closely to do with Islam and Islamism. The problem, which is safe to assume as common to all Western countries, has severe consequences on engagement issues. Policy makers who ignore the most basic features of Islam and Islamism are hardly in a position to assess a movement as complex as the Muslim Brotherhood, understand its nuances, and decipher its often ambiguous language. Yet they are often the ones who decide whom to engage.

Western governments do have analysts and experts who possess an extensive understanding of Islamism, but a series of factors impede the formation of a complete body of knowledge on the subject available to all public officials. First, in most countries such analysts are few and overburdened, struggling to keep up with the ever-evolving universe of Muslim organizations. According to an Italian government report, for example, the number of mosques and Islamic organizations went from 351 in 2000 to 696 in 2006; 39 were set up just between January and May 2007, an average of one every four days.[12] In Italy, as in all other Western countries, only a few analysts are able to navigate the complex jungle of Islamic organizations and assess their ideological nature. Worsening these capacity problems, in several countries the most gifted and experienced analysts are often lured to the private sector by higher salaries, leaving security agencies with severe gaps in institutional knowledge.

Moreover, Western intelligence agencies tend to devote only limited attention to Brotherhood offshoots. Some of them, like the FBI, Britain's MI5, and Denmark's PET, are subject to legal limitations that force them to focus only on direct threats to their countries' security. Aside from their suspected fund raising for Hamas, New Western Brotherhood organizations are generally not engaged in any activity that falls within that mandate; therefore, the agencies have only limited knowledge of them.[13] Others, like Holland's AIVD and Germany's Verfassungsschutz, do have a broader mandate to investigate not just security threats but all activities that could be considered a threat to the country's democratic order and social cohesion. These agencies do devote more attention to the Brothers, but particularly after 9/11, they have understandably directed most of their focus and manpower to the prevention of terrorist attacks.

An additional factor that prevents the formation of a widely accessible intragovernmental body of knowledge on the New Western Brotherhood is the very nature of large bureaucracies. The studies of Graham Allison, one of America's most renowned political scientists, are particularly useful in explaining the convoluted nature of government decision-making processes. Allison argues that it is often assumed that a government is a unified body that has all possible available information and makes its decisions rationally, after a straightforward process that has identified the state's interest and how best to pursue it. In reality, no government corresponds to this ideal "centrally controlled, completely informed and value maximizing" rational decision maker. Rather, Allison argues, a government is a "conglomerate of semi-feudal, loosely allied organizations," each with its own procedures, customs, priorities, and personalities.[14]

Applied to the assessment and engagement of the New Western Brothers, Allison's theory explains why information does not circulate among various governmental institutions. In many cases, intelligence agencies do not share their knowledge unless prompted, due to an institutional bias that stresses sometimes excessive secrecy. In other cases, government officials do not bother to contact intelligence agencies for an assessment. Bureaucratic sluggishness, jurisdictional obstacles, and intragovernmental rivalries also contribute to enormous problems in information sharing. Countries with large populations and, consequently, large bureaucracies experience particular difficulties. In the United States, for example, the overlap between state and federal authorities, geographic distances, and the enormous size of the government make information sharing particularly challenging.

The result of all these problems is that the choice of Muslim organization to engage might be made by a handful of individuals who lack any expertise on Islam and Islamism. In many cases governmental institutions will engage New Western Brotherhood offshoots after a complete and well-informed assessment process, fully aware of the nature of their interlocutor. Such a decision might be taken either because the institution is optimistic or because, whatever its assessment of the New Western Brothers, it believes that engaging them could achieve the institution's aim. But often the decision to engage New Western Brotherhood organizations is made after an uninformed assessment of their characteristics. In fact, cases in which governmental institutions engaged such organizations and later backtracked after discovering more information are not unusual.

One mistake commonly made, particularly at the local level, is to overestimate the representativeness of New Western Brotherhood organizations. Over the last few years most authorities have developed an understanding of the extreme heterogeneity of Western Muslim communities, but in the past some relied only on the most religiously orthodox cross-sections of their Muslim communities to be the spokesmen for the entire community.[15] Affected by what Danish politician Naser Khader sarcastically calls the "mullah syndrome," policy makers therefore engaged predominantly conservative Muslims, ignoring the large masses of secular and sociological Muslims.[16] This attitude only played into the hands of New Western Brotherhood organizations, which, thanks to their activism and resources, could easily persuade Western governments and publics to regard them as spokesmen for the Muslim community.

Sometimes, politicians simply fail to check the backgrounds of organizations they decide to engage, only to hastily retrace their steps after they are provided with more information. In his testimony before the Congressional Human Rights Caucus, for example, *Wall Street Journal* reporter Ian Johnson recounted how in an interview, a British member of the European Parliament told him that she enjoyed meeting with representatives of FIOE, the Brussels-based pan-European umbrella organization for the New Western Brotherhood.[17] She considered FIOE a very moderate organization, unlike the Muslim Association of Britain (MAB), whose extremism troubled her. When Johnson pointed out that MAB was a founding member of FIOE, the MP was astonished, embarrassedly admitting she had failed to make such a basic connection.

In other cases policy makers possess the necessary information but fail to process it correctly, as did former Dutch Minister of Integration Ella Vogelaar. In 2007, the Dutch newspaper *De Telegraaf* alleged that Yahiya Bouyafa, a local Muslim activist, was linked to various organizations of the global Muslim Brotherhood network and was receiving money from the Europe Trust.[18] The story was particularly important because Bouyafa had been engaged by the Dutch Ministry of Integration as a partner in its efforts to promote integration and combat radicalization within the local Muslim community. Some members of the Dutch Parliament asked Vogelaar to publicly explain her decision to work with Bouyafa.[19]

Vogelaar's response, given during a parliamentary session, perfectly exemplifies the inability of many Western policy makers to understand the very nature of the New Western Brotherhood.[20] First, the minister responded that there was no information indicating that Bouyafa belonged to the Brotherhood, just that he was connected to a large number of Muslim organizations that sympathized with the Brotherhood. This demonstrated that Vogelaar did not understand how affiliation to the Brotherhood can be determined. Whether Bouyafa is or is not a Muslim Brother, however defined, is here irrelevant. But Vogelaar's statement clearly identifies such an affiliation as some kind of formal membership, not understanding that it is determined by personal, ideological, and financial connections.

Furthermore, Vogelaar assured the legislators that she had been informed by the security services that the organizations to which Bouyafa was linked did not "pose a threat to national security" and, therefore, had intended to keep engaging Bouyafa. By saying so, she appeared to divide the candidates for her efforts in two categories. Individuals involved in terrorist activities, who therefore pose a threat to national security, should not be engaged; all others can be used as partners. Vogelaar seemed to ignore that there could be a third category, composed of individuals and organizations that, while not involved in any terrorist activity and posing no direct threat, might have an agenda and an ideology incompatible with the Dutch government's goal of encouraging integration.

Insiders' Influence

In some cases, acknowledging their lack of expertise on Islam and Islamism, public institutions have resorted to hiring advisors from the Muslim community to fill the gap. With an understanding of the community that few people in government can match, such advisors have often been listened to with particular attention by many policy makers. The idea is obviously a good one, but it is not uncommon for advisors, in this as in any other field, to attempt to influence policy according to their own views. Given their high level of education and close ties to political establishments, it is not surprising that in several Western countries Brotherhood sympathizers have obtained such positions and have used them to further the influence of Brotherhood-linked organizations.

Personal and Political Considerations

Bureaucracies are deeply influenced by the views of some of their key personalities. Allison uses "parochial priorities and perceptions" to describe the tendency of certain individuals to sway the decisions of a bureaucracy according to their personal ideological positions and political goals.[21] The issue could not be more relevant in the field of engagement with Muslim communities. Policy implementation has often been based on the decision of a single minister or a single official; consequently, the personal views and considerations of a few powerful individuals can play a crucial role in determining which Muslim organization is engaged and how the New Western Brothers are perceived. In many cases, government officials form their opinions, along either the optimist or the pessimist line, after an intellectually honest analysis of the nature of New Western Brotherhood organizations and how best to engage the Muslim community. Nevertheless, it is not uncommon for policy makers, particularly those who participate in elections, to factor in considerations about the possible consequences of their decisions on their political careers.

One factor that clearly influences such decisions is the effect of their actions on the electorate and, more specifically, on their constituencies. The factor can work both ways. In some cases policy makers may be wary of engaging certain organizations for fear that the media and the general public might react negatively. An example of such a dynamic took place in Italy in 2007. After leaders of the Union of the Islamic Communities and Organizations of Italy (UCOII) made a series of statements that drew strong criticism from all sides of the Italian political spectrum and most of the media, mayors in various large cities that had previously entered into negotiations with UCOII to authorize the construction of new mosques suddenly withdrew their support.[22] They officially attributed the change of heart to contractual technicalities and zoning regulations, but the move is widely believed to have been dictated by the realization that large segments of the media and the public viewed UCOII in extremely negative terms.[23]

Policy makers may also be influenced by their desire for electoral success in the Muslim community. The "Muslim vote" can already determine the outcome of contested national elections in several Western countries and is likely to increase in importance, as Muslim populations are growing at a remarkably fast rate. This phenomenon is particularly significant at the local level, given the tendency of Muslims to concentrate in urban areas. In cities like Rotterdam, Amsterdam, Bradford, Malmö, and certain boroughs of London and Paris, the Muslim vote is fundamental and actively sought by all political forces. In Brussels, Muslims currently constitute 17 percent of the population, but various projections estimate they will become a majority by 2025.[24] In a country like Belgium, where Brussels' vote is often the tie-breaker in the political struggle between various political parties and between Flemings and Walloons, it is natural that all forces compete to attract Muslim voters.

Sensing an opportunity, the New Western Brothers have often tried to portray themselves as the key to this growing electoral block. Brotherhood organizations distribute guides on how to vote, organize voter registration drives, and indicate what candidates should be supported throughout their network of mosques. Western politicians running in districts with significant Muslim populations cannot be indifferent to such initiatives, and many engage in various forms of mutual support with Brotherhood organizations. In many Western countries, in fact, the Brothers have managed to establish clientelistic relations with political forces, either at the national or the local level, in which the Brothers promise to mobilize their resources in support of the party in exchange for financial and political rewards.

Many have questioned the existence of a monolithic "Muslim vote." Undoubtedly some voting patterns do exist. Muslims in Europe have traditionally voted for parties of the Left, a tendency common to most immigrant groups. But Muslims do not necessarily vote as a predetermined block, blindly casting their ballots as their coreligionaries do. Rather, their political preferences mirror the sociopolitical diversity of their communities. And it is likely that second- and third-generation Western Muslims will vote in more diverse ways in the future. Even more questionable is the New Western Brothers' claim to be able to deliver the Muslim vote. Have Muslims voted for certain parties because local Brotherhood organizations told them to, or would they have made that choice anyway? Without a definitive answer to the question, many policy makers lean toward a safe strategy and maintain their clientelistic relationships with the Brothers.

What is unquestionable is that the New Western Brothers can severely damage the standing of politicians and other public figures by accusing them of anti-Muslim sentiments and, more specifically, of Islamophobia. First used by French orientalist Etienne Dinet in 1922, the term has become common in today's political jargon.[25] Defined as "an outlook or worldview involving an unfounded dread and dislike of Muslims, which results in practices of exclusion and discrimination" in the influential 1996 report by the British-based Runnymede Trust, "Islamophobia" describes an unpleasant phenomenon that exists in all Western countries.[26]

Parts of Western society do indeed harbor an unjustified fear of Islam, and Muslims have unquestionably been subjected to acts of discrimination and racism that warrant attention. But today Islamophobia has also become a useful political weapon in the New Western Brothers' quiver. Within the Muslim community, the Brothers often exaggerate episodes of actual or perceived Islamophobia to reinforce the feeling of a "community under siege" and portray themselves as the only defenders of that community.[27] Externally, it has become an extremely effective tool to silence critics and force policy makers to work with Brotherhood organizations. The charge of Islamophobia is brought not just against those who criticize Islam. Any criticism of a New Western Brotherhood leader or organization is met with an accusation of racism and Islamophobia. In some cases the Brothers, always aware of what chords to strike, tailor their charges according to the country in which they operate. Therefore, in the United States those who criticize them are guilty of McCarthyism, in Italy of fascism, and in most others, of a postcolonial mentality.

The use of the Islamophobia weapon has unquestionably silenced many critics of the New Brothers and led many policy makers to engage them. The label of racist and Islamophobe, whether deserved or not, is hardly something that any public figure and, in particular, any politician would take lightly.[28] The result of such a tactic is perfectly exemplified by the discussion that surrounded a 2008 hearing before the U.S. House of Representatives Committee on Foreign Affairs, on whether the State Department was inadvertently funding Islamist organizations in the Middle East. Several U.S.-based New Brotherhood organizations criticized the committee's choice of witnesses and demanded that one of their experts be included, stating that doing otherwise would signal Islamophobia. Democratic Congressman Brad Sherman, the committee chairman, refused to cave in and addressed the demands during the hearing. "I think one of the greatest fears of people in the United States is somebody may call you a racist . . . they may call you an Islamophobe," stated Sherman. "And what we've seen with some of these organizations is their message is clear: 'Give us money or we'll call you an Islamophobe.'"[29] Although Sherman did not budge, other politicians might determine that the political costs of not doing so are too high.

Satisficing

Graham Allison defines "satisficing" as the tendency of overburdened bureaucracies to satisfy themselves with finding "a needle in the haystack rather than searching for the sharpest needle in the haystack."[30] Rather than seeking the optimal solution, bureaucracies often opt for those that meet the criteria of adequacy and solve pressing needs, ignoring long-term repercussions. Applied to engagement with Muslim communities, satisficing explains why in some cases Western governmental institutions decide to engage with New Western Brotherhood organizations rather than competing groups.

Western policy makers have often seen their wish to find representative, reliable, and moderate partners within the Muslim community crushed by the realization that no organization is able to meet even the first of the three requirements. As a consequence, they have often concluded that the choice was between engaging organizations that seemed vaguely close to meeting the requirements or not engaging anybody. Therefore, New Western Brotherhood organizations, which have consistently claimed to represent the majority of Western Muslims, have often been accepted as dialogue partners. "The government is always looking for organizations to talk to," explains Ursula Spuler-Stegemann, the dean of German experts on Islam, "and the Islamists are the ones coming."[31] The New Western Brothers have often been the lowest hanging fruit, the most visible and loud among Muslim organizations, and as such have been engaged by Western governments looking for the next best thing to a fully representative interlocutor.[32]

In many cases, policy makers agree with at least parts of the assessment made by pessimists and look at the New Western Brothers with a degree of suspicion. But the need to find a partner overrides such doubts. Moreover, bureaucracies tend to prefer to work with established organizations that in some way reflect their own structure. For the most part, only New Western Brotherhood organizations have the resources to be structured in a way that resembles a bureaucracy, with a legally registered status, a predefined structure, a headquarters, and a full-time professional staff. Competing organizations, lacking such structure and the visibility of the New Western Brothers, experience more difficulties in obtaining access to governments.[33] New Western Brotherhood organizations are therefore sometimes engaged as sole partners in order to satisfy the short-term need of interlocutors in the Muslim community, and only limited thought is given to what the long-term repercussions of such a relationship could be.

Change Through Engagement

Despite all the difficulties in policy making on the issue, in many cases the decision to engage New Western Brotherhood organizations is reached after a fully informed assessment, independently from personal and political considerations, and as part of a carefully thought-out plan that takes into consideration long-term implications. In many cases, in fact, a gradual engagement of New Western Brotherhood organizations is seen as the only possible way to deal with them and to influence their development in the direction desired by the government. Most government officials, while perhaps not fully embracing the pessimist point of view, recognize that there are aspects of the New Western Brotherhood's ideology that they find troubling. Yet they find themselves in front of a dilemma: how is the state to deal with organizations that do not fully recognize core Western values, yet do not advocate violence in the West and have achieved a position of significant influence?

Most officials believe that refusing any dialogue with the New Western Brothers is an ideological and impractical position. Not only have the Brothers a position of influence that cannot be ignored, but pushing them aside could also lead to a radicalization of the movement. At the same time, they acknowledge that it is at least unclear whether the New Western Brotherhood's social agenda is compatible with the goal of a cohesive society and believe that empowering them by selecting them as partners is a dangerous choice. Often government officials seem therefore to opt for a sort of middle ground; they believe that they should establish forms of permanent dialogue with Brotherhood organizations while refraining from granting them financial and political support.

Some proponents of this practical approach argue that gradual engagement enables the government to know more about the Brothers' activities and aims, cynically applying the doctrine of "keeping your friends close but your enemies closer." For the very reason that they question some of the Brothers' goals, they should maintain an open dialogue. Moreover, it is often argued that participation in the political system can have a moderating effect on the New Western Brothers.[34] In the Muslim countries where they have participated in the process, Islamist groups have abandoned, at least publicly, some of their more ideological positions. Being forced to deal with practical issues, Islamists must leave their ideological bubble, review their positions, and compromise.[35] Many policy makers at least hope that a similar process will take place with the New Western Brothers. French President Nicolas Sarkozy is among the firmest believers in this. "I am [also] convinced," he argued in his 2004 book on religion and the state, discussing his approach to French-based New Western Brotherhood organizations, "that once a 'radical' is integrated in an official structure, he loses his radicalism because he becomes part of a dialogue."[36]

French scholar Gilles Kepel, one of the foremost European experts on Islamism, while being very critical of the New Western Brothers' aims, also believes that a graduated engagement will eventually change the movement. He compares the New Western Brothers to the Euro-Communists, the various Western European Communist movements that broke with the Soviet Union in the 1970s. As the Euro-Communists began a process of moderation that made them abandon their dream of creating the dictatorship of the proletariat, the same might happen with the New Western Brothers, who will eventually abandon the dream of a global caliphate and break with the parts of their heritage that are incompatible with life in a Western democracy. "In the same way," argues Kepel, "several decades ago, the children of proletarian and communist immigrants to France from southern and eastern Europe fell under the influence of the Communist party and the trade unions, while all the time engaged in a process of gradual integration and advancement in society. Today, these French citizens belong to the *petite bourgeoisie*, having lost all links with both Marxism-Leninism and their parents' native countries."[37]

It is, of course, impossible to predict whether the New Western Brothers will undergo the same evolution. The rhetoric of some of the leaders of the new generation of Western-born Brothers seems to reinforce this view, though pessimists might argue that they are simply better skilled at deceiving Westerners. In any case, graduated engagement leading to a dilution of Islamist ideology seems to be the idea guiding many policy makers in their approach to New Western Brotherhood organizations.

Necessity or Perception of Necessity

Occasionally government officials engage New Western Brotherhood organizations because, independently from their assessment of the group, working with them on a certain issue can achieve an institutional goal. Even intelligence agencies that hold some of the most negative views on the Brothers recognize that, in some cases, it is in the state's best interest to establish forms of limited cooperation, as the Brothers are believed to be in a unique position to help the state. For the most part such cooperation has taken place over security and terrorism issues, where some governments try to turn to their advantage the reach and legitimacy that the New Western Brothers have in the Muslim community and in particular, among its most radical fringes. Based on a cold *realpolitik* approach, this analysis argues that, even if the Brothers are viewed negatively, they can be used as limited partners.

Over the last few years, for example, various governments have occasionally felt the need to seek the support of New Western Brotherhood organizations in order to diffuse tensions inside local Muslim communities. Danish authorities, for example, believe that Brotherhood-inspired networks in Denmark were crucial in keeping the calm inside the country during the 2006 Mohammed cartoon crisis. Although those very networks helped internationalize the issue by mobilizing Brotherhood groups worldwide and most Danish policy makers consider their influence on Danish Muslims in highly negative terms, Danish security services acknowledge that cooperation with the Brothers was fundamental in preventing violence inside Denmark at the height of the crisis.[38]

In some cases the cooperation on security issues has gone beyond emergency situations and has become, if not a permanent policy, an established pattern. Some Western governments try to establish a relationship with New Western Brothers in order to create a rapport with Islamist groups in the Muslim world, seeing the former as a key to the latter. In other cases New Western Brotherhood organizations have been engaged as partners in the fight against terrorism. As will be extensively analyzed in chapter 8, some Western governments believe that nonviolent Islamists can lend a significant hand in fighting violent extremism among Western Muslim communities and have established various forms of cooperation with them. A similar argument has been made that the New Western Brothers can help governments fight the problems of crime and gang activities in urban areas with high concentrations of Muslim residents.

The effectiveness of these strategies is highly debated and quite difficult to determine, particularly in the long term. In implementing them, governments often seek to find a difficult balance between engaging Brotherhood organizations to achieve essential goals and avoiding empowering the Brothers' social agenda. In any case, the efforts at engagement represent an important political opportunity for the New Western Brothers, who seek to exploit all possible openings to increase their access to power and consequently their legitimacy and influence.

5

Great Britain

This second part of the book will analyze in more detail the situation in various Western countries, providing examples of some of the patterns identified in the previous chapters. It is perhaps appropriate to start with Great Britain, because Islamic revivalist organizations, mostly of South Asian origin, have traditionally been particularly active there; an analysis of their tactics reveals patterns common to most other countries. Moreover, Britain has been one of the first Western countries to attempt to craft a policy of engagement with Islamist spinoffs. The internal debate and the shifts in policy provide particularly useful insights on processes also occurring elsewhere.

The Formation of the Mawdudist Network

A Muslim presence in Great Britain dates back at least three centuries, when small groups of South Asian sailors recruited by the East India Company worked in many ports.[1] Yemeni sailors and Indian students were also present in various British cities during the nineteenth century and the first decades of the twentieth, but it was not until the first decades after the end of World War II that a sizeable Muslim population permanently settled in the country. As former colonial subjects, Indians and Pakistanis (from both West and East Pakistan, which would later become Bangladesh) enjoyed Commonwealth citizenship and could therefore reside in Britain, enjoying the economic opportunities of the country's booming economy.

Mostly seeking low-skilled jobs, Muslim immigrants settled predominantly in London and in the industrial cities of the north, creating sizeable communities in Bradford, Leicester, Oldham, and Birmingham.

Even after 1962, when the British government closed its borders to Commonwealth citizens, family reunifications and other immigration mechanisms allowed the Muslim population to grow steadily. The 2001 census, the last taken, revealed that Muslims were 1.6 million, representing 2.7 percent of the total population.[2] More recent statistics indicate that the Muslim population of Britain has increased significantly since then. Research by the Office for National Statistics indicates that between 2004 and 2008, Britain's Muslim population has grown by more than 500,000 to 2.4 million, a growth rate ten times higher than in the rest of society.[3]

Coming largely from South Asia, most British Muslims have traditionally followed schools and strains of Sunni Islam that originated in the Indian subcontinent, such as the Deobandi, Barelvi, and various Sufi orders.[4] By the 1960s, the fragmentation of the traditional social, tribal, and familial networks led these and other Muslim movements to vie for influence among the communities of South Asian Muslims in Britain by establishing mosques, schools, and in general, an infrastructure to tend to their religious and social needs.[5] As in most Western countries, the formation of an Islamic revivalist movement also took place in Britain at that time. However, the formation of Islamist networks in those other countries has to be attributed to the activism of Arab militants, whereas in Britain, it was done by members of the Pakistan-based Jamat-e-Islami (JeI). Arab activists linked to various branches of the Muslim Brotherhood established a presence in the early 1960s, giving birth to two prominent student organizations (the Muslim Students Society and the Federation of Student Islamic Societies, FOSIS), and have been quite active in various British-based Islamist organizations ever since. But both Islam and Islamism in the United Kingdom are deeply shaped by the South Asian origins of most of its adherents, who dominate in terms of numbers and influence.

As previously seen, JeI was formed in 1941 by Abul A'ala Mawdudi as the ideological correspondent of the Muslim Brotherhood in the Indian subcontinent and became a moderately successful political party in Pakistan.[6] As the British Muslim community was growing, small numbers of JeI members traveled to Britain to spread their interpretation of Islam. Unlike most Arab Brotherhood sympathizers, who had settled in the West to

escape persecution or further their studies but with no predetermined intention of establishing spinoffs of the movement, many of these activists
moved to Britain as part of a centrally approved plan by leaders in Pakistan
to spread their ideology worldwide.[7] Motivated, highly educated, and fluent in English, close disciples of Mawdudi like Khurshid Ahmad and Khurram Murad were instrumental in laying the foundations of the JeI network
in the country. The two men spent their lives shuttling between Pakistan,
where they held some of the highest political positions (Ahmad served for
decades in Parliament and even became a government minister under Zia
ul-Haq), and Britain, where they established scores of organizations.[8]

The original embryo of the Mawdudist network was the UK Islamic
Mission, established in 1962 and headquartered in Islington, a northern
area of London with a growing Muslim population.[9] Unlike Deobandis,
Barelvis, and Sufis, conservative movements that simply tried to preserve
the social and religious customs of Muslims living in Britain, JeI networks
immediately declared their political agenda. Applying Mawdudi's teachings,
the Mission defined itself as an "ideological organization" grounded in the
belief that "Islam is a comprehensive way of life which must be translated
into action in all spheres of human life."[10] Similarly, its official mission
statement declared that the organization sought to "establish the social order of Islam for the Muslims and non-Muslims living in Britain."[11] Person-
ally addressing its 1976 conference, Mawdudi praised the Mission for being
"pioneers of an Islamic movement and resolution in the Western world,"
urging them to continue their *dawa* in Britain since "there is no reason why
the rest of humanity are not persuaded to embrace Islam today."[12]

The Mission understood the importance of extending its teachings to
the largest audience possible and began creating branches throughout the
country. Today the UK Islamic Mission is a nationwide organization with
forty-nine branches and providing Islamic education to thousands of British Muslim children.[13] Following the pattern of New Brotherhood organizations throughout the West and with funds coming from the Arab Gulf,
the Mawdudist network also spawned other organizations and initiatives.
Aside from disseminating the works of Mawdudi and other Islamist thinkers, it began distributing its own publications, including *Paigham* (The
Message, in Urdu).[14] In 1982, Khurram Murad formed a steering committee of a dozen JeI activists to "present Islam to the British population as an
alternative way of life."[15] After two years of training, the activists gave life

to the Mission's youth branch, Young Muslims UK, whose national leader was Farooq Murad, Khurram's son.[16] Today Young Muslims UK, which has partly moved away from the Mawdudist organizational structure, attempts to attract the sons and daughters of Muslim immigrants through study groups, summer camps, Quran competitions, and even activities such as go-karting and paintball, all conducted in religiously oriented and sex-segregated environments.[17]

Headquartered at London's prestigious East London Mosque, the Mawdudist network has grown significantly over the years and encompasses a variety of organizations that cater to various regional constituencies or social groups but refer to the same ideological framework. Its crown jewel is the Islamic Foundation, Khurshid Ahmad's brainchild. Established in 1973 in a small two-room office in central Leicester, it has grown into one of Europe's largest institutions of Islamic knowledge; in 1990 it moved its headquarters to a sprawling mansion in rural Markfield, a few miles northwest of Leicester.[18] The Foundation has been a beacon for the spread of Islamist thought in the West, printing the works of various Islamist thinkers and serving as a bridge between South Asian and Arab activists. Some of the top Islamist thinkers from all over the world have passed through it, either to attend its many symposia or for longer sojourns as visiting fellows.

Like most other New Western Brotherhood organizations, the Mawdudist network in Britain has evolved significantly over time, displaying a sort of dual nature. On one hand, activists linked to the network, particularly among the second, British-born generation, have been involved in an effort to reinterpret and recontextualize Mawdudi's teachings. In 1988, at the Mission's annual conference, Khurshid Ahmad proclaimed that, for British Muslims who wanted "to safeguard their progeny, property, business," "the only way, safe and certain, is to convert the indigenous population to [a] Muslim majority." Today's activists seem to have abandoned these unrealistic goals and publicly avow their desire to contribute to the cohesiveness of a multireligious and democratic society.[19] The network is involved in several interfaith dialogue initiatives, works with various city councils on issues involving the Muslim community, and conducts Islamic-awareness training for British police officers. Many in the British establishment have considered its institutions moderate and reliable partners of the state. Tellingly, in a dinner to celebrate the thirty years of the Islamic Foundation, the Prince of Wales, sitting beside Ahmad, praised the organization as "all that is to be admired about Islamic scholarship in the West" and "a fine example for others to follow."[20]

Others believe that the Mawdudist network has never broken with its past. On this account, the network's apparent moderation is only a façade to deceive the British establishment. A visit to the Web site of any of the network's organizations would reveal that writings on the necessity of rejecting any political order not based on *sharia* are quite common and often written or translated by activists of the second generation. "The truth is that Islam is a revolutionary ideology which seeks to alter the social order of the entire world and rebuild it in conformity with its own tenets and ideals," reads, for example, the essay "Jihad in Islam," penned by Mawdudi in 1939 and posted on the Mission's site as of April 2009 along with more than a dozen of his other writings.[21] Sermons and lectures inside the many mosques controlled by the network have a similar tone, proclaiming the superiority of Islam and the need to turn Britain, as well as the rest of the world, into an Islamic state.[22]

This debate is today raging in Whitehall corridors and has very practical repercussions on policy making, given the importance of the Mawdudist network and its influence in the British Muslim community. Having arrived in Britain as just one of the many forces competing for influence, how did the Mawdudists manage to overshadow groups such as the Barelvis, the Deobandis, and the Sufis, which traditionally appealed to a much larger cross section of the South Asian Muslim community? Mirroring the process that took place in other countries, the reasons of their success have to be found in their activism, access to funds, and mobilization ability. But, if in other countries the process was gradual, in Britain the affirmation of Islamist organizations can be traced to a precise moment in time, which is often seen as a landmark in the relations between the West and Islam.

The Rushdie Affair and the Formation of the Muslim Council of Britain

In September 1988, publishing giant Penguin famously published *The Satanic Verses*, a novel by Indian writer Salman Rushdie.[23] In the book, Rushdie, an iconoclastic figure whose previous writings had mocked both Indian and British traditions, revisited episodes of the life of the prophet

Mohammed in terms that differed significantly from mainstream Muslim tradition. In particular, the book's title refers to the belief that some verses of the Quran had been dictated to Mohammed by the devil, who had deceived the prophet into believing they came from God. Other parts of the book poked fun at various aspects of the prophet's life and the Muslim faith, among many targets.

Rushdie, a secular Muslim intellectual more at ease in London's cultural circles than in mosques, had harshly criticized Jamat-e-Islami in the past, and the publication of *Verses* was the final stroke that led South Asian Islamists to mobilize against their arch-enemy.[24] Activists at the Islamic Foundation of Madras began a campaign to have the book banned in India and urged their colleagues at the Islamic Foundation of Leicester to do the same.[25] The director of the foundation, Manazir Ahsan, and the editor of *Impact International*, Hashir Faruqi, immediately devised a plan to mobilize British Muslims. They began by sending a communication to a large number of mosques, Muslim organizations, and community leaders to denounce the book, urging them to start a campaign to force the publisher to withdraw it and issue a formal apology.[26]

Having received positive feedback, Faruqi and Ahsan convened a meeting of more than 20 British Muslim organizations and formed the UK Action Committee on Islamic Affairs (UKACIA) to coordinate their efforts. Headed by a Saudi diplomat, Regent's Park Mosque director Mughram al Ghamdi, UKACIA was a heterogeneous group that included various sects and trends, but whose leadership was clearly reserved for Mawdudists.[27] UKACIA directed some of its efforts to the Muslim community, collecting 60,000 signatures in support of the ban on the book and encouraging British Muslims to influence public opinion by writing to their MPs and local newspapers.[28] But UKACIA also acted as de facto representative of the British Muslim community, calling on Prime Minister Margaret Thatcher to change the country's blasphemy laws and issuing a formal demand to Penguin, asking for a formal apology, the withdrawal of all the copies of the book, and pecuniary damages to be paid to a charity of its choosing.[29]

As neither Penguin nor the majority of the British establishment paid much attention, the leaders of the Mawdudist network decided to internationalize the matter by seeking the help of sympathetic Muslim governments. Ahsan traveled to Saudi Arabia, where he met with the Muslim

World League's Secretary General and other personalities to get their support.[30] Salem Azzam's Islamic Council of Europe also played a key role, contacting ruling elites throughout the Muslim world. By the end of the year, the Organization of the Islamic Conference, the transnational body that unites all Muslim countries, and individual governments had mobilized against the book, banning it and seeking similar measures from non-Muslim countries.

Despite such efforts, which were to be replicated with very similar dynamics almost twenty years later after the publication of Danish daily *Jyllands Posten*'s cartoons depicting the prophet Mohammed, neither Penguin nor the British government balked. Meanwhile, other Muslim trends had had time to organize their own actions; lacking the means, international connections, and political sophistication of the Mawdudists, they mobilized mostly at the local level. On January 14, 1989, Muslims in Bradford organized a large protest and publicly burned copies of *Verses*, generating an outcry from British pundits who compared their actions to the Nazis' infamous book burnings of the 1930s. A month later, Ayatollah Khomeini of Iran, at the urging of some of his British-based supporters who wanted to counter Saudi influence in the country, famously issued a *fatwa* calling for the death of Rushdie and anybody else connected to the book. Isolated episodes of violence followed, and various London bookshops and other sites related to Penguin were later bombed. In August, Mustafa Mazeh, a twenty-one-year-old Lebanese Shia, accidentally blew himself up in a Paddington hotel room while assembling a bomb to kill Rushdie.[31]

The Bradford book burning and Khomeini's *fatwa* attracted most of the media's attention and have become the most common snapshots of the crisis. But in hindsight, these efforts seem more like poorly organized and extemporaneous attempts on the part of competing Islamic groups to respond to the impressive mobilization of the Mawdudist network and its Saudi patrons. The novel had outraged the vast majority of British Muslims, and the Mawdudists had managed to first capture these feelings and translate them into active political mobilization. Numerically inferior to other trends and little known until then, the Mawdudists were catapulted to the forefront of the struggle for the leadership of the British Muslim community. While other trends struggled to organize a response, the politically minded and professionally trained Mawdudists fully understood how to motivate people and used all the means available in a democratic system to express the voice of the Muslim community and, simultaneously, raise their standing in it.

The Rushdie affair is rightly considered a watershed event in the history of Muslims in Britain. Even though the mobilization did not achieve its original aim to have *Verses* banned, its effects on the community and on the British public's perception of it were crucial in shaping the developments that followed. Arguably, the most notable effect was the formation of a common identity among British Muslims.[32] "It was a seminal moment in British Muslim history," argues Inayat Bunglawala. "It brought Muslims together. Before that they had been identified as ethnic communities but *The Satanic Verses* brought them together and helped develop a British Muslim identity."[33] But Dilwar Hussein of the Islamic Foundation refers to the Rushdie affair also as a "milestone in the history of Muslim organizations in the UK" because it did more: it formed a generation of Muslim leaders that shaped the future of Britain's community.[34] Throughout the first half of the 1990s, various events, from the Gulf War to the conflict in Bosnia, had reinforced the sense of identity of British Muslims, who had become increasingly more conspicuous in the public sphere.[35] They also began to voice some demands to the British state, starting with their desire to have Islamic education in schools. Answering these needs, UKACIA and its Mawdudist leadership provided the basis for the development of a permanent organization to represent the interests of the British Muslim community.

In 1995, several UKACIA leaders formed the National Interim Committee for Muslim Unity (NICMU), a temporary body whose aim was to conduct extensive research on the feasibility and characteristics of a unified representative body for British Muslims.[36] After two years of surveys and consultations, in May 1997 NICMU dissolved itself and gave birth to a new organization called the Muslim Council of Britain (MCB).[37] Originally representing 250 Muslim organizations throughout the country, MCB's structure was loosely modeled after the Board of Deputies of British Jews and other Muslim organizations operating in the West, such as the Islamic Society of North America and the American Muslim Council.[38] MCB affiliates throughout the country send delegates to the organization's general assembly, which elects the Central Working Committee, its executive body.[39] Mostly self-funded (even though the British government has often subsidized its projects), independent, and relatively well organized, MCB was designed to be the organization that expressed, in the words of Iqbal Sacranie, "a united Muslim voice."[40]

The creation of MCB represented a major step for Islam in Britain: for the first time a large number of Muslims were represented by an umbrella organization with a common leadership. The feat was particularly remarkable considering the diversity of its affiliates. MCB does not include secular Muslim organizations, but it comprises groups from various strains of Islam, including Shias, and has among its members prominent Muslim intellectuals and several Muslim MPs, even though their role is often simply nominal. While some of its affiliates trace their roots to Islamist organizations such as JeI and the Muslim Brotherhood, others are Barelvi, Deobandi, or from various traditions of non–South Asian Muslim countries, such as Somalis, Arabs, and Bosnians.

Despite such diversity, the leadership of the organization has traditionally been dominated by individuals from the Mawdudist network whose political and organizational skills have allowed them to overshadow other trends. As stated in an editorial in QNews, an influential British Muslim magazine, "a closer look at the CWC [Central Working Committee] shows that the majority belong to or have sympathies with a UK organization which is a side-kick of the Jamat-e-Islami in Pakistan."[41] Moreover, many "Rushdie children," professional activists who had honed their skills during the Rushdie affair, occupied key positions in the organization from the beginning. Manazir Ahsan, the Islamic Foundation director who had started the mobilization, became MCB's Community Affairs director, while Iqbal Sacranie, who had been UKACIA's Joint Convenor, became MCB's first Secretary General.

MCB's founding was also heralded as a positive development by British authorities, who had sought a representative for the Muslim community since the Rushdie affair. Conservative Home Secretary Michael Howard and, after Labour's landslide win in 1997, his successor Jack Straw played a key role by favoring the formation and development of MCB, which they envisioned as Whitehall's partner in all Muslim affairs. At a time when other European countries were attempting to artificially create organizations that could represent all Muslims, the British government decided that a better solution would be to simply lend its support to an organization that had been spontaneously formed at the grassroots level and that therefore had more legitimacy within the Muslim community.

If the formation of MCB responded to a need of the state, other considerations unquestionably influenced the government's support, particularly after Labour came to power. Since the early 1980s the Labour Party had begun courting the Muslim vote, hoping to use it to partly compensate for the erosion of its traditional electorate, the white working class. By then the Muslim vote had begun to have a notable importance in places like Bradford, Leicester, and inner-city boroughs of London and Birmingham. As the Conservative Party was often seen as anti-immigration, Labour consistently gained between 70 and 80 percent of the Muslim vote, which in many cases allowed it to control the entire city.[42] The trend continued throughout the 1990s, and it is estimated that four out of five Muslims voted Labour in the 1997 elections.[43]

Sensing a political opportunity, the Mawdudists soon attempted to portray themselves as capable of controlling the growing Muslim vote. Already in the 1980s Mawdudist organizations such as the Muslim Education Trust had tried to get Muslims to vote for candidates whose views were more Islamically acceptable, but such attempts had become more systematic in 1997, when UKACIA distributed a pamphlet titled *Elections 1997 and British Muslims* in mosques throughout the country.[44] The pamphlet did not endorse any party but was a clear attempt to influence the Muslim vote and, most important, to portray UKACIA as capable of delivering the Muslim electorate to British politicians.[45] Iqbal Sacranie was more explicit and outlined in a *QNews* article the need for "tactical voting," to "maximize our potential to get a return from those candidates who will not be able to make it to the Commons without our votes."[46]

The Mawdudists' electoral mobilization was not lost on Labour leaders, who were looking for ways to cement their relationship with Muslim voters. Newly appointed Home Secretary Jack Straw, whose own constituency in Blackburn had 20,000 Muslim voters in 1997, and the rest of the Labour Party began to see MCB's leaders, and particularly those from a more politically active Mawdudist background, as the vehicles that could deliver the Muslim vote and sought to establish close ties with them.[47] As part of this newly forged clientelistic relationship, Labour leaders spearheaded various initiatives that had been recommended by MCB, from officially endorsing the Runnymede Trust's report on Islamophobia to introducing legislation allowing Muslim schools to receive state funding.

Post-9/11 Tensions

Over the years MCB grew significantly in both number of affiliates and influence. Like any other organization representing a minority or an interest group, MCB regularly consulted with British officials at all levels and developed the skills to effectively participate in the system. MCB leaders lobbied to introduce pieces of legislation, organized interfaith events, and became the de facto spokesmen of British Muslims with the government and in the media. The relationship between the state and MCB was hardly without controversies. MCB's refusal to attend the annual celebrations of Holocaust Memorial Day, saying that the event needs to be more inclusive and also commemorate the victims of other ethnic massacres such as "the genocide" in the Palestinian territories and in Kashmir, had caused widespread criticism.[48] But overall, MCB was considered a representative and reliable interlocutor of the state, with a semiofficial monopoly on the relationship with the Muslim community.

Problems began to arise in September 2001, after the terrorist attacks against the United States. As issues of Islamic extremism and radicalization became priorities, the British government reached out to MCB, hoping it would endorse, or at least explain, its foreign policy decisions to the Muslim community and play a role in stemming radicalization within it. The government's demands put MCB in a bind. The organization wanted to keep its close relationship with the British establishment. At the same time, many of its leaders were highly critical of Britain's involvement in Afghanistan and, more generally, of the aims of the "War on Terror." Moreover, they understood that their own constituencies were vehemently opposed to Britain's military actions, and public displays of support for Prime Minister Tony Blair's policies could cause them to lose legitimacy among their affiliates.

Torn between their desire to preserve their relationship with the government and the need to maintain their internal support, MCB leaders struggled to find a balance.[49] On one hand, they publicly condemned attacks carried out by al Qaeda and affiliated groups. After the 2004 Madrid train bombings, for example, they wrote an open letter to all MCB affiliates urging them to sway Muslim youth away from terrorism, stating that Islam forbids such acts and that Muslims should cooperate with the police.[50] But on the other hand, many British officials started to privately complain that these very public efforts did not square with what some MCB affiliates were saying inside their mosques and, at least in the eyes of Whitehall officials, were not matched by many practical actions.[51] MCB, argued its growing number of critics, was paying lip service to the government's agenda but in reality providing no concrete help.

The July 7, 2005, bombings in London dramatically increased the tension. In the wake of the attacks, which MCB harshly condemned, British officials selected a group of influential British Muslims to form a task force to provide recommendations for the British government on how to tackle terrorism. The initiative, called *Preventing Extremism Together*, included a diverse group of Muslims, but MCB officials and affiliates clearly outnumbered members of other trends. After weeks of consultations, the task force issued its final report, which analyzed the causes of the attacks and provided short- and long-term solutions to prevent new ones.[52]

The task force constituted a watershed event in the relations between MCB and the government. Even before it could produce its report, it attracted severe criticism from all quarters, questioning the background of some members. Many argued that individuals like then MCB Media Secretary Inayat Bunglawala, who had praised Bin Laden as a "freedom fighter" only five months before 9/11, should have had nothing to do with a group established to tackle extremism.[53] "If Sir Iqbal Sacranie is the best Blair can offer in the way of a good Muslim, we have a problem," stated Salman Rushdie in regard to the recently knighted head of MCB, who had declared at the time of the Rushdie affair that capital punishment for those who insulted the prophet Mohammed was "salutary" and that death was "perhaps a bit too easy" for the Indian novelist.[54]

But criticism became more widespread and was endorsed by government officials when the task force released its report. Despite the opposition of some of its members, the task force devoted little attention to the ideology that had motivated the 7/7 bombers and other young British Muslims who had engaged in terrorist activities.[55] Rather, it stated that "the solutions lie in the medium to longer term issues of tackling inequality, discrimination, deprivation and inconsistent Government policy, and in particular foreign policy."[56] Critics argued that the MCB-driven group had avoided any introspection, ignoring undeniable issues of extremism within the Muslim community, and placed the blame for the attacks squarely on the British government and, in particular, its foreign policy.

Some of its harshest critics believed that MCB was simply exploiting the attacks, putting forward a flawed analysis of the problem and offering a series of policy recommendations that did little to solve issues of extremism and radicalization, only furthering its own agenda.[57] MCB's leaders, for example, linked the radicalization of some British Muslims to the sense of frustration they felt when Islam was attacked in the media. Pushing this argument, they began to lobby Labour leaders to introduce provisions that would have outlawed any criticism of Islam, something many MCB leaders had demanded since the days of the Rushdie affair. In 2005 the government finally introduced a bill that would have made illegal any speech that might be heard "by any person in whom it is likely to stir up racial or religious hatred," regardless of the intentions of the speaker.[58] Under such broad provisions the prosecution would have needed to prove only that there was one person likely to be influenced by such speech, and the speaker would have received a guilty conviction and prison sentence of up to seven years. Former Home Office Minister Mike O'Brien openly admitted in an editorial he wrote for *Muslim Weekly* that the bill, which did not pass in the House of Lords, had been introduced after pressure from MCB and despite strong opposition from many MPs of all political affiliations.[59]

Tony Blair's government could accept MCB's argument that racism, discrimination, and deprivation played a role in driving some British Muslims to commit acts of terror but could not tolerate that its foreign policies were being blamed for the 7/7 attacks. Britain's widely unpopular intervention in Iraq had eroded a significant portion of Labour's electorate, and the argument that the 7/7 attackers had been motivated by it had become accepted among many British citizens. MCB's analysis was seen by the Blair government as intellectually dishonest, since it did not take into consideration factors besides its foreign policy, and politically inconvenient, as it could undermine its quasi-monopoly over the Muslim electorate. Slowly, many Labour leaders started to publicly voice some of the same criticisms of MCB that had been widespread among conservatives and some sections of the British media.

But some of the harshest critics of MCB and its automatic linking of terrorism to foreign policy came, to the surprise and relief of many Labour leaders, from within the Muslim community. One of the loudest was Asim Siddiqui, the chairman of City Circle, a London-based Muslim organization comprising mostly young professionals. "The response from some UK Muslim groups (influenced by Islamist thinking) is still largely to blame foreign policy (undoubtedly an exacerbating influence but not the cause), rather than marching 'not in my name' in revulsion against terrorist acts committed in Islam's name," argued Siddiqui in the *Guardian*.

> No, it's not foreign policy that's the main driver in combating the terror-
> ists; it is their mindset. The radical Islamist ideology needs to be exposed
> to young Muslims for what it really is. A tool for the introduction of a
> medieval form of governance that describes itself as an "Islamic state"
> that is violent, retrogressive, discriminatory, a perversion of the sacred
> texts and a totalitarian dictatorship.[60]

The increasing visibility of Muslims who expressed strong criticism of MCB led British policy makers to reevaluate their stance. Had they placed all their eggs in one basket, selecting MCB as the sole representative of the Muslim community while ignoring other voices? "The overwhelming number of organisations that the Government talks to are influenced by, dominated by or front organisations for the Jemaat-e-Islami [*sic*] and the Muslim Brotherhood," stated Chetan Bhatt, a professor of sociology at Goldsmiths University, in 2005. "Their agenda is strictly based on the politics of the Islamic radical Right, it doesn't represent the politics or aspirations of the majority of Muslims in this country."[61] As they began to meet with groups and individuals not involved with MCB, government officials noticed that large segments of the British Muslim population perceived MCB leaders as a clique of wealthy, politicized, middle-aged South Asian men with little understanding of the realities and needs of the community.[62] A 2006 survey of 1,000 British Muslims conducted by Channel 4 indicated that only 4 percent of them felt represented by MCB, and a similar poll conducted by the Policy Exchange think tank raised that number to just 6 percent.[63] Women, youths, and organizations representing various Islamic trends, like the Sufis, were particularly vocal in stating that MCB did not represent them.

As British authorities began to suspect they had overestimated MCB's representativeness, they also questioned whether MCB had two other attributes governmental partners are generally required to possess: reliability and moderation. Throughout 2005 and 2006 a series of high-profile journalistic investigations showed repeated instances in which MCB affiliates preached ideas that clearly displeased British officials, because they were seen as directly contributing to the radicalization of British Muslims. A prime-time BBC documentary, for example, showed several cases of preachers inside MCB mosques declaring that the government's effort against terrorism was, in reality, a war against Islam. When BBC reporter John Ware asked Iqbal Sacranie to rebut these statements and state unequivocally that this was not MCB's position, Sacranie refused.[64] And while MCB officials publicly stated that it was an "Islamic duty" to prevent terrorism, Mohammed Naseem of the MCB-affiliated Birmingham Mosque reportedly declared that "the official explanation of 7/7 does not make sense" and that Muslims should not be blamed for it.[65]

The gap between what MCB's leadership publicly stated and what some of its affiliates preached could be explained by the fact that MCB is an umbrella for a very diverse array of Muslim organizations, some of which might espouse views not shared by MCB's leaders.[66] But if those leaders did not publicly espouse conspiracy theories or argue that the British government was waging a war against Islam, their rhetoric was nevertheless judged dishonest and counterproductive by many commentators and policy makers. Particularly irksome to British policy makers was MCB's constant accusation that Muslims were unjustly and disproportionally targeted by British authorities in their effort to stop terrorism. British Muslim journalist Kenan Malik perfectly captured the dynamic in a piece he wrote for *The Spectator* in February 2005:

A total of 21,577 had been stopped and searched under the terror laws. The vast majority of these—14,429—were in fact white. Yet when I interviewed Iqbal Sacranie, general secretary of the Muslim Council of Britain, he insisted that "95–98 per cent of those stopped and searched under the anti-terror laws are Muslim." The real figure is actually 15 per cent. But however many times I showed him the true statistics he refused to budge. I am sure he was sincere in his belief. But there is no basis for his claim that virtually all those stopped and searched were

Muslim—the figures appear to have been simply plucked out of the sky. There is disproportion in the treatment of Asians. Asians make up about 5 per cent of the population, but 15 per cent of those stopped under the Terrorism Act.[67]

Data released by the City of London support Malik's claim. In 2003/04 searches of "Asian people," a term that generally indicates Muslim as well as non-Muslim South Asians, under the 2000 Terrorism Act were 11.5 percent of the total.[68] Considering that Muslims constitute 8.5 percent of the entire London population and 12 percent of the city's residents between 16 and 24 years of age, the age range most likely to be stopped in searches, the data reveal that Muslims were indeed searched proportionally more than other groups, but only by a negligible margin. Despite these data, MCB leaders have often stated that British Muslims are singled out and have compared their situation to that of Jews in Germany in 1930.[69]

Ruth Kelly's "Revolution"

By the first months of 2006 large sections of the British establishment, from the media to various think tanks, had begun to attack MCB and its virtual monopoly over the relationship with the government. As the debate over integration and radicalism in the Muslim community raged, spurred by continuous arrests of British Muslims involved in terrorist activities, the Conservative Party's National and International Security Policy Group began to work on a report that attacked the government for its ongoing support of MCB.[70] "Policy makers should stop assuming that the loudest voices and the most organised elements within the Muslim community necessarily represent the Muslim population as a whole," later argued Tory leader David Cameron. "There's a danger that groups with agendas aimed at separation rather than integration are deferred to when they should be challenged."[71]

Political pressure and a genuine reevaluation of MCB's role and nature led the British government to drastically reassess its position. Many policy makers in Whitehall, even among those who traditionally supported the organization, began to see MCB as part of the problem, rather than as the solution. Not only had MCB not delivered what the British government had expected, but the organization had also become a political liability, with criticism mounting every time controversial statements made by MCB affiliates were reported in the press. Senior policy makers began to publicly acknowledge that the government's strategy had been flawed and that appointing MCB as their exclusive interlocutor had been a mistake.[72]

The culmination of this process of detachment from MCB took place in the summer of 2006, after a couple of faux pas by the group's leadership. In June, Muhammad Abdul Bari, MCB's newly elected Secretary General, publicly defended arranged marriages as a "wonderful system" and "a way of parents helping to guide their children to make the right choices."[73] The statement was widely considered as inopportune, coming at a time when authorities had revealed they were dealing with hundreds of cases of "honor killings," many caused by young Muslim brides' refusal to enter into arranged marriages. In August, after authorities thwarted a plot hatched by a cell of British-born Muslims to blow up a dozen aircraft en route to the United States, MCB and other Muslim leaders sent a letter to the Prime Minister urging him to change foreign policy in order to defeat terrorism.[74] Labour ministers, eager to challenge any link between the two phenomena, harshly condemned the letter, publicly calling it "dangerous and foolish" and "the gravest possible error."[75]

On October 11, 2006, Secretary of State for Communities and Local Government (DCLG) Ruth Kelly gave a speech that, in the eyes of many, made official the British government's shift of policy toward MCB. Announcing the criteria that her department, which had been tasked with the bulk of outreach initiatives, would would apply in selecting its partners, Kelly stated that organizations that did not subscribe to some basic, "non-negotiable values" would not receive any support. "Over time we will support those that stand up for our shared values and not support those who don't," said Kelly. "It is only by defending our values that we will prevent extremists radicalising future generations of terrorists."[76] Singling out its refusal to participate to Holocaust Memorial Day, Kelly announced that MCB would no longer receive the financial support it had previously had from the British state.

Kelly's position stemmed from two considerations.[77] First, she believed MCB to be a "false gatekeeper," an organization whose claim of representativeness was widely overblown. MCB, according to Kelly, represented only a section of the British Muslim community, and by engaging only with it policy makers were not hearing all voices. Moreover, MCB was dominated by individuals whose ideology put it in direct opposition to most of the aims of the British government. Kelly, admitting that most civil servants had engaged Muslim organizations without the slightest knowledge of their ideological underpinnings, stated that simply condemning acts of terrorism carried out by al Qaeda should not have been enough to qualify an organization as a partner. While organizations were free to espouse any position they wanted, only those that promoted a value system compatible with the vision of cohesive society endorsed by the government should receive public funding. Kelly placed MCB, which had received 200,000 pounds in the previous two years, outside that category.[78]

Having shattered MCB's monopoly, Kelly sought to reach out to other Muslim organizations to implement the government's comprehensive plan to defeat extremism and encourage integration among the community. DCLG began to fund groups that had been formed in earlier years, in some cases with the stated goal of posing an ideological alternative to MCB.[79] But it soon became clear that no organization had the nationwide reach of MCB, making the search for partners extremely difficult. Authorities have attempted to obviate this problem by artificially forming various advisory structures to give a voice to under-represented segments of the Muslim community, such as the National Muslim Women's Advisory Group, and by operating at the local level.[80] In July 2007, the government unveiled a 70 million-pound program to combat extremism and allocated the majority of the funds to local grassroots organizations.[81]

The shift from an MCB monopoly to a diversity of interlocutors in the Muslim community has been difficult. Authorities, lacking uniform guidelines indicating what characteristics a potential partner should possess, have had problems identifying interlocutors at the local level. Moreover, Kelly's position is not an official government policy, but shaped the attitudes of just her department. While her successor, Hazel Blears, and several other ministers have followed her line, other top government officials and departments have defended MCB and still work with it. As chapter 8 will show, different sections of the British government often have diverging priorities that influence their decisions about organizations to engage.

As for MCB, the "Kelly crisis" generated a heated internal debate and led its leadership to rethink its tactics. Although it criticized the minister for seeking only Muslims who blindly endorsed the government's policies, MCB reversed some of its most controversial positions, including the refusal to attend Holocaust Memorial Day.[82] MCB also cleverly attempted to raise its appeal among British policy makers by portraying itself as the gateway to the world of Islamic finance. As the British government was passing measures to turn London into the world's capital of the fast-growing *sharia*-compliant financial system, MCB, along with the Organization of the Islamic Conference and the Islamic Development Bank, sponsored the inaugural Islamic Finance and Trade Conference. Attracting some of the wealthiest individuals and institutions from the Arab Gulf, the conference was officially acknowledged by then Chancellor of the Exchequer Gordon Brown, Tory leader David Cameron, the Duke of York, and other top British dignitaries hoping to attract much-needed petrodollars to London.[83] In 2008 MCB hosted the second, equally high-profile conference on Islamic finance.[84]

But a new conflict between MCB and the British government emerged at the beginning of 2009. In February, two hundred Muslim clerics and activists, mostly linked to the global Muslim Brotherhood network, met in an Istanbul hotel to celebrate the "victory" in the "malicious Jewish Zionist war over Gaza" the preceding month.[85] The participants, united under the name of Global Anti-Aggression Campaign, signed a joint statement defining as "a declaration of war" any country's support of Israel or the deployment of ships to patrol the "Muslim waters" in front of Gaza and prevent the smuggling of arms into it. British authorities, who were considering deploying British ships to the Gaza coastline, were dismayed to find out that one of the signatories was Daud Abdullah, MCB's deputy secretary general, and immediately called for his resignation.[86] In what became a very public dispute, MCB rejected the request, which it considered an attempt by the government to exert undue influence over an independent organization.[87] On March 13, DCLG Secretary Hazel Blears sent a letter to MCB formally announcing the suspension of the government's relations with the organization.[88] MCB officials criticized this action, stating that the government should not seek partners who "parrot its own views on what are the main drivers behind the phenomenon of violent extremism" but are "universally derided among British Muslims as stooges."[89] Abdullah subsequently threatened to sue Blears, accusing her of "bullying" and stating that he did not call for or support attacks against British troops.[90]

Blears' decision came only days before the release of CONTEST 2, the updated counterterrorism strategy elaborated by the British government. While never mentioning MCB, the strategy made it clear that the government would no longer support views that "fall short of supporting violence and are within the law, but which reject and undermine our shared values and jeopardise community cohesion."[91] A press release issued by the Home Office in February, also not directly mentioning MCB, seemed to emphasize the change:

> Our strategy to prevent people becoming terrorists is not simply about tackling violent extremism. It is also about tackling those who espouse extremist views that are inconsistent with our shared values. Decisions on which organisations to fund are taken very carefully and are subject to robust scrutiny. We are clear that we will not continue to fund groups where we have evidence of them encouraging discrimination, undermining democracy and being ambiguous towards terrorism.[92]

Although MCB is not a proper New Western Brotherhood organization, given the heterogeneity of its affiliates, a large section of its leadership does fall into that category, and engagement patterns with the British government provide useful lessons for other Western countries. Political considerations, security-related concerns, and pressure from media outlets and think tanks have deeply influenced the relationship between British policy makers and MCB, turning it from monopolistic reliance to bitter distrust. A misjudgment of the role and nature of MCB seems to be the reason for the government's shifts. On one hand, it was unfair for the government, after 9/11, to ask an organization whose official role was simply to represent the Muslim community to endorse its policies and push it aside once it did not. On the other hand, policy makers had initially endorsed MCB out of their own political considerations and satisfied themselves with the group's claim to represent the majority of British Muslims, but had never fully assessed the veracity of this claim or the views of MCB leaders and affiliates.

As in most Western countries, the situation in Britain is in constant evolution. In January 2010, DCLG's new secretary, John Denham, reversed Blear's decisions and restored the government's ties with MCB. A DCLG spokeswoman motivated the decision by emphasizing that MCB had "stated its categorical opposition to attacks on British defence interests and confirmed its unwavering support for British troops across the world."[93] Predictably, Tory leaders criticized the decision as "appeasement of extremists by a bunch of politicians scared witless of losing their seats" before the forthcoming national elections.[94] These dynamics highlight the personal and political factors influencing the convoluted relationship between MCB and the British government. Predicting future developments is difficult. It seems improbable that British authorities will revert to the monopolistic model, selecting just one representative of the Muslim community. Commenting on the decision to cut ties to MCB, Sadiq Khan, the Minister for Community Cohesion, said that "the days of lazy politicians just speaking to one or two powerful community groups or leaders are gone."[95] However, it is also likely that MCB, given the limited reach of its competitors and the considerable leverage it still holds, will remain one of the government's main interlocutors.

Multiculturalism and Islamism

While over the last fifty years several Western countries have resorted to applying various typologies and concepts of the multicultural model of integration, the British experience with multiculturalism is uniquely old, dating back to the colonial administration of India in the second half of the nineteenth century. When, in 1857, British colonial forces deposed the last Moghul emperor, Indian Muslims, who had ruled over the Hindu majority for centuries, suddenly found themselves a ruled minority. Some movements, like the Deobandis, found pious isolationism the solution to this frustrating development; in contrast, modernists like Sayyid Ahmad Khan viewed Islam and modernity as perfectly compatible and encouraged Muslims to learn English and other "modern" subjects useful in order to succeed in colonized India.[96]

Khan's school of thought soon found a base in the Uttar Pradesh city of Aligarh, where it established the renowned Mohammedan Anglo Oriental College (later Aligarh Muslim University). The result of Khan's vision was the creation of secularized Muslim elites who presented themselves as useful middlemen between the British colonialists and the Muslim population.[97] As British administrators were looking at ways to rule India's huge territory without getting involved in the complex internal affairs of its extremely diverse population, Aligarh-educated intellectuals sought to convince them that Indian Muslims possessed a separate political status, the preservation of which would be in the British best interest. The political bargain that emerged generated what Gilles Kepel has referred to as "the first manifestation of political communalism in the history of the modern world."[98] This vision was "promoted by political leaders who wished to attain power by presenting themselves as the exclusive representatives of a 'community' reduced to a single will, by unifying heterogeneous populations on the basis of a sociological definition of their 'Muslimness,'" and was soon adopted by British administrators.[99] In what appeared to be a mutually convenient deal, Muslim leaders guaranteed the British that order would be maintained inside the community and spared them the unwanted and resource-consuming task of administering its daily life.

The communalist model adopted in colonized India found a new application in postwar Britain.[100] Having devised a system in which Welsh, Scottish, and Northern Irish could be British citizens while maintaining their strong, particular identities, British policy makers thought that nonwhite immigrants could become a sort of fourth minority community. Even when this broad category was divided into blacks/West Indians, Indians, and Muslims, authorities believed that communities could fit into the existing framework of dual identity. Members of each community would have citizenship and equal rights, but would not be asked to adopt the social and moral code of the majority as long as they respected the law of the land. Rather than a collectivity of individuals united by the same values, British authorities opted for a "federation of communities," each living separately according to their own values.[101]

The British multicultural model has traditionally relied heavily on community leaders who act as trusted intermediaries between the community and the state, to whom the latter can delegate the administration of various services. In colonial India this role was often occupied by the Aligarh-educated secularized elites, whose knowledge of the English language and customs rendered them close to British administrators. No such class existed among the masses of poorly educated South Asian immigrants in postwar Britain. This situation created the opportunity for the Mawdudists, thanks to their superior resources, organizational skills, and good understanding of the British political system, to surpass other groups in the competition for the role of community leaders. Multiculturalism, which not only allows various groups to keep their identity but actively encourages them to do so, constituted a political gold mine for the Mawdudists, who, like all Islamist groups, thrive on identity politics. Moreover, it provided them with an unprecedented opportunity to spread their influence inside the Muslim community by portraying themselves as the reliable delegates the British state was seeking.

An analysis of the dynamics within the Bengali community of East London perfectly exemplifies the phenomenon. Having established a presence already in the 1850s, Bengalis began settling in Tower Hamlets and other parts of East London in large numbers in the 1950s, making it today the area with the highest proportion of Muslim residents in Britain (36.4 percent, according to the 2001 census, 90 percent of whom are of Bengali descent).[102] Throughout the 1960s and 1970s Bengalis framed their identity mostly in racial terms. Although Islam was an important part of life for many of them, Bengalis considered themselves simply part of the nonwhite minority and used secular, often socialist, ideology to combat issues of discrimination, poverty, and racism. Islamists had always been present in the neighborhood, but were mostly overshadowed by secular and nationalistic forces.

The 1981 Brixton race riots, which involved mostly Caribbean youths, and other episodes of interethnic tension attracted significantly increased attention among British policy makers for ethnic and religious minorities. The Scarman Report, issued in the wake of the Brixton riots, called for policies that supported differential treatment according to cultural differences. At the local level, the newly elected leader of the Greater London Council, Ken Livingstone, also decided that the diversity of various ethnic and religious communities should be emphasized. Livingstone and city councils in areas with large minority populations began to focus less on issues of discrimination and economic equality and more on identity politics and greater recognition of diversity.[103] In the words of Kenan Malik, himself a longtime militant of the British far Left, "where once the left had argued that everyone should be treated equally, despite their racial, ethnic, religious or cultural differences, now it pushed the idea that different people should be treated differently *because* of such differences."[104] From the denial of equal rights, racism came to be seen as the denial of the right to be different.

By the late 1980s and early 1990s, the British establishment began to embrace the concept of "Muslim community" and decided to create more connections with religious organizations. Institutions such as the JeI-linked East London Mosque and others were actively sought by authorities as ideal partners to deliver social welfare programs.[105] Local authorities, like the Greater London Council's Ethnic Minorities Unit, began to increasingly rely on them to administer programs against drugs, crime, and gang activities, hoping that their religion-based approach would appeal to young Muslims.[106] Islam came to be seen as an antidote to social malaises that plagued the Asian community. The funds received from councils, combined with the funds already received from wealthy overseas donors, allowed Mawdudist organizations to significantly alter the balance of power in East London as secular organizations struggled to compete.

Multicultural policies have, therefore, played a key role in helping Islamist organizations become the modern-day "village strongmen" representing the Muslim community with the British state, the educated and professional elite to which the establishment could delegate the administration of day-to-day life.[107] According to the many critics of multiculturalism, these very policies also fostered the development of organizations that led Muslims to express themselves only through their Muslim identity and prevented them from forming a sense of allegiance to Britain. "The close relationship between mosques and social services," argues Kepel, "has encouraged the emergence of a certain type of leader who has an interest in perpetuating the community boundary, since it makes them indispensable as intermediaries."[108]

"Why should a British citizen who happens to be Muslim have to rely on clerics and other leaders of the religious community to communicate with the Prime Minister?" asks Bengali Nobel prize winner Amartya Sen.[109] "Mainstream politicians have come, in effect, to abandon their responsibilities for engaging directly with Muslim communities," argues Kenan Malik. "Instead, they have subcontracted out those responsibilities to so-called community leaders. . . . Rather than appealing to Muslims as British citizens, and attempting to draw them into the mainstream political process, politicians of all hues today prefer to see them as people whose primary loyalty is to their faith and who can be politically engaged only by other Muslims."[110]

Sen, Malik, and other critics of British multiculturalism believe that, by empowering a leadership that uses identity politics to create "ethnic fiefdoms," fostering their own agenda and furthering their own position, British authorities prevented young British Muslims from feeling they had a stake in British society and developing a sense of belonging in it.[111] This analysis is strikingly similar to those of historians who analyzed British communalist policies in colonial India. "By treating the Muslims as a separate group, [the colonial government] divided them from the Indians," wrote David Page in his 1982 book *Prelude to Partition*. "By granting them separate electorates, it institutionalized that division. This was one of the most crucial factors in the development of communal politics. Muslim politicians did not have to appeal to non-Muslims; non-Muslims did not have to appeal to Muslims. This made it difficult for a genuine Indian nationalism to emerge."[112]

Similarly, Ed Husain, a London-born Muslim who left the militant group Hizb ut Tahrir after renouncing Islamist ideology, provides a firsthand account of how multicultural policies contributed to his radicalization in modern-day Britain:

Islamic communities are segregated. Many Muslims want to live apart from mainstream British society; official government policy has helped them do so. I grew up without any white friends. My school was almost entirely Muslim. I had almost no direct experience of "British life" or "British institutions." So it was easy for the extremists to say to me: "You see? You're not part of British society. You never will be. You can only be part of an Islamic society." The first part of what they said was true. I wasn't part of British society: nothing in my life overlapped with it.[113]

In his memoirs, published in 2007, Husain reiterated this message by describing his life inside the Islamic Society of East London's Tower Hamlets College, a JeI-dominated Muslim student organization he led before joining the more radical Hizb ut Tahrir:

In the multicultural Britain of the 1980s and 1990s we were free to practice our religion and develop our culture as we wanted. Our teachers left us alone, so long as we didn't engage in public expressions of homophobia or intimidation of non-Muslims. But Britishness and the British values of democracy, tolerance, respect, compromise, and pluralism had no meaning for us. Like me, most of the students at the college had no real bond with mainstream Britain. Yes, we attended a British educational institution in London, but there was nothing particularly British about it. It might as well have been in Cairo or Karachi. Cut off from Britain, isolated from the Eastern culture of our parents, Islamism provided us with a purpose and a place in life. More importantly, we felt as though we were the pioneers, at the cutting edge of this new global development of confronting the West in its own backyard.[114]

The writings of Muslim commentators like Sen, Malik, and Hussein have heavily influenced the British debate on multiculturalism, which reached the center of the national stage after the 2001 race riots in various northern English cities, the 9/11 attacks, and the 7/7 bombings.[115] Although advocates of the traditional multicultural model are still quite vocal, the majority of the British establishment seems to agree with the warning of Trevor Philips, chairman of the Commission for Racial Equality, who famously said in 2005 that Britain was "sleepwalking into segregation" along racial and religious lines.[116] Large segments of the population and the political elites seem to agree that multiculturalism should entail treating people equally despite differences, not treating them differently because they are different. Moreover, there is a growing understanding that ethnic communities are no less heterogeneous than the white community, and pretending that one person or one organization can represent all their diverse interests is pure fiction. Given this wide consensus, Britain is slowly reviewing its multicultural model. In any case, its implementation during the previous two decades provides an invaluable example of the ability of Islamist groups to take advantage of favorable political conditions to further their agenda.

The Iraq War, Qaradawi, and the Left

While South Asians linked to JeI have traditionally dominated the British Islamist scene, since the early 1960s a significant number of Arab activists linked to various Middle Eastern offshoots of the Muslim Brotherhood have settled in London, where they have continued their activities with remarkable energy. Particularly prominent among them due to experience, connections, and charisma is Kamal Helbawy, one of the New Western Brothers' most dynamic leaders.[117] Born in 1939 in northern Egypt, Helbawy joined the Brotherhood when he was still in secondary school and has been a leading member ever since. Over the years, he became involved in Islamic activities throughout the world. In 1972 he was one of the founders and the first executive director of the Saudi-based World Assembly of Muslim Youth (WAMY), and in the 1980s he lived between Afghanistan, where he served as "adviser to the mujahedeen leadership," and Pakistan, where he chaired the Arabic studies department and worked at a lecturer on *dawa* at the Institute of Policy Studies, Khurshid Ahmad's think tank.

In the mid-1990s, Helbawy was sent by the Egyptian Brotherhood's *shura* council to Great Britain to establish the Global Information Centre, the Brotherhood's first office in the West. London, traditionally a hub for both Western and Arab media, was the ideal location for a body deputized to promote the positions of the Brotherhood on a global scale, and Helbawy, who was fluent in English and had previously lived in London (directing Finsbury Park's Muslim Welfare House in the early 1980s), was the ideal person to run it. Helbawy soon had a personal falling out with the Egyptian Brotherhood's leadership and the center became inactive, but he was deeply involved in Islamic activities inside Britain. Reinforcing the links to JeI networks he had built in Pakistan, Helbawy served as a trustee of the Islamic Foundation of Leicester and became active in MCB, of which he was a founding member and a member of the Central Working Committee from 2000 to 2004.

Helbawy's major achievement since moving to Britain has unquestionably been the creation of his own organization, the Muslim Association of Britain (MAB).[118] Founded in 1997 to unite various ethnic Arab activists, MAB is a quintessential New Western Brotherhood organization in its origins, ideology, connections and methodology. Aside from Helbawy, MAB's leadership includes experienced political activists from various Middle Eastern countries such as Mohammed Sawalha, whom IslamOnline identifies as a member of the "political committee of the International Organization of the Muslim Brotherhood;" Anas al Tikriti, the son of the leader of the Iraqi branch of the Brotherhood; and Azzam Tamimi, the former director of the parliamentary office of the Islamic Action Front, Jordan's Brotherhood offshoot.[119] Its leaders, whose rhetoric deeply reflects their past experiences, are involved in a myriad of initiatives, running small think tanks and small television stations catering to Muslims, publishing magazines, and frequently speaking at conferences in Britain and abroad. A founding member of MCB, MAB is also a key member of the Federation of Islamic Organizations in Europe, the Western Brothers' Brussels-based pan-European organization.

During its first years, MAB, despite the activism of its leaders, had only limited reach at the grassroots level; it was often unable to bridge the ethnic gap and attract South Asian sympathizers. A major opportunity to increase its importance presented itself in 2002, as tensions built up between the United States and Iraq. In the months preceding the conflict, antiwar activists began mobilizing in most Western countries, organizing massive protests against the possibility of a U.S. attack. In Britain, the largest and most active groups formed the Stop the War Coalition (STWC), a partnership of various organizations led by the Socialist Workers Party and the Communist Party of Britain. Formed in the wake of the 2001 war in Afghanistan, STWC found new energy in its effort to protest the widely more unpopular conflict in Iraq and sought to attract Muslim organizations to increase and diversify its ranks.[120]

Despite their strong opposition to the war, MCB leaders were reluctant to directly participate in high-profile demonstrations, afraid to jeopardize their still good relationship with the government.[121] STWC leaders, looking for alternatives, set their sights on MAB after a large anti-Israel protest it had organized in central London in April 2002. The event made headlines for its strong tones, the presence of emblems of Hamas and Hezbollah, and the burning of Israeli and American flags. But STWC leaders were more impressed by the number of participants (10–15,000 according to Scotland Yard, 80,000 according to Helbawy).[122] Even though large organizations such as MCB, the UK Islamic Mission, and STWC itself had supported it, the event had been organized by MAB, and it was remarkable that an organization with just 400 members could mobilize such large crowds, clear proof of its leadership's professionalism and skills.[123]

Eager to find a Muslim partner and impressed with its mobilization abilities, STWC leaders asked MAB to join the coalition.[124] The offer generated intense internal debate, as MAB leaders weighed the benefits of extending their message on a much larger level and the potential costs of an alliance with Marxists, atheists, and homosexuals, particularly among the most conservative segments of the Muslim community.[125] In the end, MAB agreed to enter a form of partnership on an equal basis, cooperating closely but remaining an autonomous bloc with its own agenda. It also imposed as necessary conditions for its participation the presence of *halal* food, faith-sensitive accommodations, and gender-segregated meetings and demonstrations.[126] STWC leaders, over some members' protests, reportedly agreed to all the conditions.[127]

MAB and STWC held their first joint protest in September 2002, attracting a large number of demonstrators in central London. This and other events were characterized by MAB's determination, embraced by STWC, to link the opposition to the war in Iraq to the Palestinian issue. MAB leaders, who have often openly expressed support for Hamas, imposed as a slogan for the movement the dual statement "No war in Iraq, justice for Palestine," arguing that the two events are deeply interconnected.[128] Similarly, MAB's leaflets and placards read FREEDOM FOR PALESTINE, STOP THE WAR IN IRAQ; STWC had the same two slogans but in reverse order.[129]

The cooperation with unlikely bedfellows, particularly on the extreme Left, has been a recurrent tactic for the Brothers in various parts of the world, from the Middle East to the West. The global post–9/11 tensions only increased these contacts among political forces that, while harboring diametrically opposed visions on many issues, particularly on the role that religion should play in society, are united by their antipathy toward the United States and Israel. Capitalizing on these sentiments and always seeking opportunities to further its agenda, in 2002, for example, the Egyptian Brotherhood hosted in Cairo the first anti-Zionist International Conference. Participants, including prominent Western leaders of the extreme Left, signed the "Cairo Declaration Against U.S. Hegemony and War on Iraq and in Solidarity with Palestine," a document that defined Palestinian attacks against Israel as legitimate acts of liberation and stated that all participants in the movement must reaffirm their "resolve to stand in solidarity with the people of Iraq and Palestine, recognizing that war and aggression against them is but part of a U.S. project of global domination and subjugation."[130]

The Brothers' willingness to cooperate with political forces with which they have little in common is another proof of their flexibility and sophisticated political strategy. MAB leaders openly acknowledge these ideological differences but say that there are "greater objectives" to be achieved by establishing a temporary partnership with the extreme Left.[131] Conversely, it seems that the STWC leaders' decision was based on less clear premises. "The anti-war coalition, in order to work with the Muslim community, has decided to work with Islamists," complained Ansar Ahmed Ullah, an East London–based Bengali community leader.[132] Like other British Muslims, he argues that STWC was desperately seeking any Muslim partner and, ignoring the internal dynamics of the community, chose to side with the one that was the most active and vociferous. By doing so, STWC not only allied itself with an organization whose stance on many issues is directly incompatible with its own but also failed to engage the many secularist groups inside the Muslim community that would have been equally interested in participating in antiwar activities, but were put off by the presence of Islamists.

In any case, the cooperation between MAB and STWC was quite successful, as hundreds of thousands of demonstrators participated in their events. Hoping to capitalize on the momentum they had generated, the leaders of the two organizations decided to make their partnership more permanent. In January 2004, they created a new political formation called RESPECT/The Unity Coalition, which participated in London's mayoral elections and, in 2005, in national and European elections. Hoping to sway disaffected Labour voters opposed to the war and banking on polls suggesting that more than half of traditional Muslim supporters of Labour intended to vote against Tony Blair, RESPECT ran in England and Wales on a platform based on socialism and opposition to "occupation" in Iraq and Palestine.[133] Its candidates included far Left leaders like "Old Labour" MP George Galloway and Socialist Workers Party leader Lindsey German, MAB members like Anas al Tikriti, and other Muslim activists like Mohammed Naseem, Salma Yaqoob, and Yvonne Ridley, the British journalist who had converted to Islam after being held captive by the Taliban.

Although Labour did suffer from the "Baghdad backlash" at the voting booth, RESPECT managed to chip away only a small percentage of its electorate. Despite good performances by some of its candidates in areas with a large Muslim population, George Galloway, running in East London, was the only RESPECT candidate who managed to win a seat in the 2005 national elections. Since then, the party seems to have lost traction, mired in internal disputes. MAB itself has also experienced a strong, albeit informal, internal division. Leaders of the older generation, like Helbawy, have opted for a return to their origins, arguing that the organization's involvement in political activities distracted it from its original aim of doing *dawa*. Others, like Sawalha, al Tikriti, and Tamimi, have created a parallel group called the British Muslim Initiative (BMI) and through it continue their political activities, including their cooperation with STWC.

MAB's experience with STWC was not the organization's only foray into the political scene. In July 2004, MAB played a crucial role in a heated and very public controversy centered on then Mayor of London Ken Livingstone. It started when MAB hosted in London the meeting of the European Council for Fatwa and Research, al Qaradawi's jurisprudential body. After the meeting, Livingstone, who had just been readmitted to the Labour Party after a four-year suspension, hosted a joint press conference inside London City Hall with al Qaradawi in which the two criticized the French Parliament's decision to ban the *hijab* in public schools.[134] Livingstone's decision to provide al Qaradawi with such a platform and legitimacy was harshly criticized by voices from various quarters. A coalition of diverse London organizations, including homosexual, Jewish, and Sikh groups, came together to protest the press conference, starting their mobilization weeks before it took place.[135]

MAB and MCB reacted to the controversy by strongly defending al Qaradawi. MCB issued a press release condemning the "character assassination" "orchestrated by the Zionist lobby" to defame al Qaradawi, "a voice of reason and understanding."[136] Livingstone used similar tones, praising the Egyptian cleric as "one of the most eminent and moderate Muslim scholars in the world."[137] "Sheik Qaradawi is I think very similar to the position of Pope John XXIII. An absolutely sane Islamist," stated the mayor, arguing that criticism of him was nothing than a "hysterical outburst of racism and Islamaphobia [*sic*]."[138]

As the controversy lingered for months, Livingstone commissioned a dossier on al Qaradawi, which he released in January 2005 in order to rebuff his critics. Calling him a "progressive," Livingstone said that al Qaradawi "has explicitly opposed repression of homosexuals," based on an interview the cleric had given to the *Guardian* during his visit in which he stated that Muslims "are not required" by their faith "to declare a war against homosexuality and homosexuals."[139] As for the accusations of anti-Semitism, Livingstone stated that al Qaradawi had "made it absolutely clear when he spoke at City Hall that he is totally opposed to anti-Semitism" and that he regarded "Judaism as one of the world's great religions and that

Jewish and Muslim people have lived together in peace in the Middle East for hundreds of years." Other parts of the dossier attempted to discredit al Qaradawi's critics, accusing them of relying on inaccurate translations of his sermons done by Israeli Right-wing Web sites such as the Middle East Media Research Institute (MEMRI).

In reality, it seems that Livingstone had decided to rely on a few statements al Qaradawi had made during his sojourn in London and ignore other sources. "These words spoken [by al Qaradawi] in London don't match those in Doha, which can be read on his own website," wrote the general manager of the Al Arabiyya news channel, Abdel Rahman al-Rasheed, in an editorial during the "al Qaradawi crisis."[140] In fact, wrote al-Rasheed, just two weeks before visiting London, al Qaradawi had stated on his weekly program on Al Jazeera that "the tyranny of the Jews as a sect is clear and evident, which means that while there may be some in the West who are tyrants and others who aren't, the tyranny of the Jews is overt, great and unmatched."[141] And while many of al Qaradawi's sermons used by his critics had indeed been translated by Web sites linked to Israelis (which, in any case, always provide the original footage in Arabic), the BBC's international service had translated a sermon given by the cleric at Doha's Umar Bin-al-Khattab mosque just a month before his visit to London. In it, al Qaradawi invoked: "O God, deal with your enemies, the enemies of Islam. O God, deal with the usurper, oppressor, and tyrannical Jews."[142]

It is difficult to say whether Livingstone decided to endorse and later defend al Qaradawi because he was not aware of some of the cleric's statements or because he had made a well-informed and calculated decision to do so. Atma Singh, Livingstone's advisor on South Asian issues, very much believes that the decision was strongly influenced by political considerations. Singh claims to have repeatedly advised the mayor against publicly endorsing al Qaradawi and alienating minority groups such as Jews, gays, and Sikhs. But, he says, "Livingstone was more interested in the Muslim vote and thought that by pandering to al-Qaradawi he could get it."[143]

The partnership between Livingstone and MAB continued after the al Qaradawi controversy. In 2006, for example, MAB/BMI activists organized in London the first IslamExpo, a high-profile, four-day-long Muslim fair with lectures, films, art workshops, Quran recitation shows, and a large bazaar.[144] The event, which attracted tens of thousands of visitors, received part of its funding (200,000 pounds) from Livingstone, who also officiated at the opening ceremony.[145] In 2008, as Livingstone sought to win a new term as mayor against Conservative candidate Boris Johnson, MAB/BMI leaders returned the favor and came out to support him, publishing editorials in various London newspapers, speaking at rallies, and setting up a Web site, "Muslims 4 Ken."[146] Despite these efforts, Livingstone lost the race by an 8.5 margin.

The experiences in STWC and RESPECT and MAB/BMI's involvement with Livingstone highlight a possible pattern of evolution of at least a section of the New Western Brotherhood, who seem to have established more or less permanent partnership with the extreme Left. For some, particularly among the old guard, such cooperation might be purely tactical and disposable once no longer useful. But for some British-born activists with roots in the Islamist milieu, this could represent a stable channel to express their opinions. Individuals like Osama Saeed, the young head of the Scottish chapter of MAB, and Soumaya Ghannouchi, Rachid's daughter and a prominent columnist, are two prominent examples of second-generation activists who don't fit in a predetermined category, their rhetoric mixing traditional Islamist, Marxist, and liberal-democratic concepts. Moreover, RESPECT, despite its internal problems, can be considered an important instance in which Islamists decided to express their frustration over the Iraq war and other foreign policy issues through the ballot box, rather than through violence.[147] It is arguable that parts of the movement could evolve in this direction, possibly providing supporting evidence to Kepel's claim that Western Islamists will undergo the same evolution as the Euro-Communists.

6
Germany

In May 1999, the German Parliament passed a historic piece of legislation that drastically changed the country's approach to citizenship.[1] By shifting the basis for acquiring German nationality from descent (*jus sanguinis*) to birth on German soil (*jus solis*) and making naturalizations easier, Germany finally accepted the fact that the millions of guest workers (*Gastarbeiter*) and their progeny who had settled in the country since the mid-1950s were not going to return to their countries of origin but had become a permanent part of German society. Policy makers, who passed the bill with a large majority, understood that a less restrictive citizenship law was just one component of a much-needed strategy to compensate for the country's poor record on integration. Partly because the government's effort was so late, turning the masses of poorly educated *Gastarbeiter* into full-fledged Germans has proven to be a very challenging task. Tellingly, even though the *Gastarbeiter* population is young—children under 15 with a "migration background" represent one third of all the country's minors (45 percent in cities with more than 200,000 inhabitants)—immigrants are severely overrepresented in unemployment, educational underachievement, and crime statistics.[2]

Problems have been particularly acute among the country's large Turkish community. Since the 1950s, the historically close relations between the two countries have led hundreds of thousands of unskilled workers from the Anatolian peninsula to Germany, where they have significantly contributed to the booming economy. Some returned to Turkey after years spent working in Germany's factories; many decided to stay in the country with their families. Today, according to recent estimates, 2.6 million individuals of Turkish descent live in Germany, making them by a wide margin the largest group in the country's estimated 3.8 to 4.3 million-strong Muslim community (Europe's second largest after France's).[3] Despite several success stories, overall people of Turkish descent living in Germany, whether citizens or not, severely lag behind their ethnic German counterparts in all achievement indicators, from income to education. This disparity leads many of them, even if born in Germany, to feel alienated from German society, and reportedly, two thirds see themselves as victims of discrimination.[4]

An issue that simultaneously exemplifies many German Turks' feeling of discrimination and the German state's difficulties in adapting to the needs of newcomers is the official recognition of Islam and the Muslim community. Traditionally, the German system encourages strong cooperation between the state and religious communities. The latter enjoy a vast array of privileges, including tax-free status and the right to collect a 9 percent "church tax" that members of the religious community pay to the organization.[5] But in order to receive these generous benefits, a religious community has to be recognized as a "Corporation Under Public Law" (*Körperschaft öffentlichen Rechts*—KöR), a formal requirement that can be fulfilled only if the community proves that it possesses several characteristics, including a certain number of members, a hierarchical structure, and a long-standing presence in the country.

The status of KöR and, therefore, of recognized religious community, has long been held by the Protestant Church, the Catholic Church, and the Central Council of German Jews, long-established groups that have traditionally divided among themselves the millions that the German government doles out every year. The insertion of Muslims into this mechanism, however, has been quite problematic. The system had been designed for relatively homogeneous religious groups with a widely recognized, if not elected, leadership. In substance, each religious community must be represented by only one organization that can demonstrate that it represents a majority of believers, that functions according to precise internal norms, and that has had a stable presence for some years and is likely to maintain it in the foreseeable future.

These characteristics, designated in an era when only Christian and Jewish communities existed in the country, are difficult to apply to the Muslim community, which by nature tends to be churchless. Over the years,

Muslims living in Germany have created hundreds of organizations, many of which are officially registered as formal entities. But despite several attempts by various organizations, only the Berlin-based Islamische Religionsgemeinschaft has been able to attain the status of "religious community" as a body of public right. Authorities have repeatedly rejected the requests filed by various Muslim groups on several grounds, but have mostly argued that none of them could even remotely meet the necessary requirement of representing a sizeable percentage of believers. Even when various Muslim organizations formed umbrella organizations to achieve KöR status, German authorities turned down their application. The lack of official recognition of the Muslim community, while not hampering individual and group religious rights enshrined in the German constitution, means that the Muslim community as a whole does not receive any of the state benefits that other, even smaller religious communities receive.

A Divided Community

The reasons for the lack of formal recognition are heatedly debated. German authorities argue that they are simply applying the law and that its provisions cannot be changed just for Muslims. Critics argue that it is unfair and "a contradiction in terms" to ask Muslims to organize themselves in a way that runs counter to the very nature of Islam.[6] German authorities are therefore often accused of lack of flexibility or, in some cases, of deliberately discriminating against Muslims, using a strict interpretation of the law to prevent them from obtaining the same benefits that Christians and Jews receive.

Although there might be some truth to these charges, it is unquestionable that the enormous divisions within the German Muslim community have played a key role in its failure to be officially recognized. As stated, Turks constitute roughly two thirds of Germany's Muslims, but there are also sizeable Moroccan, Palestinian, and Bosnian communities and a growing number of converts.[7] But even the Turkish community is hardly monolithic. A first division is along ethnic lines, as approximately 600,000 of the official 2.5–2.7 million Turks living in Germany are Kurds, who have often established separate organizations and mosques. Religion is a second source of fragmentation. The majority of German Turks are Sunni; there are also roughly half a million Alevis, a religious community that follows a particularistic interpretation of Islam. Shias, Ahmadis, and various Sufi groups also have their own organizations.

Finally, there are divisions along political lines, in patterns often mirroring those of political life in Turkey and other countries of origin of German Muslims. Particularly relevant is the transposition of the tensions between Kemalists and Islamists from Turkey to Germany. The animosity between the two camps—the former being supporters of modern Turkey's founder, Kemal Atatürk, and his belief in a firm separation between religion and state, and the latter nostalgic for the Caliphate and wanting Islam to play a bigger role in public life—has characterized politics in the Turkish state since its foundation in 1923.[8] Over the last thirty years these tensions have also characterized the development of organized Islam among Turkish diaspora communities throughout Europe and particularly in Germany, given the size of its Turkish population.[9]

The arrival of Turkish Islamism in Western Europe can be dated to 1971, when the Turkish military executed a bloodless coup and the Constitutional Council banned several parties, including the Millî Nizam Partisi (National Order Party).[10] This party was the brainchild of Necmettin Erbakan, a German-educated engineer and the undisputed godfather of political Islam in Turkey. After a brief sojourn in Switzerland, Erbakan returned to Turkey to form several political outfits that have attempted to survive the traditionally rigid attitudes of the Turkish state toward Islamism; he became prime minister in 1996. Some of his followers permanently settled in various European countries with a large Turkish diaspora such as France, Holland, Switzerland, Austria, and, mostly, Germany.[11]

Erbakan's activists in Europe remained connected to their leader, who in the late 1960s had founded an ideological movement called Millî Görüş (National Vision), an Islamist organization with a strong nationalistic spin.[12] The movement's main message is one of social justice and strong Turkish identity, both linked to strict adherence to the vision of Islam as a comprehensive system. Its original plan aimed at restructuring society in Turkey based on the socioreligious concept of *adil düzen* (just order), the abolition of secularism, the creation of a Greater Turkey modeled on the Ottoman Empire, and finally the establishment of an Islamic world order.

The movement's ideas attracted the scrutiny of Turkish authorities, who banned many of the political entities created by Erbakan throughout the

1980s and 1990s, but Millî Görüş activists faced no such limitations in Europe, where free speech laws and little attention from local authorities allowed them to develop extensive networks. By the second half of the 1970s Millî Görüş had established a foothold in Germany, where it established its continental headquarters; however, a national organization was established only in 1985.[13] Ten years later the group morphed into the Islamische Gemeinschaft Millî Görüş (Islamic Community Millî Görüş), based in the Cologne suburb of Kerpen.

Today, Millî Görüş can count an estimated quarter of a million members and sympathizers among the Turkish communities of virtually all Western European countries, with Germany having the lion's share.[14] Its message has found a fertile audience among the masses of poorly educated and economically disenfranchised Turks of Europe, who saw the emphasis on a strong Islamic and Turkish identity as an answer to their alienation from mainstream society. Moreover, Millî Görüş' activists, who are often university-educated professionals, have employed modern mobilization techniques to spread their message within Turkish communities. The movement claims to run between five and seven hundred mosques throughout Europe, the majority in Germany.[15] Its facilities typically follow the "paramosque" structure, offering a range of services and activities from *halal* butchers to translation services, bookstores to kindergarten, all imbued with Millî Görüş' message.

Unlike most New Western Brotherhood organizations, Millî Görüş has been relatively successful in creating a mass movement. One contributing factor has been, particularly in the first years, the lack of competition from the Turkish state. In Turkey, the state controls the country's religious life through the Ministry of Religious Affairs (Diyanet İşleri Başkanlığı, commonly referred to as Diyanet). Created by Atatürk after the abolition of the Caliphate, the Diyanet manages mosques and writes the weekly sermons delivered by the imams, keeping a tight hold on the country's religious tendencies.[16] When Millî Görüş activists began laying the foundation of their European network in the 1970s, no such competition existed, and they had much more room to operate than in Turkey.

Only in the mid-1980s did the Turkish government perceive its loss of influence among Turkish diaspora communities at the expense of Millî Görüş as a problem.[17] It therefore decided to create Diyanet İşleri Türk İslam Birliği (DITIB), the European branch of the Diyanet, to run activities for Turkish émigrés and their progeny.[18] Representing the long arm of the Turkish state, DITIB has since created a wide network of Islamic centers that seek to maintain the cultural and political links between Turkish diaspora communities and Turkey and to propagate Ankara's interpretation of Islam.

The organizational structure of today's German-Turkish community reflects this history and these divisions. The vast majority of German Turks—85 to 90 percent, according to the German government—do not belong to any mosque association or other officially recognized organization.[19] Some belong to the Alevi community or to various Sufi orders, whose organizations operate mostly at the local level. Therefore, the two largest and most visible organizations are DITIB and Millî Görüş, whose mutual dislike and opposition has traditionally divided the organized religious Turkish community. Their diametrically opposed ideological positions, combined with their inability to comprise the majority of German Muslims, has prevented the formation of an entity that could legitimately claim the status of KöR and be recognized as a religious community.

The panorama of organized Islam in Germany would not be complete without mention of the Islamische Gemeinschaft Deutschland (Islamic Society of Germany, IGD). Founded in 1960, IGD has long been headquartered in the Islamic Center of Munich, which, as seen in chapter 2, was one of the first mosques created by Muslim Brotherhood members and sympathizers in Europe. Over the years, IGD expanded throughout Germany, reportedly controlling more than 120 mosques throughout the country (a number that German authorities dispute), yet retaining strong ideological and functional connections to its origins.[20] It is, in fact, no coincidence that several senior leaders of the Egyptian Brotherhood, including its former *murshid*, Mohammed Akef, who served as the mosque's imam between 1984 and 1987, have spent extensive time in Munich.[21] In 2002, after Ghaleb Himmat, the longtime associate of Yussuf Nada and co-head of the al Taqwa Bank, left IGD's chairmanship after being designated by the United Nations as a terrorism financier, leadership passed to a charismatic 34-year-old named Ibrahim El Zayat.[22]

If IGD, thanks to its history, is a perfect example of a New Western Brotherhood organization, various characteristics make El Zayat a quintessential New Western Brother. First, mirroring a common pattern, Islamic activism is a family affair for him. His father, Farouk, left Egypt in the 1960s and settled in Germany, where he married a German convert to Islam and became the imam of a mosque in Marburg, a university town north of Frankfurt.[23] The El Zayats had six children, most of whom have also been involved in Islamic activities, from German Muslim charities to student organizations. Bilal El Zayat, for example, is a founding member of the Muslimischen Jugend Deutschland (German Muslim Youth) and an officer of the Muslim Studenten Vereinigung (Muslim Students' Union).[24] Manal El Zayat, who is married to Kamal Helbawy's son, is a graduate of IESH and has been involved in Islamic organizations in various European countries.[25]

Born in 1968, Ibrahim El Zayat is the eldest and the most active of the El Zayat children. In Germany, he was the head of the Muslim Students' Union before assuming the chairmanship of IGD. He has also been involved in pan-European organizations. From 1996 to 2002 he was the head of FEMYSO, the Brussels-based youth branch of FIOE. He is also involved in FIOE itself; he is a founding member and currently leads the office of public relations.[26] El Zayat is also affiliated with IESH, WAMY, and Islamic Relief Worldwide, holding various official titles. Fluent in several languages, he frequently attends high-profile political and interfaith events throughout Europe, speaking at the European Parliament and other prestigious venues.[27]

El Zayat's intense political life does not prevent him from being a successful businessman. He holds a master's degree in economics from the University of Marburg and runs several property investment companies.[28] One of his businesses buys properties to build mosques and advises Islamic organizations on how to obtain building permits and fulfill all the connected legal requirements. Another side of his business provides consulting services on the German real estate market to wealthy Arab investors.[29] It is no surprise that El Zayat, given his expertise and connections, sits on the board of the Europe Trust, the British-based financial arm of the New European Brothers.[30]

El Zayat, whom the head of North Rhine-Westphalia's security services, Hartwig Möller, tellingly describes as "a spider in the web of Islamist organizations," is also a board member of the Europäische Moscheebau und Unterstützungs Gemeinschaft (EMUG), the German-based company that controls and manages Millî Görüş' mosques throughout Europe.[31] His links to Millî Görüş are not surprising and are based on ideological affinities.

But, as it is often the case among the New Western Brothers, ideological, religious, and financial connections are intermingled with personal ones. El Zayat is married to Sabiha Erbakan, Necmettin's niece. The Erbakan siblings, like the El Zayats, are heavily involved in Islamic activities. Sabiha's brother Mehmet Sabri is the former leader of Millî Görüş in Germany, and Sabiha herself, German-born and university educated, has been active in the leadership of organizations for German Muslim women and in several interfaith initiatives.[32]

The personal and financial union between the leaderships of Millî Görüş and IGD is a natural consequence of their ideological affinity. Although the former caters to German Turks and the latter to Arabs, the two groups, in the words of El Zayat, "can be considered as Pan-Muslim organizations," espousing the same vision of Islam as a comprehensive system and tracing their ideological roots to the Brotherhood milieu.[33]

The Security Services and the Lack of "Ideal" Partners

The internal fragmentation of Germany's Muslim community is the foremost factor determining its lack of official recognition by the German state. However, many argue that considerations about the nature of the main organizations applying for KöR status have played a crucial role in shaping the attitudes of German authorities and led them to refuse to modify or relax their interpretation of the provisions of the law regulating religious communities.

For many years the German government relied heavily on DITIB for the management of Islam, in effect outsourcing it. Good relations with the Turkish government and an appreciation for DITIB's interpretation of Islam have traditionally led Berlin and the governments of various German states, to which most issues regarding religion and integration are constitutionally delegated, to remedy the lack of an officially recognized Muslim community by working closely with DITIB. Treaties between Germany and Turkey have allowed Diyanet imams to obtain visas and work in German mosques, where they follow the teachings and sermons imposed by Ankara.[34]

But once authorities acknowledged that Turks living in Germany were no longer *Gastarbeiter* but permanent components of German society, this solution was reconsidered. German authorities therefore, like most European governments, are faced with the dilemma of how to deal with "embassy Islam." On one hand, DITIB preaches an interpretation of Islam that is widely perceived as moderate, aimed at reconciling religion with life in a secular society, whether that is Turkey or Germany. So German authorities believe that DITIB's Islam serves as a useful counterbalance to various forms of Islamism and appreciate its usefulness. On the other hand, DITIB openly tries to reinforce the bond between Ankara and German Turks, a goal that directly clashes with the German government's attempt to instill a sense of belonging and citizenship into the German Turkish community. The idea of referring to an organization headquartered inside the Turkish embassy in Berlin as the representative of German Muslims seems increasingly at odds with the government's stated goal of building a German Islam.

In any case, DITIB, which has never formally filed a request for KöR status, is just one of the main Muslim organizations operating in Germany. Both Millî Görüş and IGD supersede two umbrella organizations (Islamrat and Zentralrat respectively) that have consistently worked for KöR designation, claiming to control a large number of mosques.[35] Authorities have repeatedly denied their requests, questioning the number of mosques they actually controlled and pointing to the existence of other organizations as proof that they did not represent "peak organizations." IGD-dominated Zentralrat, for example, claims to control almost 500 mosques, even though most analysts put the number at 200 and German authorities estimate that the organization represents no more than 3 percent of German Muslims.[36] Its request for KöR status was denied in 2001.[37]

But, aside from lack of representativeness and other formal requirements, additional considerations have clearly influenced German authorities' decision. Crucially important have been the assessments of Millî Görüş and IGD provided by German security services, at both the federal and state level. The Federal Office for the Protection of the Constitution (Bundesamt für Verfassungsschutz, BfV) and the intelligence agencies of the vast majority of the sixteen German states have openly and consistently depicted both organizations in extremely negative terms, as potential threats to German democracy. Both organizations are analyzed in the annual reports issued by federal and state intelligence agencies and labeled "foreign extremist organizations."[38]

The reports do acknowledge that Millî Görüş and IGD act within the democratic framework and do not advocate violence inside Germany. Yet the German intelligence agencies' assessment of their aims is remarkably harsh. "These 'legalistic' Islamist groups represent an especial threat to the internal cohesion of our society," reads, for example, the 2005 report from the BfV. "Among other things," it continues, "their wide range of Islamist-oriented educational and support activities, especially for children and adolescents from immigrant families, are used to promote the creation and prolifera- tion of an Islamist milieu in Germany. These endeavours run counter to the efforts undertaken by the federal administration and the *Länder* [states] to integrate immigrants. There is the risk that such milieus could also form the breeding ground for further radicalization."[39] In all their reports and public statements, German security services highlight the negative impact that the activities of Millî Görüş and IGD can have on social cohesion and, in the long term, also on security, as they encourage the formation of an "us-versus-them mentality" that is the first step on the road to violent radi- calization.[40] German authorities accuse Millî Görüş of propagating anti- Semitic ideas, actively opposing democracy, and seeking to establish a strict Islamic order that would undermine the rights of other religious groups.[41]

Millî Görüş has been particularly active in fighting these characteriza- tions. In some cases it has brought the security services of various *Länder* to court, claiming that their intelligence reports were flawed, discriminatory, and based on dated information.[42] Besides accusing the services of transla- tion errors, Millî Görüş officials claim that most of the accusations against them are based on writings in *Milli Gazete*, Millî Görüş' official publication in Turkey. German Millî Görüş officials claim that statements published in *Milli Gazete* cannot be attributed to them, since they have no functional relationship with the publication.[43] In some cases Millî Görüş has been successful, obtaining court orders enjoining the security services from reprinting certain accusations against the organization in their reports.[44] Moreover, in the last few years Millî Görüş has also engaged in an effort to present a better image to the German public. Its officials consistently publicly avow their desire to cooperate with authorities, favor the integra- tion of Turks into German society, and want to "immunise [them] against extremism and terrorism."[45]

German security services are unconvinced. The links between Millî Görüş in Germany and the mother group in Turkey, they argue, are informal but solid.[46] Erbakan, though holding no formal position, is still revered as the spiritual leader of the movement and hailed as a hero whenever he speaks at its conferences in Germany.[47] Turkish Islamist politicians regularly speak and fund-raise at Millî Görüş events in Germany, and German Millî Görüş officials often return to Turkey to run for elections there.[48] Moreover, *Milli Gazete*, though not formally linked to Millî Görüş in Germany, is widely distributed throughout the Islamic centers controlled by it. To confirm the links, German authorities quote a statement by a German Millî Görüş official: "*Millî Gazete* is our lifeline. It should be our primary task to stand up for it, to read it, and to motivate others to read it."[49] In substance, German security officials accuse Millî Görüş leaders in Germany of engaging in a quintessential outsourcing of radicalism, letting *Milli Gazete* and Turkish Millî Görüş say what they themselves also believe but cannot publicly declare.[50]

Millî Görüş' attempts to be seen as moderate partners of the state are, therefore, widely shunned by German security services, which call it "an organization with two faces."[51] "Although Milli Görüş, in public statements, pretends to adhere to the basic principles of Western democracies," reads a 1999 BfV report, "abolition of the laicist government system in Turkey and the establishment of an Islamic state and social system are, as before, among its goals."[52] Similarly, referring to the group's activities in Germany, in 2000 the BfV stated that "while in recent times the Milli Görüş has increasingly emphasized the readiness of its members to be integrated into German society and asserts its adherence to the basic law [German constitution], such statements stem from tactical calculation rather than from any inner change of the organization."[53]

A similar dynamic characterizes the relations between security services and IGD. Public reports issued by the intelligence agencies of most German states openly call the IGD an offshoot of the Muslim Brotherhood, pointing to its historical and ideological connections to the movement.[54] El Zayat admits that IGD has "roots in the Muslim Brotherhood," but states that "we are not led or dominated by the Muslim Brotherhood." He adds, "If you are talking about influence, then virtually all major Islamic organizations in the West, as well as those in the Muslim world, have been dominated by the ideas of the Islamic movement."[55]

El Zayat's public stance on the influence of the Brotherhood on IGD and himself is particularly interesting, as it exemplifies patterns present in many other Western countries. On one hand, El Zayat has publicly referred to the Brotherhood as "the most important Islamic reform movement of the twentieth century," even though he has stated that he disagrees with some of its positions.[56] "It stands for the freeing of women," he said in a 2007 interview with the *Frankfurter Allgemeine Zeitung*. "For the solution of social problems, it promotes an interpretation of the Koran adapted to the space and time—all goals to which I subscribe."[57]

On the other hand, El Zayat has staunchly denied that he is a member of the Brotherhood. In 2005, for example, he sued a member of the German Parliament who had called him "an official of the Muslim Brotherhoods," but the court rejected his claim.[58] A more embarrassing situation arose in 2008, when an Egyptian military court sentenced El Zayat to ten years *in absentia* for financing the Egyptian branch of the Brotherhood.[59] El Zayat could easily downplay the importance of the Egyptian verdict, passed by a military court and based on secret evidence. Arguably more damaging was the press release issued before the trial by Ikhwanweb, the Egyptian Brotherhood's official English-language Web site. Ikhwanweb described El Zayat as one of the "members of the Muslim Brotherhood" unjustly put on trial by the government; he contacted the site's administrators and asked them to issue a formal correction, indicating, in a subsequent posting, that he "is not a member of the Muslim Brotherhood and is not associated with any of the Muslim Brotherhood's organizations."[60]

El Zayat's position on the issue is paradigmatic of the difficulties in defining the modern Brotherhood. In all likelihood El Zayat is technically correct, as there is no publicly available evidence that he has ever been a formal "member" or "official" of the movement. A German-born citizen, he is unlikely to have undergone the same process of formal membership that takes place in Egypt or other Middle Eastern countries. At the same time, El Zayat represents the quintessential New Western Brother. His personal connections, self-professed adherence to the Brotherhood's core ideas, and his form of activism make him not a "member" but a key player in the informal network of the New Western Brothers. It is for this reason that senior members of the Egyptian Brotherhood such as Yussuf Nada, Kamal Helbawy, and Abd El Monem Abou El Fotouh speak fondly of him, detail their many contacts with him, and, while confirming that he is not a member of the Brotherhood, state that he "works for Islam in Germany and in Europe," a veiled confirmation of his role.[61]

This sort of ambiguity constitutes one of the factors that drive German security services to assess IGD's claims of moderation no differently than Millî Görüş. IGD and the IGD-dominated Zentralrat have repeatedly expressed their desire to build bridges between Muslims and German society, and have engaged in high-profile initiatives such as a campaign against forced marriages. In 2002, under increased scrutiny after 9/11, Zentralrat even released the Islamic Charta, a document in which it unconditionally accepted the predominance of German law over sharia and expressed the desire to contribute to integration. "We do not aim at establishing a clerical theocracy," stated the document. "Rather, we welcome the system existing in the Federal Republic of Germany where state and religion harmoniously relate to each other."[62] Moreover, El Zayat, the target of several negative profiles in the media, has recently kept a lower profile; a German convert, Axel Ayub Köhler, and a younger activist, Aiman Mazyek, have become the public faces of the organization.

The security services look at these initiatives with skepticism, arguing that they are just for public consumption and do not match up with what IGD and Zentralrat say inside their mosques and in their internal publications.[63] Firm in their belief that Millî Görüş and IGD are not transparent organizations, authorities have also opened several investigations against them for various financial crimes. In 2002, for example, El Zayat came under investigation for his involvement in several money-laundering activities.[64] In 2004, Millî Görüş' mosques and headquarters were raided in a money-laundering investigation.[65] A larger investigation was launched in 2009, when German authorities raided various mosques and homes connected to IGD's and Millî Görüş' leadership. Authorities suspect El Zayat and other top officials of the two organizations of being engaged in fraud, forgery, embezzlement, and other financial irregularities.[66]

The Education Dilemma

The hard line adopted by German security services has practical repercussions for the process of engagement. Although their assessment is not binding, it is nevertheless a strong signal to all branches of the German state, from the federal to the state and local level. As a consequence, many officials tasked with engaging the Muslim community find themselves in a bind. "We cannot meet with half of the Muslims in town because the Verfassungsschutz says they are a danger to our values," complains a German politician.[67] Many have criticized the blacklisting of Millî Görüş and IGD, saying that intelligence reports are "overly blunt" instruments that lead to the lumping together of all Islamist organizations, almost equating nonviolent groups with al Qaeda.[68] Others share the security services' assessment but argue that engagement with Millî Görüş and IGD is necessary, given the almost complete lack of alternatives.

A field where these problems are particularly evident is religious instruction. Article 7.3 of the federal constitution indicates that education is a matter reserved to the individual states, which have to provide religious instruction in accordance with the tenets of the religious community concerned. In substance, each state may enter in an agreement with any religious community that has pupils in the public school system, provide funds, and de facto subcontract the determination of the content and the selection of the teachers to the religious community. While most *Länder* have had no problem identifying the bodies that should teach Christianity, the lack of Muslim organizations with KöR status has generated serious problems. Which of the many Muslim groups filing an application should be considered the "religious community" to which the constitution assigns the right to teach religion to the more than 700,000 Muslim pupils in German public schools?[69]

The country's sixteen states have come up with different solutions. Some have resorted to subcontracting Islamic instruction to DITIB, even if its curriculum has little appeal to non-Turks and to Turks who disagree with its statecentric interpretation of Islam.[70] In a few cases, small Muslim communities have managed to form a truly comprehensive platform at the local level, allowing authorities to sign an agreement with them even if they did not have KöR status.[71] In most cases, however, state ministries of education are faced with a myriad of applications from various competing Muslim organizations. Almost invariably, the most complete and well-planned applications come from Islamrat and Zentralrat, whose organizational capabilities far exceed those of other groups. In light of this situation, the alternative is often between subcontracting Islamic instruction to organizations that are considered by the security services a threat to the democratic order, thus providing them with an enormous platform to spread their views to young German Muslims, or not establishing any program, reinforcing the not uncommon perception among Muslims that German authorities discriminate against Islam.[72]

These dynamics have been particularly controversial in North Rhine-Westphalia, the German state with the largest Muslim population (one in three Muslims in Germany lives there; Muslim students in the state's schools are estimated to be 310,000 out of a total of 2.9 million).[73] In the late 1970s, after extensive negotiations with various Muslim groups broke down, North Rhine-Westphalia's Ministry of Education decided that partnership with the Muslim community was impossible, since no organization could be selected as exclusive partner and infighting prevented the formation of a truly representative umbrella organization. It therefore decided to create its own curriculum and teach Islam directly, without the help of the Muslim community.[74] Architects of the program openly stated their goal of teaching a brand of Islam they deemed compatible with German values and went as far as saying they would "welcome the democratization of Islam spreading out [to the Muslim world] from Germany."[75]

Unsurprisingly, Islamrat and Zentralrat, which are both headquartered in the state, have repeatedly challenged the validity of North Rhine-Westphalia's program in court.[76] The two organizations have argued that the state unfairly interferes in a matter that the federal constitution assigned to religious communities and have sought to have their own programs approved. After an extensive legal battle in the state court system, in 2005 the case was decided by the Federal Administrative Court. It ruled that even religious organizations that do not represent all believers have a constitutional right to enter into an agreement with the state, arguing that there could be more than one religious community within Islam. The court, however, did not feel it had enough evidence to decide whether Islamrat and Zentralrat satisfied even these lowered requirements, and remanded the case to North Rhine-Westphalia's administrative court.

In its ruling, the federal court partly opened the door to the two organizations' claim, recognizing their substantive right to enter in an agreement with the state even if they did not represent the majority of Muslims. However, the rest of the ruling outlined specific characteristics that the state court should have verified before recognizing Islamrat and Zentralrat as religious communities, providing North Rhine-Westphalia with new legal tools to reject their application. Aside from structural requirements, such as number of members and length of presence in the country, the court stated that a necessary prerequisite was that the organization applying for recognition did not threaten basic constitutional principles. The state could not require that religious organizations wanting to enter into an agreement be neutral or proclaim that all religions are equal. Organizations should also be free to pray for the end of democracy and the establishment of a theocratic regime in its place. However, a religious organization is legitimately considered a threat to the constitutional order and should be rightly excluded from any cooperation with the state if it does not "leave it to the transcendental area to change the current system of things but intends to itself eliminate the foundations of the State by repeated aggressive attacks," which can also be purely verbal.[77]

Officials at North Rhine-Westphalia's Ministry of Education have since engaged both Islamrat and Zentralrat, meeting their representatives on several occasions.[78] They keep in mind the warnings of the security services, whose advice is constantly sought; however, eager to find a solution to a thorny issue, they do not rule out the possibility of partnering with the two organizations once they meet the necessary formal requirements. Meanwhile, the ministry has signed an agreement with the Alevi community, which is running its own state-sponsored Islamic education program for Alevi children in public schools despite its lack of KöR status.[79]

The legal challenges initiated by various Muslim organizations against their exclusion from education programs have generated a different outcome in the city-state of Berlin, which is subjected to slightly different constitutional provisions on the matter.[80] In the early 1980s, the city signed an agreement with the Turkish government, assigning DITIB to teach Islam in its public schools.[81] The decision was challenged by the Islamische Föderation in Berlin (Islamic Federation in Berlin, IFB), a group that had filed an application to teach its own program. After a legal battle that lasted more than fifteen years, in 1998 the administrative High Court of Berlin chose to void the city's agreement with DITIB and stated that IFB, though not a KöR, had to be recognized as a religious society that, under the city's regulations, could teach Islam.[82] Since then, despite the strong opposition of Berlin's government, IFB has been in charge of organizing Islamic education courses for thousands of Muslim pupils throughout the city.[83]

Although officially independent, the IFB is, according to German authorities, nothing more than an offshoot of Millî Görüş.[84] Several organizations that belong to the federation also belong to Millî Görüş and, according to the local Verfassungsschutz, IFB's former chairman, Nail Dural, is also the deputy chairman of Millî Görüş.[85] Many critics have also highlighted flaws in IFB's curriculum and its teachers' lack of credentials.[86] Some media reports, particularly after 9/11, took heated undertones, unjustly linking IFB to terrorism. Other critics have launched more nuanced accusations. Klaus Böger, a Berlin state senator long involved in education issues, stated: "I do not believe that they are teaching their pupils to make bombs, but I think they are rejecting our society and are teaching an intolerant form of Islam."[87] Özcan Mutlu, the Green Party's spokesman for education issues in the Berlin House of Representatives, similarly said: "I feel they do a good job in many ways, like teaching Muslim women to read and setting up programs to help children with their homework. But they also say: 'We don't belong to this society. We are different.'"[88]

IFB officials deny all charges, stating that they are groundless and politically motivated.[89] Yet harsh criticism has come also from those at the ground level who have witnessed firsthand how IFB's programs work. Marion Berning, the principal of a school in Berlin's Neukölln district where 92 percent of the student body is of immigrant descent, has publicly recounted her negative experience working with IFB.[90] Participation in Islamic education is, according to the law, voluntary; Berning states, however, that people linked to IFB stood outside school one day and handed out the forms to enroll in its classes, telling children and parents that "Allah would have punished them if they didn't enroll."[91] Moreover, contrary to the court ruling, the classes were held behind closed doors and in Turkish, rather than in German. Berning says that a few months after IFB began teaching its classes, relations in the school changed drastically, as Muslim students refused to participate in activities with students of the opposite sex or began to taunt their non-Muslim peers about their beliefs. IFB officials dispute the veracity of Berning's stories and claim that their teachings had a positive impact on the school.[92]

The Deutsche Islam Konferenz and Prospects for the Future

Issues of integration, radicalization, education, and discrimination surrounding the country's Muslim community have been at the forefront of the political debate in Germany since 9/11. To obviate to the many difficulties previous governments had faced on these matters, in 2006 the newly appointed federal Minister of the Interior, Wolfgang Schäuble, decided to create the German Conference on Islam (Deutsche Islam Konferenz, DIK).[93] DIK was designed as a four-year-long, semipermanent meeting place for government officials from the federal, state, and local levels and prominent Muslim leaders. Convened for the first time in September 2006, DIK met twice a year as a plenum and with more frequency in smaller working groups to discuss issues ranging from education to terrorism, from the construction of mosques to the recognition of the Muslim community.

Schäuble's underlying idea was that German Muslims have been unable to form a unified leadership and that DIK, by engaging them in a constant dialogue, could perhaps facilitate such a process.[94] His first, extremely challenging task was to select the participants and, as was easily predicted, each of his choices drew criticism.[95] Critics noted, for example, that inviting DITIB, a Turkish government organization, to an event designed to help form a German Islam was inconsistent. Others pointed that by inviting the leaders of Islamrat and Zentralrat he was going against the warnings of the security services. The invitation of two other organizations (the Alevi community and the VIKZ, an organization linked to the Suleymanci Turkish brotherhood) drew only limited criticism, but some questioned Schäuble's decision to flank the leaders of the five big organizations with ten unaffiliated and handpicked Muslim activists and intellectuals. The ten, whom Schäuble invited to represent the silent majority of secular or unaffiliated Muslims, have been accused of having no place in a body that is supposed to deal with religious issues. Ibrahim El Zayat charged some of them with having "strong Islamophobic views."[96]

Despite these criticisms, Schäuble's selection seems sound. While aware of the implications of inviting DITIB, Zentralrat, and Islamrat, Schäuble has displayed remarkable pragmatism, understanding that they constitute realities that cannot be ignored simply because of their flaws. In particular, the inclusion of Zentralrat and Islamrat is part of a policy aimed at cautiously reaching out to them, hoping that engagement will bring moderation and that by participating in the system, they will change positions that authorities deem incompatible with German values. Moreover, by adding ten unaffiliated individuals, Schäuble tried to balance DIK's composition, allowing the voice of the unorganized, silent majority to be heard.

DIK, whose last plenary meeting took place in June 2009, did not achieve any groundbreaking results—something about which German authorities, who had kept public expectations low from the very beginning, were not disappointed—but it represented a major first step in the establishment of a permanent dialogue between the state and German Muslims and among German Muslims.[97] One apparent result seems to be the formation of a body that unites, albeit only temporarily, four of the five participating organizations. In March 2007, DITIB, VIKZ, Islamrat, and Zentralrat joined forces to form the Coordination Council of Muslims in Germany (Koordinierungsrat der Muslime in Deutschland, KRM).[98] KRM leaders, claiming that their organizations combined represent 85 to 90 percent of German mosques and Islamic associations, clearly aim at obtaining KöR status.[99] Studies conducted by the Ministry of the Interior show another side of reality, as extensive polls among German Muslims revealed that only 25 percent felt represented by any of KRM's organizations and only 2 percent by KRM itself.[100] Authorities therefore look at KRM with cautious optimism, eager to work with it but suspecting that it is just a temporary body, set up to obtain KöR status but lacking internal unity, and likely to collapse due to internal divisions once it has achieved that goal.[101]

The formation of KRM highlights another interesting development. If the unity among Islamrat, Zentralrat, and VIKZ, which is itself a founding member of Zentralrat, is not surprising, DITIB's participation is. For decades, the harsh rivalry between Kemalist DITIB and Islamist Millî Görüş had divided the German Turkish community, preventing the formation of a unified body. DITIB's new position seems to be the direct consequence of the political change in Turkey since 2002, when the Justice and Development Party (Adalet ve Kalkınma Partisi, AKP) won the elections. AKP's leadership grew up politically in Erbakan's movements and parties, and current Prime Minister Recep Tayyip Erdoğan and President of the Republic Abdullah Gül were top leaders of Erbakan's Welfare Party (Refah Partisi) in the 1990s. Several German officials and commentators argue that the ideological change in Ankara has naturally influenced DITIB, whose positions are now less radically secularist.[102] In light of this, DITIB's alliance with Millî Görüş is not surprising.

7

The United States

The situation of both the Muslim community and the Muslim Brotherhood in the United States represents an anomaly, characterized by several differences from Europe. Wealthier and more educated, on average, than both European Muslims and non-Muslim Americans, American Muslims experienced few problems integrating into a nation that, unlike most European countries, has absorbed millions of immigrants since its birth. Moreover, enjoying the strict separation between church and state and the laissez-faire attitude toward religious pluralism that has characterized America since the Founding Fathers, they have experienced few of the problems of recognition and institutionalization of their faith that European Muslims have.[1]

American-based New Western Brotherhood networks have also been able to take advantage of these conditions and establish a presence that significantly overshadows their European counterparts' in terms of organization, funds, and almost monopolistic access to government. Finally, the American case is anomalous because of the voluminous amounts of primary information on the structure and functioning of Brotherhood networks in the country available to authorities and the public. During the 2007 trial of the Holy Land Foundation (HLF), the Texas-based charity that U.S. authorities accused of financing Hamas, federal prosecutors introduced as evidence thousands of pages of internal Brotherhood documents.[2] The documents, whose authenticity has never been contested, represent an unprecedented treasure trove of information on the otherwise extremely secretive organization.[3]

The Origins

Until the 1960s, the vast majority of Muslims living in the United States were African Americans. Although it had been present among West African slaves since the seventeenth century, Islam began to attract a significant following among black Americans in the first decades of the twentieth century, as charismatic Muslim preachers found a receptive audience among the masses of disenfranchised blacks who had immigrated from the South to the large industrial cities of the North. Movements founded at the time, such as the Moorish Science Temple and the Nation of Islam, blended tenets of the Muslim faith with teachings of other religions and fostered a strong message of racial pride, generating particularistic forms of Islam that have little in common with traditional Sunni Islam but that suited the identity needs of African Americans.[4]

Small communities of Muslim immigrants from Lebanon and other Arab countries had been settling throughout the United States since the late nineteenth century, growing in subsequent waves and fully integrating into American society. By the 1950s some of the local organizations founded by Arab Muslim immigrants formed a national umbrella organization called the Federation of Islamic Associations (FIA).[5] Mirroring countless American organizations that cater to various ethnic or religious groups, the FIA aimed to maintain the cultural heritage and the familial bonds among American Muslims of Arab descent, organizing a popular annual conference that brought together families from throughout the country.[6]

The FIA's limited goals and activities, while satisfying the needs of the fully Americanized Arab immigrants, were not enough for a new constituency that, by the early 1960s, had arrived en masse in America: Muslim students. Between the 1950s and the 1960s, more than half a million students from throughout the Muslim world, as well as other parts of Asia, Africa, and Latin America, were on hundreds of American college campuses, seeking internationally recognized degrees in medicine, engineering, and most other scientific fields.[7] The phenomenon was widely encouraged by American authorities, who saw it as an excellent opportunity for the country to form friendly relationships with the future elites of newly independent and "third world" countries. Lacking the historical links with those potential allies that many European countries had established during the colonial era, America saw the presence of hundreds of thousands of students on its campuses as the perfect way to form ties. If, as part of the Cold War chess game, Moscow was opening the doors of its educational institutions to future leaders of countries it sought to influence, so was Washington.

The scions of the urban elites of the Muslim world on U.S. college campuses established the first student organizations that could fulfill their basic religious needs.[8] Since supporters of nationalism, at the time the leading ideology in the Muslim world, had little interest in religious organizations, individuals who had had experiences in various Islamist organizations in their home countries became the main drivers behind the small student groupings that spontaneously formed on various campuses.[9] Realizing that the FIA's apolitical nature did not fulfill their vision of Islam as a comprehensive way of life, Islamist students soon felt the need to form their own national organization. In the winter of 1963, a hundred students representing fewer than twenty Muslim student organizations from various parts of the country met on the campus of the University of Illinois in Urbana-Champaign, a university town less than a hundred miles from Chicago, Indianapolis, and St. Louis, in the heart of the American Midwest.[10] The result was the creation of the Muslim Student Association (MSA), America's first national Muslim student organization.

The MSA was the brainchild of a small group of student activists who originated from various countries of the Muslim world but were united by a common vision of Islam as inherently political. They included activists from various backgrounds, including several Shias, yet a crucial role was played by members and sympathizers of various national branches of the Muslim Brotherhood who had settled in America since the 1950s.[11] Though the MSA was not a "pure" Brotherhood organization, its links to that network were strong.[12] From its inception Brotherhood members held key positions, influencing its ideology and direction. Moreover, the MSA became a sort of parallel structure of the Brotherhood, independent but representing an inexhaustible recruiting pool and a perfect avenue to disseminate its ideas.[13]

Initially affiliated with the FIA, the MSA soon overshadowed it, establishing branches on hundreds of campuses and recruiting thousands of new members and sympathizers. The FIA's activities were limited mostly to an annual meeting where members celebrated their common identity; the MSA had a much more ambitious agenda. The organization's publication, *Al Ittihad*, tackled deeper issues, from political events in the Muslim world to theological controversies, often disseminating the positions and writings of al Banna, Mawdudi, and Qutb.[14] The MSA's annual conference, often held during Labor Day weekend, attracted thousands of participants. At a time when Islam was almost invisible in America, the conferences represented a unique occasion for Muslims from all ethnic backgrounds to come together, shop at an Islamic bazaar, purchase Islamic literature, hear prominent Muslim speakers, and meet other Muslims who held a similar interpretation of their faith. The MSA also created professional subgroups, such as the Islamic Medical Association and the Islamic Association of Scientists and Engineers, and others based on ethnic origin, such as the Muslim Arab Youth Association and the Malaysian Islamic Study Group.[15] Entities such as the North American Islamic Trust, the MSA's financial holding; the Islamic Book Service; and American Trust Publications were also set up to serve the growing needs of the organization.[16]

The success of the MSA, as with most other New Western Brotherhood organizations, was due to its leaders' unrelenting activism and unparalleled access to funds. As seen, key MSA leaders such as "the three Kurds"—Barzinji, Totonji, and al Talib—developed important relations with affluent networks in the Arab Gulf, gaining access to sources of funding that no other American Muslim organization could match. "They were in a position to define American Islam," argues Inamul Haq, a professor of religion at Benedictine University. "Since they were well-connected in the Middle East, they were able to bring money to build various institutions."[17]

By the late 1970s/early 1980s MSA leaders realized that a student organization, even as sophisticated as theirs, was not enough to fulfill the needs of the growing number of Muslims who had decided to permanently relocate to America. As a consequence, they incorporated the Islamic Society of North America (ISNA), an umbrella organization to coordinate the activities of the MSA and the other groups born out of the same milieu. The evolution from student grouping to "adult" organization, serving the needs of a permanent Muslim community in the West, has characterized the evolution of Brotherhood networks in virtually all Western countries. A particularly interesting perspective on this passage in the United States comes from the internal writings and speeches of Brotherhood members operating in America that were introduced as evidence in the HLF trial. Among the various sources documenting the first years of the Brotherhood in the United States, the most authoritative and comprehensive is a lecture given to other members in Kansas City in the early 1980s by Zeid al Noman, a *masul* (official) of the Executive Office of the U.S. Muslim Brotherhood.[18]

One of the most striking aspects of al Noman's lecture is the level of organization he describes. The group had only just established a presence in the country, but al Noman outlines a formal and extremely complex structure. He explains that the group had some twenty collegial bodies and committees that operated according to a well-defined hierarchy and met regularly. While some of the committees discussed security or *dawa* methods, the organization's central bodies drafted and oversaw meticulous long-term plans of action. According to al Noman, the Brotherhood's Shura Council in the United States approved five-year plans for the group's activities and the Executive Office, to which al Noman himself belonged, put together annual work programs to implement the Shura Council's guidelines.

According to al Noman, the plan for the 1975–1980 quinquennium was simply "general work," but the plan for the 1981–1985 quinquennium unveiled a major shift in the American Brotherhood's views and perceptions of its goals. The Shura Council and the Executive Office understood that basing the movement's activities on a student organization was limiting and that a more comprehensive solution needed to be found. Only a permanent network of organizations—not a student group, which, by nature, changes in membership as its members graduate—could implement the quinquennial plans. "What the Movement should be," said al Noman, "is to become a Movement for the residents." He refers to this new phase as "the settlement of the *dawa*." The transition from the MSA to the ISNA, organizations that the Brotherhood indirectly controlled, has to be seen, therefore, in light of this change in the American Brotherhood's strategy.

Clarifications on what "settlement of the *dawa*" means come from another extremely detailed document introduced as evidence by the government in the HLF trial. Entitled *An Explanatory Memorandum on the Strategic Goals for the Group in North America*, it is an 18-page internal memorandum sent by Mohammed Akram, a member of the Shura Council of the U.S. Brotherhood, to the rest of the Shura Council in 1991.[19] Akram, who currently serves as secretary general of the International al Quds Foundation, a Lebanon-based institution headed by al Qaradawi, states that "it must be stressed that it has become clear and emphatically known that all is in agreement that we must 'settle' or 'enable' Islam and its Movement in this part of the world [America]." "Islam and its Movement," writes Akram, referring to the Muslim Brotherhood's movement, are to "become part of the homeland it lives in." He continues,

> The general strategic goal of the Brotherhood in America which was approved by the Shura [Leadership] Council and the Organizational Conference for 1987 is "enablement of Islam in North America, meaning: establishing an effective and stable Islamic Movement led by the Muslim Brotherhood which adopts Muslims' causes domestically and globally, and which works to expand the observant Muslim base; aims at unifying and directing Muslims' efforts; presents Islam as a civilization alternative; and supports the global Islamic state, wherever it is." ... The priority that is approved by the Shura Council for the work of the Brotherhood in its current and former session is "Settlement."

The step that Akram deems necessary in order to implement "the settlement of the *dawa*" is the shift from an elite movement to a popular one. While some of the group's core activities and, most importantly, its aims need to remain secret, Akram believes that, in order to create a stable and widespread presence in the country, the Brotherhood needs to open up to the outside, and particularly toward Muslim communities in North America. He states that "absorbing and winning them with all of their factions and colors in America and Canada" is crucial for the settlement project and that "the art of dealing with others" has to be learned. A mastery of "the art of coalitions, the art of absorption and the principles of cooperation" are equally important. Akram understands that, in order to spread its message to other Muslims living in the United States, the Brotherhood needs to become an open and public organization, reaching out to potential new members and allies.

But Akram also reminds the readers of his memorandum what the real aim behind the "settlement of the *dawa*" is:

> The process of settlement is a "Civilization-Jihadist Process" with all the word means. The Ikhwan [Muslim Brothers] must understand that their work in America is a kind of grand Jihad in eliminating and destroying the Western civilization from within and "sabotaging" its mis-

erable house by their hands and the hands of the believers so that it is eliminated and God's religion is made victorious over all other religions. Without this level of understanding, we are not up to this challenge and have not prepared ourselves for Jihad yet. It is a Muslim's destiny to perform Jihad and work wherever he is and wherever he lands until the final hour comes, and there is no escape from that destiny except for those who choose to slack.

Crucially important in order to advance this goal is the development of what Akram refers to as "the organizational mentality," examples of which, he says, can be found in the prophet Mohammed ("the first pioneer of this phenomenon") and Muslim Brotherhood founder Hassan al Banna ("the pioneer of contemporary Islamic *Dawa*"). "We must say that we are in a country which understands no language other than the language of the organizations," Akram writes to other members of the Shura Council, "and one which does not respect or give weight to any group without effective, functional and strong organizations."

At the local level, therefore, Akram argues that the Brothers should develop multifunctional Islamic centers, bases from which they will generate new followers like "a beehive which produces sweet honey." If the Islamic center/paramosque represents the local unit of the movement in the United States, Akram believes that the Brothers should also operate at the national level. "In order for the process of settlement to be completed," says Akram, "we must plan and work from now to equip and prepare ourselves, our brothers, our apparatuses, our sections and our committees in order to turn into comprehensive organizations in a gradual and balanced way that is suitable with the need and the reality." The last five pages of Akram's memorandum detail how the Brotherhood can and must form organizations that will, operating on different levels, further the group's agenda. He notes that most of these organizations do already exist but operate without much central control. The goal must be to merge them and coordinate their work in a cohesive manner. Finally, a one-page attachment lists 29 American Muslim organizations, including ISNA, MSA, NAIT, IIIT, and many of their subgroups, that belong to the movement and that are in need of centralized planning. The page is headlined with a hopeful comment ("imagine if they all march according to one plan") that the group should better coordinate in order to advance its goals.

While there is no available evidence suggesting that Akram's memorandum or any other similar plan was ever officially approved by the Brotherhood's Shura Council, what Akram outlines seems to mirror the development of the MSA/ISNA milieu over the last thirty years. Most of the organizations listed in the memo have substantially expanded their reach and generated myriads of offshoots. Comprising only a few hundred core activists and a few thousand members, they constitute a tightly knit network of organizations that, despite some occasional disagreements, works together under an efficient distribution of roles and has managed to overshadow competing Muslim trends and organizations to a degree that surpasses most European countries.

Headquartered in an Indianapolis suburb, ISNA is the overarching organization for many of the entities listed by Akram as belonging to the American Brotherhood, and it has focused mostly on serving the religious needs of American Muslims. The Islamic Circle of North America (ICNA), also listed by Akram, caters mostly to the South Asian population and is headed by several members and sympathizers of Jamat-e-Islami.[20] IIIT, as seen, unites some of the top minds of the global Islamist movement.[21] In the late 1970s, its founders, including the three Kurds, settled in suburban Washington, D.C., where they established an intricate array of multimillion-dollar financial, political, and religious activities.

The development of the northern Virginia-based SAAR Foundation, the holding entity for these enterprises, is paradigmatic of the New Western Brothers' ample access to financial resources. It has received substantial backing from wealthy Arab Gulf donors and particularly by the al Rajhi family, one of Saudi Arabia's wealthiest. "We asked investors to give us one large lump sum rather than smaller amounts every year," stated SAAR vice president and former MSA president Yaqub Mirza, explaining the foundation's fund-raising mechanisms in the early 1980s. "This way we were bringing in from $10 million to $20 million a year."[22] A 2002 investigative report by the *Washington Post* revealed additional details about SAAR's financial activities:

In 1984, Yaqub Mirza, a Pakistani native who received a PhD in physics from the University of Texas in Dallas, used money from the Rajhis to start SAAR in Virginia, with the goal of spreading Islam and doing charitable work. Mirza also sought out business ventures for SAAR. By

investing the Rajhis' money with Washington real estate developer Mohamed Hadid, he made SAAR one of the region's biggest landlords in the
1980s. The SAAR network also became one of South America's biggest
apple growers and the owner of one of America's top poultry firms, Mar-
Jac Poultry in Georgia. "The funds came very easily," said a businessman
who dealt with SAAR. "If they wanted a few million dollars, they called
the al-Rajhis, who would send it along."[23]

Easy access to these enormous sums made the "settlement of *dawa*" a
smooth process, and the U.S. Brothers quickly developed additional organizations. By the end of the 1980s, as the settlement phase was deemed to
be completed, the Brothers began to focus on influencing political life. In
1986, ISNA's Planning Committee stated that "in order to exert influence
on the political decision-making and legislation in North America, ISNA
should launch a campaign to educate Muslim citizens about their voting
rights and mobilize them to vote on issues affecting Islam and Muslims."[24]
Within a few years several organizations were established to increase the
network's participation in American political life. In 1990, Mahmoud Abu
Saud, a prominent Egyptian Brotherhood leader and one of the fathers of
modern Islamic banking, together with other activists, formed the American Muslim Council (AMC). The AMC was headed by the abovementioned
Abdurahman Alamoudi, who until then had served as ISNA's representative
in the Washington area and executive assistant to the president of SAAR.[25]
Based in Washington, the AMC took advantage of its leaders' wealth and
connections to establish important links to the capital's elites.

In 1992, the self-avowed head of the U.S. Brotherhood's Shura Council,
Ahmed Elkadi, an Egyptian physician who had married Abu Saud's daughter, met with other top Brotherhood activists, including the future murshid
of the Egyptian branch, Mohammed Akef, in a hotel on the Alabama–
Tennessee border. Disenchanted with the direction some groups of the network had taken, the Brothers feared a loss of influence. U.S. Brotherhood
leaders had expressed particular concern about the ISNA. "The ISNA has
developed significantly in the eighties by the Ikhwan's leadership," stated
a 1991 internal memorandum of the Shura Council, "and direction of it
started to gradually decrease due to their scarce presence."[26] A decision was
therefore made to create the Muslim American Society (MAS), a new organization to represent more directly the thinking of the Brotherhood.[27]

Incorporated in Chicago but later moved to northern Virginia, the MAS has quickly grown to a nationwide organization with 53 local chapters, even though its active membership is limited to some 1,500 individuals.[28] It runs extensive cultural programs, including a university in suburban Detroit that includes al Qaradawi on its board of trustees.[29] The MAS is also extremely active in grassroots political activities, harnessing the drive of its few members to mobilize Muslims for political purposes. In Virginia, for example, the MAS claims to have determined the 2006 senatorial race in favor of Democratic candidate Jim Webb against incumbent Senator George Allen. Its 230 volunteers claim to have registered 65,000 voters, mostly among the large Muslim community of northern Virginia. According to the MAS, the Muslim vote, which largely supported Webb, was crucial in an election that was decided by less than 8,000 votes.[30]

The MSA, the ISNA, the ICNA, the IIIT, the SAAR (now dissolved and subjected to extensive terrorism-financing investigations by U.S. authorities), the AMC, the MAS, and the jungle of acronyms and subgroups that have splintered from them form a cluster of organizations, each with its own magazine, Web site, annual conference, subdepartments, and regional branches, whose unity is revealed by common financial sources, interlocking boards of directors, and occasional participation in common initiatives.[31] The few hundred individuals who run them form a small social network united by family, business, and, most important, ideological ties. Affluent, well-connected, highly educated, and motivated, they are a clique of leaders with an ample clout but few followers. Despite their influence among American policy makers their organizations have very limited membership numbers, mostly in the few thousands. According to a 2006 study, for example, the vast majority of American Muslims do not belong to any religious organization and of the more than 2,500 registered Muslim organizations in the United States, only a few dozen belong to the ISNA.[32]

As in the case of their counterparts in Europe, the links between these organizations and the Muslim Brotherhood are sometimes contested. In 2007, after the ISNA was listed as an unindicted coconspirator by the Department of Justice in the HLF trial and Akram's memorandum indicating it as one of the groups supposed to participate in the proscribed "Civilization-Jihadist Process" was introduced as evidence, the organization issued a statement claiming that it had never been "subject to the control" of the Muslim Brotherhood.[33] In the past, other ISNA leaders had been more open about their group's ties to the Muslim Brotherhood. This is how Steve A. Johnson (also known as Faruq Abdullah), the former editor of *Islamic Horizons*, ISNA's official publication, described the organization's internal elections in 1986:

> Splits among Ikhwan factions constituting ISNA became apparent during the 1986 ISNA elections. It is alleged by some ISNA members that the nomination process was postponed several times until IIIT was able to rally enough support to ensure Ahmad Zaki's (supposedly a member of the Egyptian Ikhwan) election. Evidently, some of the old guards in the more "orthodox" Ikhwan supported Shawki Zahran over Ahmad Zaki. The Sudanese, Tunisian, and more liberal factions of the Ikhwan supported past ISNA president Qutbi Mehdi. The Malaysian students were split with the Ikhwan-modeled MISG, supporting their champion Zaki. The members of the Muslim Youth Movement of Malaysia (ABIM)—still bitter about what they took to be Ahmad Zaki's involvement in splitting the Malaysian students in America—supported Mehdi. The Sudanese attempted to rally several groups—including the American Muslims— behind Mehdi, but they had waited too long and the other factions of the Ikhwan had already launched a telephone and letter campaign to inform fellow Muslim Brotherhood members how to vote.[34]

Similarly, Shaker Elsayed, a top MAS official and also ISNA's director of education, admits that roughly 45 percent of MAS activists are members of the Brotherhood, but highlights that the MAS is operationally independent and "not administered from Egypt." "Ikhwan members founded MAS, but MAS went way beyond that point of conception."[35] Elsayed's explanation captures the nature of what we have termed New Western Brotherhood organizations. Members and sympathizers of the Brotherhood played a key role in forming and leading these groups, albeit independently, rather than as part of a centralized plot masterminded in Cairo or any other Middle Eastern city. As the years went by, these organizations adapted to the environment in which they operated, making their connections to the Middle East progressively more tenuous and, today, virtually nonexistent. "We really see that our methods and means are different from the Orient," argued American Brotherhood leader al Noman in his Kansas City lecture. "We did not take or borrow a method or a means from the Orient unless it was compatible with the reality of the Islamic Movement over here."[36] Like their European counterparts, American-based organizations that trace their origins to the Brotherhood have evolved independently, sharing the movement's general philosophy and interpretation of Islam, but adapting them to their new environment.

The Philadelphia Meeting and the Birth of CAIR

In his 1991 memorandum, Akram theorized that "the success of the Movement in America in establishing an observant Islamic base with power and effectiveness will be the best support and aid to the global Movement project."[37] The statement seems to confirm what al Qaradawi had written the year before in *Priorities*: that the Islamic Movement should take advantage of its position in the West to influence policies and public debates in those "societies that affect world politics"and that the presence of a strong and organized Islamist movement in the West is "required for defending the causes of the Muslim Nation and the Muslim Land against the antagonism and misinformation of anti-Islamic forces and trends."[38] Akram fully understood that no other Western country was more important to influence than America, given its deep involvement in the Muslim world.

Given the abundance of relevant original sources released during the HLF trial, the Brotherhood's organized attempt to influence American policy makers and public debate on the Palestinian issue is particularly revealing. In the months following the 1987 formation of Hamas, the self-proclaimed Palestinian branch of the Brotherhood, other branches and offshoots throughout the world acted to assist the newly formed organization.[39] According to documents released in the trial, in 1988 the head of the Palestine Section of the Muslim Brotherhood in the Middle East traveled to the United States, where he met with fellow Muslim Brothers to seek their support.[40] The result of the meeting was the formation of the Palestine Committee of the Muslim Brotherhood in America, a subgroup of the American Brotherhood made up mostly of members of Palestinian origin.

Reflecting the traditional pyramidal structure of Brotherhood organizations, the committee was composed of three U.S.-based organizations that had been set up to aid the Islamic movement in Palestine: the general-purpose Islamic Association for Palestine (IAP), the financial arm represented by the Occupied Land Fund (which later became the Holy Land Foundation), and the United Association for Studies and Research (UASR), a think tank on whose board Akram sat. The committee was headed by Musa Abu Marzook, a native of the Gaza Strip who had obtained his doctorate in industrial engineering in Louisiana and currently serves as the deputy chairman of the Damascus-based political bureau of Hamas.

An October 1992 internal memorandum clearly explained the Brotherhood's vision of the Israeli-Palestinian conflict:

Palestine is the one for which Muslim Brotherhood prepared armies—made up from the children of Islam in the Arab and Islamic nations to liberate its land from the abomination and the defilement of the children of the Jews and they watered its pure soil with their honorable blood which sprouted into a jihad that is continuing until the Day of Resurrection and provided a zeal without relenting making the slogan of its children "it is a Jihad for victory or martyrdom."[41]

The document also called on the committee to "increase the financial and the moral support for Hamas," to "fight surrendering solutions," and to publicize and focus on "the savagery of the Jews." Since Hamas had not yet been designated as a terrorist organization by the U.S. government, an action that would be taken in 1995, the committee and its organizations operated legally within the country, fund-raising and propagandizing for Hamas. Things began to change in August 1993, when PLO leader Yasser Arafat and Israeli Prime Minister Yitzhak Rabin signed the Oslo Peace Accords. The Palestine Committee went into fibrillation, strongly opposing the peace treaty and also fearing that Hamas could soon become the target of U.S. actions.

FBI officials, who had been keeping close tabs on members of the committee, began to monitor alarmed conversations.[42] Realizing the huge repercussions that the Oslo agreement could have had not only on the Israeli-Palestinian conflict but also on their activities inside the United States, the members decided to convene an extraordinary three-day meeting in Philadelphia. Held at a Marriott hotel near the city's airport, the closed-door meeting was attended by some twenty top leaders of the Hamas support network in the United States. Unbeknownst to the participants, the FBI had placed wiretaps inside the hotel, taping most of the conversations that took place behind the doors of the conference room. The transcripts of many conversations were introduced as evidence during the HLF trial.[43]

Attending the meeting were representatives of the three organizations making up the Palestine Committee. Following a common pattern, most were united by blood ties and lived in tightly knit communities in the three American cities that have traditionally hosted the largest clusters of Hamas supporters: Chicago, Dallas, and Washington, D.C. The IAP was represented by its president, Omar Ahmed; its director of public relations, Nihad Awad; and the head of its Washington office, Akram Kharroubi, who would later become HLF's representative in Ramallah. HLF founder and president Shukri Abu Baker, whose brother Jamal was the head of Hamas in Sudan and later in Yemen, and Dallas-based treasurer Ghassan Elashi, whose cousin is married to Marzook, also attended.[44]

The meeting, which was organized with formalities resembling a board meeting of a large corporation, opened with instructions regarding security, as participants were urged to refer to Hamas as "Samah"—its name spelled backward—or simply as "the movement" throughout the meeting and in phone conversations.[45] Then the participants began condemning the Oslo Accords, which Omar Ahmed called a treaty "between infidels and infidels."[46] Formulating a common position against the accords was not difficult, and the participants discussed ways to undermine them. Fully aware of the environment in which they operated, some stressed the necessity to frame their opposition to the peace treaty in terms that would appeal to Americans.

"It does not benefit me to show to the American people that . . . I am against the accord because I hate Abou Ammar [Yasser Arafat] and hate the [Palestinian Liberation] Organization," argued Shukri Abu Baker. Instead of "attack[ing] the [Palestinian Liberation] Organization in a personal and direct manner," the Palestine Committee and its offshoots should speak about "democracy and freedom of expression," concepts that are dear to most Americans.[47] "Make people view the [Palestinian National] Authority as collaborators," agreed Omar Ahmed, "an Authority which doesn't care for people's interests and the interest of the national rights and the people."[48] Another unidentified speaker further elaborated that the committee members should be "playing a very important tune to the average American which is the issue of democracy, the issue of representation. When you tell an American individual that, '. . . this person is not elected. He is an oppressor . . . This is a dictatorial regime' . . . Bring up Saddam Hussein's name."[49]

The participants also discussed the future of their activities, aware they could no longer openly state their support for Hamas. The U.S. government would soon ban the group, and furthermore, publicly siding with an organization that was advocating the rejection of the U.S.-brokered peace and the use of violence would have been public relations suicide. Abu Baker acknowledged that when talking to Americans, members of the cluster "cannot say . . . that I'm Hamas," because "if you're against peace, you're a terrorist."[50] Another participant said that the committee "must formulate the position of the Palestinians and the Muslims here in America to support the resistance. . . . That's a problem by itself. In the same time, not falling under the accusations of terrorism and those who harbor terrorism or tend to according to the American [definition] . . . This, really, is a true problem."[51]

The participants argued about how to incite American Muslims to support Hamas and its tactics while maintaining a façade of moderation with American authorities and media. "If you want to [talk to] the Americans, you lose the Muslims," summarized Ahmed; "if you address the Muslims, it means that you cannot reveal your address to the Americans."[52] "If someone asked you if you want to destroy Israel, what are you going to say on TV? If you give an inconclusive response which is like you didn't answer the question, someone will come to you and tell you that you have forsaken your principles."[53]

Faced with two conflicting needs, the participants opted for a two-pronged approach that differentiated between its internal and external strategy. Within the Muslim community, the committee should maintain its support for Hamas undeterred, working to aid the organization. "In the coming stage, the most important thing we can provide," said one speaker, "is to support Jihad in Palestine. I believe it is the only way if we want to bring the goals of the [Oslo peace] accord to fail."[54] Fund-raising among local Muslim communities was immediately identified as one of the key activities the group should engage in. The newly created Holy Land Foundation was to collect funds for Hamas while giving the impression that it was sending them to orphans and needy children. "We give the Islamists $100,000 and we give others $5,000," stated Abu Baker, outlining how the HLF could maintain the semblance of being a charitable organization and avoid scrutiny from authorities. HLF needed to "maintain a balance," avoid-

ing attracting attention while "stay[ing] on its legal track as far as charitable projects are concerned without going after a sentiment which could
harm the Foundation legally."[55] In the trial, U.S. authorities would argue
that using these expedients, HLF officials collected and funneled more than
$12 million to Hamas until the charity was shut down in December 2001.[56]

At the same time, meeting participants decided, the committee should
make an extensive effort to educate the American Muslim community,
convincing them that the peace accords harmed the Palestinians and that
Hamas was the only force worth supporting. Several participants argued
that the committee should be particularly active in spreading this message
among the youth. "We don't want the children of the [American Muslim]
community who are raised here in schools and in Islamic schools and
non-Islamic schools to grow up surrendering to the issue of peace with
Jews," stated one unidentified speaker. "I mean, we don't see in ten years the
growing generation in America surrendering to peace with Jews. Therefore,
there must be curricula and teaching materials which spread in Islamic
schools and in weekend schools."[57] Another speaker said that the committee should use the annual conferences and the network of Islamic schools
run by affiliated organizations such as the MAS, the ISNA, and the ICNA
to disseminate books and introduce speakers who could raise awareness of
the need to support Hamas.

While the internal strategy of the committee aimed at mobilizing the
American Muslim community to support Hamas, meeting participants
understood that they could also play an important role by influencing
American public opinion and policy makers. Ahmed, in particular, stressed
the need to increase the committee's "influence with Congress." "This can
be achieved by infiltrating the American media outlets, universities and research centers." He continued, "It is also achieved by working with Islamic
political organizations and the sympathetic ones such as . . . the American
Muslim Alliance, such as the United Muslims of America, MPAC [Mus-
lim Public Affairs Council] . . . if Muslims engage in political activism in
America and started to be concerned with Congress and public relations
we will have an entry point to use them to pressure Congress and the deci-
sion-makers in America."[58]

The development of a carefully crafted media strategy, defending Hamas
without giving the impression of supporting violence, was deemed one
of the most important aspects of the committee's public relations cam-

paign. Ahmed spoke of "broadcasting the Islamic point of view in U.S. media," adding that "when Nihad appeared on CNN and talked in the way he spoke, this greatly reduces the severity of allegations of radicalism."[59] Ahmed's statement referred to the appearance, a few weeks earlier, of IAP public relations director Nihad Awad on *CNN Crossfire*, when he advanced Hamas' point of view with words that were palatable to the American public.[60] In the meeting, the media-savvy Awad followed up Ahmed's words with a presentation on the media strategy, stressing the importance of "training and qualifying individuals in the branches and the communities on media activism through holding special courses on media," and of writing op-eds in prominent American newspapers.[61] This plan has long been followed by U.S.-based Hamas activists upon their return to the Middle East. Former U.S. Palestine Committee head Musa Abu Marzook and former UASR director Ahmed Yousef, currently senior political adviser to Palestinian Prime Minister Ismail Haniya, have published several editorials in prominent American newspapers such as *The Washington Post*, *The New York Times*, and the *Los Angeles Times*, using tones that are quite different from those used in Arabic.[62]

Discussions at the meeting made clear that participants fully understood that when dealing with the general public and policy makers, they needed to take a more nuanced position. "We can't, as an American organization, say we represent Samah [Hamas spelled backward]," explained Omar Ahmed. "Can we go to the Congressman and tell him," he asked sarcastically, "'I am Omar Yehya [Ahmed], Chairman of the Union [IAP], Yassir Arafat doesn't represent me, but [Hamas spiritual leader Sheik] Ahmad Yasin does'?" Other participants agreed that dissimulating the committee's real aims and feelings when dealing with Americans was a necessary tactic. "I swear by Allah that war is deception," said Abu Baker. "We are fighting our enemy with a kind heart. . . . Deceive, camouflage, pretend that you're leaving while you're walking that way. Deceive your enemy." "I agree with you, politics is a completion of war," said Ahmed, displaying a remarkable knowledge of Clausewitz. Ahmed further elaborated on Baker's position, comparing the deception the group was to use with the head fake used by basketball players: "He makes a player believe that he is doing this while he does something else."[63]

Other participants heeded the calls for dissimulation. One argued: "In my opinion, we must form a new organization for activism which will be neutral because we are placed in a corner, we are placed in a corner. It is known who we are, we are marked and I believe that there should be a new neutral organization which works on both sides."[64] Another unidentified speaker agreed, highlighting the need for a new organization to be "an official U.S. cover representing the Islamic community" and also a "cover for the existing organizations in case they got dissolved."[65] Abu Baker stated that the group "should start right now . . . begin thinking about establishing alternative organizations . . . whose Islamic hue is not very conspicuous."[66]

Abu Baker, worried about impending U.S. actions against Hamas and its support network inside the country, emphasized the need to camouflage the identity of the new organization the participants had decided to create. "Let's not hoist a large Islamic flag and let's not be barbaric-talking. We will remain a front so that if the thing [the U.S. government ban on Hamas] happens, we will benefit from the new happenings instead of having all of our organizations classified and exposed." "I was telling our brother Aboul Hassan [Abdelhaleem Ashqar] about Al Aqsa Organization," he added, stressing the need to avoid Arabic names that could intimidate the public. "Why Al Aqsa Educational? When you go to Oxford they will ask you: 'Sir, what is Aqsa?' Make it the 'Palestinian General Education Academy.' Make yourself a big name like that and give it a media twinkle and there is no need for Al Aqsa, Al Quds, Al Sakhra and all that stuff."[67]

In order to be able to continue their activities in the United States, the participants agreed that a new organization with no evident ties to Hamas and operating in ways that would make it appear moderate should be founded. The amended bylaws of the Palestine Committee, drafted in 1991, had already expressed the wish to establish one additional organization in the future. "It is hoped that it will become an official organization for political work and its headquarters will be in Washington, God's willing. . . . It represents the political aspect to support the cause politically on the American front."[68]

Basing their judgment on ample evidence, U.S. authorities have publicly stated they believe that organization to be the Council on American Islamic Relations (CAIR), which was founded in Washington, D.C. a few months after the Philadelphia meeting.[69] In fact, IAP president Omar Ahmed and public relations director Nihad Awad, both members of the Palestine Committee who had attended the Philadelphia meeting, became, respectively, CAIR's chairman emeritus and executive director. Rafeeq Jabar, who had been IAP president, also became a founding director of CAIR, while for-mer IAP employee Ibrahim Hooper became CAIR's director of commu-nications.[70] Ghassan Elashi, the treasurer of the Holy Land Foundation, became the founding board member of CAIR's Texas chapter, and, as evidence introduced in the Dallas trial showed, the HLF also transferred funds to CAIR for "consulting services."[71] Finally, a July 1994 internal mem-orandum of the Palestine Committee recognized CAIR, together with IAP, UASR, and HLF, as a part of the committee.[72]

Within a few years of its founding, CAIR achieved remarkable successes. It currently employs some seventy full-time staffers in its large headquar-ters located three blocks from Capitol Hill, has thirty offices in nineteen states, and dubs itself the country's largest civil rights organization, whose stated mission is to "enhance understanding of Islam, encourage dialogue, protect civil liberties, empower American Muslims, and build coalitions that promote justice and mutual understanding."[73] Thanks to a combina-tion of unrelenting activism, moderate public façade, and abundant for-eign funding, CAIR soon became the de facto representative of the Ameri-can Muslim community, regularly contacted by media and policy makers on any issue related to Islam.

Omar Ahmed boasted in a 1999 interview in a Saudi magazine:

CAIR has become a center of information for the highest ranking of-ficials in the US. For example, if the American President wants to meet one of the Muslims in Phoenix, Arizona, it is CAIR that gives the White House a list of some of the names in that city. This has happened sev-eral times. In other cases, we were contacted by the Presidential Advisory Board on Equity and Diversity to invite us to break the Ramadan fast meals in the White House. We are the ones who invite those whom we see fit to represent the Muslims in this invitation.[74]

Although this claim may have been partly motivated by his desire to boost the credentials of his organization in the eyes of potential donors, facts back Ahmed's assertion that CAIR soon became the most important rep-resentative of the Muslim community when dealing with the American government. Its officials have traditionally enjoyed unparalleled access to the White House, the State Department, Congress, and the Department of Justice. CAIR has also been the only Muslim organization to offer training on Islam to all sorts of public institutions, from the FBI to the Transportation Security Administration, the Department of Homeland Security, and the Marine Corps. From the White House all the way down to law enforcement agencies at the local level, CAIR has successfully portrayed itself as a moderate and mainstream Muslim organization with which the government should partner.

Similarly, other organizations belonging to the U.S. Brotherhood's network, many of them specifically mentioned as member organizations in Akram's memorandum, have become mainstream and fully embraced by America's political, religious, and cultural establishment. They regularly appear on television as spokesmen for the American Muslim community and brief members of Congress and their staffers. They lecture at America's most prestigious universities and attend high-profile interfaith meetings, warning about Islamophobia and preaching tolerance and dialogue. They form partnerships with all sorts of organizations, from the American Civil Liberties Union to conservative Christian groups, from Jewish organizations to the antiwar movement.

Despite this widespread acceptance, several prominent voices inside and outside the U.S. government have repeatedly expressed criticism of CAIR and other American-based New Western Brotherhood organizations. The differing opinions lead to a status quo that can only be described as schizophrenic. Congressman John D. Dingell, for example, has publicly praised the group, saying, "CAIR and I have a long history of cooperation and my office door is always open to my friends so that I can be of assistance to the causes that CAIR promotes."[75] Senator Richard Durbin, in contrast, has called CAIR "unusual in its extreme rhetoric and its association with groups that are suspect."[76] While Congressman Bob Filner has said that "far too often, the remarkable work and achievements of organizations such as CAIR are overlooked," Senator Chuck Schumer has condemned the group for its "ties to terrorism" and "intimate connections with Hamas."[77]

These statements beget the question: How is it possible that four congressmen, all of them Democrats and all of them privy to the same information, could reach such diametrically opposing conclusions on CAIR's nature and aims? The answer is not easy to find, and the issue is hardly limited to Democratic congressmen or to CAIR. Both sides of the political spectrum and virtually all departments and agencies of the federal government have been unable to reach a consistent assessment of the nature of

CAIR and all other Brotherhood-linked organizations in the United States, creating confusing and sometimes embarrassing situations.

A recent mishap at the Department of Justice perfectly exemplifies the problem. In the beginning of August 2007, federal prosecutors trying the case against the Holy Land Foundation listed the ISNA as an unindicted coconspirator, introducing evidence about its ample ties to the Muslim Brotherhood (including Akram's memorandum, which listed the ISNA as the first Brotherhood organization in the country). At exactly the same time, the department's Civil Rights Division invited a top ISNA official to a high-profile speech by then-Attorney General Alberto Gonzales in Washington and, a few days later, cosponsored ISNA's annual conference in Chicago, sending representatives to staff a booth.[78]

The two actions denote a staggering lack of cohesive strategy.[79] Designating the ISNA as an unindicted coconspirator makes the effort of the civil rights division to reach out to the organization highly unlikely to succeed. By the same token, legitimizing ISNA by cosponsoring one of its events while another section of the department is trying to link the organization to the largest terrorism financing case in America's history severely undermines the prosecution's argument.[80] What *is* the Department of Justice's position on the ISNA? Does it consider it part of a U.S.-based Muslim Brotherhood network engaged in a "Civilization-Jihadist Process" and an integral part of a sophisticated terrorism financing ring? Or does it consider it a legitimate and moderate Muslim organization, to which it should reach out and which it has no qualms publicly endorsing?

The Counterterrorism Conundrum

Inconsistencies in assessing and engaging New Western Brotherhood organizations are common to virtually all American governmental institutions. It is particularly interesting to examine the difficulties the FBI has experienced. Before and after 9/11, the FBI conducted several investigations against individual members of the U.S. Brotherhood network, collecting an abundance of information only partly exemplified by the hundreds of documents introduced as evidence in the HLF trial. Based on this information, many top FBI officials have publicly stated their negative assessment of CAIR and other affiliated organizations. Among the most vocal, Steven

Pomerantz, former Assistant Director and former Chief of the Counterterrorism Section of the FBI, has publicly stated:

> It is clear from a review of CAIR's statements and activities that one of
> its goals is to further the agenda of radical Islamic terrorist groups by
> providing political support. By masquerading as a mainstream public
> affairs organization, CAIR has taken the lead in trying to mislead the
> public about the terrorist underpinnings of militant Islamic movements,
> in particular, Hamas. . . . Unfortunately, CAIR is but one of a new gen-
> eration of new groups in the United States that hide under a veneer of
> "civil rights" or "academic" status but in fact are tethered to a platform
> that supports terrorism. The degree to which these groups are able to de-
> ceive the American public and intimidate writers and counter-terrorist
> officials will be a significant ingredient in whether this country will be
> rendered more vulnerable to terrorism in future years.[81]

This assessment outlined in 1998 and the many investigations into the
activities of New Western Brotherhood organizations do not square with
the close relationship established by the FBI after 9/11. Since 2001, CAIR has
been engaged by the FBI as one of its most important partners in the Muslim
community and given preferential treatment. Aside from regular meetings,
which the Bureau has held with all sorts of Muslim organizations, CAIR officials have often conducted private sensitivity training sessions on Islam for
FBI field offices, and FBI officials have attended CAIR fund-raising events
to express their appreciation. While several field offices have conducted investigations targeting CAIR officials and affiliated organizations, FBI officials have at the same time publicly thanked CAIR for its role in "keep[ing]
the nation safe" and praised its "commitment to maintaining a dialogue
leading to the frank and honest exchange of ideas."[82] The inconsistencies in
the FBI's assessment and behavior are the consequence of a combination
of factors that operate concurrently but need to be examined separately.[83]

Optimistic Point of View

Like virtually any other Western institution dealing with New Western
Brotherhood organizations, the FBI comprises people who, like Pomerantz,

harbor very negative views of the movement and others who subscribe to the optimist point of view. Given the lack of centralized assessment and engagement policy, the actions of various sections and field offices have been influenced by the positions their leaders hold. The counterterrorism section of the Bureau's Washington field office, for example, was led from 2002 to 2005 by now retired Special Agent Michael Rolince, who has been a strong defender of CAIR and affiliated organizations. "'Of all the groups, there is probably more suspicion about CAIR, but when you ask people for cold hard facts, you get blank stares," said Rolince to *The New York Times* in March 2007, months before the HLF documents were made public.[84] It is probably not a coincidence that the Washington field office sent CAIR a commendation letter praising its "dedication in representing the heart of the Muslim American community."[85]

Knowledge/Access to Information

Even though, as the HLF trial showed, the FBI has gathered an impressive amount of intelligence on organizations of the U.S. Brotherhood network, that information has not been disseminated within the Bureau for a long time. Many FBI agents, analysts, and, most important, managers who have not worked directly on Brotherhood-related cases have been unaware of the subject of the Philadelphia meeting, Akram's memorandum, or other pieces of information about the network's activities and agenda. No central directive instructed the thousands of FBI officials, who have traditionally focused on hard crime and terrorism and for the most part have little knowledge of the nuances of Islam and Islamism, how to assess and engage Brotherhood-derived organizations, whose ambiguous nature is difficult to decipher.

In some cases this lack of centralized cohesive strategy has generated uninformed decisions that many FBI officials privately criticize. Interviewed for this book a few months after the HLF documents were made public, a senior FBI official in charge of counterterrorism at the field office of a major metropolitan center stated he had "heard about them" but never actually seen them. After reading some, he stated that he'd had "no idea whatsoever" that CAIR had that history and in all likelihood, he would have not reached out to the organization had he known.[86]

Condemnation of Terrorism

Before 9/11, U.S. organizations tracing their origins to the Brotherhood kept an ambiguous position toward various Islamist groups involved in what the U.S. government considers terrorism. While condemning acts of violence in general terms, they regularly praised the actions of Hamas and Hezbollah and occasionally also endorsed positions and organizations that U.S. authorities would consider more radical. An editorial in the March/April 1996 issue of *Islamic Horizons*, the ISNA's official publication, for example, read: "Muslim children need to know and honor not only those martyrs who are laying down their lives in Algeria, Bosnia, Chechenya [*sic*], Kashmir, Palestine, and Mindanao, but also those who are sacrificing their livelihoods to establish the rule of Allah in lands now held hostage to the whims of despots."[87] In July 1999, almost a year after al Qaeda had destroyed two American embassies in East Africa, *al-Talib*, a newspaper published by the MSA at the University of California–Los Angeles, referred to Osama bin Laden as a "great Mujahid (someone who struggles in Allah's cause)," instructed readers to "defend our brother" Osama bin Laden, and "refer to him as a freedom fighter, someone who has forsaken wealth and power to fight in Allah's cause and speak out against oppressors."[88]

Yet, immediately after 9/11, CAIR, ISNA, and other affiliated organizations engaged in a consistent and very public condemnation of terrorism and, in particular, the actions of al Qaeda. Five days after the attacks CAIR took out a full-page advertisement in *The Washington Post* to condemn the attacks.[89] CAIR also started the "Not In The Name Of Islam" initiative, an online petition to denounce acts of terror that reportedly has been signed by almost 700,000 people.[90] The Fiqh Council of North America, the network's jurisprudential body, has issued a widely publicized *fatwa* condemning terrorism and even decreed it is legitimate for American Muslims to fight in the U.S. army in Afghanistan.[91] ISNA officials have repeatedly stated that Muslims have a responsibility to condemn "political violence committed in the name of Islam" and lately even included Hamas and Hezbollah among the groups whose actions should not be accepted.[92] Virtually all the organizations of the cluster have declared their desire to help authorities in any possible way to prevent terrorist attacks and defeat radicalization inside the American Muslim community.

Critics have argued that these statements are little more than posturing, clever tactical moves dictated by an understanding of the post–9/11 environment. With the FBI and the rest of the U.S. government in overdrive to hunt down terrorists, they say, the New American Brothers had two options: be seen as either part of the problem or part of the solution. By presenting themselves as the latter, a moderate force that might disagree with U.S. foreign policies but fully rejects terrorism, they could strengthen their position, increase their access to the government and the rest of the American establishment, and consequently become the de facto representatives of the American Muslim community.

Critics point to several inconsistencies in the New American Brothers' stance as proof of their suspicions. In some cases, individuals linked to the network who had publicly condemned terrorism when speaking in America have been caught peddling a very different line in private or in the Middle East. The case of Abdurahman Alamoudi, the AMC leader who is currently serving a twenty-three-year sentence for his participation in an al Qaeda plot, is unique in its drama but not isolated. Critics take the case of Salah Sultan as another example of the duplicitous nature of the New American Brothers. A Columbus, Ohio resident, Sultan is a member of the board of trustees of the MAS, a member of the European Council for Fatwa and Research, and a signatory of the Fiqh Council of North America's *fatwa* condemning terrorism.[93] In May 2006, less than a year after signing the *fatwa*, Sultan appeared on Risala, a Saudi TV station, and, speaking in Arabic, argued that he did not believe al Qaeda was behind 9/11. "The entire thing was of a large scale and was planned within the U.S.," he claimed, "in order to enable the U.S. to control and terrorize the entire world, and to get American society to agree to the war declared on terrorism—the definition of which has not yet been determined."[94]

Although cases like those of Alamoudi and Sultan represent the most visible manifestations of the New American Brothers' duplicitous position of terrorism, they are not the only cases. Moreover, according to pessimists, their systematic condemnation of virtually all actions taken by law enforcement agencies since 9/11 constitutes not only an additional proof of their true colors but also an obstacle to counterterrorism efforts. CAIR in particular has been consistent in downplaying the legitimacy of arrests of al Qaeda operatives inside the country, attributing the government's actions to discrimination, sloppy police work, and a "general policy of targeting Muslims because they are Muslims."[95] In several cases, particularly when counterterrorism actions targeted U.S.-based individuals and entities linked to Hamas, CAIR officials suggested that the U.S. government was not engaged in a "war on terror" but rather a "war on Islam." Many would argue that this characterization could potentially have a devastating impact on the feelings of Muslims in America and worldwide.[96]

Though probably displeased by these statements, FBI officials, particularly in the upper management, cannot overlook the importance of public condemnations of al Qaeda coming from American Muslim leaders. "CAIR might condemn terrorism for self-serving purposes, in order to get acceptance by the FBI, the government and the media, but it is still better than nothing," argues a former senior FBI official. "Imagine if after 9/11 it had said nothing," he adds, "or, even worse, if it had supported al Qaeda."[97] Whether tactical or heartfelt, public condemnations of terrorism are extremely helpful to the FBI, whose institutional mandate of preventing terrorist attacks is unquestionably aided by the New American Brothers' calls to American Muslims to reject violence.

Satisfacing

In order to understand the FBI's close relationship with CAIR and affiliated groups it is necessary to comprehend the situation in which the Bureau found itself immediately after 9/11. In the wake of the attacks, the FBI drastically shifted most of its attention and resources to finding individuals and terrorist cells hidden among a community of which the Bureau knew close to nothing. As had happened when it had focused on the Italian mafia, the FBI slowly sought to build knowledge on and develop sources within a community (ethnic in case of the Italian community, religious in the case of the Muslim community) that it aimed to partner with rather than alienate. Aggressive law enforcement operations became a trademark of the post–9/11 FBI, but a partnership with the community, built on the common interests of preventing acts of terror as well as potential backlash and discrimination against Muslims, was also deemed to be a necessary tool of a comprehensive counterterrorism strategy.[98]

Yet, from the very beginning, besides experiencing enormous difficulties in building a broad institutional knowledge on even the most basic tenets of both Islam and Islamism, the FBI faced severe challenges in gaining the trust of the Muslim community. Like most Muslim immigrants in Europe, many American Muslims come originally from countries where law enforcement and intelligence agencies are corrupt, ruthless, and deeply distrusted by the local population. These experiences have left many with an almost indelible fear of any intelligence agency, making cooperation between Western security services and local Muslim communities extremely challenging. The FBI, in particular, is also perceived among some segments of the American Muslim community as an almost almighty and all-knowing entity whose sole goal is to "get Muslims." This reputation, generated more by a combination of Hollywood movies and urban legends rather than by direct knowledge of the Bureau's capabilities and aims, created an additional challenge to its outreach effort.

The only possible solution for the FBI was to find leaders in the Muslim community who could help. The task proved difficult. Affluent, well integrated, and living scattered throughout a huge country, the vast majority of American Muslims do not belong to any religious organization or are simply engaged in local mosque associations. With few exceptions, the only groups that have a national profile, capable of operating offices in Washington and branches throughout the country, tend to be those belonging to the New American Brotherhood. Given the absence of "embassy Islam" in the country, only the New Brothers have had the means and motivations to create high-profile, nationwide organizations. Despite very low membership numbers—CAIR declared in 2006 that it had fewer than 1,700 members, though it had claimed more in the past—and the fact that the members do not represent large sections of the American Muslim population (such as Iranians and African Americans), they are the next best thing to a representative of the American Muslim community, possessing at least the structure to make such claim.[99]

While acknowledging these limits, the FBI leadership consciously decided that, at least in the short term, engaging with CAIR and affiliated organizations was the only alternative to an almost complete lack of contacts with the Muslim community. "I think the community looks upon the major groups—whether it's ISNA, the Islamic Society in North America, MPAC, the Muslim Public Affairs Council, or any other of the other groups, AADC

[American-Arab Anti-discrimination Committee]—as trusted agents,"
stated FBI Public Affairs Assistant Director John Miller in a 2007 interview
with National Public Radio. "And the fact that they talk to us and we talk to
them certainly brings the FBI into a better light in the community, where,
I think, to start this conversation, we have to admit that there is [a] good
degree of suspicion and discomfort."[100] Despite a heated internal debate
within the Bureau over the issue, the FBI's upper management decided that
the partnership was valuable to its counterterrorism strategy. "We now have
partners in the Arab-American and Muslim communities," added Miller in
congressional testimony. "Some have become publicly declared allies in our
efforts to condemn terrorism. They have become our bridge to many who
viewed the FBI with either contempt, or worse, fear."[101]

New American Brotherhood organizations seized the opportunity and
presented themselves as the ideal partners the government was looking
for. "American Muslims can be of great help in fighting terrorism and extremism, and in bridging the deepening divide between the United States
and the Muslim world," argues Louay Safi. "American Muslims have deep
understanding of both Muslim and American cultures, and are well-
positioned to help reconcile Islam and the West."[102] Safi's argument appeals
immensely to American officials, who have been desperately trying to project a positive image of their country to Muslims in America and throughout the world. But Safi, who has served as research director for IIIT, executive director of ISNA's Leadership Development Center, and president
of the Association of Muslim Social Scientists, also knows that not all
American Muslims belong to an organizational apparatus that could make
them viable candidates for structural partners of the U.S. government, a
competition in which the New American Brothers have an enormous
advantage.[103]

Since no formal guidelines were issued by FBI headquarters, each of the
fifty-six field offices had ample latitude in how to engage the local Muslim community.[104] In some cases, field offices reached out to a very wide
range of interlocutors, which included New Brotherhood organizations
but also many other voices, from mosque leaders to representatives of various ethnic communities. Other field offices relied more extensively on the
established New Brotherhood groups. A similar policy was followed, for
the most part, at the national level, where only New Western Brotherhood
organizations have an extensive structure.

Institutional Mandate

Arguably one of the most important factors determining the FBI's decision to establish close relations with New American Brotherhood organizations is its institutional mandate. As the Attorney General's Guidelines for the FBI clearly state, the agency's core mission is to investigate violations of federal law, use all possible means within the law to prevent terrorist attacks, and gather intelligence on potential terrorist activities.[105] Unlike many European intelligence agencies, the FBI therefore focuses solely on violent extremism and activities that could lead to a criminal act. The activities of Brotherhood-linked networks, which do not aim at using violence inside the United States, do not fall within this very narrowly defined mandate. The Bureau might investigate if they suspect the network of collecting funds for a designated terrorist entity, as in the case of the HLF, or if its members are engaged in other criminal activities, as in the case of Alamoudi. But in general, the Brothers, not posing a direct security threat to the United States, are not an immediate target.[106]

Moreover, as various governmental inquiries have highlighted, the FBI currently lacks the analytical capabilities to produce wide-ranging strategic assessments on national security matters.[107] Although it employs hundreds of analysts of excellent quality, the FBI is, by nature and tradition, mostly a "guns and cars" institution, focused on arresting criminals and terrorists rather than looking at long-term trends and potential threats of more a oblique and political nature. This became evident at a Senate hearing convened in September 2007 to discuss the government's engagement of CAIR and ISNA after their designation as unindicted coconspirators and the release of the HLF documents. Basing his analysis on those documents, a few days before the hearing Pentagon Joint Staff Analyst Stephen Coughlin had penned and circulated within government circles an official memorandum on the HLF trial that categorized the organizations involved as "threat entities" engaged in domestic subversion. Coughlin, whose report caused a heated controversy, also warned that outreach to these organizations "can cause those responsible for its success to so narrowly focus on the outreach relationship that they miss the surrounding events and lose perspective."[108]

Addressing the issue before the senatorial panel, FBI Director Robert Mueller stated that, in substance, the Bureau is not involved in a war of ideas and that outreach to groups such as CAIR is a useful part of its counterterrorism strategy. Asked whether the FBI has a responsibility to consider the ideological background of some of the organizations it engages and the consequences of partnering with them, he said: "I would say no, that it would not be our responsibility for [dealing with groups from] any religion to engage in the war of ideas." The FBI must rather "explain that once one goes over the line and it becomes not a war of ideas but a criminal offense, this is what you can expect, and . . . elicit the support of those in whatever religious community to assist us in assuring that those who cross that line are appropriately investigated and convicted."[109] Muller made clear that the FBI's priority is to establish ties to the Muslim community in order to gather information on possible terrorist activities. The repercussions of engaging, and therefore legitimizing and empowering, certain organizations over others are largely beyond the Bureau's institutional mandate.

The FBI's narrow focus on terrorism is, for the most part, a consequence of its own past. Throughout the 1950s and 1960s, it employed extremely aggressive tactics, often skirting the law, to monitor and contrast various movements that were deemed "anti-American," from Communist (or perceived Communist) organizations to African American activists, including Martin Luther King Jr. In the following decades various congressional task forces, including the famous Church Committee, investigated the FBI's excesses and various legislative acts were passed to limit the Bureau's ability to monitor "subversive" groups. As a consequence, today's FBI is bound by severe legal limitations and an institutional culture that prevent it from focusing on anything beyond criminal acts and direct threats to national security. Additionally, in the case of Brotherhood networks, any assessment of their ideology necessitates a stance on extremely sensitive issues of religion and ethnic minorities, a political minefield the FBI seeks to avoid.

Personal Goals

As in any other institution, most FBI employees tend to adopt behaviors that, while fulfilling the organization's goals, also maximize their chances of advancing their position within it. Traditionally focused on building criminal cases, the FBI tends to evaluate the performance of its agents on the number of arrests and convictions obtained. As the HLF trial showed, several successful cases against Brotherhood-linked organizations have been built by the FBI since 9/11. But agents know that they are more likely to advance by pursuing investigations on other matters that pose a more immediate threat to national security, require less complex and time-consuming investigative work, and are less politically sensitive. In an organization whose weltanschauung is based on obtaining convictions and staying away from thorny ideological issues, investigating Brotherhood networks is hardly a recipe for fast career advancement. In the words of a former FBI agent, "investigating jihadists gets you a promotion, investigating Brothers gets you a headache."[110]

The priorities of managers involved in outreach are quite different. Officers in charge of establishing relationships with the Muslim community or any other ethnic or religious group are often evaluated on the basis of the number of meetings they set up every year. Engagement partners are screened, but the outreach officers have several bureaucratic incentives to keep their pool of potential invitees as large as possible. The term "satisficing" perfectly captures the reality in which outreach officers, once they have established that their invitees are not criminals or terrorists, have little interest in asking deeper questions about their organization's nature and the long-term repercussions of the engagement efforts. The tension between the Department of Justice's Civil Rights Division and its Counterterrorism Section after the designation of CAIR and ISNA as unindicted coconspirators in the HLF trial is a quintessential example of this phenomenon.[111] Very similar dynamics are at work within the FBI.

Changes?

In November 2008, a Dallas jury found all defendants in the HLF trial guilty of providing material support to a designated foreign terrorist organization, and a federal judge later imposed stiff sentences—including a sixty-five-year prison term for Shukri Abu Baker and Ghassan Elashi.[112] But the impact of the trial was much wider. In the fall of 2008, the FBI formally cut its ties to CAIR, sending a communication to all its field offices urging them to stop all meetings with chapters of the organization "until certain issues are addressed by CAIR's national headquarters."[113] In a letter sent to various congressmen, the Bureau specifically mentioned the evidence in the HLF trial as the reason for its decision, stating that until "we can resolve whether there continues to be a connection between CAIR or its executives and HAMAS, the FBI does not view CAIR as an appropriate liaison partner."[114] The move received the public support of some congressmen, who argued that the FBI's decision should become governmentwide policy.[115] Organizations linked to CAIR reacted strongly, accusing the FBI of "McCarthy-era tactics" and threatening to suspend their relations with the Bureau.[116] ISNA issued a press release stating that the decision to sever ties to CAIR, which it described as its "respected sister organization," could lead to "the marginalization of mainstream Muslim organizations."[117] Doubts remain as to why the FBI, which had been in possession of the information presented at the HLF trial since the mid-1990s, decided to act only after the trial and sentencing were over. Whether the decision will be permanent and signifies a shift in U.S. government policies toward New Western Brotherhood organizations is hard to tell. The United States, partly because of the sheer size of its bureaucratic apparatus, has adopted some of the most erratic assessment and engagement strategies, ranging from enthusiastic partnerships to aggressive law enforcement pursuit of Brotherhood leaders. It is difficult to predict which direction each of its many branches will lean in the future.

Arguably equally difficult to assess is the evolution of New American Brotherhood organizations. In the 1990s, leaders of the network openly expressed positions similar to those outlined by Akram. "Ultimately we can never be full citizens of this country," stated Ihsan Bagby, director of ISNA's Tarbiyah department and member of CAIR's National Board of Directors, "because there is no way we can be fully committed to the institutions of this country. We can be citizens in the sense that we try to influence American policy."[118]

The positions publicly espoused today by leaders of the same organizations are completely different. While striving to maintain a strong Islamic identity among American Muslims, they openly speak of Americanization of Islam and the need for Muslims to be active and loyal citizens. Organizations linked to the network consistently praise the foundations of the American system, where people of all faiths can freely practice their religion and citizens are treated equally and fairly. U.S.-based New Brotherhood scholars have made major efforts to reconcile Islamic values with the ideals of democracy and pluralism and pledge full allegiance to America.[119]

This change in rhetoric triggers the usual debate between optimists and pessimists. It must be noted that a new generation of American-born activists is slowly replacing the foreign-born founders of the network and their views cannot be exactly the same as their predecessors'. It is indeed difficult to think of Ingrid Mattson, the soft-spoken Canadian-born convert who in 2006 became ISNA's first female president, as part of the "Civilization-Jihadist Process" envisioned by Akram almost twenty years ago. At the same time, many of the founding leaders, including those who at the Philadelphia meeting advocated deceiving Americans through fake moderation, are still very much active, and it is premature to rule out the possibility that the network's current rhetoric might be part of that strategy. It is not easy for the U.S. government, as for any of its European counterparts, to assess which of the two positions best captures the current status of the movement.

8

The Brothers and Terrorism

Firefighters or Arsonists?

Since September 11, 2001, security considerations and terrorism have almost inevitably become the prisms through which most issues involving Western Muslim communities have been viewed. During the months following the attacks, policy makers, fearing imminent further attacks, understandably focused on uncovering and dismantling terrorist networks. Yet, over the last few years, and particularly after the attacks in Madrid and London and the arrests of hundreds of European and American Muslims who had been involved in terrorist activities, many governments have understood that simply dismantling terrorist networks without preventing the radicalization of potential new militants is like playing a never-ending game of "whack-a-mole": an exercise in policing can have temporary benefits but does not go to the root of the problem.

In light of these considerations, authorities on both sides of the Atlantic have started thinking about more comprehensive counterterrorism policies. While still devoting large and much needed resources to repression, authorities consider contrasting and preventing radicalization among Muslim communities necessary components of a security strategy aimed at providing results in the long term. Many Western governments have therefore enacted counter-radicalization programs, whose characteristics and complexity vary significantly from country to country. However, all of them consider the active participation of Muslim leaders and organizations a crucial element, necessary to provide legitimacy and appeal to their initiatives.

This idea has been criticized by some commentators. Kenan Malik, for example, has challenged the widespread "belief that Muslims constitute a distinct community with its own views and beliefs" and that only Muslim leaders can successfully engage them in order to defeat extremism.[1] Aside from these criticisms, the search for partners in the security field has been more complicated and controversial than the search for partners in any other endeavor, attracting unprecedented attention from the media and generating intense debates within governments. In particular, policy makers and experts incessantly debate the role that New Western Brotherhood organizations, given their prominence in the Muslim community and ideological proximity to violent extremists, should play in comprehensive counterterrorism strategies. Can nonviolent Islamists be engaged and used as partners against violent radicalization? Can they contrast the appeal of jihadists? In substance, are they part of the problem or the solution?

The Brothers as Firewall?

Many scholars and policy makers, even some who do not embrace the optimist point of view, believe that the Brothers could play a crucial role in undermining the legitimacy and appeal of al Qaeda and other violent Islamist groups among young Muslims in both the Muslim world and the West. Supporters of this position argue that political Islam is a reality whose widespread popularity should be acknowledged.[2] Islamism is today a global ideology that, in its very diverse forms, attracts millions of Muslims. A sensitive analysis, argue supporters of engagement, should distinguish between Islamist groups that engage in violence and those that do not, harnessing the appeal of the latter against the former. Western policy makers might disagree with many of the nonviolent Islamists' positions but should acknowledge that they do not pose a threat to the West. They should take advantage of nonviolent Islamists' condemnation of al Qaeda, establishing various forms of cooperation against a common enemy.

These scholars and analysts believe that the movement can serve as a firewall against al Qaeda-style radicalization.[3] Hypothetically envisioning radicalization as a continuum whose terminal point is defined by the embracing of al Qaeda's worldview and violent tactics, they identify the Brothers as a force that can stop the process halfway. According to an influential 2007 *Foreign Affairs* article by Robert Leiken and Steven Brooke, the Brotherhood "works to dissuade Muslims from violence, instead channeling them into politics and charitable activities."[4] The Brothers do adopt positions that are, in certain cases, extremely antagonistic toward the West and could be labeled "radical." But they do not advocate violence against the West and actively condemn those who do. Western policy makers should be pragmatic and try to exploit this. The fact that Salafists harshly criticize the Brothers and that some jihadist leaders, including Ayman al Zawahiri, have even accused them of apostasy because of their abandonment of jihad and support of democracy is seen by supporters of engagement as additional proof of the common ground that the West can find with the movement.[5]

The Brothers' role as firewall is, according to some scholars, particularly effective because of the legitimacy the movement enjoys at the grassroots level and among the most conservative fringes of the Muslim world. Only the Brothers are in a position to intellectually engage angry young men on the path toward radicalization and sway them from violence. "Muslim 'moderates' can't defeat bin Ladenism since they don't speak to the same audience with the same language and passions," argues former CIA official Reuel Marc Gerecht.[6] Muslim Brotherhood leaders publicly agree. "We're better able to conduct an intellectual confrontation, and not a security confrontation, with the forces of extremism and fanaticism," stated the head of the Islamic Action Front, the Jordanian Brotherhood party, in an interview he gave to Leiken and Brooke.[7]

Although it has never officially been formulated as a policy by any Western government, the idea of forging cooperation with the Brothers has appealed to many policy makers, particularly after 9/11. The hypothetical engagement of nonviolent Islamists in the Muslim world has been difficult, given the opposition of local regimes. Western governments have experienced fewer problems in establishing various forms of security-focused contact with Western-based Brotherhood legacy groups. Most approaches have been timid, low profile, and not part of a well-defined strategy. Yet they represent an application of the "firewall model" advocated by scholars like Leiken, Brooke, and Gerecht.

Like the MAB, the IGD, and the CAIR, since 9/11 New Western Brotherhood organizations have consistently issued public statements denouncing al Qaeda's actions, urging Muslims to reject its violent tactics and calling for calm during the many domestic and international crises that have taken place. Many Western policy makers have publicly praised these positions, considering them extremely important in deescalating tensions. The fact that organizations that can reach large segments of Western Muslim communities and possess high levels of legitimacy among some of their most conservative fringes adopt these positions is something that no Western government can ignore. Whether its overall nature and aims seem positive or negative, the movement's public position on the use of violence in the West makes it a useful ally of any government seeking to address pressing security needs.

These considerations have led some Western governments to establish limited forms of cooperation with New Western Brotherhood offshoots. One of the best known examples is the takeover of the North London Central Mosque, better known as the Finsbury Park mosque. Originally founded as a mainstream, moderate mosque for the large Muslim community of north London, Finsbury Park was taken over by the notorious Egyptian cleric Abu Hamza al Masri and a small group of followers in the mid-1990s.[8] After physically intimidating the mosque's trustees, Abu Hamza turned the place into what intelligence agencies from various countries considered the undisputed headquarters of jihadist activities in Europe. Scores of individuals linked to al Qaeda, from shoe bomber Richard Reid to the so-called twentieth hijacker, Zacarias Moussaoui, passed through its doors and hundreds of militants were recruited by Abu Hamza inside to fight or train with al Qaeda in places such as Afghanistan and Chechnya. British authorities kept the mosque under surveillance for years, but only in January 2003, after it became apparent that it had been used by a cell of North African militants planning an attack in Britain, was the decision made to swoop in on Finsbury Park.[9] After a dramatic night raid uncovered items such as military manuals, handguns, combat clothing, hundreds of stolen and forged documents, and even three nuclear, chemical, and biological warfare protection suits in the basement of the mosque, authorities decided to shut it down.

The decision was unpopular among the local Muslim community and boosted support for Abu Hamza, who began holding his Friday sermons in the middle of the street across from the mosque. Even after Abu Hamza's arrest in May 2004 his supporters held sway in the area surrounding the mosque, creating a tense situation for the entire neighborhood. At this point British officials became convinced that the mosque had to be reopened and turned to somebody who would be accepted by the community.[10] Officials from Scotland Yard, the Charity Commission, and Islington Council approached Kamal Helbawy and the leaders of the Muslim Association of Britain. After lengthy consultations, MAB leaders accepted British authorities' offer to take over the mosque. On a cold morning in February 2005, some seventy to eighty MAB activists arrived at the mosque, while police officers stood ready a few blocks away. A confrontation with Abu Hamza's supporters ensued, but after a few hours of tension and some minor scuffles, MAB activists physically secured the mosque.

The MAB's takeover of Finsbury Park has been touted by British authorities as a major accomplishment. Abu Hamza's supporters no longer have a base, and what was a "suicide factory," as a book that profiled the mosque called it, has become a thriving community center. During Abu Hamza's reign only a few dozen people, most of them hardcore followers of the radical cleric, used to attend Friday services; today the mosque welcomes more than a thousand worshippers every week. Moreover, Finsbury Park's new leadership has established excellent relations with the local community and even participates in interfaith forums. Muslim and non-Muslim residents of the neighborhood are enthusiastic about the change and law enforcement officials are relieved to be able to divert the human and financial resources needed to monitor Abu Hamza's supporters elsewhere. By turning Finsbury Park over to MAB, British authorities have unquestionably removed a major center for terrorist recruitment and preparation of attacks on British soil, bringing a problematic situation under control. Under such extraordinary circumstances, they deemed that only a quintessential Western Brotherhood organization like MAB had the legitimacy and street credibility to be accepted by the local Muslim community.

While never a full-fledged policy, the formation of various kinds of partnership with nonviolent Islamists in order to stem violent radicalization has been advocated by various branches of the British government. A 2005 internal memorandum from the Foreign Office on Yussuf al Qaradawi's visit to London perfectly exemplifies this line of thinking. While the Foreign Office admitted that Qaradawi's open support for suicide bombings in Iraq and Palestine was troubling, it also acknowledged that "they are not unusual or even exceptional amongst Muslims" in both the Middle East and the United Kingdom. Endorsing the cleric's visit, the Foreign Office praised al Qaradawi's role in "promoting mainstream Islam" and suggested that "having individuals like Qaradawi on our side should be our aim."[11]

Particularly since 7/7, this reasoning has led British authorities to establish various forms of partnership with individuals and organizations belonging to the Mawdudist network or Brotherhood spinoffs inside the country, subsidizing some of their activities. In 2005, for example, the Home and Foreign Office created "The Radical Middle Way," a series of itinerant public lectures, seminars, and workshops aimed at young British Muslims. The program included a diverse array of speakers, but the Western Brothers have a prominent role in it.[12] In other cases organizations linked to the East London mosque have directly received public funding for various counter-radicalization programs.

Like Britain, France has experimented with partnerships with nonviolent Islamists for security purposes. In the early 1990s, French authorities became seriously concerned by the surge of criminal activity, unemployment, and in general, sense of disenfranchisement that pervaded the *banlieues*, the housing projects that surround most French cities. The tensions, which became more visible during various spates of civic unrest in which mobs torched cars and attacked police officers, were particularly high among the country's Muslim population, Europe's largest.

The traditional partner of the French government for all "Islamic issues" had been, since its foundation in 1922, the Grande Mosquée de Paris.[13] Controlled by the Algerian government, it is a quintessential example of embassy Islam, moderate, secular, and with good access to the government.[14] But French authorities soon realized that the Grande Mosquée had virtually no following in the *banlieues*, where most Muslims perceived its leadership as out of touch with their reality.[15] Conversely, organizations such as the UOIF, France's "branch" of the New Western Brotherhood, had managed to establish a solid presence at the grassroots level, running extensive *dawa*/social services programs and engaging in initiatives to sway young Muslims from crime and drugs. These observations led French authorities to a shift in policy, as they began to perceive the work done by the UOIF as beneficial in solving the problems of the *banlieues*.[16]

One of the most prominent advocates of this new approach was Dounia Bouzar, an anthropologist and government consultant on integration issues. Bouzar's argument is condensed in a book she published in

2001, *L'Islam des Banlieues*.[17] The choice of the title is telling, because it was meant to contrast with the title of the celebrated 1987 book by French scholar Gilles Kepel, *Les Banlieues de l'Islam*.[18] In his work, Kepel had described how the UOIF and other organizations ideologically close to the Brotherhood had taken advantage of the social and economic disenfranchisement of young Muslims who lived in the *banlieues* in order to Islamize them, replacing their sense of French citizenship with a strong Muslim identity. In her book, Bouzar makes the opposite argument. As the subtitle, "Islamic Preachers: New Social Workers?" suggests, Bouzar sees the work of Brotherhood spinoffs and other *dawa* organizations in a positive light.

In her book, written amid the tensions between Muslim youth and the police in the northern city of Lille that followed the death of a young local Muslim in 2000, Bouzar argues that traditional, state-salaried social workers do not possess the necessary background to be effective in neighborhoods with large Muslim populations. Muslim preachers, however, live in those neighborhoods, have a deep knowledge of their dynamics, and understand the cultural background of their residents. They are therefore in an ideal position to exert a positive influence, as renewed piety can be a factor that favors integration, allowing young Muslims to take pride in their Islamic identity and, at the same time, live in harmony with French society. Preachers, therefore, are the ideal "new social workers," possessing the language, legitimacy, and drive to sway youngsters away from crime and drugs and to a life of piety and active citizenship.

"The mosque," argues Bouzar, "not only allows the practice of religion but also presents itself as a convivial space that allows a general organization and the creation of new networks of solidarity."[19] It is a space where families can be sure their children are sheltered from drugs and crime, and where preachers, who have become their "role models, friends and confidants," can steer them the right way.[20] New Western Brotherhood organizations such as the UOIF, whose paramosque structure closely resembled Bouzar's vision, were quick to point out that their work could help public institutions in combating the social malaises of the *banlieues*.[21] This thinking became widely accepted and the "new social workers'" *dawa* came to be seen as the best solution to the problems of troubled neighborhoods.[22] The perception that nonviolent Islamist organizations could succeed where the state had failed led many French policy makers, particularly at the local level, to provide financial and political support to them.

"All of a sudden it was enough to add the word 'Muslim' to the name of an association to benefit from a subsidy," recalls Paris-based antiracism activist Nadia Amiri.[23] Many others also criticized this approach, pointing out that several branches of the French government itself had expressed concerns about UOIF's nature and agenda. For example, the Conseil d'État, the country's highest administrative court, has referred to the organization as "a federation to which are affiliated many extremist movements which reject the essential values of French society."[24] French intelligence agencies have traditionally held similar views.[25]

Yet this security-based partnership was widely implemented, albeit never as a formal policy and not across the board, and received a boost after 9/11.[26] If during the 1990s some French policy makers envisioned UOIF activists as "social pacificators" keeping order in the *banlieues*, the emergence of terrorism and radicalization as state priorities added a new responsibility.[27] "The reality is that the UOIF does, on the ground, a work that is useful against the most dangerous enemies of the Republic: the Salafists," then Interior Minister Nicolas Sarkozy wrote in his book *La République, les Religions, l'Espérance*.[28] Sarkozy's statement underscores his pragmatic views. While acknowledging that in some ways the UOIF does not share French ideals on integration, he believes the organization respects the basic values of the state, such as the *laïcité* (the concept of a secular society), and considers it a necessary partner.[29] Given the Grande Mosquée's limited influence, the UOIF represents the only counterbalance to the criminal subculture and the Salafist ideology that, according to French authorities, would otherwise dominate in the *banlieues*.

The culmination of this partnership took place in fall 2005, when the *banlieues* became the theater for continued clashes between youths and the police. Even though Islamist groups, whether of the Brotherhood or the Salafi strain, had nothing to do with the riots, Muslims represented a large portion of those involved.[30] On November 6, the UOIF issued a public *fatwa* condemning violence and urging Muslims to return to calm.[31] Although this had little to no impact on the riots, which continued for weeks, French authorities (and particularly Sarkozy, whose harsh comments, according to many critics, had contributed to the violence) could not ignore the fact that the UOIF was trying to present itself as a reliable and much needed partner to manage the *banlieues*. The episode sanctioned a fifteen-year-long strategy on the part of the group's leadership—started after its

Bordeaux-based cadres decided to break with the founders' confrontational approach—for the organization to be seen as a potential partner of the French state.[32]

Or Foxes Guarding the Henhouse?

The 2005 UOIF *fatwa* has been criticized by some who have compared it to the religious edicts issued by Egyptian and Saudi clerics at the behest of their governments, a comparison particularly controversial in a country that has made laicism one of its cornerstones.[33] More generally, the criticism of Sarkozy has been raised against all Western governments that, with varying degrees of intensity, have flirted with the idea of partnering with nonviolent Islamists for security purposes. Even assuming that nonviolent Islamists can indeed sway some young Muslims from committing acts of terrorism or engaging in criminal activities, argue the critics, such short-term gains in the security field are offset by the long-term implications of such a partnership. While opposing acts of terror in the West, nonviolent Islamists have views and goals that are incompatible with those of the secular and multifaith societies of modern Europe. Seeing them as part of the problem rather than the solution, critics argue that governments should not legitimize and empower them. The long-term repercussions of such engagement on social cohesion and integration would be much greater than the yet-to-be-proven short-term gains tin preventing acts of terrorism.

Some of the earliest and harshest critics of this approach are social workers from France, the country that first experimented with informal partnerships with Western Brotherhood organizations, where the long-term impact is easier to detect. Many point to the fact that crime and the sense of disenfranchisement that plagued the *banlieues* have not been reduced. Most important, others point to the negative social developments that the Brothers' influence has brought. One particularly loud voice has been that of the women's association *Ni Putes Ni Soumises* (Neither Whores Nor Submissive), a feminist group traditionally linked to the French Left. "In the 1980s [in the *banlieues*], there were mixed marriages and sexuality was treated in far less intolerant terms," recounts a *Ni Putes Ni Soumises* militant. Then, she says, as Brotherhood organizations began their government-subsidized activities, the social climate changed significantly:

"Today, there is nothing left in these neighborhoods: no sense of life, no love, nothing but prohibition."[34]

A similar view is held by Father Christian Delorme, the liaison to the Muslim community for the diocese of Lyon, who has worked for decades in some of the city's most troubled neighborhoods. Starting in the 1980s, Father Delorme was active in organizing protests and popular marches against the discrimination North Africans faced in France and was among the most vocal backers of government support for the activities of Islamic organizations in the *banlieues*, arguing that more piety would have a beneficial effect.[35] But by the end of the 1990s, he became convinced that not all Muslim organizations were the same. "There is an Islam of the families, which is for the most part an Islam of hospitality and piety," said the clergyman in a 2001 interview with *Le Monde*, stating that the majority of French Islam is, as such, "neither static not dominating."[36]

> What I criticize is the work of hardening of the religious identity operated by some organizations that have an interest in discrediting such popular Islam; I am thinking in particular at the current of the Muslim Brothers. . . . I came to understand that they were dangerous when I saw that they cut the ties between the young and their families, explaining that their parents did not practice the true Islam, that they were not on the right path. I also understood that they wormed their way into institutions, taking advantage of secularism, using the rhetoric of secularism, but using it only as a means; for basically they were against integration, and the identity they sought was that of a community of Muslims, living autonomously in the Republic, like a potent countervailing power.[37]

Such testimonies provide ammunition to those who argue that the social engineering program envisioned by the Brothers, which entails a rejection of many core Western values, is the main problem. Senior security officials in various Western countries embrace the view that identifying the problem as only violent groups is self-deceiving. Alain Grignard, deputy head of the Belgian police's antiterrorism unit and a professor of Islamic studies at Brussels Free University, calls al Qaeda an "epiphenomenon," the most visible aspect of a much larger threat: political Islam.[38] Alain Chouet, the former head of DGSE, the French external intelligence agency, agrees with Grignard and believes that "Al-Qaeda is only a brief episode and an expedient instrument in the century-old existence of the Muslim Brotherhood. The true danger is in the expansion of the Brotherhood, an increase in its audience. The wolf knows how to disguise itself as a sheep."[39]

According to this view, political Islam, like any other totalitarian movement, has two wings: one, represented by groups like al Qaeda, more impatient and action-prone that seeks to use violence to achieve its goals, and another, constituted by the Brothers, that does not completely rule out the use of violence but aims at employing the appropriate strategy at the right time and place. Disagreements between the two wings exist, often with visceral undertones. But they should be considered as dissent among fellow travelers who share similar worldviews and aims but disagree on which tactics to employ.

Seasoned strategic thinkers, nonviolent Islamists since 9/11 have attempted to benefit from what is known in social movement theory as the "positive radical flank effect."[40] According to the theory, more moderate wings of a political movement improve their bargaining position when a more radical fringe emerges. The positive radical flank effect would explain why the presence of al Qaeda and other jihadist groups has led Western governments to see nonviolent Islamists more benignly and even to consider establishing partnerships with them. The severe and prolonged terrorist threat, critics say, has led some Western governments to lower the threshold of what is acceptable and to endorse extremist organizations as long as they oppose violence in the West. "Al Qaeda was the best thing that happened to these groups," argues *Wall Street Journal* reporter Ian Johnson. "Nowadays, our bar is so low that if groups aren't al Qaeda, we're happy. If they're not overtly supporting terrorism, we think they're okay. We don't stop to think where the terrorism comes from, where the fish swim."[41]

The New Western Brothers have seized this unprecedented opportunity by presenting themselves as sworn enemies of the jihadists, loyal partners of the state in stemming violent extremism and social unrest. But, according to critics, their real aim is to use the financial support and political legitimacy they seek simply to further their own agenda. The New Western Brothers have little actual knowledge of the Western jihadist underworld. Second-generation, homegrown jihadist clusters, which represent the largest security threat to the West, pay little attention to what the Brothers say and condemn them as "sellouts." Moreover, even assuming that some short-term results against the radical wing can be achieved by engaging with the moderate one, in the long term, if the movement's goals are incompatible with those of the state, no permanent alliance can be found. To the contrary, there is a risk that the moderate wing will unduly benefit from the state's support and expand its reach well beyond where it could have gone on its own, to the larger Muslim community.

The Brothers have used this strategy in the past, convincing Middle Eastern leaders to support them as an alternative to other inimical forces in more than one case. In the 1970s, for example, Anwar Sadat relaxed the traditional repressive policies of the Egyptian government toward the Brotherhood, believing that the group could effectively contrast with the appeal of leftist organizations, which he perceived as his main opponents.[42] In Saudi Arabia, the royal family, although never allowing a formal branch of the organization to be established on its soil, financially supported the Brothers for decades, considering them useful allies against secular regimes and Iran's attempts to export its militant interpretation of Shiism. And even the Israeli government, in the 1980s, tolerated and indirectly supported the growth of Hamas, the Palestinian branch of the Brotherhood, in order to weaken Arafat's PLO.[43]

In all these cases, Middle Eastern regimes have come to regret their decision, finding themselves fighting the very forces they have unleashed. "All our problems come from the Muslim Brotherhood," stated Prince Na'if Ibn Abdul Aziz, Saudi Arabia's Interior Minister, in 2002. "We have given too much support to this group. The Muslim Brotherhood has destroyed the Arab world."[44] Today, argue critics, Western governments risk making the same mistake, relying on the Brothers in order to possibly achieve short-term security results and ignoring the much more dangerous long-term effects of empowering them.

The Brothers and Violence

Over the past few years, and particularly since 9/11, the New Brothers, both in the Muslim world and in the West, have been consistent in denouncing terrorism. Top clerics of the movement have issued *fatwas*, signed petitions, and publicly stated that terrorism, violence, and suicide bombings are barbaric acts that are diametrically opposed to the teachings of Islam. Such very public condemnations have gained the praise of many Westerners, pleased to find common ground with Muslim scholars on such important issues.

Yet, a deeper analysis of such condemnations gives reasons to pause. Although a universally accepted definition of terrorism does not exist, most would identify the killing of civilians for political reasons by that term. The New Western Brothers, however, have a quite different interpretation. During the July 2003 meeting of the European Council for Fatwa and Research, held in Stockholm, al Qaradawi laid out five categories of terrorism, including "terror that is permitted by Islamic law" and "martyrdom operations." After ruling that Israeli society as a whole can be defined as "invaders" and therefore can be legitimately targeted, al Qaradawi stated that "those who oppose martyrdom operations and claim that they are suicide are making a great mistake."[45] The ruling expanded on a point made during a 2002 episode of al Qaradawi's high-profile Al Jazeera program *Life and Religion*, when he stated that there was no such a thing as an Israeli civilian and hence any target in Israel, man, woman, or child, was legitimate. Moreover, he applauded the use of children as suicide bombers, declaring that "the Israelis might have nuclear bombs, but we have children bombs."[46]

The reasoning behind such statements is that the acts of those who resist an occupation, whatever their targets, are justified both morally and under Islamic law. The argument applies not only to Palestine but also to all other Muslim territories deemed under occupation, including Chechnya, Kashmir, and Iraq. Issuing a *fatwa* decreeing that it is not permissible for Arab countries to cooperate with the United States in the "War on Terror," Mawlawi noted that in most cases acts dubbed terrorism by Washington are in fact "jihad and legitimate right," such as resistance operations in Palestine, Iraq, and Afghanistan.[47] Similarly, in 2004, al Qaradawi issued a *fatwa* justifying attacks against all American citizens in Iraq, including civilians, pronouncing that "there is no difference between US military personnel and civilians in Iraq since both have come to invade the country," and since "civilians are actually there to serve the US occupying forces."[48] Therefore, the New Brothers' endorsement of the killing of American contractors in Iraq or of Israeli children would not violate their public condemnation of terrorism, as those acts constitute legitimate resistance.

The positions of al Qaradawi and Mawlawi, who head the European Council for Fatwa and Research, are embraced by the vast majority of New Western Brothers. In some cases they justify violence through legalistic arguments, stating that international law sanctions peoples' right to self-determination. In other cases, in order to appeal to Westerners on an emotional level, they compare the actions of Hamas fighters to those of Nelson Mandela, who was also once labeled a terrorist.[49] Ahmad al Rawi, the head of FIOE, the European Brothers' Brussels-based umbrella organization, expressed the most common position of New Western Brothers when he told the *Wall Street Journal* that suicide bombings in Iraq and Israel are justified because Muslims "have the right to defend themselves."[50]

The Brothers' open support for violence is, however, limited to conflicts in which Muslims are fighting for the liberation of lands they deem theirs and could be analyzed in light of the never-ending "one man's terrorist is another man's freedom fighter" debate.[51] Supporters of engagement argue that the Brothers endorse only a defensive jihad and have consistently condemned the attacks of 9/11, the London and Madrid bombings, and most other attacks perpetrated by al Qaeda and affiliated groups over the last few years. The pessimists contend that the Brothers' condemnation of violence is not only selective but also purely tactical. Consummate strategic thinkers, the Brothers understand that the violent tactics employed by al Qaeda are, at least for the time being, ineffective. The West will not collapse because of random terrorist attacks, and the current balance of power is such that any attack can have only counterproductive consequences. The Brothers' condemnation of terrorism, argue the pessimists, has to do more with a cold calculation of how best to achieve the movement's goals than with a deep-seated repudiation of violent means.

Indeed, argue the pessimists, the idea of using violence only when it is deemed the most fruitful tactic dates back to the teachings of Hassan al Banna. The Brotherhood's founder focused most of his attention on what he called "jihad of the pen and of the voice," urging Muslims to employ peaceful means to achieve their goals. Even though the word "jihad" makes some Western commentators shake, in this case it simply signifies an effort to please God, spreading the Brotherhood's message with words and writings. But al Banna is also clear in declaring that if words and writings do not suffice, then violence will be necessary: "the Muslim Brotherhood will use force only when there would be no other course open for it."[52] He states with equal clarity that all other efforts are necessary and praisewor-thy, but "armed combat for the cause of God" is the highest stage of jihad, a step that Muslims must take in order to achieve the Islamic order if other means have failed.[53] Al Banna never managed to develop a comprehensive doctrine for the use of violence, perhaps due to his premature death, but he seems clear in stating that violence can be used to pursue the movement's goals, only as last resort and, most important, when the movement is suf-ficiently prepared to do so. Other top Brotherhood thinkers have expressed similar views. Said Hawwa, a senior leader of the Syrian Brotherhood, wrote in the 1980s that "the Muslim Brotherhood would surely use force, but only at the time when there would be no other course open for it, and when they would be fully satisfied that they have equipped themselves with the strength of faith, belief, unity and organization."[54] In light of such state-ments, the Brothers' accommodationist turn of the 1970s could be seen as dictated by awareness of the movement's military inferiority to the regime it opposed.

Nevertheless, argue some optimists, the Brotherhood is known for its flexibility and lack of dogmatism. The positions of al Banna and other senior Brotherhood members, though considered with deference, are not necessarily accepted by the new generations, who have repeatedly affirmed their right to contribute to the evolution of the movement's ideology. Yet, an analysis of the writings and speeches of New Brotherhood leaders shows an almost identical rejection of violence based purely on an evaluation of the current balance of power. Among the many sources confirming this position, particularly important for authoritativeness and completeness are the writings of al Qaradawi. His 1987 book, translated into English by IIIT, *Islamic Awakening Between Rejection and Extremism*, has often been touted as a seminal text that proves the Islamist movement's moderation.[55] Extensive sections are devoted to the condemnation of religious extrem-ism and violence, which, according to al Qaradawi, plague part of today's Muslim youth. Al Qaradawi criticizes young Muslims for being too liberal with the practice of *takfir* and for their excessive dogmatism, arguing that moderation, tolerance, and flexibility are crucial attributes a good Muslim must possess.

Yet, in other sections, al Qaradawi has softer words for the "extremist youth," arguing that they have "good intentions and sincerity" toward Al-lah.[56] The blame for their violent actions has to be laid elsewhere. "What we actually need," states the cleric, "is the unflinching courage to admit that our youth have been forced to what we call 'religious extremism' through our own misdeeds."[57] The "misdeed" that leads young Muslims to violence is the older generation's inability to establish an Islamic state. Those who use violence have good souls and are aiming for the right goals. Their only mistake, caused by their young age, is being too impatient and choosing the wrong methods.[58] Had the older generation established an Islamic state, no such problem would exist. And, while the movement is at fault, the blame for such failure "can basically be attributed to the imposition on Muslim societies of secularism—an alien trend which is at odds with all that is Islamic."[59] The cleric states that "contemporary crusaders" have infiltrated the Muslim world to spread Marxism and secularism in order to prevent the spread of Islamic ideals and keep Muslims subjugated. "Muslim youth are also aware that all of these negative attitudes towards Islamic causes— locally and internationally—are initiated by foreign forces, and carried out by some Muslim rulers who act as mere puppets manipulated by Zionist, Christian, or atheist powers."[60]

In *Islamic Awakening* al Qaradawi provides a veiled justification for violence; in his 2000 book, *Priorities of the Islamic Movement in the Coming Phase*, he is more explicit about the purely tactical nature of his rejection of violence against the West and secular Muslim rulers.[61] Al Qaradawi criticizes Qutb and other theorists who seek to violently confront those who oppose the creation of an Islamic state and, more generally, the Islamic movement.[62] His criticism is not that the Qutbist approach is un-Islamic, but rather that it will not take the movement anywhere. "How can we talk of launching offensives to subject the whole world to our Message," asks al Qaradawi, "when the only weapons we can muster are those given us by them [those against whom we want to launch our offensive jihad] and when the only arms we can carry are those they agree to sell us?"[63] Violent confrontation is rejected not because it is wrong, immoral, or against his interpretation of Islamic texts, but simply because it is at present ineffective. It is a moral duty in places where Muslims are, according to al Qaradawi's interpretation of events, under direct attack, such as in Palestine, Kashmir, and Iraq. In those cases his endorsement of jihad is open and constant, urging fellow Muslims all over the world to aid their brothers. In other places, such as against secular Muslim rulers, jihad is ineffective and gives an excuse to foreign forces to intervene. The Islamic movement, argues al Qaradawi, should be more strategic and forgo the use of violence against secular Muslims rulers and the West until its strength matches that of its enemies.

Al Qaradawi's positions provide ammunition to those who believe that the Brothers are, consciously or not, applying the doctrine advocated by Italian Marxist philosopher and activist Antonio Gramsci. Gramsci, writing in the 1920s and '30s, believed that anticapitalist activists should have applied a two-pronged strategy to seize power.[64] First, they should have waged a nonviolent "war of position," becoming the dominant voices in the mass media, in education, and on the streets. This position of cultural hegemony would have allowed the revolutionary vanguard to indoctrinate the masses and lay the groundwork for the second part of his strategy, a full-fledged "war of manoeuvre" entailing an armed insurrection against the ruling classes. Today's Brothers, argue pessimists, apply the same gradualist plan, having understood that al Qaeda's confrontational strategy is admirable but premature.[65] As, in the Quran, Allah instructed the prophet Mohammed and his early followers not to wage war against the Meccans until they could match their enemies' military might, the Brothers argue that today, Muslims who want to establish an Islamic order have to patiently build their strength before initiating any confrontation.[66]

Even though the books of al Qaradawi and other scholars that openly advocate violence, such as Fathi Yakan or Mawlawi, are translated and distributed throughout their networks, most New Western Brothers tend to avoid publicly discussing issues of violence, limiting their statements to a general but stern condemnation of all acts of terrorism. But some private documents and conversations on the matter have surfaced, confirming some of the pessimists' doubts. A noteworthy example is Abdurahman Alamoudi, the American Muslim leader arrested in 2003. In a phone call with an associate secretly taped by U.S. authorities before his arrest, Alamoudi expressed his feelings about al Qaeda's bombings of the American embassies in Kenya and Tanzania in 1998:

> I think that the attacks that are being executed by Bin Laden and other Islamic groups are wrong especially hitting the civilian targets. For example, bombing the American embassy in Kenya in which many African Muslims have died and not a single American died. You killed 500 Africans and injured 5,000 and then you said we exploded an Ameri-

can embassy! This is not good and this gives a bad image of the Muslims and Arabs, and even inside America itself. What is the result you achieve in destroying an embassy in an African country? I prefer to hit a Zionist target in America or Europe or elsewhere but not like what happened at the Embassy in Kenya. I prefer, honestly, like what happened in Argentina.[67]

Asked by his interlocutor what he meant by "what happened in Argentina," Alamoudi began praising the 1994 bombing of the Buenos Aires Jewish Community Center, which he described as a "worthy operation." "You have to choose the target so as not to put the Muslim[s] in an uncomfortable situation," he added. "We should not go to the military solution unless we were forced to do that."

Alamoudi's tactical thinking on the use of violence was even more evident in a speech he delivered, unaware of being taped, at a conference of the Islamic Association of Palestine in Chicago in 1996:

I think our attitude toward America should change. We have a chance, in America, to be the moral leadership of America. The problem is when? It will happen, it will happen, I have no doubt in my mind, Muslims sooner or later will be the moral leadership of America. It depends on me and you, either we do it now or we do it after a hundred years, but this country will become a Muslim country. And I (think) if we are outside this country we can say "oh, Allah destroy America," but once we are here, our mission in this country is to change it. And the prophet told us that there are three ways of changing things, either by your hand or your mouth or within yourself, and we can change it by our hand and by our mouth, but positively. There is no way for Muslims to be violent in America, nowhere at all. We have other means to do it. You can be violent anywhere else but in America.[68]

The emphasis on "other means to do it," say the pessimists, perfectly encapsulates Alamoudi's and the New Western Brothers' position. Violence, even against civilians, is perfectly acceptable as long as it does not create negative repercussions for the movement. But for now, the use of violence in the West is counterproductive and the movement should use political engagement to achieve its goals.

Determining Factors

Even though no country can be said to have adopted a cohesive and definitive policy and the debate is ongoing within virtually every Western government, it is apparent that the decision to partner with nonviolent Islamists is closely linked to the definitions of extremism and radicalization that the authorities have formally or informally adopted. Authorities that tend to closely associate these concepts with the use of violence are more likely to be open to some form of partnership with nonviolent Islamists. That is the case in Great Britain, where the initial aim of PREVENT, the government's counter-radicalization program introduced in 2003, was to "stop people from becoming or supporting terrorists or violent extremists."[69] As a consequence, for several years various Islamist organizations that rejected violence inside the country were engaged as partners and received funding from the British government.

Other countries adopt a broader interpretation of what constitutes extremism, and consequently of what the aim of their counter-radicalization programs should be. Dutch authorities, for example, define radicalization as "the growing preparedness to wish to or to support fundamental changes . . . in society that do not fit within our democratic system of law."[70] The Netherlands' domestic security services, AIVD, specifically state that violence is not necessarily part of the extremism they are monitoring among segments of the Dutch Muslim community. "There is no threat of violence here," states a 2007 AIVD report, "nor of an imminent assault upon the Dutch or Western democratic order, but this is a slow process which could gradually harm social cohesion and solidarity and undermine certain fundamental human rights."[71] Consequently, Dutch authorities are much more reluctant than their British counterparts to partner with nonviolent Islamists but have not completely ruled out the possibility of doing so in extraordinary circumstances.[72]

The definition of extremism and therefore of the goal of the counter-radicalization strategy is shaped by various factors. The single most important factor is the security threat facing the country. Governments dealing with a relatively high level of radicalization among their Muslim population and a severe threat of a terrorist attack are more likely to focus simply on violent radicalization rather than more general and less immediately visible threats to social cohesion. Eager to use any tool that can stop an attack, they are likely to be more open to the idea of partnering with non-violent Islamists. In other words, the higher the terrorist threat, the lower the level at which the bar of partner acceptability is set.

Great Britain seems to be a perfect case in point. Since 9/11 Great Britain has been targeted multiple times by terrorists linked to or sympathizing with al Qaeda. Thanks to a combination of luck and impressive skills on the part of British authorities, terrorists have been able to successfully strike only once, but the threat has dimensions that are unparalleled in any other European country. In 2008, for example, British security services estimated that 2,000 individuals, mostly British citizens or residents, were involved in al Qaeda-influenced terrorist activities and claimed to monitor around 30 serious plots at any given moment.[73] It is no coincidence that British authorities, facing the most imminent and constant terrorist threat of any European country, have established the most extensive forms of partnership with nonviolent Islamist organizations.[74] While British officials do not consider partnering with nonviolent Islamists an established policy, cutting deals on a case-by-case basis with admittedly less-than-ideal partners is seen as an unavoidable *realpolitik* move dictated by the emergency of the severe threat.[75]

Most other European countries, not faced with a terrorist threat of such magnitude, hold more prudent positions. Dutch intelligence agencies, for example, estimate the number of individuals involved in terrorist activities in the country at just a few dozen and seem to address the issue by drawing a clear line between engaging and empowering. All sorts of voices should be engaged, as long as they do not advocate violence, since pushing nonviolent Islamists to the margins could have negative repercussions. Nevertheless, authorities feel they cannot consider them permanent partners, as these forces espouse a message that clashes with the Dutch government's ideas of democracy, integration, and social cohesion.[76]

Another factor influencing the choice of whether or not to partner with nonviolent Islamists is the institutional mandate of the body making the decision. Institutions whose mandate is simply to prevent acts of violence naturally tend to focus on violent extremism and are therefore satisfied with the short-term security gains that such partnerships can achieve. But institutions that aim at the preservation of a harmonious and cohesive society will be more careful about the long-term effects of such cooperation. They understand that occasional cooperation might be necessary in emergency situations, but they fear that the legitimacy and financial support derived from a permanent partnership with the government could unduly empower organizations whose agenda they deem negative.

The debate taking place among British authorities is particularly telling of these dynamics. Robert Lambert, the former head of the Muslim Contact Unit (MCU), the section of the London Metropolitan Police devoted to engaging the city's Muslim community, argues the "ideal yes-saying" Muslim leaders lack credibility in their communities and have no knowledge of radicalism.[77] Lambert, who was one of the masterminds of MAB's takeover of the Finsbury Park mosque, believes that only groups like MAB and even nonviolent Salafis have the street credibility to challenge the narrative of al Qaeda and influence young Muslims. He therefore advocates "police negotiation leading to partnership with Muslim groups conventionally deemed to be subversive to democracy."[78]

If the MCU understandably seeks to utilize all possible tools to fulfill its institutional mandate of preventing acts of violence, other public institutions with different mandates are more cautious. Top officials at the Home Office and DCLG, while acknowledging that the Finsbury Park takeover was, given the circumstances, a success, have argued that the British government's aim should be to target not simply "violent extremism" but all forms of radicalism.[79] Top Labour and Tory politicians have publicly stated that being against al Qaeda is not enough; they insist that Muslim organizations be treated as partners only if they adhere to "non-negotiable" British values. Government officials like Ruth Kelly, Hazel Blears, and Jacqui Smith have repeatedly stated that groups that condemn al Qaeda's violence while praising the acts of other groups considered terrorist by the British government and espousing values deemed to undermine social cohesion are also part of the problem. "They may not explicitly promote violence," said Smith, "but they can create a climate of fear and distrust where violence becomes more likely."[80] This line of thinking, as seen in chapter 5, seems to have prevailed; British authorities are progressively expanding their focus on "violent extremism" to a broader definition of the phenomenon.

The positions adopted by policy makers on the nature of the New Western Brothers also play a key role in shaping decisions. Optimists tend to favor working with the Brothers for security purposes, and many pessimists, while mindful of potential pitfalls, also argue for some forms of cooperation. An additional factor influencing the decision-making process is the analysis of the radicalization process. Despite many studies, there is no consensus among experts and policy makers on how and why radicalization takes place. Analysts debate, for example, whether integration and lack thereof are related to radicalization. Germany's Office for the Protection of the Constitution argues confidently that "a successful integration is a substantial contribution to the prevention of extremism and terrorism."[81] Others point to a lack of empirical evidence that definitely links lack of integration, radicalism, and violence.[82]

Equally debated is the role played by nonviolent Islamist organizations in relation to the radicalization process. Do such groups work as a barrier against violent radicalization or serve as conveyor belts for more extremist groups? Brotherhood officials argue the former. "If it wasn't for the Brotherhood, most of the youths of this era would have chosen the path of violence," stated a senior Egyptian Brotherhood official to Leiken and Brooke. "The Ikhwan has become a safety valve for moderate Islam."[83] Danish security services (PET) claim that in some cases, nonviolent Islamists do serve as firewalls. "It is precisely these individuals who have the best chance of influencing the attitudes of the young people who are in a process of radicalisation, in a nonviolent direction," stated PET in a 2008 report.[84]

German security services disagree, publicly stating in their annual reports that nonviolent Islamist organizations "do not carry out recruitment activities for the purpose of the violent 'Holy War' (Jihad). They might rather claim to immunise young Muslims against Jihadist indoctrination by presenting to them an alternative offer of identification. However, one has to critically ask whether their activities that are strongly directed at preserving an 'Islamic identity' intensify disintegration and contribute to the development of Islamist parallel societies."[85] Moreover, there "is the risk that such milieus could also form the breeding ground for further radicalization," laying the ideological groundwork for violent groups.[86]

Divergent opinions are a natural consequence of the difficulties in conclusively determining the impact of the Brothers on radicalization and the security environment, given the lack of clear empirical evidence. The Brothers do unquestionably serve as occasional "firefighters," determined to extinguish the flames of tension among young Muslims.[87] The New Western Brothers, in fact, have been consistent in their denunciation of the actions of al Qaeda and in calling for calm on several occasions when tensions were simmering within the Muslim community. It is arguable that, as

Leiken and Brooke believe, the Brotherhood serves as a safety valve, channeling into political activities the energy and frustration of some young Muslims who might otherwise engage in terrorism. In some cases a form of partnership with them has achieved good results, as with the Finsbury Park mosque, which the vast majority of British policy makers, even those who harshly criticize the Brothers, acknowledge as a success story. There are reasons to suspect that the New Western Brothers have adopted these positions mostly for tactical purposes, in order to gain legitimacy in the eyes of Western elites and thereby increase their influence. Even assuming that is true, no Western government can afford to ignore the short-term benefits that some of their actions bring.

If the Brothers are occasional short-term firefighters, they are arguably, at the same time, long-term arsonists. It is true that the active members of New Western Brotherhood organizations who have further radicalized and engaged in violent activities are very few. But it is also true that the Brothers provide the ideological background for further radicalization, creating a siege mentality that could be the gateway to violence. Brotherhood organizations have made mainstream a narrative of victimhood that has created a fertile environment for violent Islamists, who only have to convince potential recruits about the righteousness of their tactics. The Quilliam Foundation, a London-based think tank established in 2008 by former members of Hizb ut-Tahrir and the Mawdudist network who have rejected Islamism, stated in its launch publication that nonviolent Islamists, while condemning terrorism, "advocate separatist, confrontational ideas that, followed to their logical conclusion, lead to violence." "At the very least," it added, their rhetoric "provides the mood music to which suicide bombers dance."[88]

The Brothers, while condemning violence in the West, spread concepts that create the ideal breeding ground for it. By consistently alleging that Western Muslims and Islam itself are under attack, they create a siege mentality that often represents the first step toward radicalization.[89] The widespread availability of texts extolling the virtues of military jihad in their bookstores and on Web sites and their selective and geographically limited renunciation of violence could also be problematic. If Muslims in Palestine, Kashmir, and Iraq have the right to defend themselves, why not in the West, where, according to what the New Western Brothers say, they are also under attack? The Brothers do not advocate attacks against the West, but once the "*jihadi* genie" is out of the bottle, it is difficult to control.[90]

Conclusion

The Way Forward

The difficulties experienced by most Western governments in assessing and engaging New Western Brotherhood organizations are paradigmatic of the challenges posed by such a complex movement. Conceptualizing a movement that mixes politics and religion, particularly a religion about which most policy makers know little, has proven extremely difficult. In some cases, the Brothers' actions seem to reflect the moderation and pro-integration stance that Western governments are desperately looking for in their Muslim interlocutors. In others, they seem to harbor an agenda and embrace values diametrically opposed to those of a Western liberal democracy. Policy makers, eager to find solutions to urgent problems involving the Muslim community, find themselves in a bind.

Many among the pessimists call for policies that would exclude the New Western Brothers from any engagement. Considering them deceitful actors seeking to destroy the very same freedoms that have allowed them to flourish, critics argue that their organizations should be marginalized or even outlawed as subversive, the political wings of a global Islamist insurgency. While highlighting troubling aspects of the Western Brothers' nature and agenda that unquestionably need to be addressed, this position is unrealistic and, arguably, dangerous.

Although their claims of representativeness are often overblown, New Western Brotherhood organizations do represent a significant cross-section of the Muslim community. If the aim of a government is to hear all voices, it makes little sense to exclude an important one. Talking only to those Muslim leaders whose positions square with the government's and pretending that more confrontational voices do not exist is hardly a constructive policy. When they act outside of the law, as when they provide financial support to groups designated as terrorist, Western Brotherhood organizations should be prosecuted. But since most of their activities are abundantly within the law, nonviolent Islamists are a reality that cannot be ignored and should be engaged. Moreover, more pragmatically, marginalization could trigger a dangerous radicalization of the movement, pushing it to embrace more extremist positions and perhaps even violence.

A diametrically opposite approach, advocated by some optimists, sees the New Western Brothers as reliable partners the state should engage in order to favor integration and stem radicalization among Western Muslims. Only the Brothers, according to some, possess the grassroots reach and the credibility to effectively influence large segments of the Muslim community. On this account, the Brothers, while seeking to maintain the Islamic identity of Western Muslims, have views and aims compatible with those of Western governments.

This approach is also problematic. The previous chapters have presented ample evidence showing that the aims of the New Western Brothers do not necessarily correspond to those publicly stated in dialogues with Western establishments. Assigning an almost monopolistic control of the community to a handful of self-appointed leaders whose aims are, at best, unclear seems naïve. It would reinforce the position of the movement within Western Muslim communities, aiding its effort to make its interpretation of Islam mainstream. There is the risk that, thanks to the support of the government, a vocal minority would be able to further marginalize competing forces and exercise undue influence over a community that, for the most part, does not embrace the Brothers' conservative and politicized version of Islam. The potential repercussions of this hypothetical shift for security and social cohesion are debatable, but providing the New Western Brothers with a blank check seems overly optimistic.

The experiences of the last few years have led some Western policy makers to consider a third option, which entails cautious engagement of New Western Brotherhood organizations. Most governments are now refuting the monopolistic approach. Increasingly aware of the extreme diversity of Western Muslim communities, they try to speak to a wider range of voices, proactively seeking to connect with traditionally underrepresented groups. Looking beyond the "bearded communalist shepherds" who have often monopolized access to institutions, policy makers are progressively trying to broaden the spectrum of government interlocutors.[1] New Western Brotherhood organizations do represent a section of the community, but their activism and visibility should not be mistaken for universal representativeness.

Moreover, there is a growing awareness of the need for a more refined approach. There are indeed significant advantages in not isolating New Western Brotherhood organizations, for example, good results in the security field. And, even though nobody can exactly predict long-term developments, it is arguable that engagement can lead to a moderation of the movement, as Sarkozy believes. Isolation, in contrast, could have negative repercussions, further radicalizing the organizations and allowing them to be seen as "martyrs" in the Muslim community.[2] But engagement needs to be based on a firm understanding of the history, characteristics, connections, *modus operandi*, and, most important, aims of the Brothers. Only an informed engagement can lead to a realistic and constructive rapport.

Finally, many policy makers increasingly understand the difference between engagement and empowerment. Establishing a permanent dialogue and even occasional and limited forms of partnership with New Western Brotherhood organizations can produce several positive outcomes. But entrusting them with undue powers that would give them the keys to the Muslim community appears to be an option that most Western governments are no longer willing to choose. The evolution of the relationship between the British government and the Mawdudist network is, from this point of view, emblematic. Striking the right balance between engagement and empowerment is not easy, but necessary in order to avoid granting legitimacy and influence to organizations with limited representativeness whose agenda is not necessarily compatible with those of Western governments.

Crucially important in policy development is the uncertain evolutionary path New Western Brotherhood organizations will follow. The organizations established some forty years ago by the pioneers are undergoing a significant change, as leadership is slowly being passed to a new generation of Western-born activists, who will inevitably add their perspectives. Today it is not unreasonable to speak of some of these organizations as "post-Brotherhood," even though the real meaning of this expression is still to be defined. Will the New Western Brothers become a "Muslim church in

Europe, which will pose little or no security threat, but will push for conservative moral and social values," as French scholar Olivier Roy theorizes?[3] Or are the pro-democracy and pro-integration statements of the new generation just a carefully devised smokescreen for the movement's real aims of a "Civilization-Jihadist Process," as outlined by Akram and other older Brotherhood leaders? Only time will tell, and it is not unlikely that different wings of the movement will go in separate and even opposing directions. But for the time being, given this uncertainty, a policy of cautious and informed engagement appears to be the most appropriate.

Notes

1. Who Speaks for Western Muslims?

1. Alamoudi's resume, introduced as evidence in *U.S. v. Abdurahman Muhammad Alamoudi*, U.S.D.C. of Eastern Virginia, Case 03–1009M. Before founding the American Muslim Council, Alamoudi held leadership positions in the Muslim Student Association (MSA) and the Islamic Society of North America (ISNA).

2. *American Muslim Council: Our First Five Years*, report by the AMC, 1996, 5.

3. Mohamed Nimer, "Muslims in American Public Life," in Yvonne Yazbeck Haddad, ed., *Muslims in the West: From Sojourners to Citizens* (Oxford: Oxford University Press, 2001), 176–77.

4. See, for example, "AMC Hosts Interfaith Heritage Banquet," *The AMC Report* 6, no. 1 (January 1996).

5. "Arrested Muslim Activist Helped Pick Chaplains for U.S. Military," *Washington Times*, September 30, 2003.

6. Joseph Braude, "Moderate Muslims and Their Radical Leaders," *The New Republic*, February 27, 2006; Ahmed Yousef, *American Muslims: A Community Under Siege* (Springfield, VA: UASR Publishing Group, 2004).

7. Department of Justice press release on the sentencing of Alamoudi, October 15, 2004.

8. Treasury Department press release, July 14, 2005, http://www.treas.gov/press/releases/js2632.htm.

9. Interview with U.S. Department of Homeland Security official, Washington, D.C., May 2008.

10. As reported in the affidavit of U.S. Immigration and Customs Enforcement Special Agent Brett Gentrup in *U.S. v. Abdurahman Muhammad Alamoudi*,

U.S.D.C. of Eastern Virginia, Case 03–1009M, September 30, 2003. In reality, 12 American citizens died on that day, even though the majority of the 224 victims were citizens of Kenya and Tanzania.

11. Original speech available at http://www.investigativeproject.org/article/218 (accessed October 14, 2008).

12. *American Muslim Council*, 9.

13. Bernard Lewis, *Islam and the West* (New York and Oxford: Oxford University Press, 1993), 3–25.

14. Joel S. Fetzer and J. Christopher Soper, *Muslims and the State in Britain, France and Germany* (New York: Cambridge University Press, 2005), 64.

15. Jørgen Nielsen, Muslims in Western Europe (Edinburgh: Edinburgh University Press, 2004), vii, 8–21, 24–27, 40–44.

16. Joceline Cesari, *When Islam and Democracy Meet: Muslims in Europe and in the United States* (New York: Palgrave Macmillan, 2004), 11–16.

17. The exact number is highly debated and is virtually impossible to establish with certainty. 15 million is the estimate by the 2004 U.S. Department of State International Religious Freedom Report, as well as by a 2005 study by the Pew Research Center entitled *An Uncertain Road: Muslims and the Future of Europe*.

18. Nielsen, *Muslims in Western Europe*, 121.

19. This process is excellently described, for example, by Philip Lewis in his study of Bradford's Muslim community. See Philip Lewis, *Islamic Britain: Religion, Politics and Identity Among British Muslims* (London: I. B. Tauris, 1994).

20. Aslam Abdullah and Gasser Hathout, *The American Muslim Identity: Speaking for Ourselves* (Pasadena, CA: Multimedia Vera International, 2003), 25–27.

21. Cesari, *When Islam and Democracy Meet*, 16.

22. *Muslim Americans: Middle Class and Mostly Mainstream*, Pew Research Center, May 22, 2007, 24–25; *Western Muslim Minorities: Integration and Disenfranchisement*, CAIR Policy Bulletin, April 2006.

23. The term "governance of Islam" has been used by Marcel Maussen to describe "various ways and patterns of regulation, steering and accommodation of Islam in Western Europe." The same concept applies to North America. See Marcel Maussen, *The Governance of Islam in Western Europe: A State of the Art Report*, IMISCOE working paper No. 16, December 2006, 5.

24. See, for example, Matthias Koenig, "Incorporating Muslim Migrants in Western Nation States: A Comparison of the United Kingdom, France and Germany," *Journal of International Migration and Integration* 6 (2): 219–34; Silvio Ferrari, "The Secularity of the State and the Shaping of Muslim Representative Organizations in Western Europe," in Jocelyne Cesari and Sean McLoughlin, eds., *European Muslims and the Secular State* (Aldershot: Ashgate, 2005).

25. Fetzer and Soper, *Muslims and the State in Britain, France and Germany*, 1–21.

26. For a comprehensive overview of the different approaches adopted by each European country, see Brigitte Marechal, "Dealing with European States," in Brigitte Marechal, Stefano Allievi, Felice Dassetto, and Jørgen Nielen, *Muslims in the Enlarged Europe* (Leiden/Boston: Brill, 2003), 153–80.

27. Jytte Klausen, *The Islamic Challenge: Politics and Religion in Western Europe* (New York: Oxford University Press, 2005), 81.

28. Carolyn M. Warner and Manfred W. Wenner, "Religion and the Political Organization of Muslims in Europe," *Perspectives on Politics* 4, no. 3 (September 2006): 457–79.

29. Jan Rath, Rinnus Pennix, Kees Groendendijk, and Astrid Meyer, "The Politics of Recognizing Religious Diversity in Europe: Social Reactions to the Institutionalization of Islam in the Netherlands, Belgium and Great Britain," *Netherlands Journal of Social Sciences* 35 (1): 53–70; Philip Lewis, *Islamic Britain*, 52.

30. Cesari, *When Islam and Democracy Meet*, 154.

31. Warner and Wenner, "Religion and the Political Organization of Muslims in Europe."

32. Interview with Turkish government official, Istanbul, June 2008; Ali Bardakoglu, "'Moderate Perception of Islam' and the Turkish Model of the Diyanet: The President's Statement," *Journal of Muslim Minority Affairs* 24, no. 2 (October 2004).

33. Brigitte Marechal, "The Question of Belonging," in Brigitte Marechal, Stefano Allievi, Felice Dassetto, and Jørgen Nielen, *Muslims in the Enlarged Europe* (Leiden/Boston: Brill, 2003), 100; Bernard Godard and Sylvie Taussig, *Les Musulmans en France* (Paris: Robert Laffont, 2007), 35. A 2007 survey conducted in Denmark, for example, showed that only 5 percent of Danish Muslims went to a mosque or spoke with an imam at least once a month, and half seldom or never participated to religious ceremonies (Kirsten Nilsson, "Imamers indflydelse er begrænset," *Politiken*, March 12, 2007). A 2008 survey of young Dutch Muslims of Moroccan descent revealed 72 percent rarely or never visited a mosque ("Marokkaanse jongeren willen soepeler geloof," *EenVandaag*, September 29, 2008).

34. Marechal, "The Question of Belonging," 9–10.

35. Interview with Geneive Abdo, Washington, D.C., October 2008; Jocelyne Cesari, "Islam in France: The Shaping of a Religious Minority," in Yvonne Yazbeck Haddad, ed., *Muslims in the West: From Sojourners to Citizens* (Oxford: Oxford University Press, 2001), 41–42.

36. The Bradford Council of Mosques, an elected body representing various Islamic trends present in the British city, is a good example of a relatively repre-

sentative organization at the local level. In the German state of Lower Saxony the Landesverband Shura-Niedersachsen seems to have similar characteristics.

37. Yorgos Christidis, "The Muslim Minority in Greece," in Gerd Nonneman, Tim Niblock, and Bogdan Szajkowski, eds., *Muslim Communities in the New Europe* (Berkshire, UK: Ithaca Press, 1996); interview with Greek politician, Washington, D.C., June 2007; interview with Kostas Lavdas, Medford, MA, October 2007.

38. Similarly, Marcel Maussen uses the terms "representative" and "reasonable." See Maussen, *The Governance of Islam in Western Europe*, 36.

39. Interview with Anna Seleny, Medford, MA, November 2007; Anwar Alam, "Muslim Minority, Multiculturalism and Liberal State: A Comparison of India and Europe," paper released by the Université Paris 1—Panthéon-Sorbonne.

40. Marechal, "Dealing with European States," 156.

41. Jonathan Birt, "Good imam bad imam: civic religion and national integration in Britain after 9/11," *The Muslim World* 4 (96): 687–705.

42. Ferrari, "The Secularity of the State."

43. Jonathan Laurence, "Integrating Islam: A New Chapter in 'Church-State' Relations," report for the Transatlantic Task Force on Immigration and Integration, October 2007.

44. Klausen, *The Islamic Challenge*, 5.

45. Sayeed Hawwa, a senior leader of the Syrian branch of the Muslim Brotherhood, described an Islamist organization as "that which works for the establishment of Islam in the sphere of individual, family or the entire world." Sayeed Hawwa, *The Muslim Brotherhood* (Kuwait: International Islamic Federation of Student Organizations/Al Faisal Islamic Press, 1985), 14.

46. A similar division has been made by other scholars. See Anthony McRoy, *From Rushdie to 7/7: The Radicalisation of Islam in Britain* (London: Social Affairs Unit, 2006), 4 and Part III; and Jeffrey M. Bale, "Hiding in Plain Sight in 'Londonistan,'" in Michael Innes, ed., *Denial of Sanctuary: Understanding Terrorist Safe Havens* (Westport, CT: Praeger, 2007), 139–51.

47. Amel Boubekeur, "Political Islam in Europe: A Changing Landscape," in Amel Boubekeur, Samir Amghar, and Michael Emerson, eds., *European Islam: The Challenges for Public Policy and Society* (Brussels: CEPS/Open Society Institute, 2007).

2. The Western Brotherhood

1. Ali Rahnema, "Introduction," in Ali Rahnema, ed., *Pioneers of Islamic Revival* (London: Zed Books, 1994), xlv–xlvii.

2. Jamal Barzinji, "History of the Islamization of Knowledge and Contributions of the International Institute of Islamic Thought," in Amber Haque, ed., *Muslims and Islamization in North America: Problems and Prospects* (Beltsville, MD: Amana Publications, 1999), 16; David Commins, "Hasan al-Banna, 1906–1949," in Ali Rahnema, ed., *Pioneers of Islamic Revival* (London: Zed Books, 1994).

3. Although many books have been written on the Muslim Brotherhood and its early activities, the most comprehensive and widely read remains Richard P. Mitchell, *The Society of the Muslim Brothers* (New York: Oxford University Press, 1969).

4. Brynjar Lia, *The Society of the Muslim Brothers in Egypt: The Rise of an Islamic Movement, 1928–1942* (Reading, UK: Ithaca Press, 1998), 32–40.

5. Mitchell, *The Society of the Muslim Brothers*, 223; Robert S. Leiken and Steven Brooke, "The Moderate Muslim Brotherhood," *Foreign Affairs* (March/April 2007):108.

6. Hassan al Banna, "The New Renaissance," in John J. Donahue and John L. Esposito, eds., *Islam in Transition: Muslim Perspectives* (New York: Oxford University Press, 1982), 79.

7. Hassan al Banna, quoted in Lia, *The Society of the Muslim Brothers in Egypt*, 202.

8. Mitchell, *The Society of the Muslim Brothers*, 232–33.

9. *Five Tracts of Hasan al-Banna (1906–1949): A Selection from the Majmu'at Rasa'il al-Imam al-Shahid Hasan al-Banna*, trans. and annotated by Charles Wendell (Berkeley: University of California Press, 1978), 48.

10. William L. Cleveland, *A History of the Modern Middle East* (Boulder, CO: Westview, 2004), 302.

11. Dennis J. Sullivan and Sana Abed-Kotob, *Islam in Contemporary Egypt: Civil Society vs. the State* (Boulder, CO: Lynne Rienner, 1999), 42.

12. Khurshid Ahmad, "Mawdudi's Model for Islamic Revival," in Muhammad Mumtaz Ali, ed., *Modern Islamic Movements: Models, Problems and Perspectives* (Kuala Lumpur: Noordeen, 2000); interview with Husain Haqqani, Boston, February 2006.

13. Jamal A. Badawi, "Approaches to Muslim Reawakening: Al-Banna's Approach," in Muhammad Mumtaz Ali, ed., *Modern Islamic Movements: Models, Problems and Perspectives* (Kuala Lumpur: Noordeen, 2000).

14. Saeed Hawwa, *The Muslim Brotherhood* (Kuwait: International Islamic Federation of Student Organizations/Al Faisal Islamic Press, 1985), 2.

15. Olivier Roy, *The Failure of Political Islam* (Cambridge, MA: Harvard University Press, 1996), 110–13.

16. Ziad Abu-Amr, *Islamic Fundamentalism in the West Bank and Gaza* (Bloomington and Indianapolis: Indiana University Press, 1994), 2–4.

17. Mitchell, *The Society of the Muslim Brothers*, 30–64.

18. Tewfiq Aclimandos, *Officiers et Freres Musulmans*, Centre d'études et de documentation économiques, juridiques et sociales, Etudes et documents, n°1/2 (2001): 61–125; Ataf Lutfi Al-Sayyid Marsot, *A History of Egypt: From the Arab Conquest to the Present* (Cambridge: Cambridge University Press, 1985), 127–31.

19. Mitchell, *The Society of the Muslim Brothers*, 105–33.

20. Gilles Kepel, *Muslim Extremism in Egypt* (Berkeley and Los Angeles: University of California Press, 1986), 26–35.

21. Sayyid Qutb, *Islam: The Religion of the Future* (Delhi: Markazi Maktaba Islami, 1974), 67.

22. Kepel, *Muslim Extremism in Egypt*, 36–59.

23. The Arabic word *jihad*, literally meaning struggle, can be used to describe various phenomena. Traditionally, scholars identify as "greater *jihad*" man's internal struggle to reach perfection and please God and as "lesser *jihad*" Muslims' duty to take up arms to defend Islam.

24. Sullivan and Abed-Kotob, *Islam in Contemporary Egypt*, 43.

25. For an excellent overview of Qutb's life and influence, see Lawrence Wright, *The Looming Tower: Al Qaeda and the Road to 9/11* (New York: Knopf, 2006), 7–31.

26. Interview with Barbara Zollner, London, December 2008; John O. Voll, "Fundamentalism in the Sunni Arab World," in Martin E. Marty and R. Scott Appleby, eds., *Fundamentalisms Observed* (Chicago: University of Chicago Press, 1991).

27. Barbara Zollner, *The Muslim Brotherhood: Hasan Al-Hudaybi and Ideology* (London: Routledge, 2008); Emmanuel Sivan, *Radical Islam: Medieval Theology and Modern Politics* (New Haven: Yale University Press, 1985), 107–11.

28. Barbara Zollner, "Prison Talk: The Muslim Brotherhood's Internal Struggle During Gamal Abdel Nasser's Persecution," *International Journal of Middle Eastern Studies* 39 (2007): 411–33.

29. John L. Esposito, *The Islamic Threat: Myth or Reality?* (New York and Oxford: Oxford University Press, 1999), 140–41; Kepel, *Muslim Extremism in Egypt*, 62–63.

30. The expression "Neo Muslim Brethren" is used by various scholars to describe the accommodationist wing that developed in the late 1960s/early 1970s. Among them, see Kepel, *Muslim Extremism in Egypt*, 62–63.

31. For an extensive history of the founding of the Muslim World League and other pan-Islamic organizations, see Reinhard Schulze, *Islamischer Internationalismus im 20. Jahrhundert: Untersuchungen zur Geschichte der Islamischen Weltliga* (Leiden: Brill, 1990); see also John L. Esposito, ed., *The Oxford Encyclopedia of the Modern Islamic World* (New York/Oxford: Oxford University Press, 1995), 2:207–209. A detailed list of *dawa* projects financed by the MWL since the 1960s can also be found in most issues of the *Muslim World League Journal*.

32. Jocelyne Cesari, *When Islam and Democracy Meet: Muslims in Europe and in the United States* (New York: Palgrave MacMillan, 2004), 143.

33. For the life of Said Ramadan, see: M. H. Faruqi, "Les Frères Musulmans: Politique de 'Rabbaniyya,' les Prières avant le Pouvoir," Islamic Center of Geneva, http://www.cige.org/historique.htm (accessed January 21, 2005); Tariq Ramadan, "Une Vie Entière," http://membres.lycos.fr/oasislam/personnages/tariq/tariq.html (accessed May 4, 2007); Tariq Ramadan, "4th August . . . 10 Years," http://www.tariqramadan.com/spip.php?page=imprimer&id_article=371 (accessed May 28, 2009).

34. Abu-Amr, *Islamic Fundamentalism in the West Bank and Gaza*, 3.

35. Interview with Husain Haqqani, Boston, April 2006.

36. Interview with official at the Landesverfassungsschutz Baden-Württemberg, Stuttgart, November 2008.

37. See, for example, Kenneth R. Timmerman, *Preachers of Hate: Islam and the War on America* (New York: Crown Forum, 2003).

38. Schulze, *Islamischer Internationalismus im 20. Jahrhundert.*

39. Ian Johnson, "The Brotherhood's Westward Expansion," *Current Trends in Islamist Ideology*, February 5, 2008; interview with Ian Johnson, Berlin, November 2008; interview with Stefan Meining, Munich, May 2009; interview with Bavarian Landesamt für Verfassungsschutz officials, Munich, May 2009.

40. The history of the Munich mosque, central to an understanding of the early days of the Brotherhood in Europe, is being told in two forthcoming books written by Stefan Meining and Ian Johnson. I thank both of them for allowing me to see the extensive documentation they have obtained from German public archives.

41. Ian Johnson, "The Beachhead: How a Mosque for Ex-Nazis Became Center of Radical Islam," *The Wall Street Journal*, July 12, 2005; Zwischen Halbmond und Hakenkreuz, *ARD* documentary, July 19, 2006.

42. Filing of the Moscheebau Kommission, Munich Amtsgericht, March 29, 1960; filings of the Islamische Gemenischaft in Deutschland from 1973 to 2002, Munich Amtsgericht; interview with Bavarian Landesamt für Verfassungsschutz officials, Munich, May 2009; interview with Stefan Meining, Munich, May 2009; interview with Ian Johnson, Berlin, November 2008.

43. Interview with Bavarian Landesamt für Verfassungsschutz, Munich, May 2009; interview with Stefan Meining, Munich, May 2009.

44. Interview with Yussuf Nada, Campione d'Italia, July 14, 2008.

45. Ibid. Extensive interviews with Nada about his life have also been published by the Egyptian paper *al Misri al Yawm* (May 25–30, 2008) and by Al Jazeera ("Century Witness," from August 4 to September 29, 2002).

46. Interview with Yussuf Nada, Campione d'Italia, July 14, 2008.

47. Interview with Yussuf Nada, Campione d'Italia, July 14, 2008.

48. "Recent OFAC Actions," U.S. Department of the Treasury, Office of Foreign Assets Control, November 7, 2001. In March 2010 the UN removed Nada from the list.

49. Muslim scholars have traditionally debated the two concepts, often developing subcategories and diverging opinions. See, for example, Khaled Abou El Fadl, "Striking a Balance: Islamic Legal Discourse on Muslim Minorities," in Yvonne Yazbeck Haddad and John L. Esposito, eds., *Muslims on the Americanization Path?* (New York: Oxford University Press, 2000).

50. Wasif Shadid and Sjoerd van Koningsveld, "Loyalty to a Non-Muslim Government," in W. A. R. Shadid and P. S. van Konignsveld, eds., *Political Participation and Identities of Muslims in Non-Muslim States* (Kampen: Kok Pharos, 1996); Xavier Ternisien, *Les Frères Musulmans* (Paris: Fayard, 2005), 190–92.

51. "London Conference of Islamic Centres and Bodies in Europe," *Impact International*, May 25–June 7, 1973.

52. John Lawton, "Muslims in Europe: The Presence," *Saudi Aramco World* (January/February 1979):3–8.

53. Phone interview with Maha Azzam, March 2009; "Islamic Council of Europe: 'Foundations Well Laid,'" *Impact International*, May 26–June 8, 1978.

54. People Section, *Impact International*, October 28–November 10, 1977. Salem Azzam was a relative of Abdel Rahman Azzam, the first Secretary General of the League of Arab States (whose daughter married the eldest son of King Faysal of Saudi Arabia) and Dr. Abdal-Wahab Azzam, president of Cairo University and founder of King Saud University, in Riyadh.

55. "Spectrum: A Roll Call of UK Islamic Groups—Islam and Britain," *Times of London*, August 17, 1987.

56. "Islamic Council of Europe: Progress and Plans," *Impact International*, September 10–23, 1976; "News from the Muslim World League," *Muslim World League Journal*, July 1974.

57. Cesari, *When Islam and Democracy Meet*, 147.

58. Sylvain Besson, *La Conquête de l'Occident* (Paris: Seuil, 2005), 114.

59. http://www.jamaat.org/leadership/pka.html (accessed January 17, 2008).

60. John L. Esposito and John O. Voll, *Makers of Contemporary Islam* (Oxford University Press, 2001), 45–46.

61. Annual filings of the Islamische Gemeinschaft in Süddeutschland, Amtsgericht, Munich, 1983.

62. Interview with Yussuf Nada, Campione d'Italia, July 14, 2008 and Mohamed Nimer, *The North American Muslim Resource Guide: Muslim Community Life in the United States and Canada* (New York: Routledge, 2002), 161–62.

63. Barzinji, "History of the Islamization of Knowledge and Contributions of the International Institute of Islamic Thought," 13–21; Leif Stenberg, *The Islamiza-*

tion of Science: Four Muslim Positions Developing an Islamic Modernity (New York: Coronet Books, 1996), 157–58.

64. Ilyas Ba-Yunus and Kassim Kone, *Muslims in the United States* (Westport, CT: Greenwood Press, 2006), 49; http://www.msanational.org/about/history/ (accessed September 24, 2008); interviews with MSA members, Chicago, December 2002.

65. Larry Poston, *Islamic Da'wah in the West* (New York: Oxford University Press, 1992), 79; interview with Yussuf Nada, Campione d'Italia, July 14, 2008; John Mintz and Douglas Farah, "In Search of Friends Among the Foes: U.S. Hopes to Work with Diverse Group," *Washington Post*, September 11, 2004.

66. Ahmad Totonji, "World Assembly of Muslim Youth," *Impact International*, October 22–November 11, 1976; "IIFSO Conference: No Proclamations, No Self-Congratulations, Just Sharing of Experience," *Impact International*, August 12–15, 1977.

67. John L. Esposito, ed., *The Oxford Encyclopedia of the Modern Islamic World* (New York/Oxford: Oxford University Press, 1995), 2:207–209.

68. "ISNA Recognizes IIIT VP Dr. Jamal Barzinji for Pioneering Service," September 8, 2008, http://www.iiit.org/NewsEvents/News/tabid/62/articleType/Article View/articleId/90/Default.aspx, (accessed September 24, 2008); Steven Merley, *The Muslim Brotherhood in the United States*, research monograph for the Hudson Institute, April 2009, 9–10; "Muslim Students' Associations Hold Annual Convention," *Muslim World League Journal*, November/December 1965.

69. http://www.nait.net/ (accessed September 24, 2008).

70. Barzinji, "History of the Islamization of Knowledge and Contributions of the International Institute of Islamic Thought," 18.

71. "Pangs and Process of Self-Discovery," *Impact International*, October 14–27, 1983; interview with ISNA official, Chicago, December 2002; Poston, *Islamic Da'wah in the West*, 104.

72. Gutbi Mahdi Ahmed, "Muslim Organizations in the United States," in Yvonne Yazbeck Haddad, ed., *The Muslims of America* (Oxford: Oxford University Press, 1991), 14–18.

73. Interview with Yussuf Nada, Campione d'Italia, July 14, 2008. One of the companies was Nada International, one of the many entities set up by Nada in Liechtenstein. Both Barzinji and al Talib served on its board of trustees for years.

74. Interview with Yussuf Nada, Campione d'Italia, July 14, 2008.

75. Barzinji, "History of the Islamization of Knowledge and Contributions of the International Institute of Islamic Thought," 13–21; Muhammad Shafiq, *Growth of Islamic Thought in North America* (Brentwood, MD: Amana Publications, 1994), 87.

76. Ismail Raji al-Faruqi, "Islamizing the Social Sciences," *Muslim World League Journal*, August 1977.

77. Shafiq, *Growth of Islamic Thought in North America*, 28; http://www.iiit.org/AboutUs/AboutIIIT/tabid/66/Default.aspx (accessed September 8, 2008); Merley, *The Muslim Brotherhood in the United States*, 26.

78. For an extensive biography of Ismail Faruqi, see Shafiq, *Growth of Islamic Thought in North America*. See also Esposito and Voll, *Makers of Contemporary Islam*, 23–35.

79. http://www.iiit.org/AboutUs/OfficesAffiliates/tabid/68/Default.aspx (accessed September 24, 2008).

80. See Letter from Office of the Assistant Secretary of Defense to Abdurahman Alamoudi, Executive Director, American Muslim Council, September 12, 1996; Cordoba University, http://www.siss.edu/Newsletter/FirstMAMCAConference8–8-00.htm (accessed through www.archive.org).

81. Speech by HRH The Prince of Wales during his visit to the Islamic Foundation, 24 January 2003, http://www.princeofwales.gov.uk/speeches/multiracial_24012003.html (accessed April 22, 2005).

82. Mitchell, *The Society of the Muslim Brothers*, 172–73.

83. Interview with Dr. Abd El Monem Abou El Fotouh, Cairo, December 2008; interview with Barbara Zollner, London, December 2008.

84. Interview with Dr. Abd El Monem Abou El Fotouh, Cairo, December 2008.

85. Wendy Kristianasen, "A Row in the Family," *Le Monde Diplomatique*, April 2000.

86. Interview with Kamal Helbawy, London, December 2008; Israel Elad Altman, *Strategies of the Muslim Brotherhood Movement*, 1928–2007, monograph for the Hudson Institute, January 2009, 5–6; interview with Israel Elad Altman, Paris, May 2009.

87. Altman, *Strategies of the Muslim Brotherhood Movement*, 1928–2007, 5–6.

88. Leiken and Brooke, "The Moderate Muslim Brotherhood," 115.

89. Interview in *Asharq Al-Awsat*, December 11, 2005.

90. Cited in Hillel Fradkin, "The History and Unwritten Future of Salafism," *Current Trends in Islamist Ideology*, November 25, 2007.

91. For an extensive analysis of how the Palestinian branch of the Muslim Brotherhood became Hamas, see Azzam Tamimi, *Hamas: A History from Within* (Northampton, MA: Olive Branch Press, 2007), 10–51; and Abu-Amr, *Islamic Fundamentalism in the West Bank and Gaza*, 1–22.

92. Interview with John Voll, Washington, October 2008; for a definition of "transnational activism" see Sidney Tarrow, *The New Transnational Activism* (Cambridge: Cambridge University Press, 2005).

93. Interview with MB Deputy Chairman Mohamed Habib in *al Ahrar Daily*, as reported by the Muslim Brotherhood's official Web site, June 16, 2008, http://

www.ikhwanweb.com/Article.asp?ID=17267&LevelID=1&SectionID=0   (accessed August 1, 2008).

94. Brigitte Maréchal, *The Muslim Brothers in Europe: Roots and Discourse* (Leiden/Boston: Brill, 2008), 179.

95. Tariq Ramadan, *Aux Sources du Renouveau Musulman* (Lyon: Tawhid, 2002), 11.

96. *Al-Sharq al-Awsat* (London), December 11, 2005.

97. Interview with Yussuf Nada, Campione d'Italia, July 14, 2008.

98. Interview with Dr. Abd El Monem Abou El Fotouh, Cairo, December 2008.

99. Ternisien, *Les Frères Musulmans*, 110–11.

100. Interview with Mohammed Akef, Alwihdah Web site, January 14, 2004, http://www.alwihdah.com/view.asp?cat=3&id=50.

101. Besson, *La Conquête de l'Occident*, 100.

102. For an explanation of the concept of *dawa* and its evolution, see Dale F. Eickelman and James Piscatori, *Muslim Politics* (Princeton: Princeton University Press, 1996), 35–36.

103. The term "paramosque" has been coined by Prof. Larry Poston. See Poston, *Islamic Da'wah in the West*, 94–97; see also Carrie Rosefsky Wickham, *Mobilizing Islam: Religion, Activism, and Political Change in Egypt* (New York: Columbia University Press, 2002), 98.

104. Mohammed Akram, An Explanatory Memorandum on the Strategic Goals for the Group in North America, Government Exhibit 003–0085 in *United States v. Holy Land Foundation et al.*, 3:04-cr-240 (ND, Tex.).

105. Wickham, *Mobilizing Islam*, 130.

106. John O. Voll, "Relations Among Islamist Groups," in John L. Esposito, ed., *Political Islam: Revolution, Radicalism, or Reform?* (Boulder, CO: Lynne Rienner, 1997).

107. Interview with Yussuf Nada, Campione d'Italia, July 14, 2008.

108. Roy, *The Failure of Political Islam*, 110–13.

109. Khurshid Ahmad wrote extensive treatises on Islamic banking while living in England. Gamal Attia was based for a long time in Luxembourg, where he was involved in several high-profile financial activities. Mahmoud Abu Saud, who founded Alamoudi's American Muslim Council, penned most of his writings while living in Florida.

110. Filings with the Erhvervs- og Selskabsstyrelsen (Danish Commerce and Companies Agency), April 7, 1983; annual reports of the International Islamic Bank, 1982–1996, Erhvervs- og Selskabsstyrelsen.

111. Extract from the Central Register of Charities Maintained by the Charity Commission for England and Wales, http://www.charity-commission.gov.uk (accessed July 21, 2008).

112. Ibid.

113. Bret Stephens, "Benedict's Opposite," *The Wall Street Journal*, September 26, 2006.

114. Gudrun Krämer, "Drawing Boundaries: Yusuf al-Qaradawi on Apostasy," in Gudrun Krämer and Sabine Schmidtke, *Speaking for Islam: Religious Authorities in Muslim Societies* (Leiden: Brill, 2006), 186–209.

115. For an extensive profile of al Qaradawi's life and works, see Bettina Gräf and Jakob Skovgaard-Petersen, eds., *The Global Mufti: The Phenomenon of Yusuf Al-Qaradawi* (New York: Columbia University Press, 2009).

116. Husan Tammam, "Yusuf Qaradawi and the Muslim Brothers: The Nature of a Special Relationship," in Bettina Gräf and Jakob Skovgaard-Petersen, eds., *The Global Mufti: The Phenomenon of Yusuf Al-Qaradawi* (New York: Columbia University Press, 2009), 55–74.

117. Raymond William Baker, *Islam Without Fear: Egypt and the New Islamists* (Cambridge, MA: Harvard University Press, 2003); Bettina Gräf, "The Concept of Wasatiyya in the Work of Yusuf al-Qaradawi," in Bettina Gräf and Jakob Skovgaard-Petersen, eds., *The Global Mufti: The Phenomenon of Yusuf Al-Qaradawi* (New York: Columbia University Press, 2009), 213–28. It must be noted that al Qaradawi's rejection of violence is not absolute, as he has consistently endorsed acts of violence in places where Muslims are under occupation, such as Palestine, Chechnya, and Iraq. The matter will be treated at length in chapter 8.

118. Al Qaradawi's refusal in 2004 was not the first, as he had turned down the group's leadership also in 1976; see Jakob Skovgaard-Petersen, "Yusuf Al-Qaradawi and Al-Azhar," in Bettina Gräf and Jakob Skovgaard-Petersen, eds., *The Global Mufti: The Phenomenon of Yusuf Al-Qaradawi* (New York: Columbia University Press, 2009), 37.

119. Al Jazeera, January 12, 2004.

120. "Qaradawi: 'MB Asked Me to Be a Chairman,'" Ikhwanweb, September 5, 2006, http://www.ikhwanweb.net/Article.asp?ID=3537&SectionID=0 (accessed August 19, 2008).

121. Alexandre Caeiro and Mahmoud al-Saify, "Qaradawi in Europe, Europe in Qaradawi? The Global Mufti's European Politics," in Bettina Gräf and Jakob Skovgaard-Petersen, eds., *The Global Mufti: The Phenomenon of Yusuf Al-Qaradawi* (New York: Columbia University Press, 2009).

122. Interview with a FIOE representative, Brussels, June 2008.

123. http://www.eu-islam.com/en/templates/Index_en.asp (accessed September 26, 2008).

124. *Power, Development and Prosperity*, 2007 FIOE report obtained by the author during a visit to FIOE's headquarters in Brussels, June 2008.

125. http://www.euro-muslim.com/en_about_us.aspx (accessed June 6, 2009).

126. Ibid.

127. http://www.eu-islam.com/en/templates/Index_en.asp (accessed September 26, 2008).

128. http://www.iesh.org/index.php?option=com_content&task=view&id=50& Itemid=102&lang=en (accessed August 2, 2008); Franck Fregosi, "Les Filières Nationales de Formation des Imams en France," in Franck Fregosi, ed., *La Formation des Cadres Religieux Musulmans en France* (Paris: L'Harmattan, 1998), 108–13.

129. http://www.femyso.net/about.html (accessed September 28, 2008).

130. Interview with EU official, Brussels, June 2008.

131. Ian Johnson, "How Islamic Group's Ties Reveal Europe's Challenge," *The Wall Street Journal*, December 29, 2005.

132. Interview with a FIOE representative, Brussels, June 2008.

133. "The Muslim Brotherhood in Europe and a Course of Reviews, UK an Example," Ikhwanweb, August 12, 2008, http://ikhwanweb.com/Article.asp?ID=17575 &SectionID=67 (accessed August 28, 2008).

134. Interview with Akef in Besson, *La Conquête de l'Occident*, 100.

135. See, for example, Azzam S. Tamimi, *Rachid Ghannouchi: A Democrat Within Islamism* (New York: Oxford University Press, 2001), 170.

136. Maréchal, *The Muslim Brothers in Europe*, 168–73.

137. Kristianasen, "A Row in the Family."

138. See chapter 5 for an analysis of the situation in Great Britain.

139. Amel Boubekeur, "Post-Islamist Culture: A New Form of Mobilization?" *History of Religions* 47, no. 1 (2007): 75–94.

140. Maréchal, *The Muslim Brothers in Europe*, 78.

3. Aims and Methods

1. The debate is perfectly summarized in an article by Jonathan Dahoah-Halevi with the telling title, "The Muslim Brotherhood: A Moderate Islamic Alternative to al-Qaeda or a Partner in Global *Jihad*?" *Jerusalem Center for Public Affairs* 558 (November 1, 2007).

2. Lecture by Carry Wickham at Harvard University's Weatherhead Center for International Affairs, February 26, 2005; Carry Wickham, "Democratization and Islamists—Auto-Reform," Ikhwanweb, June 15, 2006, http://www.ikhwanweb.com/ Article.asp?ID=4112&SectionID=81 (accessed October 13, 2008).

3. Robert S. Leiken and Steven Brooke, "The Moderate Muslim Brotherhood," *Foreign Affairs* (March/April 2007).

4. Amr Al-Chobaki, "Future of Muslim Brotherhood," June 13, 2007, http://www .ikhwanweb.com/article.php?id=814&ref=search.php.

5. *Ad-Dawa* magazine, January 1981, quoted in Sayed Mahmoud Al-Qumni, "The Muslim Brotherhood's Initiative as a Reform Program: A Critical Review," paper presented at the conference on Islamic reform, Brookings Institution, October 5–6, 2004. http://www.brookings.edu/fp/research/projects/islam/cairopaper1.pdf (accessed October 7, 2008).

6. Interview with Dr. Abd El Monem Abou El Fotouh and Dr. Hesham El Hamamy, Cairo, December 2008; Israel Elad Altman, "Current Trends in the Ideology of the Egyptian Muslim Brotherhood," *Current Trends in Islamist Ideology*, December 29, 2005.

7. Amel Boubekeur, *Political Islam in Algeria*, Center for European Policy Studies working document 268, May 2007.

8. Quoted in Al-Qumni, "The Muslim Brotherhood's Initiative as a Reform Program."

9. Quoted in Al-Qumni, "The Muslim Brotherhood's Initiative as a Reform Program."

10. Amr Hamzawy, "Regression in the Muslim Brotherhood's Platform?" *Daily Star*, November 1, 2007.

11. Nathan J. Brown and Amr Hamzawy, *The Draft Party Platform of the Egyptian Muslim Brotherhood: Foray Into Political Integration or Retreat Into Old Positions?* Carnegie Papers, Middle East Series, Number 89, January 2008.

12. Various members of the Egyptian Brotherhood claim that the role of this body is still debated internally and should be seen not as binding but as simply advisory. Interview with Dr. Abd El Monem Abou El Fotouh and Dr. Hesham El Hamamy, Cairo, December 2008. Some scholars believe that Islamists simply seek to create bodies of judicial review to confirm legislation's compatibility with *sharia*, like bodies in most Western constitutional systems (see, for example, Noah Feldman, *The Fall and Rise of the Islamic State* [Princeton and Oxford, Princeton University Press, 2008], 11–15, 120–23).

13. Various members of the Egyptian Brotherhood claim that the group's position on the issue was also misinterpreted. Rather than banning women and non-Muslims from being heads of state, they would not introduce them as candidates, but since they accept the democratic process, they would accept the election of anybody by the majority. Interview with Dr. Abd El Monem Abou El Fotouh and Dr. Hesham El Hamamy, Cairo, December 2008.

14. Maggie Michael, "Egypt's Brotherhood Party Details Platform Akin to That of Iran," *Associated Press*, October 11, 2007.

15. Azzam S. Tamimi, *Rachid Ghannouchi: A Democrat Within Islamism* (New York: Oxford University Press, 2001), v–vii, 63–104.

16. See, for example, Quran, Surat al Shura, 42/37–38 or Imran 3/159.

17. See, for example, Bassam Tibi, *The Challenge of Fundamentalism: Political Islam and the New World Disorder* (Berkeley: University of California Press, 1998), 173–77.

18. Mohamed Elhachmi Hamdi, *The Politicization of Islam: A Case Study of Tunisia* (Boulder, CO: Westview Press, 1998)., 102–105.

19. John L. Esposito and John O. Voll, *Makers of Contemporary Islam* (Oxford/New York: Oxford University Press, 2001), 115.

20. Ibid.

21. Tamimi, *Rachid Ghannouchi*, 77.

22. Dahoah-Halevi, "The Muslim Brotherhood."

23. Refaat al-Said, *Against Illumination* (Cairo: 1996), cited in Magdi Khalil, "Egypt's Muslim Brotherhood and Political Power: Would Democracy Survive?" *Middle East Review of International Affairs Journal* 10, no. 3 (March 2006): 44–52.

24. John L. Esposito, *The Islamic Threat: Myth or Reality?* (New York and Oxford: Oxford University Press, 1999), 211.

25. Altman, "Current Trends in the Ideology of the Egyptian Muslim Brotherhood."

26. "Muslim Brotherhood Supreme Guide: Bin Laden is a Jihad Fighter," Middle East Media and Research Institute (MEMRI), Special Dispatch #2001, July 25, 2008.

27. "How Islam Views Pluralism and Democracy," IslamOnline, July 30, 2002, http://www.islamonline.net/servlet/Satellite?c=FatwaE&cid=1119503545626&pagename=IslamOnline-English-Ask_Scholar%2FASELayout (accessed August 11, 2008).

28. *Fatwa* issued by Qaradawi on the IslamOnline site, February 4, 2000, http://www.islamonline.net/completesearch/english/FatwaDisplay.asp?hFatwaID=5638 through the Way Back Machine (accessed through www.archive.org, August 18, 2008).

29. Ibrahim El Houdaiby, "Why Are Western Officials Hesitant to Talk to Moderate Islamists?" *Daily Star*, November 7, 2007.

30. John L. Esposito, "Practice and Theory," *Boston Review* (April/May 2003), http://www.bostonreview.net/BR28.2/esposito.html (accessed July 24, 2008).

31. "Homosexuality Is a Major Sin," *fatwa* session with Sheik Yusuf al Qaradawi on IslamOnline, December 6, 2003, http://www.islamonline.net/servlet/Satellite?pagename=IslamOnline-English-Ask_Scholar/FatwaE/FatwaE&cid=1119503543878 (accessed September 21, 2009).

32. Yusuf al-Qaradawi, "Apostasy: Major and Minor," IslamOnline,http://www.islamonline.net/English/contemporary/2006/04/article01c.shtml (accessed July 24, 2008).

33. Gudrun Krämer, "Drawing Boundaries: Yusuf al-Qaradawi on Apostasy," in Gudrun Krämer and Sabine Schmidtke, eds., *Speaking for Islam: Religious Authorities in Muslim Societies* (Leiden: Brill, 2006), 200–209.

34. Samir Amghar, "Europe Puts Islamists to the Test: The Muslim Brotherhood (France, Belgium and Switzerland)," *Mediterranean Politics* 13, no. 1 (March 2008): 63–77.

35. Interview with Dr. Abd El Monem Abou El Fotouh, Cairo, December 2008.

36. Interview with Kamal Helbawy, London, December 2008; interview with UOIF president Lhaj Thami Breze, La Courneuve, May 2009.

37. Quoted in *Qu'est-ce que l'UOIF?* (Paris: Éditions l'Archipel, 2006), 19.

38. Philip Lewis, *Islamic Britain: Religion, Politics and Identity Among British Muslims* (London: I. B. Tauris, 1994), 191–92.

39. *First Collection of Fatwas,* trans. Anas Osama Altikriti, European Council for Fatwa and Research, date unspecified.

40. "Islam's Stance on Homosexual Organizations," *fatwa* session on Islam Online with Taha Jabir al Alawani, May 17, 2004, http://www.islamonline.net/servlet/Satellite?pagename=IslamOnline-English-Ask_Scholar/FatwaE/Fatwa E&cid=1119503545314 (accessed February 17, 2009).

41. Interview with Kamal Helbawy, London, December 2008.

42. See, for example, Anthony R. Oberschall, *Social Conflict and Social Movements* (Englewood Cliffs, NJ: Prentice Hall, 1973); Donatella della Porta and Mario Diani, *Social Movements: An Introduction* (Malden, MA: Blackwell, 1999); John D. McCarthy and Mayer N. Zald, "Resource Mobilization and Social Movements: A Partial Theory," *The American Journal of Sociology* 82, no. 6 (May 1977): 1212–1241; Bob Edwards and John D. McCarthy, "Resources and Social Movement Mobilization," in David A. Snow, Sarah A. Soule, and Hanspeter Kriesi, eds., *The Blackwell Companion to Social Movements* (Oxford: Blackwell, 2004), 116–52.

43. For two excellent and groundbreaking applications of social movement theory to Islamist groups (albeit only in the Muslim world), see Quintan Wiktorowicz, ed., *Islamic Activism: A Social Movement Theory Approach* (Bloomington: Indiana University Press, 2004) and Carrie Rosefsky Wickham, *Mobilizing Islam: Religion, Activism, and Political Change in Egypt* (New York: Columbia University Press, 2002).

44. Yusuf al Qaradawi, *Priorities of the Islamic Movement in the Coming Phase* (Swansea, UK: Awakening Publications, 2000).

45. Ibid.

46. Wasif Shadid and Sjoerd van Koningsveld, "Religious Authorities of Muslims in the West: Their Views on Political Participation," in Wasif Shadid and P. S.

van Koningsveld, eds., *Intellectual Relations and Religious Authorities: Muslims in the European Union* (Leuven: Peeters, 2002), 149–70.

47. http://www.iumsonline.org/english/index.shtml (accessed May 5, 2009); Jakob Skovgaard-Petersen, "Yusuf Al-Qaradawi and Al-Azhar," in Bettina Gräf and Jakob Skovgaard-Petersen, eds., *The Global Mufti: The Phenomenon of Yusuf Al-Qaradawi* (New York: Columbia University Press, 2009), 45–47.

48. *First Collection of Fatwas.*

49. http://islamireland.ie/about-us (accessed May 29, 2009); http://www.e-cfr.org/en/ECFR.pdf (accessed May 29, 2009).

50. Xavier Ternisien, *Les Frères Musulmans* (Paris: Fayard, 2005), 197–98.

51. Closing remarks at the council session in Stockholm, July 2003. As quoted in Sylvain Besson, *La Conquete de l'Occident* (Paris: Editions du Seuil, 2005), 124.

52. Alexandre Caeiro, "The European Council for Fatwa and Research," presentation at the Fourth Mediterranean Social and Political Research Meeting, European University Institute, Montecatini Terme, March 19–23, 2003; Alexandre Caeiro and Mahmoud al-Saify, "Qaradawi in Europe, Europe in Qaradawi? The Global Mufti's European Politics," in Bettina Gräf and Jakob Skovgaard-Petersen, eds., *The Global Mufti: The Phenomenon of Yusuf Al-Qaradawi* (New York: Columbia University Press, 2009).

53. *Fatwa 3, Resolutions and Fatwas (Second Collection)*, ed. Anas Osama Altikriti and Mohammed Adam Howard, European Council for Fatwa and Research, date unspecified.

54. *Fatwa 4, Resolutions and Fatwas (Second Collection).*

55. Quran, Surah at-Taghabun ayah 16.

56. "Living Islam in the West: An Interview with Shaykh Faisal Mawlawi," *Palestinian Times*, no. 98, http://www.palestinetimes.net/issue98/articles.html#7 (accessed March 21, 2006).

57. *Fatwa 26, Resolutions and Fatwas (Second Collection).*

58. *Fatwa 17, Resolutions and Fatwas (Second Collection).*

59. *Fatwa 21, First Collection of Fatwas.*

60. *Fatwa 32, First Collection of Fatwas.*

61. Yusuf al Qaradawi, *Le Licite et l'Illicite en Islam* (Paris: Editions al Qalam, 1992), 207. The book was first published in Arabic in 1960.

62. Ternisien, *Les Frères Musulmans*, 312.

63. *Fatwa 16, Resolutions and Fatwas (Second Collection).*

64. Resolution 5/15, Final Statement of the Fifteenth Ordinary Session of The European Council for Fatwa and Research, Istanbul, June 29–July 3, 2005.

65. al Qaradawi, *Priorities.*

66. M. Ali Kettani, "The Problems of Muslim Minorities and Their Solutions," in *Muslim Communities in Non-Muslim States* (London: Islamic Council of Europe, 1980), 103.

67. al Qaradawi, *Priorities*.

68. Quintan Wiktorowicz, "Introduction: Islamic Activism and Social Movement Theory," in Quintan Wiktorowicz, ed., *Islamic Activism: A Social Movement Theory Approach* (Bloomington: Indiana University Press, 2004).

69. Salwa Ismail, *Rethinking Islamist Politics: Culture, the State and Islamism* (London: I. B. Tauris, 2003), 34–39.

70. The term has been used, for example, as the title of a 2004 book by Ahmed Yousef describing the U.S. Muslim community. Yousef, who served for years as director of the Fairfax, VA-based think tank United Association for Studies and Research (UASR), later became chief political adviser to Hamas Prime Minister Ismail Haniyeh. See Ahmed Yousef, *American Muslims: A Community Under Siege* (Springfield, VA: UASR Publishing Group, 2004).

71. These are the words used by the Muslim Association of Britain to define its aims. See http://www.mabonline.info/english/modules.php?name=About (accessed February 8, 2007).

72. Bettina Gräf, "IslamOnline.net: Independent, Interactive, Popular," *Arab Media and Society* 4 (Winter 2008); "IslamOnline Opens Washington Office," IslamOnline.net, December 27, 2008, http://www.islamonline.net/servlet/Satellite?c=Article_C&cid=1230121266417&pagename=Zone-English-News/NWE Layout (accessed February 10, 2009); Bettina Gräf, "The Concept of *Wasatiyya* in the Work of Yusuf al-Qaradawi," in Bettina Gräf and Jakob Skovgaard-Petersen, eds., *The Global Mufti: The Phenomenon of Yusuf Al-Qaradawi* (New York: Columbia University Press, 2009), 225.

73. al Qaradawi, *Priorities*. See also Yusuf al Qaradawi, *Islamic Awakening Between Rejection and Extremism* (Herndon, VA: International Institute of Islamic Thought, 1991), where he quotes the *hadith* "a believer to another believer like a building whose different bricks enforce one another" as proof of the God-mandated duty for collective work (91).

74. Document published in appendix of Besson, *La Conquete de l'Occident*.

75. See chapter 5.

76. Gilles Kepel, *Allah in the West: Islamic Movements in America and Europe* (Palo Alto, CA: Stanford University Press, 1997), 187.

77. "La France Face à ses Musulmans: Émeutes, Jihadisme et Dépolitisation," report by the International Crisis Group, March 9, 2006, 6–9.

78. Interview with UOIF president Lhaj Thami Breze, La Courneuve, May 2009; Xavier Ternisien, "'Prière Nationale' Musulmane à La Courneuve pour Concilier

Solidarité et Revendication du Voile," *Le Monde*, September 5, 2004; Vincent Geisser and Aziz Zemouri, *Marianne et Allah: Les Politiques Français face à la "Question Musulmane"* (Paris: La Découverte, 2007), 116.

79. Ternisien, *Les Frères Musulmans*, 127.

80. Interview with UOIF president Lhaj Thami Breze, La Courneuve, May 2009; *Qu'est-ce que l'UOIF?* (Paris: Éditions l'Archipel, 2006), 19–20.

81. *Qu'est-ce que l'UOIF?*, 20.

82. Gilles Kepel, *The War for Muslim Minds: Islam and the West* (Cambridge, MA: Harvard University Press, 2004), 283.

83. For an overview of what, according to the Islamic movement, Muslims can contribute to the West, see Kamal el-Helbawy, "Cementing Relations Between Muslim Citizens and Governments in the West: The United Kingdom as a Case Study," *Islamism Digest* 3, no. 9 (September 2008).

84. Interview with UOIF president Lhaj Thami Breze, La Courneuve, May 2009.

85. al Qaradawi, *Priorities*.

86. For a detailed analysis of the Muslim Brotherhood's strategy toward Palestine, see Ziad Abu-Amr, *Islamic Fundamentalism in the West Bank and Gaza* (Bloomington and Indianapolis: Indiana University Press, 1994), 23–52.

87. Document published in appendix of Besson, *La Conquete de l'Occident*.

88. The Covenant of the Islamic Resistance Movement (Hamas), August 18, 1988. Available in English at: http://avalon.law.yale.edu/20th_century/hamas.asp (accessed May 5, 2009).

89. *United States v. Holy Land Foundation et al.*, 3:04-cr-240 (ND, Tex.). The case will be extensively examined in chapter 7.

90. Interview with Dr. Kamal Helbawy, Al-Masry al-Youm, February 2, 2009, http://www.almasry-alyoum.com/printerfriendly.aspx?ArticleID=197210 (accessed February 9, 2009).

91. Mary Habeck, *Knowing the Enemy* (New Haven: Yale University Press, 2006), 31–32.

92. Sayyeed Abdul-Ala Maududi, *Jihad in Islam* (Lahore, Pakistan: Islamic Publications), 9.

93. Interview with Peter Mandaville, Washington, October 2008.

94. "An Explanatory Memorandum on the Strategic Goals for the Group in North America," Government Exhibit 003–0085 in *United States v. Holy Land Foundation et al.*, 3:04-cr-240 (ND, Tex.).

95. Interview with Yussuf Nada, Campione d'Italia, July 14, 2008.

96. Jason Trahan, "'Smoking Gun' Holy Land Foundation Trial Document Still Viral, Spawns a New Film," *Dallas Morning News*, May 23, 2009.

97. Besson, *La Conquete de l'Occident*, 151.

98. "New Muslim Brotherhood Leader: Resistance in Iraq and Palestine Is Legitimate; America Is Satan, Islam Will Invade America and Europe," Middle East Media and Research Institute (MEMRI), Special Dispatch No. 655, February 4, 2004.

99. Yousef al-Qaradawi, MAYA Conference, 1995, Toledo, Ohio. Transcript available at: http://www.investigativeproject.org/profile/167#_ftn3 (accessed October 9, 2008).

100. "Leading Sunni Sheikh Yousef al-Qaradhawi and Other Sheikhs Herald the Coming Conquest of Rome," Middle East Media and Research Institute (MEMRI), Special Dispatch No. 447, December 6, 2002.

101. Larry Poston, *Islamic Da'wah in the West* (New York: Oxford University Press, 1992), 81–83. Mourad's most famous works are *The Islamic Movement in the West: Reflections on Some Issues* (1981) and *Da'wah Among Non-Muslims in the West* (1986).

102. Cited in Poston, *Islamic Da'wah in the West*, 82. The works on *dawa* of Shamim Siddiqi, an Indian-born activist who joined Jamat-e-Islami in 1952 and then moved to the United States in 1976, are posted on his own Web site, http://www.dawahinamericas.com/ (accessed September 3, 2008).

103. Khurram Murad, "Islamic Movement in the West: Reflections on Some Issues," in Muhammad Mumtaz Ali, ed., *Modern Islamic Movements: Models, Problems and Perspectives* (Kuala Lumpur: Noordeen, 2000), 274.

104. Shamim A. Siddiqi, "Islamic Movement in America: Why?" in Amber Haque, ed., *Muslims and Islamization in North America: Problems and Prospects* (Beltsville, MD: Amana Publications, 1999).

105. Ibid.

106. Ahmad Husain Sakr, "The Future of Islam in North America," *Muslim World League Journal* (April 1975); Sakr's biography can be found on his personal Web site: http://www.ahmadsakr.com/bio.html (accessed June 9, 2009).

107. For the Brothers' belief that "the future belongs to Islam," see, among many, Wickham, *Mobilizing Islam*, 172.

108. Taha Jaber Al-Alwani, "The Participation of Muslims in the American Political System," Islamonline.net, http://www.islamonline.net/english/Politics/2000/1/Article7.shtml (accessed January 22, 2009).

109. Brigitte Maréchal, *The Muslim Brothers in Europe: Roots and Discourse* (Leiden/Boston: Brill, 2008), 269.

110. "Muslims Participating in US Local Councils," *fatwa* session with Muzammil Siddiqi, IslamOnline.net, October 1, 2003, http://www.islamonline.net/servlet/Satellite?pagename=IslamOnline-English-Ask_Scholar/FatwaE/FatwaE&cid=1119503544898 (accessed January 26, 2009). The second part of the argu-

ment had been expressed by Siddiqi, using identical words, in a Q&A session with readers published in the October 18, 1996, issue of the American magazine *Pakistan Link*.

4. The Governments' Dilemma

1. John Mintz and Douglas Farah, "In Search of Friends Among the Foes: U.S. Hopes to Work with Diverse Group," *Washington Post*, September 11, 2004.

2. See, for example, Alexandre Caeiro and Mahmoud al-Saify, "Qaradawi in Europe, Europe in Qaradawi? The Global Mufti's European Politics," in Bettina Gräf and Jakob Skovgaard-Petersen, eds., *The Global Mufti: The Phenomenon of Yusuf Al-Qaradawi* (New York: Columbia University Press, 2009), 111.

3. Olivier Roy, *Secularism Confronts Islam* (New York: Columbia University Press, 2007), 94–98.

4. The expression is used, for example, by the British MP Michael Gove in his book *Celsius 7/7* (London: Phoenix, 2006), 84–113.

5. Antoine Sfeir, *Les Réseaux d'Allah: Les Filières Islamistes en France et en Europe* (Paris: Plon, 2001), 51.

6. Alain Chouet, "The Association of Muslim Brothers: Chronicle of a Barbarism Foretold," http://alain.chouet.free.fr/documents/M_B.htm (accessed July 21, 2008).

7. Report of the Comité Permanent de Contrôle des Services de Renseignements et de Sécurité (Comité R) to the Belgian Parliament, July 19, 2002, http://www.senate.be/www/?MIval=/publications/viewPubDoc&TID=33618007&LANG =fr#2–1171/1_112 (accessed November 12, 2008).

8. *The Radical Dawa in Transition: The Rise of Islamic Neoradicalism in the Netherlands*, AIVD, February 2008, https://www.aivd.nl/actueel-publicaties/aivd-publicaties/the-radical-dawa-in, 51.

9. Jeff Stein, "Democrats' New Intelligence Chairman Needs a Crash Course on al Qaeda," *Congressional Quarterly*, December 8, 2006.

10. Jeff Stein, "Can You Tell a Sunni from a Shiite?" *New York Times*, October 18, 2006.

11. Maurice Chittenden and Tom Baird, "MPs Don't Know their Sunnis from their Shi'ites," *Sunday Times*, January 7, 2007.

12. 59th Report of CESIS (Executive Committee for the Intelligence and Security Services) to the Italian Parliament, 2007, 71.

13. This is a frank admission that has been made to the author, on several separate occasions, by American, British, and Danish intelligence officials.

14. Graham T. Allison, *Essence of Decision: Explaining the Cuban Missile Crisis* (Boston: Little, Brown, 1971), 67.

15. Gilles Kepel, *The War for Muslim Minds* (Cambridge, MA: Harvard University Press, 2004), 286–87.

16. Conversation with Naser Khader, Boston, April 2007.

17. "The Muslim Brotherhood in Europe," testimony of Ian Johnson before the Congressional Human Rights Caucus, February 9, 2006.

18. Joost de Haas, "Moskeeen in de ban van Moslimgroep," *De Telegraaf*, March 24, 2007.

19. Questions from the PVV MPs Geert Wilders and Raymond de Roon and answers from Ella Vogelaar, August 7, 2007, http://www.pvv.nl/index.php?option=com_content&task=view&id=737 (accessed September 5, 2008); interviews with Dutch officials and journalists, Amsterdam and The Hague, May 2008.

20. Interviews with Dutch officials and journalists, Amsterdam and The Hague, May 2008.

21. Allison, *Essence of Decision*, 81.

22. See chapter 6.

23. See, for example, Alessandra Arachi, "Stop alla Moschea: 'Chi la Finanzia?' Genova Chiama Amato, Unione Divisa," *Corriere della Sera*, September 25, 2007; Magdi Allam, "La Moschea di Bologna e i Cedimenti di Cofferati," *Corriere della Sera*, December 6, 2007; Diego Pistacchi, "Ronchi: No alla Moschea degli Intolleranti," *Il Giornale*, February 3, 2009; interviews with members of the Federazione dell'islam italiano, Rome, May 2009.

24. Corinne Torrekens, "La gestion locale de l'islam à Bruxelles," *Cahiers de la sécurité*, P 8° 5663.—(2006–07/09) n°62, p.139–160; Stéphane Kovacs, "L'islam, première religion à Bruxelles dans vingt ans," *Le Figaro*, March 21, 2008.

25. Jocelyne Cesari, *Securitization and Religious Divides in Europe: Muslims in Western Europe After 9/11*, http://euro-islam.info/ei/wp-includes/pdf/securitization_and_religious_divides_in_europe.pdf (accessed February 14, 2009).

26. *Islamophobia: A Challenge for Us All*, Runnymede Trust, 1997.

27. Munira Mirza, Abi Senthilkumaran, and Zein Ja'far, *Living Apart Together: British Muslims and the Paradox of Multiculturalism*, report for the Policy Exchange, 2007, 18.

28. Bassam Tibi, *Islamische Zuwanderung, Die gescheiterte Integration* (Munich: DVA, 2002), 135; interview with Bassam Tibi, Boston, October 2008.

29. "Foreign Aid and the Fight Against Terrorism and Proliferation: Leveraging Foreign Aid to Achieve U.S. Policy Goals," hearing held by the U.S. House of Representatives Committee on Foreign Affairs, Subcommittee on Terrorism, Nonproliferation, and Trade, July 31, 2008.

30. Allison, *Essence of Decision*, 72.

31. Carla Powers, "New Imams," *Newsweek*, January 17, 2006.

32. Brigitte Marechal, "Dealing with European States," in Brigitte Marechal, Stefano Allievi, Felice Dassetto, and Jørgen Nielen, *Muslims in the Enlarged Europe* (Leiden/Boston: Brill, 2003), 180.

33. Stefano Allievi, "Muslims and Politics," in Brigitte Marechal, Stefano Allievi, Felice Dassetto, and Jørgen Nielen, *Muslims in the Enlarged Europe* (Leiden/Boston: Brill, 2003), 198.

34. Jonathan Laurence, "Integrating Islam: A New Chapter in 'Church-State' Relations," report for the Transatlantic Task Force on Immigration and Integration, October 2007.

35. See, for example, Amel Boubekeur, "Political Islam in Algeria," Centre for European Policy Studies working paper no. 268, May 2007.

36. Nicolas Sarkozy, *La République, les Religions, l'Espérance* (Paris: Éditions du Cerf, 2004), 100.

37. Gilles Kepel, *Jihad: The Trail of Political Islam* (Cambridge, MA: Harvard University Press, 2002), 369–70.

38. Interview with Hans Jørgen Bonnichsen, former head of operations of Danish domestic intelligence (PET), Copenhagen, November 2008; John Hansen and Kim Hundevadt, *Provoen og Profeten: Muhammed Krisen Bag Kulisserne* (Aarhus: Jyllands-Postens Forlag, 2006); Pernille Ammitzbøll and Lorenzo Vidino, "After the Danish Cartoon Controversy," *Middle East Quarterly* 14, no. 1 (Winter 2007).

5. Great Britain

1. Philip Lewis, *Islamic Britain: Religion, Politics and Identity Among British Muslims* (London: I. B. Tauris, 1994), 11. An even smaller presence of Muslim converts and merchants can be dated back to the late sixteenth century: see Nabil Matar, *Islam in Britain, 1558–1685* (Cambridge: Cambridge University Press, 1998).

2. UK Census 2001, http://www.statistics.gov.uk/census2001/census2001.asp (accessed January 15, 2009).

3. Data included in Richard Kerbaj, "Muslim Population Rising 10 Times Faster Than Rest of Society," *Times of London*, January 30, 2009.

4. According to the 2006 MINAB booklet *Good Practice Guide for Mosques and Imams in Britain*, 68 percent of British Muslims are of South Asian origin.

5. Lewis, *Islamic Britain*, 10–48; Jørgen S. Nielsen, "Transnational Islam and the Integration of Islam in Europe," in Stefano Allievi and Jørgen S. Nielsen, *Muslim Networks and Transnational Communities in and Across Europe* (Leiden: Brill, 2003), 35.

6. For a comprehensive history of the JeI, see Seyyed Vali Reza Nasr, *The Van-guard of the Islamic Revolution: The Jama'at-i Islami of Pakistan* (Berkeley: University of California Press, 1994).

7. John L. Esposito and John O. Voll, *Makers of Contemporary Islam* (Oxford University Press, 2001), 39–46.

8. Ibid.

9. *Muslims in London*, report published by the Greater London Authority, October 2006.

10. UK Islamic Mission, *An Introduction*, as quoted in Gilles Kepel, *Allah in the West: Islamic Movements in America and Europe* (Palo Alto: Stanford University Press, 1997), 131.

11. UK Islamic Mission annual report 1976/1977, as published in the *Muslim World League Journal*, April 1978.

12. As published in the *Muslim World League Journal*, July 1976.

13. UK Islamic Mission annual report 2004/2005, copy in possession of the author, 2–3.

14. Lewis, *Islamic Britain*, 103.

15. Anthony McRoy, *From Rushdie to 7/7: The Radicalisation of Islam in Britain* (London: Social Affairs Unit, 2006), 119.

16. Lewis, *Islamic Britain*, 104.

17. http://www.ymuk.net/ (accessed May 5, 2009).

18. http://www.islamic-foundation.org.uk/ (accessed May 5, 2009).

19. Quoted in Lewis, *Islamic Britain*, 102.

20. Speech by HRH The Prince of Wales during his visit to the Islamic Foundation, January 24, 2003, http://www.princeofwales.gov.uk/speechesandarticles/a_speech_by_hrh_the_prince_of_wales_during_his_visit_to_the_2024889013.html (accessed May 28, 2009).

21. http://www.ukim.org/dawahBooks/jihad.pdf (accessed April 15, 2009).

22. See, for example, "Dawah: Our Purpose, Our Goal," Fiaz Hussein, UK Islamic Mission National Dawah Committee, speech at the 2003 annual conference of the Islamic Mission, http://ukim.org/dawah/dawah%20our%20purpose%20our%20goal.PDF (accessed April 15, 2009).

23. Salman Rushdie, *The Satanic Verses* (New York: Viking, 1989).

24. Malise Ruthven, *A Satanic Affair: Salman Rushdie and the Wrath of Islam* (London: Hogarth Press, 1991), 65–66.

25. Ibid., 91–92.

26. M. M. Ahsan and A. R. Kidwai, eds., *Sacrilege Versus Civility: Muslim Perspectives on The Satanic Verses Affair* (Leicester: Islamic Foundation, 1993), 335–37; Kepel, *Allah in the West*, 130–46.

27. Philip Lewis, "The Bradford Council for Mosques and the Search for Muslim Unity," in Steven Vertovec and Ceri Peach, eds., *Islam in Europe: The Politics of Religion and Community* (London: MacMillan, 1997), 103–29.

28. "UK Muslims Act Against Infamous Book," interview with Manazir Ahsan, *Saudi Gazette*, December 15, 1988.

29. "The Fuss About Fatwa Evades the Real Issue: Sacrilege," interview with Iqbal Sacranie, *Impact International*, March 12/April 8, 1993.

30. "UK Muslims Act Against Infamous Book."

31. Anthony Loyd, "Tomb of the Unknown Assassin Reveals Mission to Kill Rushdie," *Times of London*, June 8, 2005.

32. Rana Kabbani, "Dislocation and Neglect in Muslim Britain's Ghettos," *Guardian*, June 17, 2002.

33. Andrew Anthony, "How One Book Ignited a Culture War," *Guardian*, January 11, 2009.

34. Dilwar Hussain, "The Holy Grail of Muslims in Western Europe," in John L. Esposito and Francois Burgat, eds., *Modernizing Islam: Religion in the Public Sphere in Europe and the Middle East* (New Brunswick: Rutgers University Press, 2003), 229.

35. Steven Vertovec, "Muslims, the State, and the Public Sphere in Britain," in Gerd Nonneman, Tim Niblock, and Bogdan Szajkowski, eds., *Muslim Communities in the New Europe* (Berkshire, UK: Ithaca Press, 1996), 170–73.

36. Interview with Dr. Muhammad Abdul Bari, MCB Secretary General, London, December 2008.

37. 10 *Years of Working for the Common Good*, MCB brochure.

38. http://www.mcb.org.uk/downloads/MCB_achievments.pdf (accessed January 15, 2009).

39. *MCB: Representing Muslims & Serving the Nation*, MCB brochure.

40. Iqbal Sacranie, quoted in McRoy, *From Rushdie to 7/7*, 12.

41. Faraz Mohammed, "MCB: Dad's Muslim Army," *Q-News*, April 1998, 21.

42. Steven Vertovec, "Islamophobia and Muslim Recognition in Britain," in Yvonne Yazbeck Haddad, ed., *Muslims in the West: From Sojourners to Citizens* (Oxford: Oxford University Press, 2001), 29; Alan Travis, "Muslims Abandon Labour Over Iraq War," *Guardian*, March 15, 2004.

43. Nadeem Azam, "Election Analysis," *Q-News*, June 1997.

44. Kepel, *Allah in the West*, 116; "Elections 1997 and British Muslims," *QNews*, March 14, 1997.

45. *Impact International*, April 1997.

46. Iqbal Sacranie, "Why You Should Exercise Your Vote," *QNews*, March 1997, 26.

47. "MCB Hosts Luncheon Meeting with Jack Straw," December 2, 1998, http://www.mcb.org.uk/media/archive/news021298.html (accessed March 2, 2009).

48. "Holocaust Memorial Ceremony—MCB regrets exclusion of Palestinian tragedy." MCB press release, January 26, 2001, http://web.archive.org/web/20050314235755/http:/www.mcb.org.uk/news260101.html (accessed January 14, 2009).

49. Interview with Dr. Muhammad Abdul Bari, London, December 2008.

50. MCB Community Guidelines to Imams and British Muslim Organisations, March 31, 2004, http://www.mcb.org.uk/media/presstext.php?ann_id=80 (accessed January 16, 2009).

51. Interview with Baroness Neville-Jones, London, December 2008; interview with Home Office officials, London, December 2008.

52. *Preventing Extremism Together*, Working Group's report, August–October 2005, http://www.communities.gov.uk/documents/communities/pdf/152164.pdf (accessed March 3, 2009).

53. Alasdair Palmer, "Top Job Fighting Extremism for Muslims Who Praised Bombers," *Telegraph*, August 20, 2005; David Cesarani, "A Way out of This Dead End," *Guardian*, September 16, 2005.

54. Salman Rushdie, "Bring on the Islamic Reformation," *Washington Post*, August 8, 2005; *A Question of Leadership*, BBC 1, August 21, 2005; "The Fuss About Fatwa Evades the Real Issue: Sacrilege," interview with Iqbal Sacranie in *Impact International*, March 12/April 8, 1993.

55. Interview with Baroness Kishwer Falkner, Cambridge (MA), March 2006; interview with Haras Rafiq, London, January 2007.

56. *Preventing Extremism Together*, 3.

57. Interview with Dean Godson, London, December 2008.

58. Racial and Religious Hatred Bill, British Parliament, http://www.parliament.the-stationery-office.co.uk/pa/cm200506/cmbills/011/06011.i-i.html (accessed May 4, 2009).

59. Mike O'Brien, "Labour and British Muslims: Can We Dream the Same Dream?" *Muslim Weekly* 58 (2004). O'Brien wrote: "The Muslim Council of Britain has been at the forefront of lobbying the Government on issues to help Muslims. Recently Iqbal Sacranie, the General Secretary of the Council, asked Tony Blair to declare that the Government would introduce a new law banning religious discrimination. Two weeks later, in the middle of his speech to the Labour Party Conference, Tony Blair promised that the next Labour Government would ban religious discrimination."

60. Asim Siddiqui, "Not in Our Name," *Guardian*, July 3, 2007.

61. Quoted in Martin Bright, *When Progressives Treat with Reactionaries: The British State's Flirtation with Radical Islam*, report published by the Policy Exchange, 2006, 25.

62. Interview with Ruth Kelly and various DCLG and Home Office officials, London, December 2008.

63. "Attitudes to Living in Britain: A Survey of Muslim Opinion," *Channel 4 Dispatches*, August 7, 2006, http://www.imaginate.uk.com/MCC01_SURVEY/Site%20Download.pdf; Munira Mirza, Abi Senthilkumaran, and Zein Ja'far, *Living Apart Together: British Muslims and the Paradox of Multiculturalism*, report for the Policy Exchange, 2007, 6.

64. *A Question of Leadership.*

65. Alasdair Palmer, "Not in Their Name?" *Sunday Telegraph*, July 8, 2007.

66. Interview with Dr. Muhammad Abdul Bari, MCB's Secretary General, London, December 2008.

67. Kenan Malik, "The Islamophobia Myth," *The Spectator*, February 2005.

68. *Muslims in London.*

69. Tom Harper, "Ministers Compared to Nazis Over Islam Stigma," *Telegraph*, December 18, 2006.

70. Conservative Party's National and International Security Policy Group's interim report on national cohesion, January 2007.

71. Graeme Wilson, "Cameron Attacks Muslim Hardliners," *Telegraph*, January 31, 2007.

72. "How the Government Lost the Plot," *The Economist*, February 26, 2009.

73. Alice Thomson, "British Should Try Arranged Marriages," *Telegraph*, June 10, 2006.

74. http://news.bbc.co.uk/2/hi/uk_news/4786159.stm?ls (accessed January 13, 2009).

75. Ned Temko, "Beckett Rejects Link Between Foreign Policy and Terrorism," *Observer*, August 13, 2006.

76. Philippe Naughton, "Funding Cut-off Threat by Minister Angers Muslim Groups," *Times of London*, October 11, 2006.

77. Interview with Ruth Kelly, London, December 2008.

78. Interview with Ruth Kelly, London, December 2008; Toby Helm, "Back British Values or Lose Grants, Kelly Tells Muslim Groups," *Telegraph*, October 12, 2006.

79. That is the case, for example, of the British Muslim Forum and the Sufi Muslim Council.

80. *Preventing Violent Extremism: Next Steps for Communities*, report by the Department for Communities and Local Government, July 2008, 31.

81. Ibid., 16.

82. Helm, "Back British Values or Lose Grants, Kelly Tells Muslim Groups"; *Representing the Muslims, Serving the Nation*, 2006/07 MCB activity report; Vikram Dodd, "Muslim Council Ends Holocaust Memorial Day Boycott," *Guardian*, December 3, 2007.

83. Program of the 2006 Islamic Finance and Trade Conference, copy in possession of the author.

84. Program of the 2008 Islamic Finance and Trade Conference, copy in possession of the author.

85. Bill Law, "Clerics Urge a New Jihad Over Gaza," *BBC News*, February 17, 2009; Vikram Dodd, "Government Suspends Links with Muslim Council of Britain Over Gaza," *Guardian*, March 23, 2009; the text of the declaration and a list of signatories can be found at http://www.islammessage.com/articles.aspx?cid=1&acid=26&aid=7295 (accessed March 27, 2009).

86. Jamie Doward, "British Muslim Leader Urged to Quit Over Gaza," *The Observer*, March 8, 2009.

87. "MCB Rejects Hazel Blears' Baseless Accusations," MCB press release, March 26, 2009; Vikram Dodd, "Government Suspends Links with Muslim Council of Britain Over Gaza," *Guardian*, March 23, 2009.

88. Letter from Hazel Blears to MCB Secretary General Muhammad Abdul Bari, March 13, 2009, http://image.guardian.co.uk/sys-files/Guardian/documents/2009/03/23/blears_letter.pdf (accessed March 27, 2009).

89. Inayat Bunglawala, "Engagement with Extremists Is Right," *Guardian*, February 26, 2009.

90. "Muslim Leader Sues Blears on Gaza," *BBC News*, April 4, 2009.

91. *The United Kingdom's Strategy for Countering International Terrorism (CONTEST 2)*, HM Government, March 2009.

92. Home Office statement regarding the BBC program *Muslim First, British Second*, February 16, 2009, http://news.bbc.co.uk/panorama/hi/front_page/newsid_7888000/7888793.stm (accessed February 25, 2009).

93. Tom Whitehead, "Government Ties with MCB Restored but not for Deputy," *The Telegraph*, January 15, 2010.

94. James Forsyth, "The Government Caves in to the Muslim Council of Britain," *The Spectator*, January 15, 2010.

95. Richard Kerbaj, "Government Moves to Isolate Muslim Council of Britain with Cash for Mosques," *Times of London*, March 30, 2009.

96. Moin Shakir, *Khilafat to Partition: A Survey of Major Political Trends Among Indian Muslims During* 1919–1947 (Delhi: Ajanta, 1983), 208.

97. Dr. Padmasha, *Indian National Congress and the Muslims: 1928–1947* (New Delhi: Rajesh, 1980), 11–17.

98. Kepel, *Allah in the West*, 94.

99. Kepel, *Allah in the West*, 94.

100. Jonathan Paris, "Discussion Paper on Approaches to Anti-Radicalization and Community Policing in the Transatlantic Space," paper prepared for the Wei-

denfeld Institute conference, Washington, June 2007; interview with Jonathan Paris, London, December 2008.

101. Amartya Sen, *Identity and Violence: The Illusion of Destiny* (New York: Norton, 2006), 118.

102. *Muslims in London.*

103. Mirza, Senthilkumaran, and Ja'far, *Living Apart Together*, 22–23.

104. Kenan Malik, *From Fatwa to Jihad: The Rushdie Affair and Its Legacy* (London: Atlantic Books, 2009), xix.

105. Delwar Hussain, "Bangladeshis in East London: From Secular Politics to Islam," *Open Democracy*, July 6, 2006, http://www.opendemocracy.net/democracy-protest/bangladeshi_3715.jsp (accessed January 7, 2009).

106. John Eade and David Garbin, "Changing Narratives of Violence, Struggle and Resistance: Bangladeshis and the Competition for Resources in the Global City," *Oxford Development Studies* 30, no. 2 (2002).

107. Carla Power, "New Imams," *Newsweek*, January 17, 2006; Sean McLoughlin, "Islam, Citizenship and Civil Society: 'New' Muslim Leadership in the UK," presentation at the European Muslims and the Secular State in a Comparative Perspective conference, European Commission/Network of Comparative Research on Islam and Muslims in Europe, June 30/July 1, 2003.

108. Kepel, *Allah in the West*, 114.

109. Sen, *Identity and Violence*, 78.

110. Kenan Malik, "What Muslims Want," Channel 4, August 7, 2006.

111. Malik, *From Fatwa to Jihad*, 67.

112. David Page, *Prelude to Partition: The Indian Muslims and the Imperial System of Control*, 1920–1932 (New York: Oxford University Press, 1982), 260.

113. Palmer, "Not in Their Name?"

114. Ed Husain, *The Islamist* (London: Penguin, 2007), 74–75.

115. For a good overview of the British debate on multiculturalism, see Jonathan Sacks, *The Home We Build Together: Recreating Society* (London: Continuum, 2007).

116. "Britain 'Sleepwalking to Segregation,'" *Guardian*, September 19, 2005.

117. For information on Helbawy's life: interview with Kamal Helbawy, London, December 2008; Dr. Helbawy's personal Web site, http://www.khelbawy.com/about.html) (accessed March 5, 2009).

118. http://mabonline.net/?page_id=2 (accessed January 7, 2009).

119. http://www.islamonline.net/Arabic/news/2004–03/19/article08.shtml (accessed March 5, 2009); Michael Whine, "The Advance of the Muslim Brotherhood in the UK," *Current Trends in Islamist Ideology* 2 (September 2005).

120. Richard Phillips, "Standing Together: The Muslim Association of Britain and the Anti-war Movement," *Race & Class* 50, no. 2 (2008): 101–13.

121. Salma Yaqoob, "British Islamic Political Radicalism," in Tahir Abbas, ed., *Islamic Political Radicalism: A European Perspective* (Edinburgh: Edinburgh University Press, 2007).

122. Interview with Kamal Helbawi, London, December 2008; "Angry Scenes at Anti-Israel Demo," BBC, April 13, 2002.

123. *http://www.ihrc.org.uk/show.php?id=294* (accessed May 5, 2009); Phillips, "Standing Together."

124. Interview with Kamal Helbawi, London, December 2008; Phillips, "Standing Together."

125. Phillips, "Standing Together."

126. Phillips, "Standing Together."

127. Interview with antiwar activist, London, December 2008; for the debate in extreme Left circles, see, for example, Jane Kelly and Karen O'Toole, "Alliances and Coalitions in Britain: 'Stop the War' and 'Respect,'" ISG Political Committee, April 2005, http://www.internationalviewpoint.org/spip.php?article672 (accessed March 2, 2009).

128. Interview with Kamal Helbawy, London, December 2008.

129. Phillips, "Standing Together."

130. Cairo Declaration, December 27, 2002, http://www.counterpunch.org/cairo 1227.html (accessed March 3, 2009); "American Anti-War Movement Leader Meets with Radical Anti-Zionists in Cairo," Anti-Defamation League, December 29, 2003, http://www.adl.org/Israel/ramsey_clark.asp (accessed March 3, 2009).

131. Phillips, "Standing Together."

132. Phillips, "Standing Together."

133. Alan Travis, "Muslims Abandon Labour Over Iraq War," *Guardian*, March 15, 2004.

134. *Why the Mayor of London Will Maintain Dialogues with All of London's Faith Communities*, dossier published by the Greater London Authority, January 2005.

135. "Mayor Livingstone and Sheikh Qaradawi: A Response by a Coalition of Many of London's Diverse Communities," document in possession of the author.

136. "MCB Decries Character Assassination of Dr Al-Qaradawi," July 7, 2004, http://www.mcb.org.uk/media/presstext.php?ann_id=102 (accessed January 12, 2009).

137. Mayor's statement at MQT on the visit of Dr. Al Qaradawi, City of London, July 15, 2004, http://www.london.gov.uk/view_press_release.jsp?releaseid=3862 (accessed August 18, 2008).

138. Ibid.; Richard Ford, "Livingstone Likens Bomb Apologist to Reformer Pope John," *Times of London*, September 14, 2005.

139. *Why the Mayor of London Will Maintain Dialogues with All of London's Faith Communities.*

140. Abdel Rahman al-Rasheed, "Qaradawi: Moderate and Extremist," *Arab News,* July 17, 2004.

141. Ibid.

142. BBC Monitoring International Reports, Near/Middle East: "Round-up of Friday Sermons," June 4, 2004 (published June 7, 2004). Qaradawi's sermons calling for the killing of Jews have been many over the years. One of the most direct is arguably one delivered in January 2009, in which Qaradawi said: "Throughout history, Allah has imposed upon the [Jews] people who would punish them for their corruption. The last punishment was carried out by Hitler. By means of all the things he did to them—even though they exaggerated this issue—he managed to put them in their place. This was divine punishment for them. Allah willing, the next time will be at the hand of the believers." ("Sheikh Yousuf Al-Qaradhawi: Allah Imposed Hitler On the Jews to Punish Them—'Allah Willing, the Next Time Will Be at the Hand of the Believers,'" MEMRI, February 3, 2009).

143. "Mayor Culpa," *Private Eye,* March 21, 2008.

144. http://islamexpo.info/index.php?option=com_frontpage&Itemid=1 (accessed March 6, 2009).

145. David Rich, "The Muslim Brotherhood in Great Britain," unpublished paper. The event's largest sponsor was the Qatari National Council for Culture, which donated almost a million pounds. For Livingstone's presence at the conference, see http://islamexpo.info/images/stories/programme_2070617.30.pdf.

146. http://www.muslimsforken.blogspot.com/ (accessed January 7, 2009); "Open Letter: Give Ken a Third Term," *Guardian,* January 3, 2008, http://www.guardian.co.uk/commentisfree/2008/jan/03/supportingkenlivingstoneas (accessed January 7, 2009).

147. Yaqoob, "British Islamic Political Radicalism."

6. Germany

1. http://www.london.diplo.de/Vertretung/london/en/06/other_legal_matters/Reform_Germanys_citizenship_seite.html (accessed March 11, 2009).

2. *Muslimisches Leben in Deutschland,* report by the Federal Ministry of Interior for the Deutsche Islam Konferenz, June 2009, 232–36; "Two Unamalgamated Worlds," *The Economist,* April 3, 2008.

3. *Muslimisches Leben in Deutschland,* 57–84.

4. "Two Unamalgamated Worlds."

5. Yasemin Karakasouglu and Gerd Nonneman, "Muslims in Germany," in Gerd Nonneman, Tim Niblock, and Bogdan Szajkowski, eds., *Muslim Communities in the New Europe* (Berkshire, UK: Ithaca Press Paperbacks, 2006); Carolyn M. War-

ner and Manfred W. Wenner, "Religion and the Political Organization of Muslims in Europe," *Perspectives on Politics* 4, no. 3 (September 2006): 457–79.

6. "Islam and Muslims in Germany: An Overview by Ibrahim El-Zayyat," *Islamism Digest* 3, no. 1 (January 2008).

7. For numbers: Federal Ministry of the Interior, http://www.bmi.bund.de/nn _1026710/Internet/Content/Themen/Deutsche_Islam_Konferenz/DatenUndFak ten/Islamkonferenz_Kurzinfo_en.html (accessed September 8, 2008).

8. M. Hakan Yavuz, *Islamic Political Identity in Turkey* (New York: Oxford University Press, 2003).

9. For a general overview of German Muslim organizations, see Nils Feindt-Riggers and Udo Steinbach, *Islamische Organisationen in Deutschland* (Hamburg: Deutsches Orient-Institut, 1997).

10. David Shankland, *Islam and Society in Turkey* (Huntingdon: Eothen Press, 1999), 87–90.

11. Stephen Kinzer, *Crescent and Star: Turkey Between Two Worlds* (New York: Farrar, Straus & Giroux, 2001), 63–64; Amel Boubekeur, "Political Islam in Europe: A Changing Landscape," in Amel Boubekeur, Samir Amghar, and Michael Emerson, eds., *European Islam: The Challenges for Public Policy and Society* (Brussels: CEPS/Open Society Institute, 2007); interview with Turkish activist, Cologne, July 2007.

12. Lars Pedersen, *Newer Islamic Movements in Western Europe* (Aldershot: Ashgate, 1999), 56–9.

13. http://www.igmg.de/verband/islamic-community-milli-goerues/historical-development-of-the-igmg.html?L=.html.html.html (accessed May 2, 2009).

14. Boubekeur, "Political Islam in Europe"; annual report of the Office for the Protection of the Constitution, 2006, 213.

15. Annual report of the Office for the Protection of the Constitution, 2008, 210; annual report of the Bavarian Verfassungsschutz, 2008, 47; *Islamistische Organisationen in Nordrhein-Westfalen*, publication by the Ministry of the Interior of Nordrhein-Westfalen, November 2008, 63.

16. Ali Bardakoglu, "'Moderate Perception of Islam' and the Turkish Model of Diyanet: The President's Statement," *Journal of Muslim Minority Affairs* 24, no. 2 (October 2004).

17. Werner Schiffauer, "From Exile to Diaspora: The Development of Transnational Islam in Europe," in Aziz Al-Azmeh and Effie Fokas, eds., *Islam in Europe: Diversity, Identity and Influence* (Cambridge: Cambridge University Press, 2007).

18. Interview with Turkish government official, Istanbul, June 2008; Bardakoglu, "'Moderate Perception of Islam' and the Turkish Model of Diyanet."

19. German Islam Conference (DIK), document provided by officials at the Federal Ministry of the Interior, Berlin, November 2008, http://www.bmi.bund.de/nn

_1026710/Internet/Content/Themen/Deutsche_Islam_Konferenz/DatenUndFak ten/Islamkonferenz_Kurzinfo_en.html (accessed September 8, 2008).

20. "Islam and Muslims in Germany"; interview with official at the Landesver-fassungsschutz Baden-Württemberg, Stuttgart, November 2008; interview with Bavarian Landesamt für Verfassungsschutz officials, Munich, May 2009.

21. *Islamistische Organisationen in Nordrhein-Westfalen*, 44; Ian Johnson, "The Brotherhood's Westward Expansion," *Current Trends in Islamist Ideology*, February 5, 2008.

22. Filing of the Islamische Gemenischaft in Deutschland at the Munich Amts-gericht, February 28, 2002.

23. Interview with Kamal Helbawy, London, December 2008; interview with Yussuf Nada, Campione d'Italia, July 14, 2008; interview with German security authorities, Cologne, April 2005; filing of the Islamische Gemeinschaft Mar-burg/Omar Ibn al-Khattab Moschee at the Frankfurt Ausländeramt, January 25, 1990.

24. Interview with German security authorities, Cologne, April 2005.

25. Interview with Kamal Helbawy, London, December 2008; interview with German security authorities, Cologne, April 2005.

26. Interview with German security authorities, Cologne, April 2005; http://p9445.typo3server.info/56.0.html (accessed November 21, 2008).

27. See, for example, the seminar on integration and diversity organized by Alli-ance of Liberals and Democrats of Europe: http://www.alde.eu/index.php?id=129& detail=16367&album=0 (accessed May 5, 2009).

28. "Islam and Europe: Ibrahim El-Zayyat Discusses the Future," *Islamism Di-gest* 3, no. 2 (February 2008): 16.

29. Uta Rasche, "Spinne im Netz der Muslime in Deutschland: Die Macht des Ibrahim El Zayat," *Frankfurter Allgemeine Zeitung*, May 11, 2007.

30. Extract from the Central Register of Charities Maintained by the Charity Commission for England and Wales, http://www.charity-commission.gov.uk (ac-cessed July 21, 2008); Rasche, "Spinne im Netz der Muslime in Deutschland."

31. Andrea Brandt, "Wendiger Weltmann," *Der Spiegel*, March 25, 2008; interview with German security authorities, Cologne, April 2005; Helmut Frangenberg and Detlef Schmalenberg, "El-Zayat, der Herr der Moscheen," *Kölner Stadt-Anzeiger*, March 20, 2009; *Islamistische Organisationen in Nordrhein-Westfalen*, 44.

32. Biography of Sabiha Erbakan-El Zayat: http://www.pferdt.de/wp-content/uploads/2006/08/participants_fotoprofile.pdf (accessed March 17, 2009)

33. "Islam and Muslims in Germany."

34. Jonathan Laurence, "Islam and Citizenship in Germany," Transatlantic Dia-logue on Terrorism, Center for Strategic and International Studies, Washington, DC, September 2007.

35. Interview with official at the Landesverfassungsschutz Baden-Württemberg, Stuttgart, November 2008; interview with Federal Ministry of the Interior officials, Berlin, November 2008; "Islam and Identity in Germany," report by the International Crisis Group, March 14, 2007, page 10.

36. http://zentralrat.de/2593.php#beauftragte (accessed November 21, 2008); "Islam and Identity in Germany," 10; "Islam and Muslims in Germany"; Warner and Wenner, "Religion and the Political Organization of Muslims in Europe," 467; *Islamunterricht*, publication provided by the North Rhine-Westphalia Ministry of Education, Düsseldorf, November 2008; interview with official at the Landesverfassungsschutz Baden-Württemberg, Stuttgart, November 2008; interview with Federal Ministry of the Interior officials, Berlin, November 2008.

37. Jytte Klausen, *The Islamic Challenge: Politics and Religion in Western Europe* (New York: Oxford University Press, 2005), 31–33.

38. Annual report of the Office for the Protection of the Constitution, 1999, 165; *Islamistischer Extremismus and Terrorismus*, publication by the Landesamt für Verfassungsschutz Baden-Württemberg, April 2006; *Islamische Gemeinschaft in Deutschland Innenministerium, Nordrhein-Westfalen* http://www.im.nrw.de/sch/580.htm (accessed March 11, 2009); annual report of the Landesamt fur Verfassungsschutz, Hansestadt Hamburg, 2001; *Islamismus*, report by the Landesamt fur Verfassungsschutz, Hessen, http://www.verfassungsschutz-hessen.de/downloads/islam.pdf (accessed January 24, 2008).

39. Annual report of the Office for the Protection of the Constitution, 2005, 190.

40. Interview with official at the Landesverfassungsschutz Baden-Württemberg, Stuttgart, November 2008.

41. See, among the many reports of German security services, the 2008 report by the Bavarian Verfassungsschutz, 43–45.

42. Interview with Burhan Kesici, head of the Islamic Federation of Berlin, Berlin, November 2008; interview with official at the Landesverfassungsschutz Baden-Württemberg, Stuttgart, November 2008; interview with Federal Ministry of the Interior officials, Berlin, November 2008;

43. Rainer Sollich, "Dialogue with Extremists?" *Deutsche Welle*, July 21, 2006.

44. See, for example, Milli Görüş' 2005 press release on their case against the Verfassungsschutz of North Rhine-Westphalia, "Verfassungsschutz NRW räumt Verbreitung von Unwahrheiten," December 17, 2005, http://www.igmg.de/verband/presseerklaerungen/newsdetails-presse/verfassungsschutz-nrw-raumt-verbreitung-von-unwahrheiten-ein/3.html (accessed September 12, 2008); report for the first semester of 2003 of the Verfassungsschutz of the Ministry of the Interior of Bavaria, 43.

45. "Two Unamalgamated Worlds."

46. Annual report of the Office for the Protection of the Constitution, 2006, 213–16; interview with official at the Landesverfassungsschutz Baden-Württemberg, Stuttgart, November 2008; interview with Federal Ministry of the Interior officials, Berlin, November 2008; interview with Bavarian Landesamt für Verfassungsschutz officials, Munich, May 2009; interview with Nordrhein-Westfalen Ministry of the Interior officials, Düsseldorf, May 2009; annual report of the Bavarian Verfassungsschutz, 2008, 48–50.

47. Annual report of the Office for the Protection of the Constitution, 2006, 213; interview with Bavarian Landesamt für Verfassungsschutz officials, Munich, May 2009.

48. Interview with official at the Landesverfassungsschutz Baden-Württemberg, Stuttgart, November 2008; interview with Federal Ministry of the Interior officials, Berlin, November 2008; see also Valerie Amiraux, "Turkish Political Islam and Europe: Story of an Opportunistic Intimacy," in Stefano Allievi and Joergen S. Nielsen, eds., *Muslim Networks and Transnational Communities in and Across Europe* (Leiden/Boston: Brill, 2003); Martin Spiewak and Wolfgang Ochatius, "Mit Koran und Grundgesetz," *Die Zeit,* February 4, 1999.

49. Annual report of the Office for the Protection of the Constitution, 2006, 213–16.

50. Interview with official at the Landesverfassungsschutz Baden-Württemberg, Stuttgart, November 2008; interview with Federal Ministry of the Interior officials, Berlin, November 2008; interview with Bavarian Landesamt für Verfassungsschutz officials, Munich, May 2009.

51. *Islamistische Organisationen in Nordrhein-Westfalen,* 71.

52. Annual report of the Office for the Protection of the Constitution, 1999, 165.

53. Annual report of the Office for the Protection of the Constitution, 2000, 198.

54. *Islamisticher Extremismus and Terrorismus,* publication by the Landesamt für Verfassungsschutz Baden-Württemberg, April 2006, 29; *Islamistische Organisationen in Nordrhein-Westfalen,* 42–43; annual report of the Landesamt fur Verfassungsschutz, Hansestadt Hamburg, 2001, 46; *Islamismus,* report by the Landesamt fur Verfassungsschutz, Hessen, http://www.verfassungsschutz-hessen.de/downloads/islam.pdf (accessed January 24, 2008)

55. "Islam and Muslims in Germany."

56. Rasche, "Spinne im Netz der Muslime in Deutschland"; "Wie Friedlich Sind Muslime?" *Die Welt,* September 7, 2008.

57. Rasche, "Spinne im Netz der Muslime in Deutschland," http://www.islam.de/844.php.

58. "Kristina Köhler gewinnt Verfahren gegen El Zayat," press release on Kristina Köhler's Web site, November 16, 2005, http://www.kristina-koehler.de/presse/mitteilungen/2005/kristina-koehler-gewinnt-verfa/ (accessed March 17, 2009).

59. Interview with Egyptian government official, Cairo, December 2008.

60. "Ibrahim El Zayat Says He Is Not a Member of the Muslim Brotherhood," Ikhwanweb, May 6, 2007, http://www.ikhwanweb.com/Article.asp?ID=752&SectionID=78 (accessed November 24, 2008 (later removed and available at: http://www.muslimbrotherhood.co.uk/Home.asp?zPage=Systems&System=PressR&Press=Show&Lang=E&ID=6372 [accessed May 28, 2009]).

61. Interview with Yussuf Nada, Campione d'Italia, July 14, 2008; interview with Kamal Helbawy, London, December 2008; interview with Dr. Abd El Monem Abou El Fotouh, Cairo, December 2008.

62. http://zentralrat.de/3037.php (accessed November 22, 2008).

63. Interview with official at the Landesverfassungsschutz Baden-Württemberg, Stuttgart, November 2008; interview with Federal Ministry of the Interior officials, Berlin, November 2008; interview with Bavarian Landesamt für Verfassungsschutz officials, Munich, May 2009; interview with Nordrhein-Westfalen Ministry of the Interior officials, Düsseldorf, May 2009.

64. Interview with German security authorities, Cologne, April 2005; Ian Johnson, "How Islamic Group's Ties Reveal Europe's Challenge," *Wall Street Journal*, December 29, 2005.

65. In 2004: see copy of the search warrant available at www.igmg.de/download/040930-Durchsuchungsbeschluss-bayern.pdf (accessed February 15, 2005); in 2008, see Udo Beißel, "Razzia bei Milli Görüs," *Kölner Stadt-Anzeiger*, August 26, 2008.

66. Bavarian police Web site, March 10, 2009, http://www.polizei.bayern.de/muenchen/news/presse/aktuell/index.html/89241 (accessed March 11, 2009); Ralph Hub, "Razzia in der Moschee in Freimann," *Abendzeitung*, March 10, 2009; Helmut Frangenberg, "Ermittlungen gegen Islam-Funktionäre," *Kölner Stadt-Anzeiger*, March 19, 2009.

67. Klausen, *The Islamic Challenge*, 43.

68. "Islam and Identity in Germany," 16.

69. Albrecht Fuess, "Islamic Religious Education in Western Europe: Models of Integration and the German Approach," *Journal of Muslim Minority Affairs* 27, no. 2 (August 2007).

70. "Islam and Identity in Germany," 7.

71. That is the case, for example, in Lower Saxony with the Landesverband Shura-Niedersachsen and in the Bavarian city of Erlangen.

72. Interview with official at the Landesverfassungsschutz Baden-Württemberg, Stuttgart, November 2008; interview with Federal Ministry of the Interior officials,

Berlin, November 2008; interview with Ulla Ohlms and other officials at the North Rhine-Westphalia Ministry of Education, Düsseldorf, November 2008; interview with Burhan Kesici, head of the Islamic Federation of Berlin, Berlin, November 2008; see also Joel S. Fetzer and J. Christopher Soper, *Muslims and the State in Britain, France and Germany* (New York: Cambridge University Press, 2005), 108.

73. *Muslimisches Leben in Deutschland; Islamunterricht,* publication provided by the North Rhine-Westphalia Ministry of Education, Düsseldorf, November 2008; interview with Ulla Ohlms and other officials at the North Rhine-Westphalia Ministry of Education, Düsseldorf, November 2008.

74. Margrete Søvik, "Islamic Religious Instruction in North-Rhine-Westphalia (1979–1999): Constructing a German Muslim Identity Between Authenticity and Responsibility," in Stephen G. Ellis and Ann Katherine Isaacs, eds., *Citizenship in Historical Perspective* (Pisa: Pisa University Press, 2006), 318–24.

75. Klaus Gebauer, architect of the North Rhine-Westphalia's program, interviewed in Fetzer and Soper, *Muslims and the State in Britain, France and Germany,* 114; Jørgen Nielsen, *Muslims in Western Europe* (Edinburgh: Edinburgh University Press, 2004), 38.

76. For an extensive analysis of the legal cases, see: Søvik, "Islamic Religious Instruction in North-Rhine-Westphalia (1979–1999)," 326; Diana Zacharias, "Access of Muslim Organizations to Religious Instruction in Public Schools: A Comment on the Decision of the Federal Administrative Court of 23 February 2005," *German Law Journal* 6, no. 10: 1319–34.

77. Ibid., 1332.

78. Interview with Ulla Ohlms and other officials at the North Rhine-Westphalia Ministry of Education, Düsseldorf, November 2008.

79. Interview with Ulla Ohlms and other officials at the North Rhine-Westphalia Ministry of Education, Düsseldorf, November 2008; *Alevitischer Religionsunterricht,* report by the North Rhine-Westphalia Ministry of Education, copy in possession of the author.

80. Article 141 of the Federal Constitution, the so-called Bremen Clause, exempts the city-states of Berlin and Bremen from applying sections of Article 7. See Zacharias, "Access of Muslim Organizations to Religious Instruction in Public Schools."

81. Lars Pedersen, *Newer Islamic Movements in Western Europe* (Aldershot: Ashgate, 1999), 27–31.

82. *Islamische Föderation in Berlin: Die Kinder sind unsere Zukunft,* brochure provided by the Islamic Federation of Berlin; Fetzer and Soper, *Muslims and the State in Britain, France and Germany,* 115.

83. Interview with Burhan Kesici, head of the Islamic Federation of Berlin, Berlin, November 2008.

84. Interview with official at the Landesverfassungsschutz Baden-Württemberg, Stuttgart, November 2008; interview with Federal Ministry of the Interior officials, Berlin, November 2008; see also Pedersen, *Newer Islamic Movements in Western Europe*, 78–88.

85. Gilbert Schomaker, "Senat Will Islamkunde an Schulen mit Neuen Argumenten Stoppen," *Berliner Zeitung*, July 29, 2000.

86. Steven Pfaff and Anthony J. Gill, "Will a Million Muslims March?: Muslim Interest Organizations and Political Integration in Europe," *Comparative Political Studies* 39 (2006): 803–28.

87. Richard Bernstein, "Lessons of Islam in German Classrooms," *New York Times*, June 30, 2004.

88. Ibid.

89. Interview with Burhan Kesici, head of the Islamic Federation of Berlin, Berlin, November 2008.

90. Interview with Marion Berning, Berlin, November 2008; Bernstein, "Lessons of Islam in German Classrooms."

91. Interview with Marion Berning, Berlin, November 2008.

92. Interview with Burhan Kesici, head of the Islamic Federation of Berlin, Berlin, November 2008.

93. Interview with Federal Ministry of the Interior officials, Berlin, November 2008; brochures provided to the author by the officials. For more information on the initiative, see its official Web site: http://www.deutsche-islam-konferenz.de/cln _092/SubSites/DIK/DE/Startseite/home-node.html?_nnn=true (accessed March 11, 2009).

94. Interview with Federal Ministry of the Interior officials, Berlin, November 2008.

95. For a good commentary on these issues, see Markus Wehner, "Am Tisch mit Islamisten und Orthodoxen," *Frankfurter Allgemeine Zeitung*, March 12, 2008.

96. "Islam and Muslims in Germany."

97. See remarks of Minister of the Interior Wolfgang Schäuble at the beginning of DIK's last plenary session, June 25, 2009.

98. http://www.bmi.bund.de/nn_1026710/Internet/Content/Themen/Deutsche _Islam_Konferenz/DatenUndFakten/Islamkonferenz_Kurzinfo_en.html (accessed September 8, 2008).

99. "Official Recognition of Islam in Germany?" *Der Spiegel*, April 16, 2007; "Islam and Muslims in Germany."

100. *Muslimisches Leben in Deutschland*, 173.

101. Interview with official at the Landesverfassungsschutz Baden-Württemberg, Stuttgart, November 2008; interview with Federal Ministry of the Interior officials, Berlin, November 2008.

102. Interview with official at the Landesverfassungsschutz Baden-Württemberg, Stuttgart, November 2008; interview with Federal Ministry of the Interior officials, Berlin, November 2008; interview with Turkish journalist, Istanbul, June 2008.

7. The United States

1. Jocelyne Cesari, *When Islam and Democracy Meet: Muslims in Europe and in the United States* (New York: Palgrave MacMillan, 2004), 80.

2. *United States v. Holy Land Foundation et al.*, 3:04-cr-240 (ND, Tex.). The documents are available at the NEFA Foundation's Web site: http://www.nefafoundation .org/hlfdocs.html.

3. Interview with Barry Jonas, trial attorney for the Department of Justice Counterterrorism Section and prosecutor in the HLF case, Washington, DC, June 2009. The most interesting documents, outlining the history, structure, and aims of the Muslim Brotherhood in the United States, were found by authorities in the home of Ismael Selim Elbarasse, a close associate of Hamas leader Musa Abu Marzook. Elbarasse, a resident of Annandale (Virginia), was detained in August 2004 by Maryland police after he and his wife were caught videotaping the Chesapeake Bay Bridge.

4. Edward E. Curtis, *Islam in Black America* (Albany: State University of New York Press, 2002); Robert Dannin, *Black Pilgrimage to Islam* (New York: Oxford University Press, 2002); Aminah Beverly McCloud, *African American Islam* (New York: Routledge, 1995).

5. Aslam Abdullah and Gasser Hathout, *The American Muslim Identity: Speaking for Ourselves* (Pasadena, CA: Dawn, 2003), 25–30; Ilyas Ba-Yunus and Kassim Kone, *Muslims in the United States* (Westport, CT: Greenwood Press, 2006), 46–49; Gutbi Mahdi Ahmed, "Muslim Organizations in the United States," in Yvonne Yazbeck Haddad, ed., *The Muslims of America* (Oxford: Oxford University Press, 1991), 12–14.

6. Ba-Yunus and Kone, *Muslims in the United States*, 47.

7. History of ISNA, documentary available at http://www.isna.net/ISNAHQ/ pages/Documentary.aspx (accessed March 22, 2009).

8. Abdullah and Hathout, *The American Muslim Identity*, 25–30; Karen Leonard, "South Asian Leadership of American Muslims," in Yvonne Yazbeck Haddad, *Muslims in the West: From Sojourners to Citizens* (Oxford: Oxford University Press, 2001), 234.

9. Gutbi Mahdi Ahmed, "Muslim Organizations in the United States," 14–16.

10. Ba-Yunus and Kone, *Muslims in the United States*, 49.

11. Steve A. Johnson, "The Muslims of Indianapolis," in Yvonne Yazbeck Haddad and Jane Idleman Smith, eds., *Muslim Communities in North America* (Albany: State University of New York Press, 1994), 270–71.

12. Noreen S. Ahmed-Ullah, Sam Roe, and Laurie Cohen, "A Rare Look at Secretive Brotherhood in America," *Chicago Tribune*, September 19, 2004; "A Little Taste of History," MSA-National Web site (archive), http://web.archive .org/web/20060118061004/http://www.msa-national.org/about/history.html (accessed October 29, 2007); "Ikhwan in America," Government Exhibit 003–0089 in *United States v. Holy Land Foundation*.

13. "Ikhwan in America," Government Exhibit 003–0089 in *United States v. Holy Land Foundation*.

14. Kambiz Ghanea Bassiri, *Competing Visions of Islam in the United States* (Westport, CT: Greenwood Press, 1990), 26.

15. Mohamed Nimer, *Muslim Community Life in the United States and Canada* (New York: Routledge, 2002), 64.

16. Johnson, "The Muslims of Indianapolis," 270–72.

17. Ahmed-Ullah, Roe, and Cohen, "A Rare Look at Secretive Brotherhood in America."

18. "Ikhwan in America," Government Exhibit 003–0089 in *United States v. Holy Land Foundation*.

19. "An Explanatory Memorandum on the Strategic Goals for the Group in North America," Government Exhibit 003–0085 in *United States v. Holy Land Foundation*.

20. Leonard, "South Asian Leadership of American Muslims," 238.

21. Johnson, "The Muslims of Indianapolis," 270–71.

22. Harry Jaffe, "Unmasking the Mysterious Mohamed Hadid," *The Business of Washington*, March 1988, http://www.mohamedhadid.com/press.php?id =200403280001 (accessed April 15, 2009); Steven Merley, *The Muslim Brotherhood in the United States*, research monograph for the Hudson Institute, April 2009, 28.

23. Douglas Farah and John Mintz, "U.S. Trails Va. Muslim Money, Ties," *Washington Post*, October 7, 2002.

24. Quoted in Steve A. Johnson, "Political Activity of Muslims in America," in Yvonne Yazbeck Haddad, ed., *The Muslims of America* (Oxford: Oxford University Press, 1991), 111.

25. *American Muslim Council: Our First Five Years*, report by the AMC, 1996; Alamoudi's resume, introduced as evidence in *U.S. v. Abdurahman Muhammad Alamoudi*, U.S.D.C. of Eastern Virginia, Case 03–1009M, September 30, 2003.

26. Muslim Brotherhood Shura Council, "Shura Council Report on the Future of the Group," Government Exhibit 003–0003 in *United States v. Holy Land Foundation*.

27. Interview with Yussuf Nada, Campione d'Italia, July 14, 2008; Ahmed-Ullah, Roe, and Cohen, "A Rare Look at Secretive Brotherhood in America"; http://www.masnet.org/aboutmas.asp (accessed April 6, 2009); Testimony of Steven Emerson before the U.S. House of Representatives Committee on Foreign Affairs, Subcommittee on Terrorism, Proliferation, and Trade, July 31, 2008, 24; Merley, *The Muslim Brotherhood in the United States*, 60. Elkadi is married to Iman Abu Saud, the daughter of Brotherhood leader Mahmoud Abu Saud. Yussuf Nada claims to have arranged the marriage.

28. MAS articles of incorporation, filed in Illinois, June 11, 1993 (file number 5735–189–6); Ahmed-Ullah, Roe, and Cohen, "A Rare Look at Secretive Brotherhood in America."

29. http://www.masnet.org/university.asp (accessed April 1, 2009).

30. "MAS Freedom Foundation Outlines Successful 2006 Election Strategy to Washington, DC Press Corps," MAS press release, November 14, 2006; Audrey Hudson, "Muslim Group Touts Local Political Clout," *Washington Times*, October 1, 2007; Abdus Sattar Ghazali, "American Muslims in 2006 Elections," Al Jazeera, November 16, 2006.

31. An example of interlocking board membership is Sayyed Syeed. Holding a Ph.D. in sociolinguistics from Indiana University, Syeed has been president of MSA, secretary general of IIFSO, founder and secretary general of ISNA, editor-in-chief of the *American Journal of Islamic Social Sciences*, member of the Board of Advisors of CAIR, and Director of Academic Outreach at IIIT.

32. Ba-Yunus and Kone, *Muslims in the United States*, 49.

33. "ISNA Statement of Position: Who We Are and What We Believe," http://www.isna.net/Documents/ISNAHQ/ISNA-Statement-of-Position-Who-we-Are-and-What-We-Believe.pdf (accessed April 6, 2009).

34. Quoted in Johnson, "Political Activity of Muslims in America," 121.

35. Ahmed-Ullah, Roe, and Cohen, "A Rare Look at Secretive Brotherhood in America"; for Elsayed's affiliation to ISNA, see http://www.islamonline.net/livedialogue/english/Guestcv.asp?hGuestID=dRJ4eJ (accessed April 3, 2009).

36. "Ikhwan in America," Government Exhibit 003–0089 in *United States v. Holy Land Foundation*.

37. "An Explanatory Memorandum on the Strategic Goals for the Group in North America," Government Exhibit 003–0085 in *United States v. Holy Land Foundation*.

38. Yusuf al Qaradawi, *Priorities of the Islamic Movement in the Coming Phase* (Swansea, UK: Awakening Publications, 2000).

39. Interview with former Muslim Brotherhood member, Boston, November 2008; Government's Trial Brief in *United States v. Holy Land Foundation*.

40. Government Exhibit 1B33/0003188 in *United States v. Holy Land Foundation*.

41. Government Exhibit 1B64/0000377–0000383 in *United States v. Holy Land Foundation*.

42. Interview with former FBI official, Washington, DC, June 2009.

43. The wiretaps of the Philadelphia meeting were introduced as evidence in the 2007 Holy Land Foundation trial through dozens of separate documents, all publicly available (see http://www.nefafoundation.org/hlfdocs.html). For a detailed summary of the wiretaps, see Josh Lefkowitz, "The 1993 Philadelphia Meeting: A Roadmap for Future Muslim Brotherhood Actions in the U.S.," NEFA Foundation report, November 15, 2007.

44. Superseding Indictment in *United States v. Holy Land Foundation*.

45. Government Exhibit 016–0049 in *United States v. Holy Land Foundation*.

46. Government Exhibit 016–0071 in *United States v. Holy Land Foundation*.

47. Government Exhibit 016–0087 in *United States v. Holy Land Foundation*.

48. Government Exhibit 016–0051 in *United States v. Holy Land Foundation*.

49. Government Exhibit 016–0087 in *United States v. Holy Land Foundation*.

50. Government Exhibit 016–0087 in *United States v. Holy Land Foundation*.

51. Government Exhibit 016–0051 in *United States v. Holy Land Foundation*.

52. Government Exhibit 016–0069 in *United States v. Holy Land Foundation*.

53. Government Exhibit 016–0069 in *United States v. Holy Land Foundation*.

54. Government Exhibit 016–0063 in *United States v. Holy Land Foundation*.

55. Government Exhibit 016–0057 in *United States v. Holy Land Foundation*.

56. Department of Justice press release on the sentencing of HLF leaders, May 27, 2009, http://www.usdoj.gov/opa/pr/2009/May/09-nsd-519.html (accessed June 9, 2009).

57. Government Exhibit 016–0067 in *United States v. Holy Land Foundation*.

58. Government Exhibit 016–0075 in *United States v. Holy Land Foundation*.

59. Government Exhibit 016–0075 in *United States v. Holy Land Foundation*.

60. *CNN Crossfire*, September 10, 1993.

61. Government Exhibit 016–0069 in *United States v. Holy Land Foundation*.

62. Ahmed Yousef, "Engage with Hamas: We Earned Our Support," *Washington Post*, June 20, 2007; Ahmed Yousef, "Pause for Peace," *New York Times*, November 1, 2006; Mousa Abu Marzook, "Hamas' Stand," *Los Angeles Times*, July 10, 2007.

63. Rob Dreher, "CAIR and Hamas," *Dallas Morning News*, August 8, 2007.

64. Government Exhibit 016–0067 in *United States v. Holy Land Foundation*.

65. Government Exhibit 016–0059 in *United States v. Holy Land Foundation*.

66. Government Exhibit 016–0067 in *United States v. Holy Land Foundation*.

67. Government Exhibit 016–0067 in *United States v. Holy Land Foundation*.

68. Government Exhibit 1B64/0000377–0000383 in *United States v. Holy Land Foundation*.

69. FBI Special Agent Laura Burns testimony in the HLF trial, quoted in Jason Trahan, "FBI: CAIR Is a Front Group, and Holy Land Foundation Tapped Hamas Clerics for Fundraisers," *Dallas Morning News*, October 7, 2008.

70. Text from Lawsuit Response in *Council on American-Islamic Relations, Inc. v. Andrew Whitehead*, no. CL04–926, Virginia: In the Circuit Court for the City of Virginia Beach, April 30, 2004.

71. Check from the Holy Land Foundation to CAIR introduced as evidence in *United States v. Holy Land Foundation*; Testimony of Matthew Epstein before the United States Senate Judiciary Committee, Subcommittee on Terrorism, Technology, and Homeland Security, September 10, 2003: http://www.cair.com/PDF/urbanlegends.pdf (accessed April 8, 2009).

72. Government Exhibit 1B64/0000412 in *United States v. Holy Land Foundation*.

73. http://www.cair.com/AboutUs/VisionMissionCorePrinciples.aspx (accessed March 24, 2009); "25 Facts about CAIR," http://www.cair.com/AboutUs/25FactsAboutCAIR.aspx (accessed April 1, 2009).

74. Interview with Omar Ahmed, *Ukaz Weekly*, January 19, 1999, 20–21.

75. "What They Say About CAIR," CAIR Pennsylvania, http://pa.cair.com/index.php?Page=whattheysay&Side=about (accessed June 16, 2009).

76. U.S. Senate Subcommittee on Terrorism, Technology and Homeland Security, *Terrorism: Two Years After 9/11, Connecting the Dots*, September 10, 2003.

77. "What They Say About CAIR"; Subcommittee on Terrorism, *Terrorism: Two Years After 9/11*.

78. Michael Isikoff and Mark Hosenball, "An Unwelcome Guest," *Newsweek*, August 8, 2007; *Justice Denied: Waste and Mismanagement at the Department of Justice*, report by the office of Senator Tom Coburn (R-MD), October 2008; "US Sponsors Islamic Convention," *Washington Times*, August 27, 2007.

79. Interview with Jeffrey Breinholt, Deputy Chief of the Counterterrorism Section, U.S. Department of Justice, Washington, D.C., June 2009.

80. See, for example, the letter written by Congressman Pete Hoekstra and Congresswoman Sue Myrick to Attorney General Alberto Gonzales on the matter on August 28, 2007.

81. Steven Pomerantz, "Counterterrorism in a Free Society," *Journal of Counterterrorism & Security International* (Spring 1998).

82. Carl Whitehead, Special Agent in Charge, FBI Tampa Field Office, speaking at the CAIR 2006 Tampa Banquet; John Miller, FBI Public Affairs Assistant Director, interviewed in "FBI Official and Imam Discuss Homegrown Terror," NPR, May 16, 2007; "What They Say About CAIR," http://www.cair.com/AboutUs/WhatTheySayAboutCAIR.aspx (accessed April 4, 2009).

83. Interviews and conversations with former and current FBI agents between 2004 and 2009.

84. Neil MacFarquhar, "Scrutiny Increases for a Group Advocating for Muslims in the U.S." *New York Times*, March 14, 2007.

85. "What They Say About CAIR," http://www.cair.com/AboutUs/WhatThey SayAboutCAIR.aspx (accessed April 4, 2009).

86. Interview with FBI official, Washington, D.C., December 2007.

87. *Islamic Horizons* (March/April 1996).

88. *Al Talib* (July 1999).

89. "CAIR's Anti-Terrorism Campaigns," http://www.cair.com/American Muslims/AntiTerrorism.aspx (accessed April 9, 2009).

90. http://www.cair.com/AboutUs/25FactsAboutCAIR.aspx (accessed March 30, 2009).

91. http://www.fiqhcouncil.org/FatwaBank/tabid/176/ctl/Detail/mid/600/xmid/ 25/xmfid/3/Default.aspx (accessed March 30, 2009).

92. Ingrid Mattson, "My Islam: Freedom and Responsibility," *Islamica Magazine* 20 (2007): 51; http://www.isna.net/articles/Press-Releases/ISNA-STATEMENT-OF-POSITION-Who-we-are-and-what-we-believe.aspx (accessed March 30, 2009).

93. Fiqh Council of North America Issues Fatwa Against Terrorism, http:// www.theamericanmuslim.org/tam.php/features/articles/fiqh_council_of_north _america_issues_fatwa_against_terrorism/ (accessed April 8, 2009); Sultan's biography, http://www.islamonline.net/livedialogue/english/Guestcv.asp?hGuestID= kfi572 (accessed April 8, 2009); Salah Sultan's personal Web site, http://www.salah soltan.com/main/index.php?_5nm (accessed May 28, 2009).

94. "Columbus, Ohio Muslim Leader Says 9/11 Planned by Americans, Praises the Wanted Al-Qaeda-Linked Yemenite Sheikh Al-Zindani," MEMRI Special Dispatch 1168, May 19, 2006.

95. Dan Mihalopoulos, "Abuse of Post–9/11 Detainees Detailed," *Chicago Tribune*, July 22, 2003.

96. On December 4, 2001, after the assets of the HLF were frozen, CAIR declared: "We ask that President Bush reconsider what we believe is an unjust and counterproductive move that can only damage America's credibility with Muslims in this country and around the world and could create the impression that there has been a shift from a war on terrorism to an attack on Islam." See "Freeze on Group's Assets Questioned by U.S. Muslims," CAIR Press Release, December 4, 2001, http:// lists.madimc.org/pipermail/mapc-discuss/2001-December/000370.html (accessed April 8, 2009). In December 2002, after the arrest of four Dallas-based individuals whom the U.S. government accused of financing Hamas, CAIR Dallas issued a press release saying: "We are concerned that these charges result from what appears to be a 'war on Islam and Muslims' rather than a 'war on terror.' Recent actions by

the Department of Justice have brought into question the intention of arrests such as these. We, as American Muslims are facing an uphill battle in defending our own government's foreign policy, as well as the, so-called, war on terrorism, while being targeted by our own law enforcement agencies." See "DFW Muslim Leaders Issue Statement Regarding Elashi Family Arrests," CAIR-Dallas press release, December 19, 2002, http://www.faithfreedom.org/forum2/viewtopic.php?t=2810&sid=271e44f238 356ca4d63c67a56824f933 (accessed April 8, 2009).

97. Interview with former FBI official, Washington, D.C., June 2008.

98. Interviews with FBI officials, Washington, D.C., June and October 2008.

99. Audrey Hudson, "CAIR Concedes Membership Down," *Washington Times*, August 22, 2007.

100. Interviewed on NPR, May 16, 2007.

101. "Countering Radicalization," FBI Web site, http://www.fbi.gov/page2/may07/radicalization051007.htm (accessed April 2, 2009).

102. Louay Safi, *Blaming Islam: Examining the Religion Building Enterprise*, report for the Institute for Social Policy and Understanding, 2006, 5.

103. Louay Safi's personal Web site: http://louaysafi.com/content/view/9/37/ (accessed April 8, 2009).

104. Interview with FBI officials, Washington, D.C., October 2008 and June 2009; Marisa Taylor, "FBI Struggles to Win Trust of Muslim, Arab Communities," *McClatchy Newspapers*, November 21, 2006.

105. *The Attorney General's Guidelines for Domestic FBI Operations*, http://www.justice.gov/ag/readingroom/guidelines.pdf (accessed June 16, 2009).

106. Interview with Richard Marquise, former senior FBI Special Agent, Boston, March 2009.

107. See, for example, the report of the Commission on the Intelligence Capabilities of the United States Regarding Weapons of Mass Destruction, March 31, 2005. At page 454 the report states that "the FBI is still far from having the strong analytic capability that is required to drive and focus the Bureau's national security work. Although the FBI's tactical analysis has made significant progress, its strategic capabilities—those that are central to guiding a long-term, systematic approach to national security issues—have lagged."

108. "Inside the Ring," *Washington Times*, September 14, 2007.

109. Ibid.

110. Interview with former FBI official, Washington, D.C., June 2009.

111. Interview with Jeffrey Breinholt, Deputy Chief of the Counterterrorism Section, U.S. Department of Justice, Washington, D.C., June 2009.

112. Department of Justice press release on the sentencing of HLF leaders, May 27, 2009, http://www.usdoj.gov/opa/pr/2009/May/09-nsd-519.html (accessed June 9, 2009).

113. Joseph Abrams, "FBI Cuts Ties with CAIR Following Terror Financing Trial," Fox News, January 30, 2009.

114. Letter from Richard C. Powers, FBI Assistant Director, Office of Congressional Affairs, to Senator Jon Kyl, April 28, 2009.

115. See, for example, the letter written by Senators Schumer (D-NY) and Kyl (R-AZ) to the FBI stating their support for the FBI's decision.

116. http://www.icna.org/index.php?option=com_content&view=article&id=80 (accessed March 30, 2009).

117. "A Call for FBI Accountability," http://www.isna.net/articles/News/A-Call-for-FBI-Accountability.aspx (accessed March 31, 2009).

118. Quoted in Johnson, "Political Activity of Muslims in America," 115.

119. Qamar-ul Huda, "Conflict Prevention and Peace-Building Efforts by American Muslim Organizations Following September 11," *Journal of Muslim Minority Affairs* 26, no. 2 (August 2006): 188.

8. The Brothers and Terrorism: Firefighters or Arsonists?

1. Kenan Malik, *From Fatwa to Jihad: The Rushdie Affair and Its Legacy* (London: Atlantic Books, 2009), 121.

2. Fareed Zakaria, "Radical Islam Is a Fact of Life; How to Live with It," *Newsweek*, March 9, 2009.

3. Remarks of Prof. Marc Lynch, George Washington University, May 12, 2008; reiterated on Prof. Lynch's blog, http://abuaardvark.typepad.com/abuaardvark/2008/05/assessing-the-m.html (accessed October 9, 2008).

4. Robert S. Leiken and Steven Brooke, "The Moderate Muslim Brotherhood," *Foreign Affairs* (March/April 2007): 112.

5. Ibid., 107; see, for example, the writings of the influential Syrian Jihadist scholar Abu Basir Al-Tartousi, who has repeatedly called al Qaradawi an apostate.

6. Interview with Reuel Marc Gerecht, American Enterprise Institute, http://www.aei.org/publications/pubID.21739/pub_detail.asp, December 16, 2004.

7. Leiken and Brooke, "The Moderate Muslim Brotherhood," 112.

8. The history of Finsbury Park's takeover is told in Sean O'Neill and Daniel McGrory's book *The Suicide Factory: Abu Hamza and the Finsbury Park Mosque* (London: HarperCollins, 2006), 34–52.

9. Ibid., 253–64.

10. Information on the takeover of the Finsbury Park mosque was provided to the author by Kamal Helbawy, Mohammed Kuzbar, and officials at the Home Of-

fice and Scotland Yard during various interviews in London in January 2007 and December 2008.

11. British Foreign Office internal memo on Yusuf al Qaradawi, July 14, 2005, in appendix of Martin Bright, *When Progressives Treat with Reactionaries: The British State's Flirtation with Radical Islam*, report published by the Policy Exchange, 2006.

12. For a list of speakers, see the Radical Middle Way's Web site: http://www .radicalmiddleway.co.uk/scholars.php (accessed March 25, 2009).

13. Web site of the Mosquée de Paris, *http://www.mosquee-de-paris.org/spip.php ?article66* (accessed October 31, 2008).

14. Jonathan Laurence and Justin Vaisse, *Integrating Islam: Political and Religious Challenges in Contemporary France* (Washington, DC: Brookings Institution Press, 2006), 101–104; Dalil Boubakeur and Virginie Malabard, *Non, l'Islam n'est pas une Politique* (Paris: Desclée De Brouwer, 2003), 78–84.

15. Nicolas Sarkozy, *La République, les Religions, l'Espérance* (Paris: Éditions du Cerf, 2004), 69; Frank Peter, "Leading the Community of the Middle Way: A Study of the Muslim Field in France," *The Muslim World* 96 (October 2006): 714.

16. Peter, "Leading the Community of the Middle Way," 707–36.

17. Dounia Bouzar, *L'Islam des Banlieues: Les Prédicateurs Musulmans: Nouveaux Travailleurs Sociaux?* (Paris: Syros la Découverte, 2001).

18. Gilles Kepel, *Les Banlieues de l'Islam* (Paris: Éditions du Seuil, 1987).

19. Bouzar, *L'Islam des Banlieues*, 110.

20. Bouzar, *L'Islam des Banlieues*, 119.

21. Marie-France Etchegoin and Serge Raffy, "La Vérité sur l'Islam en France," *Le Nouvel Observateur*, February 2, 2006.

22. Interview with French official, Paris, February 2007; interview with French official, Lyon, June 2006.

23. Caroline Fourest, *Brother Tariq: The Doublespeak of Tariq Ramadan* (New York: Encounter, 2008), 192.

24. Decision of the French Conseil d'Etat, June 7, 1999, as quoted in Fiammetta Venner, *OPA sur l'Islam de France: Les Ambitions de l'UOIF* (Paris: Calmann-Levy, 2005), 15.

25. Interview with French officials, Paris, February 2007 and May 2009.

26. Giles Kepel, *The War for Muslim Minds: Islam and the West* (Cambridge, MA: Harvard University Press, 2004), 273–74.

27. Vincent Geisser and Aziz Zemouri, *Marianne et Allah: Les Politiques Français face à la "Question Musulmane"* (Paris: La Découverte, 2007), 117.

28. Sarkozy, *La République, les Religions, l'Espérance*, 100.

29. Sarkozy, *La République, les Religions, l'Espérance*, 83.

30. Leiken and Brooke, "The Moderate Muslim Brotherhood," 118.

31. Gilles Kepel, *Beyond Terror and Martyrdom* (Cambridge, MA: Harvard University Press, 2008), 248–54.

32. Interview with UOIF president Lhaj Thami Breze, La Courneuve, May 2009; Vincent Geisser, "L'UOIF, la Tension Clientéliste d'une Grande Fédération Islamique," in Amel Boubekeur and Abderrahim Lamchichi, eds., *Musulmans de France, Confluences Méditerranée* 57 (Spring 2006): 83–101; Vincent Geisser, "'Notre Ami Sarkozy,' UOIF-UMP, Histoire d'un PACS Avorté," *Oumma.com*, November 30, 2006, http://oumma.com/Notre-ami-Sarkozy-UOIF-UMP (accessed June 10, 2009).

33. Geisser and Zemouri, *Marianne et Allah*, 119–20.

34. Quoted in Fourest, *Brother Tariq*, 191.

35. Philippe Bernard and Xavier Ternisien, "Il Faut Reconnaître la Sur-Délinquance des Jeunes Issus de l'Immigration," *Le Monde*, December 4, 2001.

36. Ibid.

37. Quoted in Fourest, *Brother Tariq*, 191.

38. As quoted in Sylvain Besson, *La Conquête de l'Occident* (Paris: Seuil, 2005), 40.

39. As quoted in Fourest, *Brother Tariq*, 103.

40. Doug McAdam, "Studying Social Movements: A Conceptual Tour of the Field," "Program on Nonviolent Sanctions and Cultural Survival," Weatherhead Center for International Affairs, Harvard University, 1992; Herbert H. Haines, "Black Radicalization and the Funding of Civil Rights: 1957–1970," in Doug McAdam and David A. Snow, *Social Movements* (Los Angeles: Roxbury, 1997), 440–41.

41. "The Muslim Brotherhood in Europe," testimony of Ian Johnson before the Congressional Human Rights Caucus, February 9, 2006.

42. Carrie Rosefsky Wickham, *Mobilizing Islam: Religion, Activism, and Political Change in Egypt* (New York: Columbia University Press, 2002), 96; Gilles Kepel, *Muslim Extremism in Egypt* (Berkeley and Los Angeles: University of California Press, 1986), 134–35.

43. Interview with Israeli officials, Jerusalem and Herzliya, July 2008.

44. As quoted in Robert Baer, *Sleeping with the Devil* (Washington, DC: Three Rivers Press, 2003), 180.

45. "Al-Qaradhawi Speaks in Favor of Suicide Operations at an Islamic Conference in Sweden," Middle East Media and Research Institute (MEMRI), Special Dispatch #542, July 24, 2003.

46. "Life and Religion," Al Jazeera, April 28, 2002.

47. Alaa Abu Elnin, "Tipping U.S. on Baathists Prohibited: Prominent Scholar," *Islam Online*, May 30, 2003, http://www.islam-online.net/english/News/2003–05/31/article07.shtml.

48. Gihan Shahine, "Fatwa Fight," *Al Ahram Weekly* 708 (September 16–22, 2004).

49. The comparison has been made by several Brotherhood leaders on different occasions, in conversation with the author.

50. Ian Johnson, "How Islamic Group's Ties Reveal Europe's Challenge," *Wall Street Journal*, December 29, 2005.

51. Leiken and Brooke, "The Moderate Muslim Brotherhood," 116.

52. Saeed Hawwa, *The Muslim Brotherhood* (Kuwait City: International Islamic Federation of Student Organizations/Al Faisal Islamic Press, 1985), 119.

53. Olivier Carré and Gerard Michaud, *Les Frères Musulmans* (Paris: Gallimard, 1983), 44.

54. Hawwa, *The Muslim Brotherhood*, 123.

55. See, for example, Joyce M. Davis, *Between Jihad and Salaam: Profiles in Islam* (New York: St. Martin's Press, 1997), 219–33.

56. Yusuf al Qaradawi, *Islamic Awakening Between Rejection and Extremism* (Herndon, VA: International Institute of Islamic Thought, 1991), 149.

57. Ibid., 15.

58. Al Qaradawi, *Islamic Awakening Between Rejection and Extremism*, 149.

59. Al Qaradawi, *Islamic Awakening Between Rejection and Extremism*, 85.

60. Al Qaradawi, *Islamic Awakening Between Rejection and Extremism*, 88–89.

61. Yusuf al Qaradawi, *Priorities of the Islamic Movement in the Coming Phase* (Swansea, UK: Awakening Publications, 2000).

62. Al Qaradawi's criticism of Qutb dates back to the 1980s. See Husan Tammam, "Yusuf Qaradawi and the Muslim Brothers: The Nature of a Special Relationship," in Bettina Gräf and Jakob Skovgaard-Petersen, eds., *The Global Mufti: The Phenomenon of Yusuf Al-Qaradawi* (New York: Columbia University Press, 2009).

63. Ibid.

64. Antonio Gramsci, *Prison Notebooks* (New York: Columbia University Press, 1992), 233–38.

65. For an application of Gramsci's concepts to the actions of Islamist movements and, in particular, Hamas, see Massimo Introvigne, *Hamas: Fondamentalismo Islamico e Terrorismo Suicida in Palestina* (Turin: Elledici, 2003).

66. Interview with former Brotherhood member, Zürich, July 2008.

67. As reported in the affidavit of U.S. Immigration and Customs Enforcement Special Agent Brett Gentrup in *U.S. v. Abdurahman Muhammad Alamoudi*, U.S.D.C. of Eastern Virginia, Case 03–1009M, September 30, 2003.

68. Audio available at http://www.investigativeproject.org/261/alamoudi-you-can-be-violent-anywhere-else (accessed April 29, 2009).

69. *The Prevent Strategy: A Guide for Local Partners in England*, HM Government, June 2008, 4.

70. *Amsterdam Against Radicalisation*, Municipality of Amsterdam, November 15, 2007.

71. *The Radical Dawa in Transition*, report by the AIVD (Algemene Inlichtingen- en Veiligheidsdienst, or General Intelligence and Security Service, the Netherlands' domestic intelligence agency), 2007, 9–10.

72. Interview with AIVD officials, The Hague, May 2008.

73. *The Prevent Strategy: A Guide for Local Partners*, 5; James Kirkup, "More than 20 Serious Terrorist Plots Against Britain Are Being Planned in Pakistan," *Daily Telegraph*, December 15, 2008.

74. Jonathan Paris, "UK Counter-Radicalisation Strategy: Accommodation to Confrontation?" paper presented at the Henry Jackson Society, July 2, 2008; interview with Jonathan Paris, New York, June 2009.

75. Interview with senior Home Office officials, London, December 2008.

76. Interview with senior Dutch officials, The Hague, May 2008.

77. Interview with Robert Lambert, London, December 2008.

78. Robert Lambert, "Empowering Salafis and Islamists Against Al-Qaeda: A London Counterterrorism Case Study," *Political Science and Politics* 41 (2008): 31–35.

79. Interviews with Home Office and DCLG officials, London, December 2008.

80. Alan Travis, "Time to Tackle the Non-Violent Extremists, Says Smith," *Guardian*, December 11, 2008.

81. *Integration as a Means to Prevent Extremism and Terrorism: Typology of Islamist Radicalisation and Recruitment*, report by the German Federal Office for the Protection of the Constitution, January 2007, 7.

82. See, for example, *Study on the Best Practices in Cooperation Between Authorities and Civil Society with a View to the Prevention and Response to Violent Radicalisation*, report by The Change Institute for the European Commission, July 2008, 35.

83. Leiken and Brooke, "The Moderate Muslim Brotherhood," 112.

84. *A Common and Safe Future: Proposal for an Action Plan to Prevent Extremist Views and Radicalisation Among Young People*, Danish Ministry of Refugee, Immigration and Integration Affairs, June 2008, 36.

85. *Integration as a Means to Prevent Extremism*, 5.

86. Annual report of the German Federal Office for the Protection of the Constitution, 2005, 190.

87. Interview with Abdul Wahid Pederesen, Copenhagen, November 2008.

88. *Pulling Together to Defeat Terror*, Quilliam Foundation, April 2008.

89. The belief that the perception of a prolonged Western attack against Islam is a key factor in the radicalization process is held by a large number of intelligence agencies and analysts. See, for example, Canadian Security Intelligence Ser-

vice, *Radicalization and Jihad in the West*, June 2006, 1; AIVD, *Recruitment for the Jihad in the Netherlands: From Incident to Trend*, December 2002, 29; and Peter R. Neumann, "Joining Al-Qaeda: Jihadist Recruitment in Europe," Adelphi Paper 339, International Institute for Strategic Studies, 46.

90. Ed Husain, *The Islamist* (London: Penguin, 2007), 119–20.

Conclusion: The Way Forward

1. Giles Kepel, *The War for Muslim Minds: Islam and the West* (Cambridge, MA: Harvard University Press, 2004), 274.

2. Sarkozy's comments on his decision to include the UOIF in the Conseil Français du Culte Musulman (CFCM, the government-created body designed to unite the representatives of the most important French Muslim organizations) further clarifies this position. "I wanted," said Sarkozy in a 2005 speech at the Académie des Sciences Morales et Politiques, "to have inside the CFCM the representation of the diversity of the practicing Muslim world, included the UOIF. And I have never regretted it. The UOIF has always respected its word. The partisans of a 'spicier' Islam have their place inside this institution, where they have brought their representativeness, without ever betraying the spirit of the authority. If the UOIF had refused to take part in it or had left it, it would have been the representativeness of the CFCM that would have been challenged. And in the *banlieues*, we would have made the UOIF an organization of martyrs, and CFCM a shell only half full. I did not want that and I assumed this responsibility."

3. Olivier Roy, *Globalized Islam: The Search for a New Ummah* (New York: Columbia University Press, 2004), 276.

Bibliography

Books

Abdullah, Aslam and Gasser Hathout. *The American Muslim Identity: Speaking for Ourselves*. Pasadena, CA: Multimedia Vera International, 2003.

Abu-Amr, Ziad. *Islamic Fundamentalism in the West Bank and Gaza*. Bloomington and Indianapolis: Indiana University Press, 1994.

Ahsan, M. M. and A. R. Kidwai, eds. *Sacrilege Versus Civility: Muslim Perspectives on the* Satanic Verses *Affair*. Leicester: Islamic Foundation, 1993.

al Qaradawi, Yusuf. *Islamic Awakening Between Rejection and Extremism*. Herndon, VA: International Institute of Islamic Thought, 1991.

———. *Le Licite et l'Illicite en Islam*. Paris: Éditions al Qalam, 1992.

———. *Priorities of the Islamic Movement in the Coming Phase*. Swansea, UK: Awakening Publications, 2000.

Allison, Graham T., *Essence of Decision: Explaining the Cuban Missile Crisis*. New York: HarperCollins, 1971.

Ba-Yunus, Ilyas and Kassim Kone. *Muslims in the United States*. Westport, CT: Greenwood Press, 2006.

Baer, Robert. *Sleeping with the Devil*. Washington, DC: Three Rivers Press, 2003.

Baker, Raymond William. *Islam Without Fear: Egypt and the New Islamists*. Cambridge, MA: Harvard University Press, 2003.

Besson, Sylvain. *La Conquête de l'Occident*. Paris: Seuil, 2005.

Boubakeur, Dalil and Virginie Malabard. *Non, l'Islam n'est pas une Politique*. Paris: Desclée De Brouwer, 2003.

Bouzar, Dounia. *L'Islam des Banlieues: Les Prédicateurs Musulmans: Nouveaux Travailleurs Sociaux?* Paris: Syros la Découverte, 2001.

Carré, Olivier and Gerard Michaud. *Les Frères Musulmans*. Paris: Gallimard, 1983.

Cesari, Joceline. *When Islam and Democracy Meet: Muslims in Europe and in the United States.* New York: Palgrave Macmillan, 2004.

Cleveland, William L. *A History of the Modern Middle East.* Boulder, CO: Westview, 2004.

Curtis, Edward E. *Islam in Black America.* Albany: State University of New York University Press, 2002.

Dannin, Robert. *Black Pilgrimage to Islam.* New York: Oxford University Press, 2002.

Davis, Joyce M. *Between Jihad and Salaam: Profiles in Islam.* New York: St. Martin's Press, 1997.

della Porta, Donatella and Mario Diani. *Social Movements: An Introduction.* Malden, MA: Blackwell, 1999.

Eickelman, Dale F. and James Piscatori. *Muslim Politics.* Princeton: Princeton University Press, 1996.

Esposito, John L. *The Islamic Threat: Myth or Reality?* New York and Oxford: Oxford University Press, 1999).

Esposito, John L., ed. *The Oxford Encyclopedia of the Modern Islamic World.* New York/Oxford: Oxford University Press, 1995, vol. 2.

Esposito, John L. and John O. Voll. *Makers of Contemporary Islam.* Oxford University Press, 2001.

Feindt-Riggers, Nils and Udo Steinbach. *Islamische Organisationen in Deutschland.* Hamburg: Deutsches Orient-Institut, 1997.

Feldman, Noah. *The Fall and Rise of the Islamic State.* Princeton and Oxford: Princeton University Press, 2008.

Fetzer, Joel S. and J. Christopher Soper. *Muslims and the State in Britain, France and Germany.* New York: Cambridge University Press, 2005.

Five Tracts of Hasan al-Banna (1906–1949): A Selection from the Majmu'at Rasa'il al-Imam al-Shahid Hasan al-Banna. Trans. and annotated by Charles Wendell. Berkeley: University of California Press, 1978.

Fourest, Caroline. *Brother Tariq: The Doublespeak of Tariq Ramadan.* New York: Encounter, 2008.

Ghanea Bassiri, Kambiz. *Competing Visions of Islam in the United States.* Westport, CT: Greenwood Press, 1997.

Geisser, Vincent and Aziz Zemouri. *Marianne et Allah: Les Politiques Français face à la "Question Musulmane."* Paris: La Découverte, 2007.

Godard, Bernard and Sylvie Taussig. *Les Musulmans en France.* Paris: Robert Laffont, 2007.

Gove, Michael. *Celsius 7/7.* London: Phoenix, 2006.

Gräf, Bettina and Jakob Skovgaard-Petersen, eds. *The Global Mufti: The Phenomenon of Yusuf Al-Qaradawi.* New York: Columbia University Press, 2009.

Gramsci, Antonio. *Prison Notebooks*. New York: Columbia University Press, 1992.

Habeck, Mary. *Knowing the Enemy*. New Haven: Yale University Press, 2006.

Hamdi, Mohamed Elhachmi. *The Politicization of Islam: A Case Study of Tunisia*. Boulder, CO: Westview Press, 1998.

Hansen, John and Kim Hundevadt. *Provoen og Profeten: Muhammed Krisen Bag Kulisserne*. Aarhus: Jyllands-Postens Forlag, 2006.

Hawwa, Sayeed. *The Muslim Brotherhood*. Kuwait: International Islamic Federation of Student Organizations/Al Faisal Islamic Press, 1985.

Husain, Ed. *The Islamist*. London: Penguin, 2007.

Introvigne, Massimo. *Hamas: Fondamentalismo Islamico e Terrorismo Suicida in Palestina*. Turin: Elledici, 2003.

Ismail, Salwa. *Rethinking Islamist Politics: Culture, the State and Islamism*. London: I. B. Tauris, 2003.

Kepel, Gilles. *Allah in the West: Islamic Movements in America and Europe*. Palo Alto: Stanford University Press, 1997.

——. *Beyond Terror and Martyrdom*. Cambridge, MA: Harvard University Press, 2008.

——. *Jihad: The Trail of Political Islam*. Cambridge, MA: Harvard University Press, 2002.

——. *Les Banlieues de l'Islam*. Paris: Le Seuil, 1987.

——. *Muslim Extremism in Egypt*. Berkeley and Los Angeles: University of California Press, 1986.

——. *The War for Muslim Minds: Islam and the West*. Cambridge, MA: Harvard University Press, 2004.

Kinzer, Stephen. *Crescent and Star: Turkey Between Two Worlds*. New York: Farrar, Straus & Giroux, 2001.

Klausen, Jytte. *The Islamic Challenge: Politics and Religion in Western Europe*. New York: Oxford University Press, 2005.

Laurence, Jonathan and Justin Vaisse. *Integrating Islam: Political and Religious Challenges in Contemporary France*. Washington, DC: Brookings Institution Press, 2006,

Lewis, Bernard. *Islam and the West*. New York and Oxford: Oxford University Press, 1993.

Lewis, Philip. *Islamic Britain: Religion, Politics and Identity Among British Muslims*. London: I. B. Tauris, 1994.

Lia, Brynjar. *The Society of the Muslim Brothers in Egypt: The Rise of an Islamic Movement, 1928–1942*. Reading, UK: Ithaca Press, 1998.

Malik, Kenan. *From Fatwa to Jihad: The Rushdie Affair and Its Legacy*. London: Atlantic Books, 2009.

Matar, Nabil. *Islam in Britain, 1558–1685*. Cambridge: Cambridge University Press, 1998.

Maududi, Sayyeed Abdul-Ala. *Jihad in Islam*. Lahore, Pakistan: Islamic Publications.

Maréchal, Brigitte. *The Muslim Brothers in Europe: Roots and Discourse*. Leiden/Boston: Brill, 2008.

Marsot, Ataf Lutfi Al-Sayyid. *A History of Egypt: From the Arab Conquest to the Present*. Cambridge: Cambridge University Press, 1985.

McCloud, Aminah Beverly. *African American Islam*. New York: Routledge, 1995.

McRoy, Anthony. *From Rushdie to 7/7: The Radicalisation of Islam in Britain*. London: Social Affairs Unit, 2006.

Mitchell, Richard P. *The Society of the Muslim Brothers*. New York: Oxford University Press, 1969.

Nasr, Seyyed Vali Reza. *The Vanguard of the Islamic Revolution: The Jama'at-i Islami of Pakistan*. Berkeley: University of California Press, 1994.

Nielsen, Jørgen. *Muslims in Western Europe*. Edinburgh: Edinburgh University Press, 2004.

Nimer, Mohamed. *Muslim Community Life in the United States and Canada*. New York: Routledge, 2002.

——. *The North American Muslim Resource Guide: Muslim Community Life in the United States and Canada*. New York: Routledge, 2002.

O'Neill, Sean and Daniel McGrory. *The Suicide Factory: Abu Hamza and the Finsbury Park Mosque*. London: HarperCollins, 2006.

Oberschall, Anthony R. *Social Conflict and Social Movements*. Englewood Cliffs, NJ: Prentice Hall, 1973.

Padmasha, Dr. *Indian National Congress and the Muslims: 1928–1947*. New Delhi: Rajesh, 1980.

Page, David. *Prelude to Partition: The Indian Muslims and the Imperial System of Control, 1920–1932*. New York: Oxford University Press, 1982.

Pedersen, Lars. *Newer Islamic Movements in Western Europe*. Aldershot: Ashgate, 1999.

Poston, Larry. *Islamic Da'wah in the West*. New York: Oxford University Press, 1992.

Qu'est-ce que l'UOIF? Paris: Éditions l'Archipel, 2006.

Qutb, Sayyid. *Islam: The Religion of the Future*. Delhi: Markazi Maktaba Islami, 1974.

Ramadan, Tariq. *Aux Sources du Renouveau Musulman*. Lyon: Tawhid, 2002.

Roy, Olivier. *Globalized Islam: The Search for a New Ummah*. New York: Columbia University Press, 2004.

——. *Secularism Confronts Islam*. New York: Columbia University Press, 2007.

——. *The Failure of Political Islam*. Cambridge, MA: Harvard University Press, 1996.

Rushdie, Salman. *The Satanic Verses*. New York: Viking, 1989.

Ruthven, Malise. *A Satanic Affair: Salman Rushdie and the Wrath of Islam*. London: Hogarth Press, 1991.

Sacks, Jonathan. *The Home We Build Together: Recreating Society*. London: Continuum, 2007.

Sarkozy, Nicolas. *La République, les Religions, l'Espérance*. Paris: Éditions du Cerf, 2004.

Schulze, Reinhard. *Islamischer Internationalismus im 20. Jahrhundert: Untersuchungen zur Geschichte der Islamischen Weltliga*. Leiden: Brill, 1990.

Sen, Amartya. *Identity and Violence: The Illusion of Destiny*. New York: Norton, 2006.

Sfeir, Antoine. *Les Réseaux d'Allah: Les Filières Islamistes en France et en Europe*. Paris: Plon, 2001.

Shafiq, Muhammad. *Growth of Islamic Thought in North America*. Brentwood, MD: Amana Publications, 1994.

Shakir, Moin. *Khilafat to Partition: A Survey of Major Political Trends Among Indian Muslims During 1919–1947*. Delhi: Ajanta, 1983.

Shankland, David. *Islam and Society in Turkey*. Huntingdon: Eothen Press, 1999.

Sivan, Emmanuel. *Radical Islam: Medieval Theology and Modern Politics*. New Haven: Yale University Press, 1985.

Stenberg, Leif. *The Islamization of Science: Four Muslim Positions Developing an Islamic Modernity*. New York: Coronet Books, 1996.

Sullivan, Dennis J. and Sana Abed-Kotob. *Islam in Contemporary Egypt: Civil Society vs. the State*. Boulder, CO: Lynne Rienner, 1999.

Tamimi, Azzam. *Hamas: A History from Within*. Northampton, MA: Olive Branch Press, 2007.

——. *Rachid Ghannouchi: A Democrat Within Islamism*. New York: Oxford University Press, 2001.

Tarrow, Sidney. *The New Transnational Activism*. Cambridge: Cambridge University Press, 2005.

Ternisien, Xavier. *Les Frères Musulmans*. Paris: Fayard, 2005.

Tibi, Bassam. *The Challenge of Fundamentalism: Political Islam and the New World Disorder*. Berkeley: University of California Press, 1998.

——. *Islamische Zuwanderung, Die gescheiterte Integration*. Munich: DVA, 2002.

Timmerman, Kenneth R. *Preachers of Hate: Islam and the War on America*. New York: Crown Forum, 2003.

Ulfkotte, Udo. *Der Krieg in unseren Staedten*. Frankfurt: Eichborn Publishing, 2003.

Venner, Fiammetta. *OPA sur l'Islam de France: Les Ambitions de l'UOIF.* Paris: Calmann-Levy, 2005.

Yavuz, M. Hakan. *Islamic Political Identity in Turkey.* New York: Oxford University Press, 2003.

Yousef, Ahmed. *American Muslims: A Community Under Siege.* Springfield, VA: UASR Publishing Group, 2004.

Wickham, Carrie Rosefsky. *Mobilizing Islam: Religion, Activism, and Political Change in Egypt.* New York: Columbia University Press, 2002.

Wiktorowicz, Quintan, ed., *Islamic Activism: A Social Movement Theory Approach.* Bloomington: Indiana University Press, 2004.

Wright, Lawrence. *The Looming Tower: Al Qaeda and the Road to 9/11.* New York: Knopf, 2006.

Zollner, Barbara. *The Muslim Brotherhood: Hasan Al-Hudaybi and Ideology.* London: Routledge, 2008.

Government Reports and Documents

Affidavit of U.S. Immigration and Customs Enforcement Special Agent Brett Gentrup in *U.S. v. Abdurahman Muhammad Alamoudi.* U.S.D.C. of Eastern Virginia, Case 03–1009M. September 30, 2003.

Akram, Mohammed. "An Explanatory Memorandum on the Strategic Goals for the Group in North America." Government Exhibit 003–0085 in *United States v. Holy Land Foundation et al.*, 3:04-cr-240 (ND, Tex.).

Algemene Inlichtingen- en Veiligheidsdienst (Netherlands). *The Radical Dawa in Transition: The Rise of Islamic Neoradicalism in the Netherlands.* February 2008. https://www.aivd.nl/actueel-publicaties/aivd-publicaties/the-radical-dawa-in.

——. *Recruitment for the Jihad in the Netherlands: From Incident to Trend.* December 2002.

Bayerische Polizei (Bavarian police). http://www.polizei.bayern.de/muenchen/news/presse/aktuell/index.html/89241 (accessed March 10, 2009).

Blears, Hazel. Letter to MCB Secretary General Muhammad Abdul Bari, March 13, 2009. http://image.guardian.co.uk/sys-files/Guardian/documents/2009/03/23/blears_letter.pdf.

British Foreign Office. Internal memo on Yusuf al Qaradawi. July 14, 2005.

Canadian Security Intelligence Service (CSIS). *Radicalization and Jihad in the West.* June 2006.

Charity Commission for England and Wales. Central Register of Charities. Europe Trust: Registered April 2004; report accessed online July 21, 2008.

Comité Permanent de Contrôle des Services de Renseignements et de Sécurité (Comité R). Report to the Belgian Parliament. July 19, 2002. http://www .senate.be/www/?MIval=/publications/viewPubDoc&TID=33618007&LANG= fr#2–1171/1_112.

Department for Communities and Local Government (London). *Preventing Violent Extremism: Next Steps for Communities*. July 2008.

Emerson, Steven. Testimony before the U.S. House of Representatives Committee on Foreign Affairs, Subcommittee on Terrorism, Proliferation, and Trade. 110th Cong., 2nd sess., July 31, 2008.

Epstein, Matthew. Testimony before the U.S. Senate Committee on the Judiciary, *Terrorism: Two Years After 9/11, Connecting the Dots*. 108th Cong., 1st sess., September 10, 2003.

Evidence in *U.S. v. Abdurahman Muhammad Alamoudi*, U.S.D.C. of Eastern Virginia, Case 03–1009M.

Executive Committee for the Intelligence and Security Services (CESIS). 59th Report to the Italian Parliament. 2007.

Federal Bureau of Investigation. *Countering Radicalization*. http://www.fbi.gov/ page2/may07/radicalization051007.htm.

Federal Ministry of the Interior for the Deutsche Islam Konferenz. *Muslimisches Leben in Deutschland*. June 2009.

German Embassy to the United Kingdom. http://www.london.diplo.de/Vertretung/ london/en/06/other_legal_matters/Reform_Germanys_citizenship_seite .html.

German Federal Ministry of the Interior. http://www.bmi.bund.de/nn_1026710/ Internet/Content/Themen/Deutsche_Islam_Konferenz/DatenUndFakten/ Islamkonferenz_Kurzinfo_en.html.

German Federal Office for the Protection of the Constitution. *Integration as a Means to Prevent Extremism and Terrorism: Typology of Islamist Radicalisation and Recruitment*. January 2007.

German Islam Conference (DIK). Document provided by officials at the Federal Ministry of the Interior, Berlin. November 2008.

Government Exhibit 016–0049 in *United States v. Holy Land Foundation et al.*, 3:04-cr-240 (ND, Tex.).

Government Exhibit 016–0051 in *United States v. Holy Land Foundation et al.*, 3:04-cr-240 (ND, Tex.).

Government Exhibit 016–0057 in *United States v. Holy Land Foundation et al.*, 3:04-cr-240 (ND, Tex.).

Government Exhibit 016–0059 in *United States v. Holy Land Foundation et al.*, 3:04-cr-240 (ND, Tex.).

Government Exhibit 016–0063 in *United States v. Holy Land Foundation et al.*, 3:04-cr-240 (ND, Tex.).

Government Exhibit 016–0067 in *United States v. Holy Land Foundation et al.*, 3:04-cr-240 (ND, Tex.).

Government Exhibit 016–0069 in *United States v. Holy Land Foundation et al.*, 3:04-cr-240 (ND, Tex.).

Government Exhibit 016–0071 in *United States v. Holy Land Foundation et al.*, 3:04-cr-240 (ND, Tex.).

Government Exhibit 016–0075 in *United States v. Holy Land Foundation et al.*, 3:04-cr-240 (ND, Tex.).

Government Exhibit 016–0087 in *United States v. Holy Land Foundation et al.*, 3:04-cr-240 (ND, Tex.).

Government Exhibit 1B33/0003188 in *United States v. Holy Land Foundation et al.*, 3:04-cr-240 (ND, Tex.).

Government Exhibit 1B64/0000377–0000383 in *United States v. Holy Land Foundation et al.*, 3:04-cr-240 (ND, Tex.)

Government Exhibit 1B64/0000412 in *United States v. Holy Land Foundation et al.*, 3:04-cr-240 (ND, Tex.)

Government's Trial Brief in *United States v. Holy Land Foundation et al.*, 3:04-cr-240 (ND, Tex.).

Greater London Authority. *Muslims in London.* October 2006.

——. *Why the Mayor of London Will Maintain Dialogues with All of London's Faith Communities.* January 2005.

HRH The Prince of Wales. Speech during visit to the Islamic Foundation, January 24, 2003. http://www.princeofwales.gov.uk/speeches/multiracial_24012003.html.

"Ikhwan in America." Government Exhibit 003–0089 in *United States v. Holy Land Foundation et al.*, 3:04-cr-240 (ND, Tex.)

Innenministerium, Nordrhein-Westfalen (Germany). *Islamische Gemeinschaft in Deutschland.* Undated. http://www.im.nrw.de/sch/580.htm.

International Islamic Bank. Annual reports, 1982–1996. Erhvervs- og Selskabsstyrelsen, Denmark.

Johnson, Ian. "The Muslim Brotherhood in Europe." Testimony the Congressional Human Rights Caucus, 109th Cong., 2nd sess., February 9, 2006.

Landesamt für Verfassungsschutz, Baden-Württemberg (Germany). *Islamistischer Extremismus and Terrorismus.* April 2006.

Landesamt fur Verfassungsschutz, Hansestadt Hamburg (Germany). Annual report, 2001.

Landesamt fur Verfassungsschutz, Hessen (Germany). *Islamismus.* Undated. http://www.verfassungsschutz-hessen.de/downloads/islam.pdf.

Mayor's statement at Mayor's Question Time on the visit of Dr. Al Qaradawi. City of London, July 15, 2004. http://www.london.gov.uk/view_press_release .jsp?releaseid=3862.

Ministry of Education, North Rhine-Westphalia (Germany). *Alevitischer Religion- sunterricht.* Undated.

——. *Islamunterricht.* Undated.

Ministry of the Interior of Nordrhein-Westfalen (Germany). *Islamistische Organi- sationen in Nordrhein-Westfalen.* November 2008.

Ministry of Refugee, Immigration and Integration Affairs (Denmark). *A Common and Safe Future: Proposal for an Action Plan to Prevent Extremist Views and Rad- icalisation Among Young People.* June 2008.

Municipality of Amsterdam. *Amsterdam Against Radicalisation.* November 15, 2007.

Muslim Brotherhood Shura Council. "Shura Council Report on the Future of the Group." Government Exhibit 003–0003 in *United States v. Holy Land Founda- tion et al.,* 3:04-cr-240 (ND, Tex.).

Office for the Protection of the Constitution (Germany). Annual reports, 1999, 2000, 2005, 2006, 2008.

Office of the Assistant Secretary of Defense, letter to Abdurahman Alamoudi, Ex- ecutive Director, American Muslim Council, September 12, 1996.

Office of Senator Tom Coburn (R-MD). *Justice Denied: Waste and Mismanagement at the Department of Justice.* October 2008.

Partij voor de Vrijheid (Netherlands). Questions from MPs Geert Wilders and Ray- mond de Roon and answers from Ella Vogelaar. August 7, 2007. http://www.pvv .nl/index.php?option=com_content&task=view&id=737.

Powers, Richard C., FBI Assistant Director, Office of Congressional Affairs. Letter to Senator Jon Kyl. April 28, 2009.

Report of the Commission on the Intelligence Capabilities of the United States Re- garding Weapons of Mass Destruction. March 31, 2005. http://www.gpoaccess .gov/wmd/pdf/full_wmd_report.pdf.

Superseding Indictment in *United States v. Holy Land Foundation et al.,* 3:04-cr-240 (ND, Tex.).

Text from Lawsuit Response in *Council on American-Islamic Relations, Inc. v. An- drew Whitehead,* no. CL04–926, Virginia: In the Circuit Court for the City of Virginia Beach, April 30, 2004.

United Kingdom. *Census* 2001. http://www.statistics.gov.uk/census2001/census2001. asp.

——. *The Prevent Strategy: A Guide for Local Partners in England.* June 2008.

——. *The United Kingdom's Strategy for Countering International Terrorism (CON- TEST 2).* March 2009.

United Kingdom. Home Office. Statement regarding the BBC program *Muslim First, British Second*. http://news.bbc.co.uk/panorama/hi/front_page/newsid _7888000/7888793.stm (accessed February 16, 2009).

United Kingdom. Parliament. "Racial and Religious Hatred Bill." June 9, 2005, Session 2005-06. http://www.parliament.the-stationery-office.co.uk/pa/cm200506/ cmbills/011/06011.i-i.html.

U.S. Congress. House of Representatives. Committee on Foreign Affairs, Subcommittee on Terrorism, Nonproliferation, and Trade. *Foreign Aid and the Fight Against Terrorism and Proliferation: Leveraging Foreign Aid to Achieve U.S. Policy Goals* (hearing). 110th Cong., 2nd sess., July 31, 2008.

U.S. Department of Justice. *The Attorney General's Guidelines for Domestic FBI Operations*. Undated. http://www.justice.gov/ag/readingroom/guidelines.pdf.

——. Press release on the sentencing of Alamoudi. October 15, 2004.

——. Press release on the sentencing of HLF leaders. May 27, 2009. http://www .usdoj.gov/opa/pr/2009/May/09-nsd-519.html (accessed June 9, 2009).

U.S. Department of State. International Religious Freedom Report. 2004. http:// www.state.gov/g/drl/rls/irf/.

U.S. Department of the Treasury. Office of Foreign Assets Control. "Recent OFAC Actions." November 7, 2001.

——. "Treasury Designates MIRA for Support to Al Qaida." July 14, 2005. http:// www.treas.gov/press/releases/js2632.htm.

U.S. Senate. Subcommittee on Terrorism, Technology and Homeland Security. *Terrorism: Two Years After 9/11, Connecting the Dots*. 108th Cong., 1st sess., September 10, 2003.

Verfassungsschutz of the Ministry of the Interior of Bavaria. Report for the first semester of 2003.

——. Annual report, 2008.

Working Groups. *Preventing Extremism Together*. August–October 2005. http:// www.communities.gov.uk/documents/communities/pdf/152164.pdf.

Journal Articles and Book Chapters

Ahmad, Khurshid. "Mawdudi's Model for Islamic Revival." In Muhammad Mumtaz Ali, ed., *Modern Islamic Movements: Models, Problems and Perspectives*. Kuala Lumpur: Noordeen, 2000, 57–76.

Ahmed, Gutbi Mahdi. "Muslim Organizations in the United States." In Yvonne Yazbeck Haddad, ed., *The Muslims of America*. Oxford: Oxford University Press, 1991, 11–24.

al Banna, Hassan. "The New Renaissance." In John J. Donahue and John L. Esposito, eds., *Islam in Transition: Muslim Perspectives* New York: Oxford University Press, 1982, 78–83.

Allievi, Stefano. "Muslims and Politics." In Brigitte Marechal, Stefano Allievi, Felice Dassetto, and Jørgen Nielen, *Muslims in the Enlarged Europe*. Leiden/Boston: Brill, 2003, 183–213.

Altman, Israel Elad. "Current Trends in the Ideology of the Egyptian Muslim Brotherhood." *Current Trends in Islamist Ideology* (December 29, 2005). http://www .hudson.org/files/publications/Ideology_of_Egyptian_Muslim_Brotherhood .pdf.

"AMC Hosts Interfaith Heritage Banquet." *The AMC Report* 6, no. 1 (January 1996).

Amghar, Samir. "Europe Puts Islamists to the Test: The Muslim Brotherhood (France, Belgium and Switzerland)." *Mediterranean Politics* 13, no. 1 (March 2008): 63–77.

Amiraux, Valerie. "Turkish Political Islam and Europe: Story of an Opportunistic Intimacy." In Stefano Allievi and Joergen S. Nielsen, eds., *Muslim Networks and Transnational Communities in and Across Europe*. Leiden/Boston: Brill, 2003, 146–69.

Ammitzbøll, Pernille, and Lorenzo Vidino. "After the Danish Cartoon Controversy." *Middle East Quarterly* 14, no. 1 (Winter 2007): 3–11.

Badawi, Jamal A. "Approaches to Muslim Reawakening: Al-Banna's Approach." In Muhammad Mumtaz Ali, ed., *Modern Islamic Movements: Models, Problems and Perspectives*. Kuala Lumpur: Noordeen, 2000, 25–34.

Bale, Jeffrey M. "Hiding in Plain Sight in 'Londonistan.'" In Michael Innes, ed., *Denial of Sanctuary: Understanding Terrorist Safe Havens*. Westport, CT: Praeger, 2007, 139–51.

Bardakoglu, Ali. "'Moderate Perception of Islam' and the Turkish Model of the Diyanet: The President's Statement." *Journal of Muslim Minority Affairs* 24, no. 2 (October 2004): 367–73.

Barzinji, Jamal. "History of the Islamization of Knowledge and Contributions of the International Institute of Islamic Thought." In Amber Haque, ed., *Muslims and Islamization in North America: Problems and Prospects*. Beltsville, MD: Amana Publications, 1999, 13–31.

Birt, Jonathan. "Good Imam Bad Imam: Civic Religion and National Integration in Britain After 9/11." *The Muslim World* 4, no. 96: 687–705.

Boubekeur, Amel. "Political Islam in Europe: A Changing Landscape." In Amel Boubekeur, Samir Amghar, and Michael Emerson, eds., *European Islam: The Challenges for Public Policy and Society*. Brussels: CEPS/Open Society Institute, 2007, 14–37.

———. "Post-Islamist Culture: A New Form of Mobilization?" *History of Religions* 47, no. 1 (2007): 75–94.

Caeiro, Alexandre and Mahmoud al-Saify. "Qaradawi in Europe, Europe in Qaradawi? The Global Mufti's European Politics." In Bettina Gräf and Jakob Skovgaard-Petersen, eds., *The Global Mufti: The Phenomenon of Yusuf Al-Qaradawi*. New York: Columbia University Press, 2009, 109–48.

Cesari, Jocelyne. "Islam in France: The Shaping of a Religious Minority." In Yvonne Yazbeck Haddad, ed., *Muslims in the West: From Sojourners to Citizens*. Oxford: Oxford University Press, 2001, 36–51.

Christidis, Yorgos. "The Muslim Minority in Greece." In Gerd Nonneman, Tim Niblock, and Bogdan Szajkowski, eds., *Muslim Communities in the New Europe*. Berkshire, UK: Ithaca Press, 1996, 153–63.

Commins, David. "Hasan al-Banna, 1906–1949." In Ali Rahnema, ed., *Pioneers of Islamic Revival*. London: Zed Books, 1994, 125–53.

Duran, Khalid. "Jihadism in Europe." *The Journal of Counterterrorism and Security International* (Fall 2000):1–5.

Eade, John and David Garbin. "Changing Narratives of Violence, Struggle and Resistance: Bangladeshis and the Competition for Resources in the Global City." *Oxford Development Studies* 30, no. 2 (2002): 137–49.

Edwards, Bob and John D. McCarthy. "Resources and Social Movement Mobilization." In David A. Snow, Sarah A. Soule, and Hanspeter Kriesi, eds., *The Blackwell Companion to Social Movements*. Oxford: Blackwell, 2004, 116–52.

El Fadl, Khaled Abou. "Striking a Balance: Islamic Legal Discourse on Muslim Minorities." In Yvonne Yazbeck Haddad and John L. Esposito, eds., *Muslims on the Americanization Path?* New York: Oxford University Press, 2000, 58–63.

el-Helbawy, Kamal. "Cementing Relations Between Muslim Citizens and Governments in the West: The United Kingdom as a Case Study." *Islamism Digest* 3, no. 9 (September 2008): 4–7.

Esposito, John L. "Practice and Theory." *Boston Review* (April/May 2003). http://www.bostonreview.net/BR28.2/esposito.html.

Ferrari, Silvio. "The Secularity of the State and the Shaping of Muslim Representative Organizations in Western Europe." In Jocelyne Cesari and Sean McLoughlin, eds., *European Muslims and the Secular State*. Aldershot: Ashgate, 2005, 11–21.

Fradkin, Hillel. "The History and Unwritten Future of Salafism." *Current Trends in Islamist Ideology* (November 25, 2007):5–19.

Fregosi, Franck. "Les Filières Nationales de Formation des Imams en France." In Franck Fregosi, ed., *La Formation des Cadres Religieux Musulmans en France*. Paris: L'Harmattan, 1998, 101–39.

Fuess, Albrecht. "Islamic Religious Education in Western Europe: Models of Integration and the German Approach." *Journal of Muslim Minority Affairs* 27, no. 2 (August 2007): 215–39.

Geisser, Vincent. "L'UOIF, la Tension Clientéliste d'une Grande Fédération Islamique." In Amel Boubekeur and Abderrahim Lamchichi, eds., *Musulmans de France, Confluences Méditerranée* 57 (Spring 2006): 83–101.

Gräf, Bettina. "IslamOnline.net: Independent, Interactive, Popular." *Arab Media and Society* 4 (Winter 2008). http://www.arabmediasociety.com/?article =576.

——. "The Concept of Wasatiyya in the Work of Yusuf al-Qaradawi." In Bettina Gräf and Jakob Skovgaard-Petersen, eds., *The Global Mufti: The Phenomenon of Yusuf Al-Qaradawi*. New York: Columbia University Press, 2009.

Haines, Herbert H. "Black Radicalization and the Funding of Civil Rights: 1957–1970." In Doug McAdam and David A. Snow, *Social Movements*. Los Angeles: Roxbury, 1997, 440–49.

Haqqani, Husain and Hillel Fradkin. "Islamist Parties: Going Back to the Origins." *Journal of Democracy* 19, no. 3 (July 2008): 13–18.

Huda, Qamar-ul. "Conflict Prevention and Peace-Building Efforts by American Muslim Organizations Following September 11." *Journal of Muslim Minority Affairs* 26, no. 2 (August 2006): 187–204.

Hussain, Dilwar. "The Holy Grail of Muslims in Western Europe." In John L. Esposito and Francois Burgat, eds., *Modernizing Islam: Religion in the Public Sphere in Europe and the Middle East*. New Brunswick: Rutgers University Press, 2003, 215–50.

"Islam and Europe: Ibrahim El-Zayyat Discusses the Future." *Islamism Digest* 3, no. 2 (February 2008): 16–18.

"Islam and Muslims in Germany: An Overview by Ibrahim El-Zayyat." *Islamism Digest* 3, no. 1 (January 2008): 13–15.

Johnson, Ian. "The Brotherhood's Westward Expansion." *Current Trends in Islamist Ideology* (February 5, 2008):71–84.

Johnson, Steve A. "Political Activity of Muslims in America." In Yvonne Yazbeck Haddad, ed., *The Muslims of America*. Oxford: Oxford University Press, 1991, 111–24.

——. "The Muslims of Indianapolis." In Yvonne Yazbeck Haddad and Jane Idleman Smith, eds., *Muslim Communities in North America*. Albany: State University of New York Press, 1994, 259–77.

Karakasouglu, Yasemin and Gerd Nonneman. "Muslims in Germany." In Gerd Nonneman, Tim Niblock, and Bogdan Szajkowski, eds., *Muslim Communities in the New Europe*. Reading: Ithaca Press Paperbacks, 2006, 241–67.

Kettani, M. Ali. "The Problems of Muslim Minorities and Their Solutions." In *Muslim Communities in Non-Muslim States*. London: Islamic Council of Europe, 1980, 91–107.

Khalil, Magdi. "Egypt's Muslim Brotherhood and Political Power: Would Democracy Survive?" *Middle East Review of International Affairs Journal* 10, no. 3 (March 2006): 44–52.

Koenig, Matthias. "Incorporating Muslim Migrants in Western Nation States: A Comparison of the United Kingdom, France and Germany." *Journal of International Migration and Integration* 6, no. 2: 219–234.

Krämer, Gudrun. "Drawing Boundaries: Yusuf al-Qaradawi on Apostasy." In Gudrun Krämer and Sabine Schmidtke, *Speaking for Islam: Religious Authorities in Muslim Societies*. Leiden: Brill, 2006, 181–217.

Lambert, Robert. "Empowering Salafis and Islamists Against Al-Qaeda: A London Counterterrorism Case Study." *Political Science and Politics* 41 (2008): 31–35.

Leiken, Robert S. and Steven Brooke. "The Moderate Muslim Brotherhood." *Foreign Affairs* (March/April 2007).

Leonard, Karen. "South Asian Leadership of American Muslims." In Yvonne Yazbeck Haddad, *Muslims in the West: From Sojourners to Citizens* Oxford: Oxford University Press, 2001, 233–49.

Lewis, Philip. "The Bradford Council for Mosques and the Search for Muslim Unity." In Steven Vertovec and Ceri Peach, eds., *Islam in Europe: The Politics of Religion and Community*. London: MacMillan, 1997, 103–28.

Marechal, Brigitte. "Institutionalisation of Islam and Representative Organisations for Dealing with European States." In Brigitte Marechal, Stefano Allievi, Felice Dassetto, and Jørgen Nielen, *Muslims in the Enlarged Europe*. Leiden/Boston: Brill, 2003, 151–82.

——. "The Question of Belonging." In Brigitte Marechal, Stefano Allievi, Felice Dassetto, and Jørgen Nielen, eds., *Muslims in the Enlarged Europe*. Leiden/Boston: Brill, 2003, 5–18.

McCarthy, John D. and Mayer N. Zald. "Resource Mobilization and Social Movements: A Partial Theory." *The American Journal of Sociology* 82, no. 6 (May 1977): 1212–41.

Murad, Khurram. "Islamic Movement in the West: Reflections on Some Issues." In Muhammad Mumtaz Ali, ed., *Modern Islamic Movements: Models, Problems and Perspectives*. Kuala Lumpur: Noordeen, 2000.

Neumann, Peter R. *Joining Al-Qaeda: Jihadist Recruitment in Europe*. Adelphi Paper 339. London: International Institute for Strategic Studies.

Nielsen, Jørgen S. "Transnational Islam and the Integration of Islam in Europe." In Stefano Allievi and Jørgen S. Nielsen, *Muslim Networks and Transnational Communities in and Across Europe*. Leiden: Brill, 2003, 28–51.

Nimer, Mohammed. "Muslims in American Public Life." In Yvonne Yazbeck Haddad, ed., *Muslims in the West: From Sojourners to Citizens*. Oxford: Oxford University Press, 2001, 169–86.

Peter, Frank. "Leading the Community of the Middle Way: A Study of the Muslim Field in France." *The Muslim World* 96 (October 2006): 707–36.

Pfaff, Steven and Anthony J. Gill. "Will a Million Muslims March?: Muslim Interest Organizations and Political Integration in Europe." *Comparative Political Studies* 39 (2006): 803–28.

Phillips, Richard. "Standing Together: The Muslim Association of Britain and the Anti-war Movement." *Race and Class* 50, no. 2 (2008): 101–13.

Pomerantz, Steven. "Counterterrorism in a Free Society." *Journal of Counterterrorism and Security International* (Spring 1998):26.

Rahnema, Ali. "Introduction." In Ali Rahnema, ed., *Pioneers of Islamic Revival*. London: Zed Books, 1994, ix–lxxxiii.

Rath, Jan, Rinnus Pennix, Kees Groendendijk, and Astrid Meyer. "The Politics of Recognizing Religious Diversity in Europe: Social Reactions to the Institutionalization of Islam in the Netherlands, Belgium and Great Britain." *Netherlands Journal of Social Sciences* 35, no. 1: 53–70.

Schiffauer, Werner. "From Exile to Diaspora: The Development of Transnational Islam in Europe." In Aziz Al-Azmeh and Effie Fokas, eds., *Islam in Europe: Diversity, Identity and Influence*. Cambridge: Cambridge University Press, 2007, 68–95.

Shadid, Wasif and Sjoerd van Koningsveld. "Loyalty to a Non-Muslim Government." In W.A.R. Shadid and P. S. van Konignsveld, eds., *Political Participation and Identities of Muslims in Non-Muslim States*. Kampen: Kok Pharos, 1996, 84–115.

——. "Religious Authorities of Muslims in the West: Their Views on Political Participation." In W.A.R. Shadid and P. S. van Koningsveld, eds., *Intellectual Relations and Religious Authorities: Muslims in the European Union*. Leuven: Peeters, 2002, 161–84.

Skovgaard-Petersen, Jakob. "Yusuf Al-Qaradawi and Al-Azhar." In Bettina Gräf and Jakob Skovgaard-Petersen, eds., *The Global Mufti: The Phenomenon of Yusuf Al-Qaradawi*. New York: Columbia University Press, 2009, 27–54.

Søvik, Margrete. "Islamic Religious Instruction in North-Rhine-Westphalia (1979–1999): Constructing a German Muslim Identity Between Authenticity and Responsibility." In Stephen G. Ellis and Ann Katherine Isaacs, eds., *Citizenship in Historical Perspective*. Pisa: Pisa University Press, 2006, 317–32.

Siddiqi, Shamim A. "Islamic Movement in America: Why?" In Amber Haque, ed., *Muslims and Islamization in North America: Problems and Prospects*. Beltsville, MD: Amana Publications, 1999, 355–61.

Tammam, Husan. "Yusuf Qaradawi and the Muslim Brothers: The Nature of a Special Relationship." In Bettina Gräf and Jakob Skovgaard-Petersen, eds., *The Global Mufti: The Phenomenon of Yusuf Al-Qaradawi.* New York: Columbia University Press, 2009, 55–84.

Torrekens, Corinne. "La gestion locale de l'islam à Bruxelles." *Cahiers de la sécurité* P 8° 5663.—(2006–07/09) n°62: 139–60.

Vertovec, Steven. "Islamophobia and Muslim Recognition in Britain." In Yvonne Yazbeck Haddad, ed., *Muslims in the West: From Sojourners to Citizens.* Oxford: Oxford University Press, 2001, 19–35.

——. "Muslims, the State, and the Public Sphere in Britain." In Gerd Nonneman, Tim Niblock, and Bogdan Szajkowski, eds., *Muslim Communities in the New Europe.* Berkshire, UK: Ithaca Press, 1996, 167–86.

Voll, John O. "Fundamentalism in the Sunni Arab World." In Martin E. Marty and R. Scott Appleby, eds., *Fundamentalisms Observed.* Chicago: University of Chicago Press, 1991, 345–402.

——. "Relations Among Islamist Groups." In John L. Esposito, ed., *Political Islam: Revolution, Radicalism, or Reform?* Boulder, CO: Lynne Rienner, 1997, 231–48.

Warner, Carolyn M. and Manfred W. Wenner. "Religion and the Political Organization of Muslims in Europe." *Perspectives on Politics* 4, no. 3 (September 2006): 457–79.

Whine, Michael. "The Advance of the Muslim Brotherhood in the UK." *Current Trends in Islamist Ideology* 2 (September 2005): 30–40.

Yaqoob, Salma. "British Islamic Political Radicalism." In Tahir Abbas, ed., *Islamic Political Radicalism: A European Perspective.* Edinburgh: Edinburgh University Press, 2007, 279–94.

Zacharias, Diana. "Access of Muslim Organizations to Religious Instruction in Public Schools: A Comment on the Decision of the Federal Administrative Court of 23 February 2005." *German Law Journal* 6, no. 10: 1319–34.

Zollner, Barbara. "Prison Talk: The Muslim Brotherhood's Internal Struggle During Gamal Abdel Nasser's Persecution." *International Journal of Middle Eastern Studies* 39 (2007): 411–33.

Newspaper Articles

Abu Marzook, Mousa. "Hamas' Stand." *Los Angeles Times,* July 10, 2007.

Ahmed-Ullah, Noreen S., Sam Roe. and Laurie Cohen. "A Rare Look at Secretive Brotherhood in America." *Chicago Tribune,* September 19, 2004.

al-Faruqi, Ismail Raji. "Islamizing the Social Sciences." *Muslim World League Journal,* August 1977.

al-Rasheed, Abdel Rahman. "Qaradawi: Moderate and Extremist." *Arab News*, July 17, 2004.

Allam, Magdi. "La Moschea di Bologna e i Cedimenti di Cofferati." *Corriere della Sera*, December 6, 2007.

"Angry Scenes at Anti-Israel Demo." BBC, April 13, 2002.

Anthony, Andrew. "How One Book Ignited a Culture War." *Guardian*, January 11, 2009.

Arachi, Alessandra. "Stop alla Moschea: 'Chi la Finanzia?' Genova Chiama Amato, Unione Divisa." *Corriere della Sera*, September 25, 2007.

"Arrested Muslim Activist Helped Pick Chaplains for U.S. Military." *Washington Times*, September 30, 2003.

Azam, Nadeem. "Election Analysis." *Q-News*, June 1997.

Beißel, Udo. "Razzia bei Milli Görüs." *Kölner Stadt-Anzeiger*, August 26, 2008.

Bernard, Philippe and Xavier Ternisien. "Il Faut Reconnaître la Sur-Délinquance des Jeunes Issus de l'Immigration." *Le Monde*, December 4, 2001.

Bernstein, Richard. "Lessons of Islam in German Classrooms." *The New York Times*, June 30, 2004.

Braude, Joseph. "Moderate Muslims and Their Radical Leaders." *The New Republic*, February 27, 2006.

"Britain 'Sleepwalking to Segregation.'" *Guardian*, September 19, 2005.

Bunglawala, Inayat. "Engagement with Extremists Is Right." *Guardian*, February 26, 2009.

Butt, Hassan. "My Plea to Fellow Muslims: You Must Renounce Terror." *The Observer*, July 1, 2007.

Cesarani, David. "A Way out of This Dead End." *Guardian*, September 16, 2005.

Chittenden, Maurice and Tom Baird. "MPs Don't Know their Sunnis from Their Shi'ites." *Sunday Times of London*, January 7, 2007.

de Haas, Joost. "Moskeeen in de ban van Moslimgroep." *De Telegraaf*, March 24, 2007.

Dodd, Vikram. "Government Suspends Links with Muslim Council of Britain Over Gaza." *Guardian*, March 23, 2009.

——. "Muslim Council Ends Holocaust Memorial Day Boycott." *Guardian*, December 3, 2007.

Doward, Jamie. "British Muslim Leader Urged to Quit Over Gaza." *The Observer*, March 8, 2009.

Dreher, Rob. "CAIR and Hamas." *Dallas Morning News*, August 8, 2007.

El Houdaiby, Ibrahim. "Why Are Western Officials Hesitant to Talk to Moderate Islamists?" *Daily Star*, November 7, 2007.

"Elections 1997 and British Muslims." *QNews*, March 14, 1997.

Etchegoin, Marie-France and Serge Raffy. "La Vérité sur l'Islam en France." *Le Nouvel Observateur*, February 2, 2006.

Farah, Douglas and John Mintz. "U.S. Trails Va. Muslim Money, Ties." *The Washington Post*, October 7, 2002.

Ford, Richard. "Livingstone Likens Bomb Apologist to Reformer Pope John." *Times of London*, September 14, 2005.

Frangenberg, Helmut. "Ermittlungen gegen Islam-Funktionäre." *Kölner Stadt-Anzeiger*, March 19, 2009.

Frangenberg, Helmut and Detlef Schmalenberg. "El-Zayat, der Herr der Moscheen." *Kölner Stadt-Anzeiger*, March 20, 2009.

Gardiner, Lisa. "American Muslim Leader Urges Faithful to Spread Islam's Message." *San Ramon Valley Herald*, July 4, 1998.

Geisser, Vincent. "'Notre Ami Sarkozy,' UOIF-UMP, Histoire d'un PACS Avorté." *Oumma.com*, November 30, 2006. http://oumma.com/Notre-ami-Sarkozy-UOIF-UMP.

Ghazali, Abdus Sattar. "American Muslims in 2006 Elections." Al Jazeera, November 16, 2006.

Gilligan, Andrew. "Pro-Ken Muslim Group Claims Boris 'Would Scrap the Koran.'" *The Evening Standard*, April 28, 2008.

Hamzawy, Amr. "Regression in the Muslim Brotherhood's Platform?" *Daily Star*, November 1, 2007.

Harper, Tom. "Ministers Compared to Nazis Over Islam Stigma." *Telegraph*, December 18, 2006.

Helm, Toby. "Back British Values or Lose Grants, Kelly Tells Muslim Groups." *Telegraph*, October 12, 2006.

"How the Government Lost the Plot." *The Economist*, February 26, 2009.

Hub, Ralph. "Razzia in der Moschee in Freimann." *Abendzeitung*, March 10, 2009.

Hudson, Audrey. "CAIR Concedes Membership Down." *Washington Times*, August 22, 2007.

——. "Muslim Group Touts Local Political Clout." *Washington Times*, October 1, 2007.

"IIFSO Conference: No Proclamations, No Self-Congratulations, Just Sharing of Experience." *Impact International* 12–15 August, 1977.

"Inside the Ring." *Washington Times*, September 14, 2007.

Interview with Mohammed Akef, *Asharq Al-Awsat*, December 11, 2005.

Interview with Youssuf Nada, *al Misri al Yawm*, May 25–30, 2008.

Isikoff, Michael and Mark Hosenball. "An Unwelcome Guest." *Newsweek*, August 8, 2007.

"Islamic Council of Europe: 'Foundations Well Laid,'" *Impact International*, May 26–June 8, 1978.

"Islamic Council of Europe: Progress and Plans." *Impact International*, September 10–23, 1976.

Jaffe, Harry. "Unmasking the Mysterious Mohamed Hadid." *The Business of Washington*, March 1988.

Johnson, Ian. "The Beachhead: How a Mosque for Ex-Nazis Became Center of Radical Islam." *The Wall Street Journal*, July 12, 2005.

——. "The Brotherhood's Westward Expansion." *Current Trends in Islamist Ideology*, February 5, 2008.

——. "How Islamic Group's Ties Reveal Europe's Challenge." *Wall Street Journal*, December 29, 2005.

Kabbani, Rana. "Dislocation and Neglect in Muslim Britain's Ghettos." *Guardian*, June 17, 2002.

Kerbaj, Richard. "Government Moves to Isolate Muslim Council of Britain with Cash for Mosques." *Times of London*, March 30, 2009.

——. "Muslim Population 'Rising 10 Times Faster than Rest of Society." *Times of London*, January 30, 2009.

Kirkup, James. "More Than 20 Serious Terrorist Plots Against Britain Are Being Planned in Pakistan." *Daily Telegraph*, December 15, 2008.

Kovacs, Stéphane. "L'islam, première religion à Bruxelles dans vingt ans." *Le Figaro*, March 21, 2008.

Kristianasen, Wendy. "A Row in the Family." *Le Monde Diplomatique*, April 2000.

Law, Bill. "Clerics Urge a New Jihad Over Gaza." *BBC News*, February 17, 2009.

Lawton, John. "Muslims in Europe: The Presence." *Saudi Aramco World*, January/February 1979, 3–8.

"London Conference of Islamic Centres and Bodies in Europe." *Impact International*, May 25–June 7, 1973.

Lloyd, Anthony. "Tomb of the Unknown Assassin Reveals Mission to Kill Rushdie." *Times of London*, June 8, 2005.

MacFarquhar, Neil. "Scrutiny Increases for a Group Advocating for Muslims in the U.S." *The New York Times*, March 14, 2007.

Malik, Kenan. "The Islamophobia Myth." *The Spectator*, February 2005.

——. "What Muslims Want." Channel 4, August 7, 2006.

"Marokkaanse jongeren willen soepeler geloof. *EenVandaag*, September 29, 2008.

Mattson, Ingrid. "My Islam: Freedom and Responsibility." *Islamica Magazine* 20 (2007).

"Mayor Culpa." *Private Eye*, March 21, 2008.

Michael, Maggie. "Egypt's Brotherhood Party Details Platform Akin to That of Iran." *Associated Press*, October 11, 2007.

Mihalopoulos, Dan. "Abuse of Post-9/11 Detainees Detailed." *Chicago Tribune*, July 22, 2003.

Mintz, John and Douglas Farah. "In Search of Friends Among the Foes: U.S. Hopes to Work with Diverse Group." *The Washington Post*, September 11, 2004.

Mohammed, Faraz. "MCB: Dad's Muslim Army." *Q-News*, April 1998.

"Muslim Leader Sues Blears on Gaza." *BBC News*, April 4, 2009.

"Muslim Students' Associations Hold Annual Convention." *Muslim World League Journal*, November/December 1965.

Naughton, Philippe. "Funding Cut-off Threat by Minister Angers Muslim Groups." *Times of London*, October 11, 2006.

"News from the Muslim World League." *Muslim World League Journal*, July 1974.

Nilsson, Kirsten. "Imamers indflydelse er begrænset." *Politiken*, March 12, 2007.

O'Brien, Mike. "Labour and British Muslims: Can we Dream the Same Dream?" *Muslim Weekly* 58 (2004).

"Official Recognition of Islam in Germany?" *Der Spiegel*, April 16, 2007

Palmer, Alasdair. "Muslim Apostates Threatened Over Christianity." *Sunday Telegraph*, December 11, 2007.

——. "Not in Their Name?" *Sunday Telegraph*, July 8, 2007.

——. "Top Job Fighting Extremism for Muslims Who Praised Bombers." *Telegraph*, August 20, 2005.

"Pangs and Process of Self-Discovery." *Impact International*, October 14–27, 1983.

"People" Section. *Impact International*, October 28–November 10, 1977.

Pistacchi, Diego. "Ronchi: No alla Moschea degli Intolleranti." *Il Giornale*, February 3, 2009.

Powers, Carla. "New Imams." *Newsweek*, January 17, 2006.

Rasche, Uta. "Spinne im Netz der Muslime in Deutschland: Die Macht des Ibrahim El Zayat." *Frankfurter Allgemeine Zeitung*, May 11, 2007.

Rushdie, Salman. "Bring on the Islamic Reformation." *The Washington Post*, August 8, 2005.

Sacranie, Iqbal. "Why You Should Exercise Your Vote." *QNews*, March 1997.

Sakr, Ahmad Husain. "The Future of Islam in North America." *Muslim World League Journal*, April 1975.

Schomaker, Gilbert. "Senat Will Islamkunde en Schulen mit Neuen Argumenten Stoppen." *Berliner Zeitung*, July 29, 2000.

Shahine, Gihan. "Fatwa Fight." *Al Ahram Weekly* 708 (16–22 September 2004).

Siddiqui, Asim. "Not in Our Name." *Guardian*, July 3, 2007.

Sollich, Rainer. "Dialogue with Extremists?" *Deutsche Welle*, July 21, 2006.

"Spectrum: A Roll Call of UK Islamic Groups—Islam and Britain." *Times of London*, August 17, 1987.

Spiewak, Martin, and Wolfgang Ochatius. "Mit Koran und Grundgesetz." *Die Zeit*, February 4, 1999.

Stein, Jeff. "Can You Tell a Sunni from a Shiite?" *The New York Times*, October 18, 2006.

——. "Democrats' New Intelligence Chairman Needs a Crash Course on al Qaeda." *Congressional Quarterly*, December 8, 2006.

Stephens, Bret. "Benedict's Opposite." *Wall Street Journal*, September 26, 2006.

Taylor, Marisa. "FBI Struggles to Win Trust of Muslim, Arab Communities." *McClatchy Newspapers*, November 21, 2006.

Temko, Ned. "Beckett Rejects Link Between Foreign Policy and Terrorism." *Observer*, August 13, 2006.

Ternisien, Xavier. "'Prière Nationale' Musulmane à La Courneuve pour Concilier Solidarité et Revendication du Voile." *Le Monde*, September 5, 1004.

"The Fuss About Fatwa Evades the Real Issue: Sacrilege." *Impact International*, March 12–April 8, 1993.

Thomson, Alice. "British Should Try Arranged Marriages." *Telegraph*, June 10, 2006.

Totonji, Ahmed. "World Assembly of Muslim Youth." *Impact International*, October 22–November 11, 1976.

Trahan, Jason. "FBI: CAIR Is a Front Group, and Holy Land Foundation Tapped Hamas Clerics for Fundraisers." *Dallas Morning News*, October 7, 2008.

——. "'Smoking Gun' Holy Land Foundation Trial Document Still Viral, Spawns a New Film." *Dallas Morning News*, May 23, 2009.

Travis, Alan. "Muslims Abandon Labour Over Iraq War." *Guardian*, March 15, 2004.

——. "Time to Tackle the Non-Violent Extremists, Says Smith." *Guardian*, December 11, 2008.

"Two Unamalgamated Worlds." *The Economist*, April 3, 2008.

"UK Muslims Act Against Infamous Book." *Saudi Gazette*, December 15, 1988.

"US Sponsors Islamic Convention." *Washington Times*, August 27, 2007.

Venner, Fiammetta and Caroline Fourest. "Le retournement incertain de Dounia Bouzar." *Pro Choix*, January 5, 2005.

Yousef, Ahmed. "Engage with Hamas: We Earned Our Support." *The Washington Post*, June 20, 2007.

——. "Pause for Peace." *The New York Times*, November 1, 2006.

Wehner, Markus. "Am Tisch mit Islamisten und Orthodoxen." *Frankfurter Allgemeine Zeitung*, March 12, 2008.

"Wie Friedlich Sind Muslime?" *Die Welt*, September 7, 2008.

Wilson, Graeme. "Cameron Attacks Muslim Hardliners." *Telegraph*, January 31, 2007.

Zakaria, Fareed. "Radical Islam Is a Fact of Life; How to Live with It." *Newsweek*, March 9, 2009.

Other Documents

A Question of Leadership. BBC 1, August 21, 2005.

Abrams, Joseph. "FBI Cuts Ties with CAIR Following Terror Financing Trial." *Fox News*, January 30, 2009.

Abu Elnin, Alaa. "Tipping U.S. on Baathists Prohibited: Prominent Scholar." May 30, 2003. http://www.islam-online.net/english/News/2003–05/31/article07 .shtml.

Aclimandos, Tewfiq. *Officiers et Frères Musulmans.* Centre d'études et de documentation économiques, juridiques et sociales, Etudes et documents, n°1/2, 2001.

Al-Alwani, Taha Jaber. "The Participation of Muslims in the American Political System." http://www.islamonline.net/english/Politics/2000/1/Article7.shtml (accessed January 22, 2009).

Al-Chobaki, Amr. "Future of Muslim Brotherhood." Ikhwanweb, June 13, 2007. http://www.ikhwanweb.com/article.php?id=814&ref=search.php (accessed January 11, 2010).

Al-Qaradawi, Yusuf, "Apostasy: Major and Minor." http://www.islamonline.net/ English/contemporary/2006/04/article01c.shtml (accessed July 24, 2008).

"Al-Qaradhawi Speaks in Favor of Suicide Operations at an Islamic Conference in Sweden." Middle East Media and Research Institute (MEMRI), Special Dispatch #542, July 24, 2003.

Al-Qumni, Sayed Mahmoud. "The Muslim Brotherhood's Initiative as a Reform Program: A Critical Review." Paper presented at the conference on Islamic reform, Brookings Institution, Washington, D.C., October 5–6, 2004.

Alam, Anwar. "Muslim Minority, Multiculturalism and Liberal State: A Comparison of India and Europe." Paper released by the Université Paris 1— Panthéon-Sorbonne.

Alamoudi, Abdurahman. Speech. http://www.investigativeproject.org/article/218 (accessed October 14, 2008).

Altman, Israel Elad. *Strategies of the Muslim Brotherhood Movement,* 1928–2007. Monograph released by the Hudson Institute, January 2009.

"American Anti-War Movement Leader Meets with Radical Anti-Zionists in Cairo." December 29, 2003. http://www.adl.org/Israel/ramsey_clark.asp (accessed March 3, 2009).

American Muslim Council. *American Muslim Council: Our First Five Years.* 1996.

An Uncertain Road: Muslims and the Future of Europe. Washington, D.C.: Pew Research Center, 2005.

"Attitudes to Living in Britain: A Survey of Muslim Opinion." *Channel 4 Dispatches.* August 7, 2006. http://www.imaginate.uk.com/MCC01_SURVEY/Site% 20Download.pdf.

Boubekeur, Amel. *Political Islam in Algeria.* Center for European Policy Studies working document 268. May 2007.

Bright, Martin. *When Progressives Treat with Reactionaries: The British State's Flirtation with Radical Islam.* Report published by the Policy Exchange, 2006.

Brown, Nathan J. and Amr Hamzawy. *The Draft Party Platform of the Egyptian Muslim Brotherhood: Foray Into Political Integration or Retreat Into Old Positions?* Carnegie Papers, Middle East Series, Number 89, January 2008.

Caeiro, Alexandre. "The European Council for Fatwa and Research." Presentation at the Fourth Mediterranean Social and Political Research Meeting, European University Institute, Montecatini Terme, March 19–23, 2003.

Council on American-Islamic Relations. http://www.cair.com/PDF/urbanlegends .pdf (accessed April 8, 2009).

——. "CAIR's Anti-Terrorism Campaigns." http://www.cair.com/American Muslims/AntiTerrorism.aspx (accessed April 9, 2009).

——. "25 Facts about CAIR." http://www.cair.com/AboutUs/25FactsAboutCAIR .aspx (accessed April 1, 2009).

——. *Western Muslim Minorities: Integration and Disenfranchisement.* CAIR Policy Bulletin, April 2006.

CAIR Pennsylvania. "What They Say About CAIR." http://pa.cair.com/index .php?Page=whattheysay&Side=about.

Cairo Declaration. Signed at summit convened by the Egyptian Popular Campaign to Confront U.S Aggression, December 27, 2002. http://www.counterpunch.org/ cairo1227.html.

"Century Witness." Al Jazeera August 4–September 29, 2002.

Cesari, Jocelyne. *Securitization and Religious Divides in Europe: Muslims in Western Europe After 9/11.* http://euro-islam.info/ei/wp-includes/pdf/securitization _and_religious_divides_in_europe.pdf (accessed February 14, 2009).

Chouet, Alain. "The Association of Muslim Brothers: Chronicle of a Barbarism Foretold." http://alain.chouet.free.fr/documents/M_B.htm (accessed July 21, 2008).

CNN Crossfire. September 10, 1993.

"Columbus, Ohio Muslim Leader Says 9/11 Planned by Americans, Praises the Wanted Al-Qaeda-Linked Yemenite Sheikh Al-Zindani." Middle East Media and Research Institute (MEMRI) Special Dispatch 1168, May 19, 2006.

Conservative Party (United Kingdom). National and International Security Policy Group. *Uniting the Country.* Interim report on national cohesion. January 2007.

Cordoba University. http://www.siss.edu/Newsletter/FirstMAMCAConference8–8- 00.htm.

Dahoah-Halevi, Jonathan. *The Muslim Brotherhood: A Moderate Islamic Alternative to al-Qaeda or a Partner in Global Jihad?* Jerusalem Center for Public Affairs, November 1, 2007, No. 558.

Erhvervs- og Selskabsstyrelsen (Danish Commerce and Companies Agency). Filings on the Islamic Bank International of Denmark. April 7, 1983.

European Council for Fatwa and Research. Final Statement of the Fifteenth Ordinary Session. Istanbul, June 29–July 3, 2005.

Faruqi, M. H. "Les Freres Musulmanes: Politique de 'Rabbaniyya,' les Prieres avant le Pouvoir." http://www.cige.org/historique.htm (accessed January 21, 2005).

"FBI Official and Imam Discuss Homegrown Terror." NPR, May 16, 2007.

Federation of Islamic Organizations in Europe. http://www.eu-islam.com/en/templates/Index_en.asp.

———. Power, Development and Prosperity. 2007.

First Collection of Fatwas. Trans. Anas Osama Altikriti. European Council for Fatwa and Research, n.d.

Forum of European Muslim Youth and Student Organisations. http://www.femyso.net/about.html.

Good Practice Guide for Mosques and Imams in Britain. Mosques and Imams National Advisory Board, 2006.

History of the Islamische Gemeinschaft Deutschland. http://www.i-g-d.com/uber%20unss2.htm.

"Holocaust Memorial Ceremony—MCB Regrets Exclusion of Palestinian Tragedy." MCB press release, January 26, 2001. http://web.archive.org/web/20050314235755/http:/www.mcb.org.uk/news260101.html.

"Homosexuality Is a Major Sin." Fatwa session with Sheik Yusuf al Qaradawi. http://www.islamonline.net/servlet/Satellite?pagename=IslamOnlineEnglish-Ask_Scholar/FatwaE/FatwaE&cid=1119503543878 (accessed September 21, 2009).

"How Islam Views Pluralism and Democracy." July 30, 2002. http://www.islamonline.net/servlet/Satellite?c=FatwaE&cid=1119503545626&pagename=IslamOnline-English-Ask_Scholar%2FASELayout.

Hussain, Delwar. "Bangladeshis in East London: from Secular Politics to Islam." Open Democracy, July 6, 2006.

Hussein, Fiaz. "Dawah: Our Purpose, Our Goal." Speech at the 2003 annual conference of the UK Islamic Mission National Dawah Committee. http://ukim.org/dawah/dawah%20our%20purpose%20our%20goal.PDF.

"Ibrahim El Zayat Says He Is not a Member of the Muslim Brotherhood." May 6, 2007. http://www.ikhwanweb.com/Article.asp?ID=752&SectionID=78.

Institut Européen des Sciences Humaines. http://www.iesh.org/index.php?option=com_content&task=view&id=50&Itemid=102&lang=en.

International Crisis Group. Islam and Identity in Germany. March 14, 2007.

———. La France Face à ses Musulmans: Émeutes, Jihadisme et Dépolitisation. March 9, 2006.

International Institute of Islamic Thought. http://www.iiit.org/AboutUs/AboutIIIT/tabid/66/Default.aspx.

International Union of Muslim Scholars. http://www.iumsonline.org/english/ index.shtml.

Interview with Dr. Kamal Helbawy. *Al-Masry al-Youm*, February 2, 2009. http:// www.almasry-alyoum.com/printerfriendly.aspx?ArticleID=197210.

Interview with MB Deputy Chairman Mohamed Habib in *al Ahrar Daily*, as reported by the Muslim Brotherhood's official Web site. June 16, 2008. (http:// www.ikhwanweb.com/Article.asp?ID=17267&LevelID=1&SectionID=0.

Interview with Mohammed Akef. January 14, 2004. http://www.alwihdah.com/ view.asp?cat=3&id=50.

Islam Expo 2006. http://islamexpo.info/index.php?option=com_frontpage&Itemid.

Islamic Cultural Center of Ireland. http://islamireland.ie/enter-the-icci/about-us/.

Islamic Federation of Berlin. *Islamische Föderation in Berlin: Die Kinder sind unsere Zukunft*. Undated.

Islamic Finance and Trade Conference. 2006 program.

———. 2008 program.

Islamic Human Rights Commission. http://www.ihrc.org.uk/show.php?id=294.

Islamic Society of North America. "A Call for FBI Accountability." http://www .isna.net/articles/News/A-Call-for-FBI-Accountability.aspx (accessed March 31, 2009).

———. "ISNA Recognizes IIIT VP Dr. Jamal Barzinji for Pioneering Service." September 8, 2008. http://www.iiit.org/NewsEvents/News/tabid/62/articleType/ ArticleView/articleId/90/Default.aspx.

———. *ISNA Statement of Position: Who We Are and What We Believe*. September 12, 2007. http://www.isna.net/Documents/ISNAHQ/ISNA-Statement-of-Position-Who-we-Are-and-What-We-Believe.pdf (accessed April 6, 2009).

Islamische Gemeinschaft in Deutschland. http://www.igd-online.de/.

———. Filing at the Munich Amtsgericht. February 28, 2002.

Islamische Gemeinschaft Marburg/Omar Ibn al-Khattab Moschee. Filing at the Frankfurt Ausländeramt. January 25, 1990.

Islamische Gemeinschaft Millî Görüş. http://www.igmg.de/verband/islamic-community-milli-goerues/historical-development-of-the-igmg.html?L=.html .html.html.

Islamische Gemeinschaft in Süddeutschland. Annual filings. Amtsgericht, Munich. 1983.

"IslamOnline Opens Washington Office." December 27, 2008. http://www.islam online.net/servlet/Satellite?c=Article_C&cid=1230121266417&pagename=Zone-English-News/NWELayout.

"Islam's Stance on Homosexual Organizations." *Fatwa* session with Taha Jabir al Alawani, May 17, 2004. http://www.islamonline.net/servlet/Satellite?pagename= IslamOnline-English-Ask_Scholar/FatwaE/FatwaE&cid=1119503545314.

Jamaat-e-Islami Pakistan. http://www.jamaat.org/leadership/pka.html.

Kelly, Jane and Karen O'Toole. "Alliances and Coalitions in Britain: 'Stop the War' and 'Respect'." International Socialist Group Political Committee, April 2005. http://www.internationalviewpoint.org/spip.php?article672.

"Kristina Köhler gewinnt Verfahren gegen El Zayat." Press release, November 16, 2005. http://www.kristina-koehler.de/presse/mitteilungen/2005/kristina-koehler-gewinnt-verfa/.

Laurence, Jonathan. "Integrating Islam: A New Chapter in 'Church-State' Relations." Report for the Transatlantic Task Force on Immigration and Integration. October 2007.

——. "Islam and Citizenship in Germany." Transatlantic Dialogue on Terrorism, Center for Strategic and International Studies, Washington, DC, September 2007.

"Leading Sunni Sheikh Yousef al-Qaradhawi and Other Sheikhs Herald the Coming Conquest of Rome." Middle East Media and Research Institute (MEMRI), Special Dispatch #447, December 6, 2002.

Lefkowitz, Josh. "The 1993 Philadelphia Meeting: A Roadmap for Future Muslim Brotherhood Actions in the U.S." Nine Eleven Finding Answers Foundation report. November 15, 2007.

"Living Islam in the West: An Interview with Shaykh Faisal Mawlawi." *Palestinian Times*, no. 98. Undated. http://www.palestinetimes.net/issue98/articles.html#7 (accessed March 21, 2006).

Louay Safi. http://louaysafi.com/content/view/9/37/.

Maher, Shiraz and Martyn Frampton. *Choosing Our Friends Wisely: Criteria for Engagement with Muslim Groups*. Report issued by the Policy Exchange. March 2009.

"MAS Freedom Foundation Outlines Successful 2006 Election Strategy to Washington, DC Press Corps." MAS press release, November 14, 2006.

Maussen, Marcel. *The Governance of Islam in Western Europe: A State of the Art Report*. International Migration, Integration and Social Cohesion, Europe working paper No. 16. December 2006.

Mayor Livingstone and Shiekh Qaradawi: A Response by a Coalition of Many of London's Diverse Communities. Document in possession of the author.

McAdam, Doug. "Studying Social Movements: A Conceptual Tour of the Field." Program on Nonviolent Sanctions and Cultural Survival, Weatherhead Center for International Affairs, Harvard University, 1992.

McLoughlin, Sean. "Islam, Citizenship and Civil Society: 'New' Muslim Leadership in the UK." Presentation at the European Muslims and the Secular State in a Comparative Perspective conference, European Commission/Network of Comparative Research on Islam and Muslims in Europe, June 30–July 1, 2003.

Merley, Steven. *The Muslim Brotherhood in the United States.* Research monograph for the Hudson Institute. April 2009.

Mirza, Munira, Abi Senthilkumaran, and Zein Ja'far. *Living Apart Together: British Muslims and the Paradox of Multiculturalism.* Report for the Policy Exchange. 2007.

Moscheebau Kommission. Filing at the Munich Amtsgericht. March 29, 1960.

Mosquée de Paris. http://www.mosquee-de-paris.org/spip.php?article66.

Muslim American Society. http://www.masnet.org/university.asp.

——. Articles of incorporation. Filed in Illinois, June 11, 1993 (file number 5735–189–6).

Muslim Americans: Middle Class and Mostly Mainstream. Pew Research Center. May 22, 2007.

Muslim Association of Britain. http://www.mabonline.info/english/modules.php? name=About.

"Muslim Brotherhood Supreme Guide: Bin Laden is a Jihad Fighter." Middle East Media and Research Institute (MEMRI), Special Dispatch #2001, July 25, 2008.

Muslim Council of Britain. http://www.mcb.org.uk/downloads/MCB_acheivments .pdf.

——. "MCB Community Guidelines to Imams and British Muslim Organisations." March 31, 2004. http://www.mcb.org.uk/media/presstext.php?ann_id=80.

——. "MCB Decries Character Assassination of Dr Al-Qaradawi." July 7, 2004. http://www.mcb.org.uk/media/presstext.php?ann_id=102.

——. "MCB Hosts Luncheon Meeting with Jack Straw." December 2, 1998. http:// www.mcb.org.uk/media/archive/news021298.html.

——. "MCB Rejects Hazel Blears' Baseless Accusations." MCB press release, March 26, 2009.

——. *Representing the Muslims, Serving the Nation.* 2006/07 activity report.

——. 10 *Years of Working for the Common Good.* 1997–2007.

Muslim Students Association. http://www.msanational.org/about/history/.

——. "A Little Taste of History." http://web.archive.org/web/20060118061004/ http://www.msa-national.org/about/history.html (accessed October 29, 2007).

Muslims for Ken. http://www.muslimsforken.blogspot.com/.

"Muslims Participating in US Local Councils." *Fatwa* session with Muzammil Siddiqi, October 1, 2003. http://www.islamonline.net/servlet/Satellite?pagename= IslamOnline-English-Ask_Scholar/FatwaE/FatwaE&cid=1119503544898.

"New Muslim Brotherhood Leader: Resistance in Iraq and Palestine is Legitimate; America is Satan, Islam Will Invade America and Europe," Middle East Media and Research Institute (MEMRI) Special Dispatch No. 655, February 4, 2004.

North American Islamic Trust. http://www.nait.net/.

"Open Letter: Give Ken a Third Term." *Guardian*, January 3, 2008.

Paris, Jonathan. "Discussion Paper on Approaches to Anti-Radicalization and Community Policing in the Transatlantic Space." Paper prepared for the Weidenfeld Institute conference, Washington, D.C., June 2007.

——. "UK Counter-Radicalisation Strategy: Accommodation to Confrontation?" Paper presented at the Henry Jackson Society, London, July 2, 2008.

"Qaradawi: 'MB Asked Me to Be a Chairman.'" September 5, 2006. http://www.ikhwanweb.net/Article.asp?ID=3537&SectionID=0.

Quilliam Foundation. *Pulling Together to Defeat Terror*. April 2008.

Radical Middle Way. http://www.radicalmiddleway.co.uk/scholars.php.

Ramadan, Tariq. "Une Vie Entiere." http://membres.lycos.fr/oasislam/personnages/tariq/tariq.html.

Resolutions and Fatwas (Second Collection). Ed. Anas Osama Altikriti and Mohammed Adam Howard. European Council for Fatwa and Research. n.d.

Rich, David. "The Muslim Brotherhood in Great Britain." Unpublished paper.

"Round-up of Friday Sermons." BBC Monitoring International Reports, Near/Middle East. June 4, 2004 (published June 7, 2004).

Runnymede Trust. *Islamophobia: A Challenge for Us All*. 1997.

Safi, Louay. *Blaming Islam: Examining the Religion Building Enterprise*. Report for the Institute for Social Policy and Understanding. 2006.

Schäuble, Wolfgang, Minister of the Interior. Remarks at the beginning of DIK last plenary session, June 25, 2009.

"Sheikh Yousuf Al-Qaradhawi: Allah Imposed Hitler On the Jews to Punish Them—'Allah Willing, the Next Time Will Be at the Hand of the Believers.'" Middle East Media and Research Institute (MEMRI), Special Dispatch #2224. February 3, 2009.

The Change Institute for the European Commission. *Study on the Best Practices in Cooperation Between Authorities and Civil Society with a View to the Prevention and Response to Violent Radicalisation*. July 2008.

The Covenant of the Islamic Resistance Movement (Hamas). August 18, 1988. Available in English at: http://avalon.law.yale.edu/20th_century/hamas.asp.

"The Muslim Brotherhood in Europe and a Course of Reviews, UK an Example." August 12, 2008. http://ikhwanweb.com/Article.asp?ID=17575&SectionID=67.

UK Islamic Mission. Annual report 2004/2005. Copy in possession of the author.

"Verfassungsschutz NRW räumt Verbreitung von Unwahrheiten." Milli Görüş press release, December 17, 2005. http://www.igmg.de/verband/presseerklaerungen/newsdetails-presse/verfassungsschutz-nrw-raumt-verbreitung-von-unwahrheiten-ein/3.html.

Wickham, Carry. "Democratization and Islamists—Auto-Reform." June 15, 2006. http://www.ikhwanweb.com/Article.asp?ID=4112&SectionID=81.

Young Muslims UK. http://www.ymuk.net/.

Zentralrat. http://zentralrat.de/2593.php#beauftragte.

Zwischen Halbmond und Hakenkreuz. ARD documentary. July 19, 2006.

Index